SAT*

success

PRE

TEST

PETERSON'S

THOMSON LEARNING

Australia • Canada • Mexico • Singapore • Spain • United Kingdom • United States

PETERSON'S
™
THOMSON LEARNING

About Peterson's

Founded in 1966, Peterson's, a division of Thomson Learning, is the nation's largest and most respected provider of lifelong learning online resources, software, reference guides, and books. The Education Supersite^{SM} at petersons.com—the Web's most heavily traveled education resource—has searchable databases and interactive tools for contacting U.S.-accredited institutions and programs. CollegeQuest® (CollegeQuest.com) offers a complete solution for every step of the college decision-making process. GradAdvantage^{TM} (GradAdvantage.org), developed with Educational Testing Service, is the only electronic admissions service capable of sending official graduate test score reports with a candidate's online application. Peterson's serves more than 55 million education consumers annually.

Thomson Learning is among the world's leading providers of lifelong learning, serving the needs of individuals, learning institutions, and corporations with products and services for both traditional classrooms and for online learning. For more information about the products and services offered by Thomson Learning, please visit www.thomsonlearning.com. Headquartered in Stamford, Connecticut, with offices worldwide, Thomson Learning is part of The Thomson Corporation (www.thomson.com), a leading e-information and solutions company in the business, professional, and education marketplaces. The Corporation's common shares are listed on the Toronto and London stock exchanges.

Contents

CONTENTS

Acknowledgments

SAT materials selected from *10 Real SATs* by College Entrance Examination Board, 1997. Reprinted by permission of the College Entrance Examination Board and Educational Testing Service, the copyright owners.

From *Economics and Sociology: Redefining their Boundaries* by R. Swedberg. Copyright © 1990 by Princeton University Press.

From "Carriers of Extinction" by Carl Zimmer in *Discover*, July 1995. Copyright © 1995 by Carl Zimmer. Reprinted with permission of *Discover Magazine*.

From *Jane Austen* by J. Dwyer. Copyright © 1989 by J. Dwyer. Reprinted by permission of Continuum Publishing Group.

From "Ethnicity and Identity in America" by Alan Jabbour from *Folklife Center News*, Spring 1993, Volume XV, no. 2. Published by the American Folklife Center of the Library of Congress.

From "Folklife Exhibition Celebrates Italian-American Ties and Attachments" by James Hardin in *Folklife Center News*, Spring 1993, XV, no. 2. Published by the American Folklife Center of the Library of Congress.

From "The Folklorist Becomes the Folk" by Francesca McLean from *Folklife Center News*, Spring 1993, XV, no. 2. Published by the American Folklife Center for the Library of Congress.

About the CD

At the end of this book, you will find a CD that will take you to the gateway to our SAT test-preparation Web site. On this site you will find practice tests, tutorials, and exercises to help you study for the SAT I examination. Once you log on to the site, you will have unlimited access for 90 days.

The first thing you must do is write down the 10-digit number that is printed on the CD itself. Once you have done that, you can insert the CD into your computer. On most machines the program will launch itself and take you right to our Web site, www.petersons.com. You will be asked to enter that 10-digit number, so keep it handy. You will then be assigned a user name and password that enables you to take the test over again or stop at any point and come back at another time. Just make sure you keep a record of your user name and password.

We suggest that you begin by taking the diagnostic test at the beginning of the book. Once you have an idea of how you did and where to focus your studying, review the material in the book, and then supplement your studies with the online lessons. Then take the other tests in the book and on line. Very little has been left to chance here, and you have been given a wide range of preparatory materials, both on line and in this book. Try to review as much as possible.

Introduction

You may be intimidated by the SAT—it's long, it's important, and it's not like the tests you've taken at school. Luckily, the test is predictable, and this book will show you how to use that predictability to your advantage. By opening this book you've taken your first step toward SAT success.

SAT Success 2002 is a complete test-prep system for the SAT I Reasoning Test. The book contains three full-length tests: a diagnostic and two practice tests. These simulations of the real exam are meant to be taken under timed conditions. They will give you an approximate idea of how you'll score on the real thing, as well as a sense of the three-hour test-taking experience. There are three Red Alert sections: SAT Overview, Math, and Verbal. Red Alerts consist of the most important, concentrated test-prep advice. There are two instructional units: Math and Verbal. These provide more in-depth information about the question types and strategies for approaching them. There are eighteen Practice Sets: nine in the Math Unit and nine in the Verbal Unit. They are organized by question type and content matter, providing extra practice in these areas. The third set in each group consists of real SAT questions from previous administrations of the test. There are two Reference Sections: Math and Verbal. The Math Reference section contains the facts, formulas, and figures that are fair game on the test. The Verbal Reference section contains a comprehensive list of common SAT vocabulary words, "word teams" grouped by theme and vocabulary-expanding "root and prefix teams." Don't feel you need to read these sections through cover to cover, memorizing as you go along. Scan through them to get a sense of their scope, and use them throughout your prep as necessary.

Start by taking the Diagnostic Test using one of the answer sheets found at the back of this book. Don't worry if you've never seen an SAT before. The specifics of the different sections and question types will be addressed in the SAT Overview Red Alert. It's important to take the test first so you can see your progress as you work through the book. There's a work sheet for scoring the exam that will give you a scaled score. Your actual score isn't as important as using the test to hone in on your strengths and weaknesses and focus your prep accordingly. Don't worry if you aren't satisfied with your Diagnostic score; that's where this book comes in.

The way you use this book will vary according to a number of factors, including your familiarity with the test, your math and reading skills, and the amount of time you have to prepare. Three study-plans follow. Use them as guides, but feel free to adjust them according to your needs.

STUDY PLANS

	Bare Bones	Middle of the Road	The Whole Nine Yards
Diagnostic Test	Required. Take under timed conditions. Score, using results to determine trouble spots you might study in the optional sections.	Required. Take under timed conditions. Score, using results to determine trouble spots you might study in the optional sections.	Required. Take under timed conditions. Score, using results to focus study.
Overview Red Alert	Required	Required	Required
Math Red Alert	Required	Required	Required
Verbal Red Alert	Required	Required	Required
Practice Test 1	Optional	Optional	Required. Take under timed conditions. Score, using results to focus further study.
Math Unit	Optional	Required. Study trouble spots, and do relevant practice sets.	Required. Study unit, and do all practice sets.
Verbal Unit	Optional	Required. Study trouble spots, and do relevant practice sets.	Required. Study unit, and do all practice sets.
Math Reference	Optional	Optional	Required
Verbal Reference	Optional	Optional	Required
Practice Test 2	Optional	Required. Take under timed conditions. Score, using results to focus last minute review.	Required. Take under timed conditions. Score, using results to focus last minute review.

Diagnostic Test

Section 1

Time—30 Minutes
25 Questions

Solve the following problems, select the best answer choice for each and fill in the corresponding oval on the answer sheet. Use your test booklet for scratchwork.

Notes:

1. You may use a calculator. All of the numbers used are real numbers.

2. Figures accompany some problems. Assume that each has been drawn accurately and lies in a plane, unless the instructions indicate otherwise.

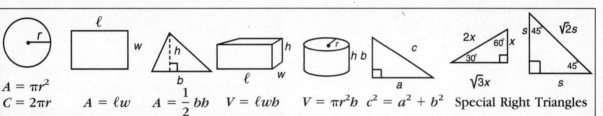

$A = \pi r^2$
$C = 2\pi r$ $\quad A = \ell w \quad A = \dfrac{1}{2} bh \quad V = \ell wh \quad V = \pi r^2 h \quad c^2 = a^2 + b^2$ Special Right Triangles

The number of degrees of arc in a circle is 360.
The measure in degrees of a straight angle is 180.
The sum of the measures in degrees of the angles of a triangle is 180.

1. Which of the following pairs (x, y) satisfies the inequality $y \le x^2$?

   (A) (0, 1) $0 \le 1 \quad 1 \le 0$
   (B) (2, 5) $5 \le 4$
   (C) (−1, 3) $3 \le 1$
   (D) (−3, 4) $4 \le 9$
   (E) (−1, 2) $2 \le 1$

Test No.	Score
1	90
2	75
3	95
4	90
5	85

75, 90, 96, 95
↓
85

2. The table above shows the scores Olga received on each of the tests. What was Olga's median test score?

   (A) 75
   (B) 85
   (C) 87
   (D) 90
   (E) 95

GO ON TO THE NEXT PAGE

3. A boy bicycles 1 mile south and then 2 miles east. Bicycling in which of the following directions will bring him back to his starting point?

   (A) 2 miles west and 1 mile north
   (B) 2 miles east and 1 mile north
   (C) 1 mile west and 2 miles north
   (D) 2 miles west and 1 mile south
   (E) 3 miles north

4. A right triangle that is also an isosceles triangle has a 90° angle and an $x°$ angle.
   $x =$

   (A) 35
   (B) 45
   (C) 55
   (D) 75
   (E) 90

5. If the area of the rectangle above is 20, what is the value of a?

   (A) 4
   (B) 5
   (C) 6
   (D) 16
   (E) 80

   a

   5

6. Which of the following is (are) equivalent to $\dfrac{x^{12}}{x^3}$?

   I. $x^{12} - x^3$
   II. $(x^4)(x^5)$
   III. $(x^3)^2$

   (A) I only
   (B) II only
   (C) I and II only
   (D) II and III only
   (E) I, II, and III

7. Five teenagers share the lifeguard position at the local pool. They rotate shifts, which are always assigned in the following order: Ariel, Brian, Cameron, Deb, Eli. Who is assigned to the 243rd shift?

   (A) Ariel   1, 2, 3, 4, 5
   (B) Brian
   (C) Cameron
   (D) Deb
   (E) Eli

8. Two numbers, a and b, can be arranged in two different orders, (a, b) and (b, a). In how many different orders can three numbers be arranged?

   (A) 2   abc   acb
   (B) 3   cba
   (C) 4   bca
   (D) 5   bac
   (E) 6   cab

x + 3y = 12y
-3y   -3y

9. If $x + 3y = 4(3y)$, then $x =$

(A) 3y
(B) 4y
(C) 9y
(D) 12y
(E) It cannot be determined from the information given.

10. What is the area of the right triangle formed by halving a square with perimeter 36 along its diagonal?

(A) 9
(B) 18
(C) $18 + 9\sqrt{2}$
(D) 40.5
(E) 81

$a^2 + b^2 = c^2$

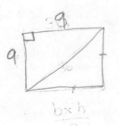

$x^2 + x^2 = 36^2$
$2x^2 = 36^2$

$\frac{b \times h}{2}$

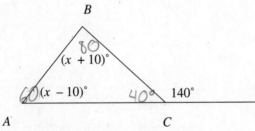

Note: Figure not drawn to scale.

11. In the figure above, what is the measure, in degrees, of angle *ABC*?

(A) 40
(B) 50
(C) 60
(D) 70
(E) 80

$180° = 40 + (x+10) + (x-10)$

$180° = 40 + 2x$

$x = 70$

12. If $a = x$ and $b = y$ and $xy = 0$, then which of the following is true?

(A) $a = 0$
(B) $b = 0$
(C) $a = 0$ and $b = a$
(D) $a = 0$ or $b = 0$
(E) None of the above

13. If $156.00 is divided among 3 people in the ratio of $\frac{1}{2} : \frac{1}{3} : \frac{1}{4}$, what is the *difference* between the greatest share received and the least share received?

(A) $34.67
(B) $36
(C) $39
(D) $48
(E) $72

$78
$- 39

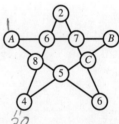

20

14. If the sums of four circles along any line segment of the star above are equal, then $B =$

(A) 3
(B) 4
(C) 6
(D) 7
(E) It cannot be determined from the information given.

GO ON TO THE NEXT PAGE

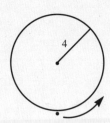

15. A bug starts walking around a circle with a radius of 4. If after having taken four steps, he has walked around 25% of the circle, how long are each of his steps?

(A) $\dfrac{2}{\pi}$

(B) $\dfrac{4}{\pi}$

(C) π

(D) $\dfrac{\pi}{4}$

(E) $\dfrac{\pi}{2}$

16. Of the total number of days in a week, what fraction of them occur only 52 times in a leap year?

(A) $\dfrac{1}{7}$

(B) $\dfrac{2}{7}$

(C) $\dfrac{3}{7}$

(D) $\dfrac{4}{7}$

(E) $\dfrac{5}{7}$

17. If the volume of a cube is 64, what is its surface area?

(A) 4

(B) 96

(C) 128

(D) 256

(E) 384

18. Martha makes g gallons of jam and divides it evenly among j jars. If 3 gallons of jam remain after she fills the jars, in terms of g and j, how many gallons of jam are in each jar?

(A) $\dfrac{j-3}{g+3}$

(B) $\dfrac{g}{3j}$

(C) $\dfrac{g-3}{j}$

(D) $\dfrac{3-j}{g}$

(E) $\dfrac{g+j}{3}$

8

Questions 19 and 20 refer to the following definition:

$$\begin{vmatrix} a & b \\ c & d \end{vmatrix} = \frac{1}{ad - bc}$$

19. Which of the following is undefined?

    (A) $\begin{vmatrix} 1 & 2 \\ 3 & 4 \end{vmatrix}$ $\dfrac{1}{ad - bc}$ (14)

    (B) $\begin{vmatrix} 2 & 3 \\ 5 & 7 \end{vmatrix}$

    (C) $\begin{vmatrix} 4 & 3 \\ 8 & 6 \end{vmatrix}$

    (D) $\begin{vmatrix} 2 & -2 \\ 4 & 4 \end{vmatrix}$

    (E) $\begin{vmatrix} -3 & -2 \\ 6 & -4 \end{vmatrix}$

20. $\begin{vmatrix} 4 & 4 \\ 3 & 5 \end{vmatrix}$ equals which of the following?

    (A) $\begin{vmatrix} 4 & 5 \\ 4 & 3 \end{vmatrix}$ $\dfrac{1}{20 - 12 = 8}$

    (B) $\begin{vmatrix} 2 & 0 \\ 6 & 4 \end{vmatrix}$ $12 - 20 = -8$

    (C) $\begin{vmatrix} -3 & -4 \\ -5 & 4 \end{vmatrix}$ $8 - 0 = 8$

    (D) $\begin{vmatrix} 5 & 6 \\ 5 & 2 \end{vmatrix}$

    (E) $\begin{vmatrix} 7 & 2 \\ 10 & 0 \end{vmatrix}$

21. At a casino there are three tables. The payoff at the first table is 10:1; at the second, 30:1; and, at the third, 40:1. If a woman bets $10 at each table and wins at two of the tables, what is the <u>difference</u> between her <u>maximum</u> and <u>minimum</u> possible gross winnings?

    (A) $200
    (B) $300
    (C) $400
    (D) $500
    (E) $600

     $400
    + 300
    ‾‾‾‾‾
    700

    100
    300

GO ON TO THE NEXT PAGE

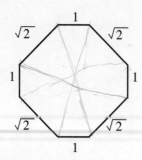

Note: Figure not drawn to scale.

22. The sides of an octagon alternate in length. As pictured above, each side with length 1 is next to a side of length $\sqrt{2}$. What is the area of the octagon?

(A) 5
(B) 6
(C) 7
(D) 8
(E) 9

23. What is the area of the square with vertices at the points (0, 2), (0, −2), (2, 0), and (−2, 0)?

(A) 4
(B) 6
(C) 8
(D) 12
(E) 16

24. After a 20% decrease, a DVD player is on sale for $400. What was its original price?

(A) $320
(B) $420
(C) $480
(D) $500
(E) $525

25. In the figure above, six equilateral triangles with sides of 1 are joined to form a hexagon. A circle is then circumscribed about the hexagon. What is the area of the shaded region?

(A) $\pi - \dfrac{\sqrt{3}}{2}$

(B) $\pi - \dfrac{3\sqrt{3}}{2}$

(C) $\pi - \dfrac{\pi\sqrt{3}}{3}$

(D) $2\pi - \dfrac{\sqrt{3}}{2}$

(E) $2\pi - 3\sqrt{3}$

STOP If you finish before time is called, you may check your work on this section only. Do not turn to any other section in the test.

Peterson's SAT Success

[This page intentionally left blank]

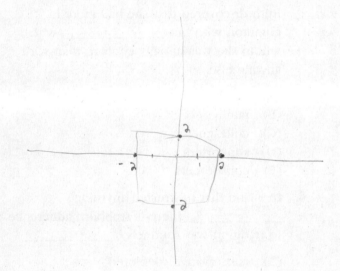

Section 2

Time—30 Minutes
36 Questions

For each question below, choose the best answer from the choices given and fill in the corresponding oval on the answer sheet.

Each sentence below has either one or two blanks in it and is followed by five choices labeled (A) through (E). These choices represent words or phrases that have been omitted. Choose the word or phrase that, if inserted into the sentence, would best fit the meaning of the sentence as a whole.

Example:
Canine massage is a veterinary technique for calming dogs that are extremely _____.

(A) inept
(B) disciplined
(C) controlled
(D) agitated
(E) restrained   Ⓐ Ⓑ Ⓒ ⬤ Ⓔ

1. Because artist Geogia O'Keefe's startling use of vibrant colors and unusual subjects proved _____ to many, acclamation for her work was understandably _____.

   (A) disturbing..forthcoming
   (B) unsettling..delayed
   (C) authentic..timely
   (D) jarring..avoided
   (E) delightful..tardy

2. _____ of the psychologist Sigmund Freud find it impossible to _____ his assertion that interpreting dreams is the key to understanding the human mind.

   (A) Opponents..dispute
   (B) Disciples..teach
   (C) Contemporaries..understand
   (D) Critics..support
   (E) Admirers..remember

3. Immersed in her work at the laboratory, Ruth discovered that she had more in common with her _____, with whom she was in daily contact, than with anyone else.

   (A) neighbors
   (B) family
   (C) colleagues
   (D) supporters
   (E) constituents

4. In a firm that mistrusted anything _____, Jerry's stubborn adherence to tradition was routinely _____.

   (A) conservative..deplored
   (B) modern..misunderstood
   (C) innovative..questioned
   (D) creative..denigrated
   (E) conventional..applauded

5. Rather than enlarging his presentation to include possible negative effects of the new vaccine, the biochemist persisted in offering only the most _____ of scenarios.

   (A) sanguine
   (B) ambiguous
   (C) pragmatic
   (D) subtle
   (E) inspiring

6. Those few paleontologists who postulated theories of warm-blooded dinosaurs have been _____ by recent discoveries that _____ this once-radical concept.

   (A) humbled..validate
   (B) ennobled..enshrine
   (C) implicated..discredit
   (D) heartened..refute
   (E) vindicated..confirm

7. Hollywood legend Jimmy Stewart privately _____ the lax morality he observed in many fellow stars, yet he never _____ any of them in public.

   (A) endorsed..criticized
   (B) encouraged..snubbed
   (C) decried..maligned
   (D) scorned..commended
   (E) discounted..persecuted

8. Only Juanita's closest friends, who knew her _____ classical music, could have guessed that she would one day become a concert violinist.

   (A) disdain for
   (B) separation from
   (C) predilection for
   (D) turmoil over
   (E) ambivalence toward

9. Bibliophiles wonder if technology will eventually turn books into _____, as out of place in the classroom as slate writing tablets.

   (A) luxuries
   (B) innovations
   (C) redundancies
   (D) curiosities
   (E) anachronisms

10. The entomologist sees daily how _____ is the lifetime of any insect he studies, especially when _____ with his own longevity.

   (A) interactive..compared
   (B) evanescent..contrasted
   (C) compelling..considered
   (D) unique..discussed
   (E) transient..confronted

GO ON TO THE NEXT PAGE

Each question below consists of two words that are related to one another in some way. Following these words are five sets of two words each, labeled (A) through (E). From these, you must choose the set that denotes a relationship *most similar* to the relationship expressed in the original set. Note also that the words in the correct answer must be in the same *order* as that in the original set.

Example:

RUNNER : SPEED ::

(A) acrobat : height
(B) dancer : grace
(C) minister : holy book
(D) waiter : order
(E) landlord : rent

11. SHAVING : WOOD ::

(A) lather : foam
(B) wax : floor
(C) raisin : bread
(D) slice : cheese
(E) wheel : car

12. BOOKS : BACKPACK ::

(A) clothing : dresser
(B) china : silver
(C) documents : portfolio
(D) relics : museum
(E) research : laboratory

13. BONNET : HEAD ::

(A) shirt : flannel
(B) necklace : jewelry
(C) mittens : snow
(D) scarf : necktie
(E) boots : feet

14. TALONS : HAWK ::

(A) pouch : marsupial
(B) tentacles : squid
(C) speed : cheetah
(D) plumage : peacock
(E) stripes : zebra

15. EDITORIAL : OPINION ::

(A) license : permission
(B) notation : postscript
(C) essay : publication
(D) headline : newspaper
(E) summary : index

16. TALENT : PRODIGY ::

(A) intuition : referee
(B) dogmatism : mediator
(C) medicine : physician
(D) proficiency : champion
(E) decency : neighbor

17. UNGUENT : SOOTHE ::

(A) ornament : embellish
(B) flea : annoy
(C) raiment : protect
(D) lecture : stupefy
(E) lotion : disguise

18. SALVAGE : DESTRUCTION ::

(A) dispute : arbitration
(B) beleaguer : enemy
(C) recoup : loss
(D) instigate : accord
(E) envy : greed

19. RETIRING : PUBLICITY ::

(A) committed : cause
(B) arbitrary : judgment
(C) temperamental: notoriety
(D) disorganized : clutter
(E) misanthropic : people

20. PRODIGIOUS : AWE ::

(A) precocious : curiosity
(B) abhorrent : revulsion
(C) demanding : withdrawal
(D) voluminous : concentration
(E) provocative : alarm

21. BULKY : GIRTH ::

(A) mellifluous : mood
(B) vocal : pitch
(C) audible : logic
(D) pungent : odor
(E) hirsute : prehistory

22. JURISPRUDENCE : LAW ::

(A) radiography : science
(B) nostalgia : heritage
(C) philosophy : tradition
(D) pedagogy : education
(E) demagoguery : history

23. DIFFIDENT : ASSERT ::

(A) vague : appeal
(B) sumptuous : deny
(C) arrogant : assume
(D) capricious : revolt
(E) ambivalent : decide

GO ON TO THE NEXT PAGE ➡

Read the passage carefully, then answer the questions that come after it. The answer to each question may be stated overtly or only implied. You will not have to use outside knowledge to answer the questions—all the material you will need will be in the passage itself.

Questions 24–36 refer to the following passage

The following is a portion of an essay by William Hazlitt (1778–1830), a prominent essayist in the Romantic movement of British literature.

Line There is a spider crawling along the matted floor of the room where I sit; he runs with heedless, hurried haste, he hobbles awkwardly toward me, he stops—he sees the
(5) giant shadow before him, and, at a loss whether to retreat or proceed, meditates his huge foe—but as I do not start up and seize upon the straggling caitiff, as he would upon a hapless fly within his toils, he takes heart,
(10) and ventures on with mingled cunning, impudence, and fear.

As he passes by me, I lift up the matting to assist his escape, am glad to get rid of the unwelcome intruder, and shudder
(15) at the recollection after he is gone. A moralist a century ago would have crushed the little reptile to death—my philosophy has gotten beyond that—I bear the creature no ill will, but still I hate the very sight of it.
(20) The spirit of malevolence survives the practical exertion of it. We learn to curb our will and keep our overt actions within the bounds of humanity, long before we can subdue our sentiments and imaginations to
(25) the same mild tone. We give up the external demonstration, the *brute* violence, but cannot part with the essence or principle of hostility. We do not tread upon the poor little animal in question (that seems barba-
(30) rous and pitiful!) but we regard it with a sort of mystic horror and superstitious loathing. It will take another hundred years of fine writing and hard thinking to cure us

of the prejudice, and make us feel toward
(35) this ill-omened tribe with something of "the milk of human kindness," instead of their own shyness and venom.

Nature seems (the more we look into it) made up of antipathies: Without some-
(40) thing to hate, we should lose the very spring of thought and action. Life would turn to a stagnant pool, were it not ruffled by the jarring interests, the unruly passions, of people. The white streak in our own
(45) fortunes is brightened (or just rendered visible) by making all around it as dark as possible; so the rainbow paints its form upon the cloud. Is it pride? Is it envy? Is it the force of contrast? Is it weakness or
(50) malice? But so it is, that there is a secret affinity with, a *hankering* after, evil in the human mind, and that it takes a perverse, but a fortunate delight in mischief, since it is a never-failing source of satisfaction.
(55) Pure good soon grows insipid, wants variety and spirit. Pain is bittersweet, which never surfeits. Love turns, with a little indulgence, to indifference or disgust: hatred alone is immortal. Do we not see this
(60) principle at work everywhere? Animals torment and worry one another without mercy: children kill flies for sport: everyone reads the accidents and offences in a newspaper as the cream of the jest: a whole
(65) town runs to be present at a fire, and the spectator by no means exults to see it extinguished. It is better to have it so, but it diminishes the interest; and our feelings take part with our passions rather than with our
(70) understandings. People assemble in crowds, with eager enthusiasm, to witness a tragedy; but if there were an execution going

forward in the next street, the theatre would be left empty . . .

(75)   We have always a quantity of superfluous bile upon the stomach, and want an object to let it out upon. How loath were we to give up our pious belief in ghosts and witches because we liked to persecute the
(80) one and frighten ourselves to death with the other! It is not the quality so much as the quantity of excitement that we are anxious about: We cannot bear a state of indifference and *ennui*: the mind seems to abhor a
(85) *vacuum* as much as ever nature was supposed to do.

24. The essayist believes that spiders possess all of the following attributes EXCEPT

(A) timidity
(B) cleverness
(C) shyness
(D) impudence
(E) generosity

25. According to the author, killing the spider is an example of

(A) human progress
(B) personal weakness
(C) heroism
(D) artistic license
(E) animal rights

26. The author assumes that his feelings about the spider are symbolic of

(A) the way humans view nature
(B) the longevity of prejudice
(C) the eternal conflict between human-kind and nature
(D) how humankind has grown more civilized
(E) the essence of humankind

27. In line 21, the phrase *practical exertion* most nearly means

(A) effort
(B) action
(C) supression
(D) attempt
(E) ill will

28. The author maintains that although we may learn to control our actions, it takes much longer to modify our

(A) surroundings
(B) behaviors
(C) feelings
(D) interests
(E) superstitions

29. According to this essayist, which human trait will live forever?

(A) indifference
(B) disgust
(C) pure good
(D) hostility
(E) love

30. Which of the following most accurately describes the author's tone in this essay?

(A) enthusiastic endorsement
(B) strong revulsion
(C) complete bewilderment
(D) general optimism
(E) resigned acceptance

31. We can infer that *the cream of the jest* (line 64) means

(A) the most intriguing or titillating bits
(B) those portions with the funniest descriptions
(C) the main focus of the newspaper reportage
(D) the only sections worth reading
(E) the most ludicrous sections

GO ON TO THE NEXT PAGE ▶

32. In line 62, the author says "children kill flies for sport," as an example of

    (A) the cruelty that is found only in the very young
    (B) a behavior that people must leave behind when they reach adulthood
    (C) a universal human trait
    (D) an action that should be punished
    (E) the inevitability of progress

33. The author uses the phrase *superfluous bile upon the stomach* (lines 75–76) to suggest

    (A) that people have an abundance of digestive juices
    (B) that no one needs to become over-wrought
    (C) that people don't really need anger or hostility
    (D) that human beings are oversupplied with hatred
    (E) that bile and a bilious temperament go hand in hand

34. The author observes that our "understandings" (line 70) are divorced from our

    (A) common sense
    (B) logic
    (C) knowledge of the facts
    (D) emotions
    (E) enthusiasms

35. The essayist maintains that the state humans are most anxious to avoid is

    (A) elation
    (B) fear
    (C) loathing
    (D) envy
    (E) boredom

36. Which of the following most nearly reflects the main conclusion in this essay?

    (A) Less is more.
    (B) Conflict is the spice of life.
    (C) Hostility is avoidable.
    (D) Persecution is delightful.
    (E) Perseverance will eventually eradicate prejudice.

S T O P If you finish before time is called, you may check your work on this section only. Do not turn to any other section in the test.

[This page intentionally left blank]

Section 3

Notes:

1. You may use a calculator. All of the numbers used are real numbers.

2. Figures accompany some problems. Assume that each has been drawn accurately and lies in a plane, unless the instructions indicate otherwise.

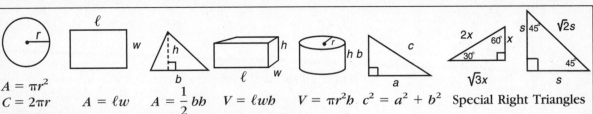

$A = \pi r^2$
$C = 2\pi r$ $\qquad A = \ell w$ $\qquad A = \dfrac{1}{2} bh$ $\qquad V = \ell wh$ $\qquad V = \pi r^2 h$ $\quad c^2 = a^2 + b^2$ $\quad$ Special Right Triangles

The number of degrees of arc in a circle is 360.
The measure in degrees of a straight angle is 180.
The sum of the measures in degrees of the angles of a triangle is 180.

Directions for Quantitative Comparison Questions

Questions 1–15 each consist of two boxed quantities, one in Column A and one in Column B. Compare them and select:

    A if the quantity in Column A is greater;
    B if the quantity in Column B is greater;
    C if the two quantities are equal;
    D if the relationship cannot be determined from the information given.

A response of E will be considered an omission.

Notes:

1. Some questions provide information about one or both of the quantities to be compared. This information is unboxed and centered above the two columns.
2. A symbol that appears in both columns represents the same value in each.
3. Letters such as x, n, and k stand for real numbers.

	EXAMPLES		
	Column A	**Column B**	**Answers**
E1	$\dfrac{1}{2}$ of 50	$\dfrac{1}{4}$ of 25	● Ⓑ Ⓒ Ⓓ Ⓔ
E2	The number of degrees in a circle	The number of degrees in a square	Ⓐ Ⓑ ● Ⓓ Ⓔ
	$x > 0$		
E3	x	$\dfrac{1}{x}$	Ⓐ Ⓑ Ⓒ ● Ⓔ

Column A	Column B

1. 2^8 | 8^2

2. $\dfrac{2 + 4 + 6 + 8}{2}$ | $\dfrac{3 + 6 + 9 + 12}{3}$

50% of y equals 180

3. y | 90

Column A	Column B

$t < s$

4. The average of t and s | s

5. The number of prime numbers between 1 and 100 | The number of odd numbers between 1 and 100

6. 18.37% of 9.15 | 9.15% of 18.37

GO ON TO THE NEXT PAGE ➤

SUMMARY DIRECTIONS

Select: A if Column A is greater;
B if Column B is greater;
C if the two columns are equal;
D if the relationship cannot be determined from the information given.

Column A	Column B

$$x^2 < 25$$
$$y^3 < 125$$

7. x y

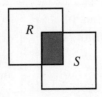

The area of the unshaded region in square R is greater than the area of the unshaded region in square S.

8. The area of square R The area of square S

Column A	Column B

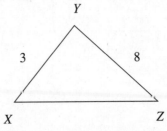

Note: Figure not drawn to scale.

9. XZ 5

$$b \neq 0$$

10. $a - b$ $a + b$

SUMMARY DIRECTIONS

Select: A   if Column A is greater;
          B   if Column B is greater;
          C   if the two columns are equal;
          D   if the relationship cannot be determined from the information given.

Column A	Column B		Column A	Column B

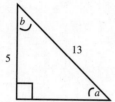

Note: Figure not drawn to scale.

Let $\boxed{n}$ be defined by the equation
$$\boxed{n} = (n + 1)^2$$

11.

a	b

13.

$\dfrac{\boxed{8}}{\boxed{4}}$	$\boxed{2}$

12.

$1{,}800^{25} - 1{,}800^{24}$	$1{,}800^{24}$

$$0 < a < x$$
$$0 < b < y$$

14.

$\dfrac{x + a}{y - b}$	$\dfrac{x - a}{y + b}$

$$a > 1$$
$$a - 1 = b$$

15.

b^2	$a^2 - 1$

GO ON TO THE NEXT PAGE

Directions for Student-Produced Response Questions

Enter your responses to questions 16–25 in the special grids provided on your answer sheet. Input your answers as indicated in the directions below.

Answer: $\frac{4}{9}$ or 4/9

Answer: 1.4
Either position is correct.

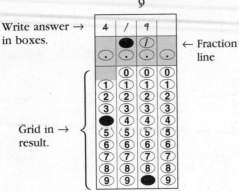

Write answer → in boxes.

← Fraction line

Grid in → result.

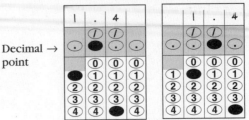

Decimal → point

Note: You may begin your answer in any column, space permitting. Leave blank any columns not needed.

- Writing your answer in the boxes at the top of the columns will help you accurately grid your answer, but it is not required. **You will only receive credit for an answer if the ovals are filled in properly.**

- Only fill in one oval in each column.

- If a problem has several correct answers, just grid in one of them.

- There are no negative answers.

- **Never grid in mixed numbers.** The answer $3\frac{1}{5}$ must be gridded as 16/5 or 3.2.

If 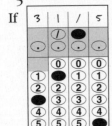 is gridded, it will be read as $\frac{31}{5}$, not $3\frac{1}{5}$.

Decimal Accuracy

Decimal answers must be gridded as accurately as possible. The answer 0.3333 . . . must be gridded as .333 or .334. **Less accurate values, such as .33 or .34, are not acceptable.**

Acceptable ways to grid $\frac{1}{3}$ = .3333 . . .

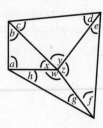

16. In the figure above, what is the value of:
$(a + b - x) + (c + d - y) + (e + f - z) + (g + h - w)$?

_____

$$4x + 3y = 15$$
$$-2x - 2y = -9$$

17. Given the two equations above, what is the value of $4x + 2y$?

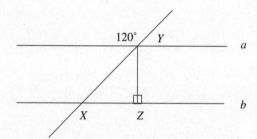

Note: Figure not drawn to scale.

18. In the figure above, line a is parallel to line b. If XY is 3, what is the value of XZ?

19. A number is said to be a "muggle" if it is the product of two consecutive integers. Grid in a muggle whose value is between 150 and 250.

_____

20. If the sum of five consecutive odd integers is 245, which is the largest of these integers?

_____

21. Two cars start off at the same point on a straight highway facing opposite directions. Each car drives for 3 miles, takes a left turn, and then drives for 4 miles. How many miles apart are the two cars?

GO ON TO THE NEXT PAGE

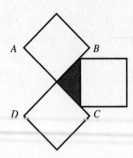

22. In the figure above, *BD* and *AC* are both line segments. Each of the three squares shown have an area of 16. What is the area of the shaded isosceles triangle?

23. A man walks 6 miles at 4 miles per hour. At what speed would he need to travel during the next $2\frac{1}{2}$ hours to have an average speed of 6 miles per hour during the complete trip?

24. The price, *x*, of a ring increases by 20% each year. How many years will it take for the price of the ring to exceed 2*x*?

25. Tickets for a certain performance cost $45 for orchestra seats and $30 for mezzanine seats. If 350 tickets were sold for a total of $12,000, how many mezzanine tickets were sold?

S T O P   If you finish before time is called, you may check your work on this section only. Do not turn to any other section in the test.

[This page intentionally left blank]

Section 4

Time—30 Minutes
31 Questions

For each question below, choose the best answer from the choices given and fill in the corresponding oval on the answer sheet.

Each sentence below has either one or two blanks in it and is followed by five choices labeled (A) through (E). These choices represent words or phrases that have been omitted. Choose the word or phrase that, if inserted into the sentence, would best fit the meaning of the sentence as a whole.

Example:
Canine massage is a veterinary technique for calming dogs that are extremely _____.

(A) inept
(B) disciplined
(C) controlled
(D) agitated
(E) restrained   Ⓐ Ⓑ Ⓒ ● Ⓔ

1. In nature, advantageous _____ are retained in successive generations: insects that thrive by tasting awful to their enemies eventually produce only offspring with that vital change.

   (A) species
   (B) mutations
   (C) fixtures
   (D) habits
   (E) patterns

2. We must _____ our schedules so that some participants will not be appearing at widely divergent times from others.

   (A) compare
   (B) individualize
   (C) synchronize
   (D) memorize
   (E) delineate

3. Rather than showering the reader with _____ of description, the writer adopted a minimalist approach and decided to offer only his _____ prose.

   (A) a welter..chattiest
   (B) a flood..finest
   (C) a torrent..sparest
   (D) historical facts..modern
   (E) a minimum..leanest

4. The sky, crackling with lightning, looked _____, a surprising departure from the weatherman's _____ forecast.

   (A) ominous..optimistic
   (B) empty..gloomy
   (C) welcoming..customary
   (D) frightening..uncertain
   (E) dire..somber

5. The eloquent and often witty speeches of Abraham Lincoln on the campaign trail contrast sharply with the _____ statements of modern political candidates, who are primarily in the business of producing television _____.

(A) ennobled..programs
(B) informative..subjects
(C) glorified..stars
(D) invigorating..sound bites
(E) prosaic..fodder

6. Successful despite—or perhaps *because* of—her _____ portrayal of her subjects, the popular portrait artist has routinely defied convention.

(A) devastating
(B) demure
(C) facile
(D) eccentric
(E) rebellious

7. From their relatively _____ appearance in classes studying British literature, Jane Austen's elegant nineteenth-century novels have made an unexpected leap into current _____ by way of the movies.

(A) scholarly..notoriety
(B) obscure..cinema
(C) demanding..fame
(D) parochial..prominence
(E) unobtrusive..parlance

8. His _____ tone of voice may have been unintentional, yet Chris's grandfather could never discuss money without expounding on the Great Depression, which had instilled in him an eternal _____.

(A) didactic..frugality
(B) patronizing..charity
(C) annoying..unease
(D) pompous..prodigality
(E) superior..inequality

9. What _____ that the word *rhetoric,* which once denoted excellence in writing and speech, should have become almost entirely _____ in connotation today.

(A) nonsense..positive
(B) irony..pejorative
(C) drivel..incomprehensible
(D) a joke..motivational
(E) an inconsistency..irrational

GO ON TO THE NEXT PAGE

Each question below consists of two words that are related to one another in some way. Following these words are five sets of two words each, labeled (A) through (E). From these, you must choose the set that denotes a relationship *most similar* to the relationship expressed in the original set.

Example:
RUNNER : SPEED ::
(A) acrobat : height
(B) dancer : grace
(C) minister : holy book
(D) waiter : order
(E) landlord : rent

10. FREEWAY : RAMP ::

(A) highway : boulevard
(B) truck : cab
(C) canal : towpath
(D) ship : gangplank
(E) plane : jetstream

11. HORSESHOE : FORGE ::

(A) cloth : spinning wheel
(B) union : mill
(C) cotton : boll
(D) tire : factory
(E) engine : hood

12. AGENT : CLIENT ::

(A) manager : staff
(B) lawyer : plaintiff
(C) firm : associate
(D) buyer : merchandiser
(E) mastermind : cohort

13. BEAVER : DAM ::

(A) termite : mound
(B) mare : foal
(C) woodchuck : groundhog
(D) bee : honey
(E) pelican : pouch

14. LANGUAGE : SLANG ::

(A) literature : Gothic
(B) limousine : sedan
(C) fresco : mural
(D) speech : polemic
(E) poetry : doggerel

15. SELFLESS : ALTRUISM ::

(A) smug : character
(B) guileless : youth
(C) stubborn : tenacity
(D) serene : temperament
(E) naive : determinism

Read each of the passages carefully, then answer the questions that come after them. The answer to each question may be stated overtly or only implied. You will not have to use outside knowledge to answer the questions—all the material you will need will be in the passage itself.

Questions 16–21 refer to the following passage.

The following passage is about Anna "Grandma" Moses, an American painter who lived from 1860–1961.

Line As technology progresses at breakneck
speed and the world becomes faster-paced
and more complex, many art appreciators
find themselves drawn to the simplicity of
(5) American primitive art. The word "primitive"
is not the insult it may appear to be. It is a
term used to describe the work of an artist
who has had no formal training. Perhaps the
most famous of American primitive artists is
(10) Anna Robertson Moses, better known as
Grandma Moses. She is known not only for
her paintings of early American life, but for a
remarkable personal circumstance. Grandma
Moses began her painting career in her late
(15) seventies and continued to paint past her
100th birthday.

    By the time she died in 1961, Moses
had lived through war and economic
depression. She had seen the world trans-
(20) formed through technology; automobiles,
television, and telephones would all have
become commonplace within her lifetime.
While she died long before the modern
computer, the fax machine, and the cellular
(25) phone had been invented, she had witnessed enormous technological progress,
and the complication that inevitably accom-
panies it. Grandma Moses painted with a
nostalgic eye to an even more innocent era.
(30) Her artistic style, unpretentious and unpolished, complemented the subject of her
work. Her paintings depict rural life:
townsfolk ice-skating, a village blanketed in
snow, a covered wagon, villagers collecting

(35) maple sugar. They evoke a combined sense
of community and connection to the land
that, by the middle of the twentieth century,
many people must have sensed to be a thing
of the past.

(40)   If Moses' subject was idealized small-
town America, her life, itself, embodied
American ideals. What, after all, could be
more a part of the American character than
self-definition? After a lifetime spent as a
(45) farm wife, Moses created a new identity for
herself as an artist. In her last years, even as
her health and vision failed, she continued
to produce her art. American culture values
entrepreneurship and self-definition;
(50) Grandma Moses epitomized these things in
her personal life, even as she tapped into
another American preoccupation: nostalgia
for our past.

        Perhaps people who seek out the
(55) American primitive work of artists like
Grandma Moses see in it more than a
depiction of a simpler life. Perhaps they
recognize in it the same values that so many
modern Americans hold dear: motivation,
(60) individuality, and a strong connection
between past and present. As primitive art
takes viewers to a simpler time, it also
reinforces the dearly held American belief
that anyone, at any age, can become a
(65) national icon.

GO ON TO THE NEXT PAGE ➤

16. Which of the following would be the best title for this passage?

(A) The Life of Grandma Moses
(B) The Many Styles of American Art
(C) A History of American Primitive Art
(D) Small-Town America: A Favorite Subject of Artists
(E) Grandma Moses: An American Artist

17. The author defines the word *primitive* (lines 7–8) in order to

(A) compare several kinds of American art
(B) clear up a possible misunderstanding
(C) broaden the reader's understanding of American history
(D) solve a long-standing mystery
(E) offer an interpretation of an art form

18. The author would most likely agree with which of the following?

(A) Grandma Moses is America's most beloved artist.
(B) People who like primitive art are unlikely to enjoy more sophisticated art.
(C) Grandma Moses lived in a time as innocent as the scenes she painted.
(D) Grandma Moses is as popular for what she represents as for her art.
(E) Americans prefer art that reminds them of the technological progress they have made.

19. In line 31, the word *complemented* most closely means

(A) praised
(B) completed
(C) matched
(D) filled up
(E) amounted to

20. The passage mentions that Grandma Moses used to be a farm wife (lines 44–45) in order to show that Moses

(A) reinvented herself
(B) overcame poverty
(C) used her rural background in her art
(D) felt deep nostalgia for simpler times
(E) was innocent of modern technology

21. The passage lists all of the following as American traits EXCEPT

(A) tendency to idealize the past
(B) entrepreneurship
(C) desire for self-definition
(D) individuality
(E) love of art

Questions 22–31 refer to the following passage.

This passage is a summary of scientific articles dealing with biorhythms/biological clocks.

Line All of us are accustomed to the idea of using clocks to alert us when we need to do important things. We rely on clocks to let us know when it is time to sleep, time to wake
(5) up, time to eat, and time to work. But scientists have discovered a different type of clock, a clock that does not have a dial, hands, or numbers, and instead of being hung on the wall, is carried within the
(10) nervous system of many animals. It is known as a biological clock, and the discovery of its influence on the everyday activities of animals has provided valuable clues about what makes creatures tick.
(15)   Many animals appear to exhibit a periodicity in their behavior. This periodicity consists of patterns of performance involving a complex interaction among their bodily systems in synchronicity with their environ-
(20) ments. Rhythms that are reactions to a 24-hour cycle of light and dark are termed circadian. Those tied to the 29-day cycle of

the moon are known as circalunar. Still others are linked to the tides, which come
(25) in two types: a 12.4-hour tide and a 24.8-hour tide. Not surprisingly, those are termed circatidal rhythms. Yet another group of beings exhibit biorhythmical patterns linked to the seasons of the year—circannual
(30) rhythms. But the most intriguing aspect of all biorhythms is their ability to reign over us even when the customary environmental cues are removed.

The biological clocks that are most
(35) familiar to scientists and non-scientists alike are the circadian rhythms that operate on a daily, or 24-hour basis. Examples of these rhythms are on all sides of us, from the squirrels with their punctual, early-morning
(40) foraging hours to the bats that swoop out of hiding to begin hunting for food in the early, early twilight. They have regular periods of wakefulness, activity, and sleep within each 24-hour period of light and dark. In labora-
(45) tory experiments, animals with pronounced circadian rhythms have been deprived of light for prolonged periods of time, yet they continue to perform their daytime tasks at the same times regardless. Apparently, no
(50) clue from the environment is necessary to prompt these animals to perform the tasks we commonly associate with daytime and nighttime.

Circannual rhythms appear to dominate
(55) certain bird species, especially warblers. If a wood warbler is kept in a laboratory where light and dark are tightly controlled, with 12 hours allotted for each, its precise annual cycle may continue undisturbed for several
(60) months longer than a year. Likewise, in certain circannual rodents such as European hedgehogs, chipmunks, and ground squir-rels, researchers note an adherence to cyclical periods of hibernation and activity
(65) even under constant laboratory periods of light and dark. Although the animals' laboratory year may vary in length from

roughly 220 to 450 days, the endogenous circannual rhythms assert their dominance
(70) over behaviors.

Research has also shown that human beings appear to have some pronounced, though very complex, biological rhythms that motivate certain behaviors in conjunc-
(75) tion with environmental cues.

What is it that causes the biological clock to tick with such a dependable regularity? Many studies have been con-ducted, all suggesting that the primary
(80) mechanism underlying behavioral periodicity is neural, meaning it is contained within the nervous system. The studies also suggest that hormones play a supporting role. In several insects, the circadian clock is apparently
(85) regulated by fibers that extend from cells in optic lobes to nerve cells, called neurons, in the thorax. Crustaceans such as crabs and crayfish depend on neurons in their eye-stalks to provide rhythmical information.
(90) Certain mollusks are dependent on seasonal chemical changes in their neurons and blood that dictate periodic levels of rest and activity.

22. This passage focuses primarily on

   (A) biorhythms of the smaller mammals
   (B) creatures with circatidal rhythms
   (C) the causes of Seasonal Affective Disorder
   (D) results of laboratory experiments on circannual rhythms of animals
   (E) periodicity in animal behavior

GO ON TO THE NEXT PAGE ▶

23. We can infer from this article that

- (A) people are better able to combat their natural rhythms than animals are
- (B) all animal behavior is based on circannual rhythms
- (C) scientists do not know the exact cause of periodicity in animal behavior
- (D) animals kept in a controlled laboratory setting would eventually lose all periodicity in their behavior
- (E) humans and animals behave according to social rules rather than according to natural ones

24. Data on biological clocks show that even if the sun did not set for an extended period of time, a circadian creature would

- (A) still require three meals a day
- (B) take more frequent naps
- (C) productively use the extra daylight hours
- (D) rest at the customary time
- (E) become cross from lack of regular sleep

25. According to this passage, animals with strong circadian rhythms

- (A) change their behaviors as soon as their environment changes
- (B) may continue circadian-based behaviors without regard to their environments
- (C) depend completely upon the position of the sun
- (D) modify their behavior only in laboratory experiments
- (E) are found primarily in parts of the world where the sun shines a great deal of the time

26. Observing test warblers in the lab where photoperiods were controlled proved to scientists

- (A) that the warblers' biological clock was preeminent
- (B) that warblers were circannual beings
- (C) that warblers required a fixed amount of darkness
- (D) that warblers utterly disregarded light and dark
- (E) that warblers were in tune with their environment

27. In line 72, *pronounced* is used to mean

- (A) articulated
- (B) unmistakable
- (C) suspected
- (D) declared
- (E) historical

28. The word *endogenous* in line 68 means

- (A) interior
- (B) induced
- (C) innate
- (D) reliable
- (E) predictable

29. All the examples in this passage serve to illustrate

- (A) the shared traits of all sentient beings
- (B) the significance of neural and hormonal changes
- (C) the universal existence of endogenous clocks
- (D) the complexity of dominant circadian rhythms
- (E) the necessity for balancing biorhythmical needs

30. According to the passage

    (A) humans are free of behavior that is linked to endogenous rhythms

    (B) humans are more strongly governed by endogenous rhythms than animals are

    (C) neither animals nor humans are affected by their environments

    (D) humans exhibit signs of endogenous rhythms

    (E) experiments performed on humans have proved the preeminence of their circannual rhythms

31. The article says all of the following EXCEPT that

    (A) the behavior of many creatures is affected by an interaction between bodily systems and the environment

    (B) animals hibernate in response to biological rhythms that interact with the seasons

    (C) humans exhibit signs of having biological clocks

    (D) laboratory tests back up circannual explanations of animal behavior

    (E) the cause of biological rhythms is exclusively neural

S T O P   If you finish before time is called, you may check your work on this section only. Do not turn to any other section in the test.

Section 5

Notes:

1. You may use a calculator. All of the numbers used are real numbers.

2. Figures accompany some problems. Assume that each has been drawn accurately and lies in a plane, unless the instructions indicate otherwise.

Reference Information

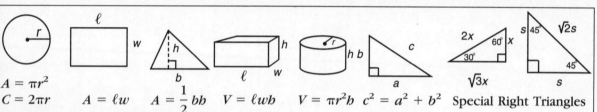

$A = \pi r^2$
$C = 2\pi r$ $\quad A = \ell w$ $\quad A = \frac{1}{2} bh$ $\quad V = \ell wh$ $\quad V = \pi r^2 h$ $\quad c^2 = a^2 + b^2$ $\quad$ Special Right Triangles

The number of degrees of arc in a circle is 360.
The measure in degrees of a straight angle is 180.
The sum of the measures in degrees of the angles of a triangle is 180.

1. If one fifth of a number is 20, then 5 times that number is

    (A) 4
    (B) 5
    (C) 20
    (D) 100
    (E) 500

2. The statement $\frac{A}{B} = C$ implies that all of the following equations are correct EXCEPT

    (A) $B = A \cdot C$
    (B) $C = A \div B$
    (C) $A = B \cdot C$
    (D) $A = C \cdot B$
    (E) All of the above statements are correct.

3. If $\frac{3}{4}$ the area of a square is 12, what is the length of a side of the square?

    (A) 3
    (B) 4
    (C) 12
    (D) 16
    (E) $\sqrt{12}$

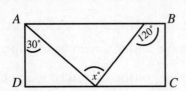

Note: Figure not drawn to scale.

4. In the figure above, *ABCD* is a rectangle.
    $x =$

    (A) 150
    (B) 125
    (C) 100
    (D) 75
    (E) 60

5. What is the average (arithmetic mean) of $a - 2$, a, $a + 2$, and $a + 4$?

    (A) 0
    (B) a
    (C) $a + 1$
    (D) $4a + 1$
    (E) $\frac{a + 1}{4}$

6. If $x = \frac{1}{2}y$ and $w = 2x$, then y written in terms of w is

    (A) $\frac{1}{4}w$
    (B) $\frac{1}{2}w$
    (C) w
    (D) $2w$
    (E) $4w$

GO ON TO THE NEXT PAGE

7. 20% of 50% of 80 is

(A) 8
(B) 20
(C) 40
(D) 50
(E) 80

9. If $b \neq a$, then $\dfrac{b}{a-b} - \dfrac{a}{b-a} =$

(A) -1
(B) 0
(C) 1
(D) $\dfrac{b-a}{a-b}$
(E) $\dfrac{a+b}{a-b}$

8. Some books are stacked beside each other on a shelf. Starting from the left, *Pride and Prejudice* is counted as the third book on the shelf, and starting from the right it is counted as the ninth book. How many books are on the shelf?

(A) 6
(B) 11
(C) 12
(D) 14
(E) It cannot be determined from the information given.

10. Sophie and Maureen bake cupcakes. Sophie coats $\dfrac{1}{2}$ of the cupcakes with chocolate frosting, and Maureen coats $\dfrac{1}{6}$ with white frosting. If 12 cupcakes remain unfrosted, how many cupcakes did they bake?

(A) 18
(B) 24
(C) 36
(D) 42
(E) 48

S T O P   If you finish before time is called, you may check your work on this section only. Do not turn to any other section in the test.

[This page intentionally left blank]

Section 6

Read each of the passages carefully, then answer the questions that come after them. The answer to each question may be stated overtly or only implied. You will not have to use outside knowledge to answer the questions—all the material you will need will be in the passage itself. In some cases, you will be asked to read two related passages and answer questions about their relationship to one another.

Questions 1–11 refer to the following passages.

Passage 1

In this passage, published in 1849, the writer reflects on the view from a canoe on a New England river.

Line   The trees made an admirable fence to the
        landscape, skirting the horizon on every
        side. The single trees and the groves left
        standing on the interval appeared naturally
(5)   disposed, though the farmer had consulted
        only his convenience, for he too falls into
        the scheme of Nature. Art can never match
        the luxury and superfluity of Nature. In the
        former all is seen; it cannot afford concealed
(10)   wealth, and is miserly in comparison; but
        Nature, even when she is scant and thin
        outwardly, satisfies us still by the assurance
        of a certain generosity at the roots. In
        swamps, where there is only here and there
(15)   an evergreen tree amid the quaking moss
        and cranberry beds, the bareness does not
        suggest poverty. The single spruce, which I
        had hardly noticed in gardens, attracts me in
        such places, and now first I understand why
(20)   people try to make them grow about their
        houses. But though there may be very
        perfect specimens in front-yard plots, their

beauty is for the most part ineffectual there,
for there is no such assurance, as in a
(25)   swamp, of kindred wealth beneath and
around them, to make them show to
advantage. As we have said, Nature is a
greater and more perfect art, the art of God;
though, referred to herself, she is genius;
(30)   and there is a similarity between her
operations and human art even in the details
and trifles. When the overhanging pine
drops into the water, the sun and water, and
the wind rubbing it against the shore, wear
(35)   its boughs into fantastic shapes, white and
smooth, as if turned in a lathe. Human art
has wisely imitated those forms into which
all matter is most inclined to run, such as
foliage and fruit. Our art leaves its shavings
(40)   and its dust about; Nature's art exhibits itself
even in the shavings and the dust which we
make, as the curled shavings drop from a
wood plane, and borings cluster round an
auger. She has perfected herself by an
(45)   eternity of practice.

Passage 2

This passage, published in 1891, consists of an imaginary dialogue that takes place in an English country house.

Cyril [coming in through the open window from the terrace]: My dear Vivian, don't coop yourself up all day in the library. It is a perfectly lovely afternoon. The air is
(50) exquisite. There is a mist upon the woods, like the purple bloom upon a plum. Let us go and lie on the grass and enjoy Nature.

Vivian: Enjoy Nature! I am glad to say that I have entirely lost that faculty. People
(55) tell us that Art makes us love Nature more than we loved her before; that it reveals her secrets to us; and that after a careful study of Corot and Constable we see things in her that had escaped our observation. My own
(60) experience is that the more we study Art, the less we care for Nature. What Art really reveals to us is Nature's lack of design, her curious crudities, her extraordinary monotony, her absolutely unfinished condition.
(65) Nature has good intentions, of course, but, as Aristotle once said, she cannot carry them out. When I look at a landscape I cannot help seeing all its defects. It is fortunate for us, however, that Nature is so imperfect, as
(70) otherwise we should have no art at all. Art is our spirited protest, our gallant attempt to teach Nature her proper place. As for the infinite variety of Nature, that is a pure myth. It is not to be found in Nature herself.
(75) It resides in the imagination, or fancy, or cultivated blindness of the person who looks at her.

Cyril: Well, you need not look at the landscape. You can lie on the grass and talk.
(80) *Vivian*: But Nature is so uncomfortable. Grass is hard and lumpy and damp, and full of dreadful crawling insects. Why, even the poorest workman could make you a more comfortable seat than the whole of Nature

(85) can. I don't complain. If Nature had been comfortable, we would never have invented architecture, and I prefer houses to the open air.

1. The author of Passage 1 uses the phrase *a certain generosity at the roots* (line 13) to suggest that

   (A) human art is merely an imitation of natural beauty
   (B) an observer must look very closely at a natural phenomenon to appreciate its beauty
   (C) nature's chief beauty lies in the way growing things are sustained by the abundance around them
   (D) natural beauty is always abundant even if the abundance is not immediately apparent
   (E) the richness of the soil from which trees and other plants grow is itself beautiful

2. For the author of Passage 1, the reason a spruce tree growing naturally in a swamp is more beautiful than a spruce tree cultivated in a front yard is that the spruce tree in the swamp

   (A) has not been spoiled by human intervention
   (B) has been worn into interesting shapes by the sun and wind
   (C) is surrounded by other naturally occurring phenomena
   (D) is more likely to be healthy and therefore beautiful
   (E) stands out against the relative poverty of its immediate environment

GO ON TO THE NEXT PAGE

3. The *overhanging pine* in line 32 is presented as an example of

   (A) a natural phenomenon that is more beautiful than anything a human artist could produce
   (B) a natural form that is similar to art produced by human beings
   (C) the beauty that results when natural processes of erosion affect growing things
   (D) the great variety of forms that natural beauty can take
   (E) the contrast between plants growing in the wild and those cultivated by humans

4. The contrast between the *shavings* and *dust* of human art and those of nature's art in lines 39–41 serves primarily to show that

   (A) human art imitates natural forms
   (B) human art is more wasteful than nature's art
   (C) nature's art is more carefully designed than human art
   (D) nature's art sometimes appears less abundant to the casual observer than human art
   (E) nature's art can make beautiful forms out of the leavings of human art

5. Which of the following does Vivian in Passage 2 see as a positive outcome of nature's limitations?

   (A) Nature's unfinished quality inspires people to create art.
   (B) Nature's monotony makes people appreciate artistic variety.
   (C) Nature's meager scope ensures that nature rarely intrudes on human life.
   (D) Studying nature is relatively easy because natural phenomena exhibit so little variety.
   (E) Observers must use their imaginations to see beauty in nature.

6. In Passage 2, Vivian mentions all of the following as defects of nature EXCEPT that nature is

   (A) full of imperfections
   (B) emotionally unsatisfying
   (C) unable to deliver on its well-meant intentions
   (D) less well designed than art
   (E) less interesting than art

7. The word *poorest* in line 83 most nearly means

   (A) most humble
   (B) most pitiable
   (C) most destitute
   (D) least valuable
   (E) least competent

8. Vivian would most likely say that the author of Passage 1 sees so much beauty in nature because he

   (A) gives nature credit for her good intentions
   (B) has too little appreciation for human art
   (C) brings the beauty to nature from his own mind
   (D) transfers his appreciation of beautiful human artifacts to similar natural phenomena
   (E) ignores the lack of comfort in natural surroundings

9. One technique that the author of Passage 1 and Vivian in Passage 2 both employ is

   (A) personification of nature as female
   (B) comparison of specific artistic and natural forms
   (C) use of nature metaphors to describe artistic endeavors
   (D) use of specific artists as examples
   (E) citation of earlier writers as authorities

10. In contrast to the tone of Passage 1, the tone of Vivian's speeches in Passage 2 is more

(A) inflammatory
(B) epigrammatic
(C) antiquated
(D) polished
(E) acerbic

11. Vivian would most likely react to the assertion by the author of Passage 1 that nature *has perfected herself by an eternity of practice* (lines 44-45) with

(A) dubious acquiescence
(B) studied indifference
(C) condescending pity
(D) lofty dismissal
(E) intense outrage

S T O P If you finish before time is called, you may check your work on this section only. Do not turn to any other section in the test.

Quick-Score Answers

Diagnostic Test					
Math			**Verbal**		
Section 1	**Section 3**	**Section 5**	**Section 2**	**Section 4**	**Section 6**
1. D	1. A	1. E	1. B	1. B	1. D
2. D	2. C	2. A	2. D	2. C	2. C
3. A	3. A	3. B	3. C	3. C	3. B
4. B	4. B	4. E	4. A	4. A	4. E
5. A	5. B	5. C	5. A	5. E	5. A
6. B	6. C	6. C	6. E	6. D	6. B
7. C	7. D	7. A	7. C	7. D	7. E
8. E	8. A	8. B	8. C	8. A	8. C
9. C	9. A	9. E	9. E	9. B	9. A
10. D	10. D	10. C	10. B	10. D	10. E
11. E	11. B		11. D	11. D	11. D
12. D	12. A		12. C	12. B	
13. B	13. B		13. E	13. A	
14. C	14. A		14. B	14. E	
15. E	15. B		15. A	15. C	
16. E	16. 0		16. D	16. E	
17. B	17. 12		17. A	17. B	
18. C	18. 1.5 or 3/2		18. C	18. D	
19. C	19. 156, 182, 210		19. E	19. C	
20. B	or 240		20. B	20. A	
21. B	20. 53		21. D	21. E	
22. C	21. 10		22. D	22. E	
23. C	22. 4		23. E	23. C	
24. D	23. 36/5 or 7.2		24. E	24. D	
25. B	24. 4		25. A	25. B	
	25. 250		26. B	26. A	
			27. B	27. B	
			28. C	28. C	
			29. D	29. C	
			30. E	30. D	
			31. A	31. E	
			32. C		
			33. D		
			34. D		
			35. E		
			36. B		

Detailed explanations to the answers for the Diagnostic Test can be found on page 389.

Scoring the Test

Check your answers to the math sections against the answer key, and record the number of correct and incorrect answers for each section in the spaces provided. For sections 1 and 5, multiply the number of incorrect answers by .25, and subtract this from the number correct. This gives you your raw scores for sections 1 and 5. For questions 1–15 in section 3, multiply the number of incorrect answers by .33, and subtract this from the number correct. For questions 16–25 in section 3, simply record the number of correct answers; these questions are Grid-ins and have no wrong answer penalty. Adding these two numbers gives you your total for section 3. Now sum the raw scores of each math section, and round the total to the nearest whole number. This is your math raw score.

Check your answers to the verbal sections against the answer key, and record the number of correct and incorrect answers in the spaces provided. Multiply the number of incorrect answers by .25, and subtract this from the number correct. Round the result to the nearest whole number. This is your verbal raw score.

Use the score chart to translate your raw scores into scaled scores. However, remember that these scores are only approximations of how you might do on the real test. Lots of factors will affect your actual SAT scores: taking the test under controlled conditions, your preparation between now and test day, etc. Use these scores to get a rough idea of your score range on the exam and to decide how to focus your SAT preparation.

Scoring Worksheet

MATH				
	Number Correct	**Number Incorrect**	**=**	**Raw Score**
Section 1	_23_	− (.25 × _0_)	=	_23_
Section 3				
1–15	_____	− (.33 × _____)	=	_____
16–25	_____	(no wrong answer penalty)	=	_____
Section 5	_____	− (.25 × _____)	=	_____
		Total Rounded Raw Score		_____
VERBAL				
Sections 2, 4, and 6	_____	− (.25 × _____)	=	_____
		Total Rounded Raw Score		_____

Score Charts

Math			
Raw Score	Math Scaled Score	Raw Score	Math Scaled Score
60	800	28	500
59	800	27	490
58	790	26	490
57	770	25	480
56	760	24	470
55	740	23	460
54	720	22	460
53	710	21	450
52	700	20	440
51	690	19	430
50	680	18	420
49	670	17	420
48	660	16	410
47	650	15	410
46	640	14	400
45	630	13	390
44	620	12	380
43	610	11	370
42	600	10	360
41	600	9	350
40	590	8	340
39	580	7	330
38	570	6	320
37	560	5	310
36	560	4	300
35	550	3	280
34	540	2	270
33	540	1	250
32	530	0	240
31	520	−1	220
30	510	−2	210
29	510	−3 and below	200

Verbal			
Raw Score	Verbal Scaled Score	Raw Score	verbal Scaled Score
78	800	37	510
77	800	36	510
76	800	35	500
75	790	34	500
74	780	33	490
73	770	32	490
72	760	31	480
71	750	30	480
70	740	29	470
69	730	28	460
68	720	27	460
67	710	26	450
66	700	25	450
65	700	24	440
64	690	23	440
63	680	22	430
62	670	21	420
61	670	20	410
60	660	19	410
59	650	18	400
58	640	17	390
57	640	16	380
56	630	15	380
55	620	14	370
54	610	13	360
53	610	12	360
52	600	11	350
51	600	10	340
50	590	9	330
49	590	8	320
48	580	7	310
47	570	6	300
46	570	5	290
45	560	4	270
44	550	3	260
43	550	2	250
42	540	1	240
41	540	0	230
40	530	−1	220
39	520	−2	210
38	520	−3 and below	200

THIS IS A TEST. IT IS ONLY A TEST.

You've heard about the SAT. You know that it has to do with getting into college, and that you'll need a couple of #2 pencils. But you may not know where the SAT comes from, how colleges use it, or what you need to do to prepare for it.

The SAT (officially the SAT I: Reasoning Test) is primarily a multiple-choice exam used for college admissions purposes. It is not prepared by colleges, high schools, or a government agency. It is published by a for-profit company (Educational Testing Services or ETS) that produces many different standardized tests.

Colleges use the SAT as a standard measuring stick to compare students from a wide variety of educational backgrounds. Given that there are many different ways that schools evaluate their students, the SAT provides a benchmark for comparison. Colleges place varying degrees of importance on SAT scores. Some don't even require them. Consult individual colleges for more information.

***Peterson's 4 Year Colleges* contains fact-filled profiles of more than 2,000 colleges and universities. It's a good place to research schools' specific SAT policies.**

The SAT can feel like an insurmountable hurdle standing between you and college, but it doesn't have to be. It's just one of many factors that a college considers in evaluating applicants and one of the few that you still have a chance to improve. The SAT is not a test of all the content you've learned since kindergarten. It tests specific content in specific ways every time it is administered. This predictability works to your advantage, as you'll see in the chapters that follow. You will go into the test knowing what types of questions you'll see, what subject matter they'll cover, and exactly how to approach them.

OVERVIEW

The SAT is a three-hour exam that is divided into seven sections: three math, three verbal, and one experimental section that can be either. The sections can appear in any order, and you'll get two ten-minute breaks. The "experimental" is used to test questions for future SATs and will not count toward your score. Since you can never be sure which section is the experimental, treat every section as though it counts.

Math	Verbal
30-minute section	30-minute section
30-minute section	30-minute section
15-minute section	15-minute section
30-minute experimental section math or verbal	

The proctor will direct you when to begin and end each section. You must work on only that section until time is called; after that, you cannot change any answers or enter additional ones in that section.

There are six different question types on the SAT, each with a specific format. The directions for the question types are always the same. Familiarize yourself with them now, so you won't need to waste time reading them on test day.

Math Question Types	Verbal Question Types
35 Five-choice Multiple Choice	19 Analogies
15 Quantitative Comparisons	19 Sentence Completions
10 Grid-ins	40 Critical Reading

These question types are distributed throughout the sections. Within each set of a particular question type (except critical reading), the level of difficulty gradually increases.

	30-Minute Section	30-Minute Section	15-Minute Section
Math	25 Five-Choice Multiple Choice	15 Quantitative Comparisons 10 Grid-ins	10 Five-Choice Multiple Choice
Verbal	13 Analogies 9 Sentence Completions 13 Critical Reading	6 Analogies 10 Sentence Completions 14 Critical Reading	13 Critical Reading

PENCIL AND PAPER

You record your responses by penciling in ovals on your answer sheet. Check every so often to make sure that you are entering your answers next to the correct question numbers. Be extra careful if you omit questions or skip around within a section. The right answers gridded in the wrong spots won't earn you any points.

Feel free to mark up your test booklet. Underline important parts of reading passages, cross out answer choices you've eliminated, make sketches for geometry questions—whatever you need to do to solve the question. No one is going to read or care about what you've written, so don't be shy. Only the ovals you mark on your answer sheet will be used to determine your score. It's also a good idea to circle questions that you skip within a section. If you have time left at the end, you'll be able to quickly find the problems you want to revisit.

SCORING

A perfect SAT score is 1600: 800 Math and 800 Verbal. These are scaled scores, which rate your performance on a scale of 200–800. When people refer to SAT scores, they are generally referring to the scaled scores. Scaled scores are generated by raw scores, which consist of the number of questions you answered correctly minus a fraction of the number you incorrectly answered. You will also receive a percentile score that shows how you performed in relation to other test-takers.

Question Type	Wrong—Answer Penalty
Five-Choice Multiple Choice	$\frac{1}{4}$ point
Quantitative Comparison	$\frac{1}{3}$ point
Grid-in	None
Analogies	$\frac{1}{4}$ point
Sentence Completions	$\frac{1}{4}$ point
Critical Reading	$\frac{1}{4}$ point

You've probably heard that there's a guessing penalty on the SAT. This isn't completely accurate. You gain a whole point for every question you get right. You lose a fraction of a point for every question you get wrong. You don't gain or lose points for questions that you omit. No one will know whether you guessed on any particular question. If you guess wrong, you lose a fraction of a point. If you guess right, you gain a point. That said, random guessing won't really get you anywhere. Statistically speaking, if you guessed haphazardly on any given section, you'd lose as many points as you'd gain. Since each question (with the exceptions noted in the chart above) has 5 choices, the odds are that in a group of 5 questions, you'd answer one correctly and the other 4 incorrectly. So, you'd gain 1 point for the right answer and lose $4\left(\frac{1}{4}\right) = 1$ point for the wrong answers and wind up with 0.

However, educated guessing can significantly raise your score. As soon as you eliminate one answer choice, you increase your odds for guessing correctly. Eliminate more than one choice, and your odds are that much better. Whenever you can eliminate one or more choices, it's worth your while to guess. Since Grid-ins don't have a wrong answer penalty, you should guess if you have any idea of the correct answer. The math and verbal chapters in this book will expose specific types of wrong answer choices so you can recognize and eliminate them on test day.

PACING

On most tests, pacing is about finishing all the questions in the given time. On the SAT, though, finishing all the questions won't necessarily earn you the most points. Unless you're aiming for a perfect score, you don't need to answer every question. If you got a 75 on a test in school, you probably wouldn't be too happy with your performance. But if you answered 75 percent or $\frac{3}{4}$ of the math questions on a typical SAT correctly, you would get a 620, a very competitive score.

POINTS IS POINTS

Remember: All questions on the SAT are worth the same number of points.

You can really boost your score by learning where it's most effective to spend your time. Difficulty level increases within each set, for all question types except Critical Reading. Obviously, hard questions take more time than easy ones. However, all questions are worth the same number of points. Don't fly through the easy questions so quickly that you make careless mistakes, only to get to the last, toughest questions, which most test-takers don't get right. Scoop up the early, easy points— don't blow questions you should get right just to get to the ones that most test-takers aren't expected to answer correctly. Remember, also, that it doesn't matter in what order you do the questions in a particular section. That means that if the section you're working on contains a Quantitative Comparison set and a Grid-in set, you can start with whichever one you feel more comfortable. Similarly, if you're faced with a reading passage you don't like the looks of, you can save it until after you've tackled the easier one.

RELATED TESTS

There are some other tests associated with the college admissions process.

PSAT

Students generally take the PSAT in their sophomore year of high school. It is very similar to the SAT, containing the same math and verbal question types in different numbers. All of the instructional material in this book can be used to prepare for the math and verbal sections of the PSAT. The test also contains a Writing Skills section. You will not be asked to write an essay, though; the Writing Skills section tests grammar and writing skills through multiple-choice questions. In addition to being good practice for the SAT, the PSAT provides a chance for students to qualify for National Merit Scholarship Corporation programs.

SAT II: Subject Tests

SAT II: Subject Tests are one-hour exams that test specific subjects. They are primarily multiple-choice tests and are marked on the 200–800 scale. Many schools require that you take one or more to be considered for admissions. The topic areas are diverse, ranging from world history to physics to Korean language.

For more information on the PSAT and the SAT II: Subject Tests, talk to your guidance counselor or visit www.collegeboard.org.

ACT

The ACT is another test used by colleges for admission purposes. Until recently, the ACT was the preferred admissions test of colleges in the Midwest. These days, most colleges in the United States accept either ACT or SAT scores. While the ACT is also a multiple-choice test, it covers a wider range of content than the SAT. The ACT contains four test sections: English, Reading, Math, and Science Reasoning.

For more information about the ACT, talk to your guidance counselor or visit www.act.org.

REGISTRATION

To register for the SAT, obtain a Registration Bulletin from your guidance counselor, complete the enclosed form, and mail it in the envelope provided. You can also register electronically by visiting College Board Online at www.collegeboard.org. Additional information about the SAT program is available at this site. To order publications, call 800-537-3160 (toll-free).

SAT I 2001–02 Test Dates

Test Date	Registration Deadline	Late Registration Deadline
October 13, 2001	September 11, 2001	September 15, 2001
November 3, 2001	September 28, 2001	October 10, 2001
December 1, 2001	October 26, 2001	November 7, 2001
January 26, 2002	December 21, 2001	January 2, 2002
March 16, 2002	February 8, 2002	February 20, 2002
May 4, 2002	March 29, 2002	April 10, 2002
June 1, 2002	April 26, 2002	May 8, 2002

The test dates above are for the Saturday administrations. Students whose religious beliefs prevent them from testing on a Saturday should consult the College Board site for alternative dates.

Special accommodations are available for students with documented disabilities. Students should contact the SAT Services for Students with Disabilities at the following address: SAT Services for Students with Disabilities, P.O. Box 6226, Princeton, New Jersey 08541-6226; Telephone: 609-771-7137 (Monday through Friday from 8:00 a.m. to 6:00 p.m. eastern standard time); TTY: 609-882-4118; E-mail: ssd@info.collegeboard.com

TEST DAY PREP TALK

Use this book as the core of your SAT preparation program and you'll be in good shape for test day. You'll have brushed up on your math and verbal skills, picked up key strategies and advice, and worked through full-length practice exams under test-like conditions. You may be tempted to study until dawn the night before the test, but the best thing you can do is to get a good night's sleep. Eat a good breakfast the morning of the test. Don't diverge too much from your daily routine, though—stick to what works for you.

Make sure you have the following items ready to go:

- admission ticket
- two #2 pencils with erasers
- four-function, scientific or graphing calculator with fresh batteries*
- identification*
- watch

Chances are that everything will go smoothly during the test, but it is possible you'll encounter a problem. If your test booklet is defective in some way or there's some kind of disturbance at the test site, notify your proctor. If the situation is not resolved to your satisfaction, contact the College Board within 24 hours.

When you've finished the test, you may be worried that you didn't do as well as you'd hoped. That's not an uncommon reaction. The test-taking experience is stressful, and you're likely to be focused on the parts of the test with which you had the most trouble. While you have the option to cancel your test score, it's probably not necessary. If you do, your test will never be scored. You probably scored higher than you think you did, and if you didn't, you can always take the test again. Many colleges look at your highest test scores. However, if you're fairly certain that something went seriously wrong, contact the College Board within 24 hours to cancel.

Now that you've gotten an overview of the SAT and read the fine print, you're ready to begin. The key to confidence on test day is to be well prepared. Study with this book and you'll face the test armed with the knowledge, strategies, and advice you need for SAT success.

---

* For specific information about what kinds of calculators and ID are acceptable, see College Board guidelines in the Registration Bulletin or College Board Online.

OVERVIEW

The SAT is a predictable exam. While the specific questions obviously change from test to test, the basic math content tested remains the same, as does the exam's format. Use this predictability to your advantage and get familiar with its ins and outs now. If you go in knowing what to expect, you'll be much more confident on test day. There are three math sections on every SAT, two 30-minute sections and one 15-minute section. In total, these three sections contain 35 five-choice multiple-choice questions, 15 Quantitative Comparison questions, and 10 Grid-in questions. That means that you'll have 60 math questions to answer in an hour and 15 minutes. Remember that in addition to the usual math and verbal sections, you'll get an extra section—the experimental. It won't count toward your score. Even if you think you can tell which section is the experimental, don't skip it, because you don't know for *sure* and it's not worth the risk.

MATH QUESTIONS

35 Multiple-Choice,
15 Quantitative Comparisons, 10 Grid-ins

While a solid grounding in the relevant math content is a must for success, it's not enough. The SAT is not a straight content test—it also involves critical thinking and math reasoning skills. Just memorizing the Pythagorean theorem won't cut it; you'll need to recognize when it's the key to solving a problem and then be able to apply it. This book will help you focus on the kind of thinking that will score you points. In the Math Red Alert, you'll be introduced to the conventions of the three math question types and some strategic insights for handling each. The Math Reference Section covers the raw content—the facts, formulas, and figures that are most often tested. It all comes together in the Math Teaching Unit, where you'll see how to apply strategies and approaches to the kinds of questions—in all content areas and question types—that show up on the SAT time and time again.

TEST TIP

Content + Knowledge + Strategic Insights = SAT Success

CALCULATORS

Definitely bring a calculator with you to the SAT, but don't feel you need to use it on every question (or at all, for that matter). Since the test isn't about performing long, mind-numbing strings of computation, a calculator won't guarantee you a perfect score. If you find yourself engaged in that kind of work, you can be sure that you've headed down the wrong path. Think through how to solve the problem first. If there's any arithmetic involved, decide whether or not using your calculator would help. Don't feel that you need the slickest, most expensive calculator on the market, either. You're better off with one that you're used to and feel comfortable with; what good is that extra functionality if you don't need it or know how to use it? Different calculators perform some functions differently, so it's important to know how yours works. For example, some calculators automatically follow the correct order of operations. If yours doesn't, you'll need to use PEMDAS to enter the operations into your calculator in the correct order. Otherwise, you'll come up with an incorrect answer. Use a calculator as you work through this book, do practice sets, take practice tests, etc. That's the best way to find out on which kinds of problems the calculator will be most useful to you.

FRESH JUICE

Make sure that your calculator has fresh batteries on test day—if it conks out midway through the test, you're on your own.

The difficulty level of the questions generally increases as you move through sets of questions in the math sections. This progression doesn't carry across question types, though; the first Grid-in is not harder than the last Quantitative Comparison it follows sequentially on the test. Obviously, harder questions will require more involved solutions, so budget your time accordingly. Be prepared for the fact that the harder questions will be, well, harder. Don't jump at tempting answer choices without thinking through the problems first. And don't beat yourself up if you can't answer some of these problems; the majority of test takers aren't expected to be able to answer them—that's why they're the hardest. All questions are worth the same number of points regardless of difficulty level. Making careless mistakes by rushing through the early, easy questions just to get a crack at the hardest ones on the section will cost you valuable points. Remember, you don't need to answer every question to get a good score.

HELP WITH MULTIPLE-CHOICE QUESTIONS

Since the directions for each question type are the same from test to test, learn them now so you don't waste time reading them on test day. Each of the math sections begins with the boxed "Reference Information" that includes some basic geometry formulas and relationships. You should already be familiar with this information and know how to use it when you sit down to take the test. Just think of it as an insurance policy in case you get a little nervous and want to make sure that the side opposite the 30° angle in a 30-60-90 right triangle is half the length of the hypotenuse. If you didn't know enough to look out for and recognize the special triangle in the first place, however, the reference information will do you little good.

TEST TIP

There are 25 multiple-choice questions on one of the 30-minute math sections and 10 on the 15-minute math section.

The five-choice multiple-choice questions (which we'll refer to as "multiple choice" from here forward) will be very important to your SAT math score. They represent more than half of all the math questions, accounting for 35 of the total of 60. As their name implies, these questions are followed by 5 possible answers, lettered (A) through (E). You need to select the correct answer and fill in its corresponding oval on your answer sheet. If you answer a multiple-choice question incorrectly, you'll lose $\frac{1}{4}$ of a point. In general, you can afford to spend a little more than a minute on each of the multiple-choice questions, but that's just a rough guide. You won't need to spend that much time on the early questions, but you'll need to spend more than that on the harder questions. Your pacing on particular questions will also depend on which content areas are your strengths and weaknesses. Multiple-choice questions can cover any of the relevant math concepts in the areas of arithmetic, algebra, and geometry or a combination of those concepts.

GENERAL APPROACH

When you approach a multiple-choice question, first read it through. Think about what the question asks and what particular math knowledge or formulas might apply. If it's a geometry question that doesn't provide a diagram, sketching one might help you to organize the given information. If it does have a diagram, mark in what you're told about it and anything else you can deduce from that. Glance at the choices. If any of them are obviously wrong, (e.g., too big or too small), eliminate them. If all the answer choices are given in a particular unit, like inches, perform your calculations in that unit as well. Solving for the correct answer in feet but then forgetting to convert it to inches could cost you points. As obvious as this might sound, make sure that you're answering the question that's asked. A question might ask you to solve for y, but in order to do so, you might have to solve for x first. It's very likely that the value of x will be a choice, there to lure in careless or hasty test takers. Be sure to follow through and answer the question that is asked.

Don't hesitate to write on your test booklet—no one will see or care what you've written. Mark up geometry figures, cross out choices you've eliminated, circle questions you've skipped and want to come back to, etc.

If one side of a triangle has length 5 and a second side has length 8, which of the following could be the perimeter of the triangle?

(A)   7
(B)   13
(C)   16
(D)   20
(E)   26

This question is about a triangle, specifically its perimeter. Remember that the perimeter of a triangle is the sum of its three sides. Since you know that two of its sides are 5 and 8, you know that its perimeter must be greater than $5 + 8 = 13$. Right off the bat, you can eliminate choices (A) and (B), so the correct answer must be among choices (C), (D), or (E). If you were stumped about what to do next, you could guess from the remaining three choices. The key to this problem is figuring out a possible length for the third side of the triangle. What rules or principles are there regarding the sides of a triangle? The third side of a triangle must be greater than the difference of the other two sides and less than their sum. So, the third side of this triangle must be between $8 - 5$ and $8 + 5$, or $3 <$ third side < 13. Subtracting 13 (the sum of the other two sides) from the remaining choices will reveal the length of the third side in each: choice (C), $16 - 13 = 3$, choice (D), $20 - 13 = 7$, and choice (E), $26 - 13 = 13$. The only side that is greater than 3 and less than 13 is 7, so choice (D) is the correct answer.

REFERENCE POINT

Triangle Inequality Theorem: The three sides of a triangle are related such that the third side must be greater than the positive difference of the other two sides, and less than their sum. *(See p. 98)*

ELIMINATING CHOICES

Sometimes when you can't solve a question, you can still do enough to eliminate one or more choices. In the question above, you really needed to remember the triangle inequality theorem to find the correct answer. But even if you didn't, just remembering how to find a triangle's perimeter would eliminate two answer choices. Remember, if you can eliminate one or more answer choice, it's worthwhile to guess. Whenever you eliminate a choice, cross it out in your test booklet. That way, if you decide to skip the question and return to it later, you won't have to retrace your footsteps to figure out what you've already excluded. Learning to eliminate unreasonable answers is one way to take advantage of the multiple-choice format. There are a couple of other ways to do so that can also help you score some points.

WORKING BACKWARDS

Sometimes you can plug the answer choices back into the question to see which is correct. This strategy works when the answer choices are numbers. While plugging in five possibilities would be time-consuming, you generally don't need to try every choice to see which is correct. And if the alternative is skipping the question, it's probably worth your while to work backwards.

CALCULATOR TIP

When you're working backward, your calculator can be a big help—use it to plug answer choices back into the question.

Tickets for a play cost $25 for floor seats and $15 for balcony seats. If 300 tickets were sold for a total of $5,500, how many balcony tickets were sold?

(A)   75
(B)   100
(C)   150
(D)   200
(E)   250

If you didn't know how to set up the equation to solve this problem, working backward would be the way to go. When you're plugging answer choices back into a question, always start with choice (C). Since SAT answer choices are usually ordered from smallest to largest (or largest to smallest) starting with the middle value can save you time. If you plug in choice (C) and it's too big, you can eliminate it as well as the two answer choices larger than it. If you were pressed for time, at this point you'd have a fifty-fifty chance of guessing correctly. Those are pretty good odds, and you only had to try one choice to get them.

START IN THE MIDDLE

When you're plugging answer choices back into a question, always start with choice (C).

Start with choice (C). If 150 balcony tickets were sold, then 150 floor seats were sold: 150 ($15 + $25) = $6,000. Ticket sales only totaled $5,500, so choice (C) is incorrect. To get a smaller total, you need fewer of the expensive tickets and more of the cheap seats. Therefore, you need a value for the balcony seats that's greater than 150, and choices (A) and (B) can be eliminated. Now there are only two choices left. If the one you try is right, it's obviously the answer. If the one you try is wrong, you know that the remaining choice must be the answer. Either way, you only need to try one more choice. Since 200 is the easier number to work with, try choice (D). If 200 balcony seats were sold, 100 floor seats were sold: 200($15) + 100($25) = $5,500, and you've got the answer.

ON THE OTHER HAND . . .

To solve this question directly, you could have set up and solved the equation below, where B is the number of balcony seats:
15B + 25(300 − B) = 5,500.

VALUES FOR VARIABLES

You can also work backward when the answer choices contain variables. Pick values for the variables and work through the problem. Then plug these values into the choices. The one that matches your result is the correct answer.

Every d days a beagle chews b bones. At this rate, how many bones will she chew in w weeks?

(A) $7bw$

(B) $\dfrac{bdw}{7}$

(C) $\dfrac{7bw}{d}$

(D) $\dfrac{bd}{7w}$

(E) $\dfrac{7d}{bw}$

This question isn't terribly difficult, but having to manipulate so many variables can be daunting. Substituting values for the variables can help by making an abstract question more concrete. Let's say that the beagle chews 4 bones every 2 days, and you want to see how many bones she'll chew in 3 weeks.

In other words, $b = 4$, $d = 2$, and $w = 3$. That means that the beagle chews 2 bones each day. Since there are 7 days in a week, you want to find how many bones she'll chew in $3(7) = 21$ days: $2(21) = 42$. Plug your values into the choices to see which gives you 42.

(A) $7(4)(3) = 84$

(B) $\dfrac{(4)(2)(3)}{7} = \dfrac{24}{7} = 3\dfrac{3}{7}$

(C) $\dfrac{7(4)(3)}{2} = \dfrac{84}{2} = 42$

(D) $\dfrac{(4)(2)}{7(3)} = \dfrac{8}{21}$

(E) $\dfrac{7(2)}{(4)(3)} = \dfrac{14}{12} = 1\dfrac{1}{6}$

Since only choice (C) gives you 42, it must be the correct answer.

CHOOSE WISELY

Don't worry that 42 sounds like a lot of bones for a little beagle to chew. It doesn't matter whether the numbers you pick make sense in the given situation. It's more important to pick values that are easy to work with.

MULTIPLE MATCHES

Sometimes the values you use will produce more than one matching answer. If this happens, try new values in just those choices until only one matches. If you don't have time to do so, you can guess from the remaining choices.

USE THE DIFFICULTY LEVEL

You've seen several ways in which the choices can help you, but they can also trip you up if you're not careful. Sometimes a choice will jump out at you before you really think the problem through. For instance, you might be tempted by choices that contain numbers from the question or simple manipulations of them. Such obvious answers are rarely correct on tougher questions; if you jump at one, you could get burned.

Increasing a number x by 20 percent and then decreasing the result by 25 percent is equivalent to

(A)   decreasing x by 5 percent
(B)   decreasing x by 10 percent
(C)   decreasing x by 22.5 percent
(D) x
(E)   increasing x by 5 percent

Easy, huh? An increase of 20 percent followed by a decrease of 25 percent—the net change must be a decrease of 5 percent, right? Wrong. That's far too obvious an answer for a hard question. You can't just add and subtract percent increases and/or decreases that are made on different original amounts. The increase is made on the original amount x, but the decrease is made on the newly increased x. To make this clear and to determine the correct answer, select a value for x. Since it's easy to find percents of 100, let $x = 100$. Increasing 100 by 20 percent yields $100 + 20 = 120$. Decreasing 120 by 25 percent or $\frac{1}{4}$ yields $120 - 30 = 90$. The only choice that yields 90 when $x = 100$ is choice (B), decreasing x by 10 percent. As you can see, this question isn't very difficult, but if you'd jumped at choice (A), you wouldn't have taken the time to solve it.

CHOOSE 100

**Pick 100 for percent problems—
it's the easiest number to find percents of.**

HELP WITH QUANTITATIVE COMPARISONS

Quantitative Comparisons may throw you off at first glance, but once you become familiar with their unusual format, they're very manageable. They account for one quarter of all the math questions, comprising questions 1–15 on the 30-minute math section that also contains 10 Grid-ins. Quantitative Comparisons are about detecting and uncovering underlying relationships, not about tedious computation. As such, they're meant to be done quickly. You should aim to spend about 10 minutes or so total on these 15 questions to allow yourself enough time for the more labor-intensive Grid-ins that

follow. If you answer a Quantitative Comparison question incorrectly, you'll lose $\frac{1}{3}$ of a point.

Directions for Quantitative Comparison Questions

Questions 1–15 each consist of two boxed quantities, one in Column A and one in Column B. Compare them and select:

A if the quantity in Column A is greater;
B if the quantity in Column B is greater;
C if the two quantities are equal;
D if the relationship cannot be determined from the information given.

A response of E will be considered an ommission.

Notes:

1. Some questions provide information about one or both of the quantities to be compared. This information is unboxed and centered above the two columns.
2. A symbol that appears in both columns represents the same value in each.
3. Letters such as x, n, and k stand for real numbers.

	EXAMPLES		
	Column A	Column B	Answers
E1	$\frac{1}{2}$ of 50	$\frac{1}{4}$ of 25	●Ⓑ©ⒹⒺ
E2	The number of degrees in a circle	The number of degrees in a square	ⒶⒷ●ⒹⒺ
	$x > 0$		
E3	x	$\frac{1}{x}$	ⒶⒷ©●Ⓔ

Quantitative Comparisons present you with values in two columns, and you're asked to determine how they are related: one value may be larger, they may be equal, or their relationship may be impossible to determine. The directions above approximate those that you'll see on the test. The four possible answer choices are not reprinted for each question, so learn what they mean now. You'll have enough on your mind on test day without worrying which lettered oval means what. Note that there is no choice (E) for Quantitative Comparisons. However, your answer sheet will contain ovals marked (A) through (E), so be careful never to bubble in this choice; a response of (E) will be treated as an omission.

CHOOSE

(A) if the quantity in Column A is greater
(B) if the quantity in Column B is greater
(C) if the quantities are equal
(D) if the relationship cannot be determined

DETERMINING WHEN CHOICE (D) IS CORRECT

Before you can internalize the answer choices, you need to understand them. If the quantity in Column A is always greater, choice (A) is correct; if the quantity in Column B is always greater, choice (B) is correct; if the quantities are always equal, choice (C) is correct; and if the relationship cannot be determined, choice (D) is correct. The first three choices are pretty self-explanatory, but choice (D) needs a little more clarification. Look at this example:

Column A	Column B
n	n^2

At first glance, you might assume that the value in Column B is greater. It can be—if $n = 2$, then Column A contains 2 while Column B contains 4, which is obviously larger. But what if $n = 1$? Then both columns contain 1 and are equal. And if $n = \frac{1}{2}$? Then Column A contains $\frac{1}{2}$, and Column B contains $\left(\frac{1}{2}\right)^2 = \frac{1}{4}$, making A greater. Since all of these relationships are possible, the answer must be choice (D). In fact, as soon as you find that more than one relationship exists, grid in choice (D) and move on.

REFERENCE POINT

When a positive fraction less than 1 is squared, the resulting value is always smaller than the original fraction. *(See p. 84)*

GUESSING

There are some cases where you can see at a glance that choice (D) can't be correct. Because the relationship between numbers is definite, if both columns contain only numeric quantities, choice (D) can't be right. Say you're asked to compare 300^{150} and 150^{300}. Even if you have no idea how to find these values, you know that each does have a definite value. Therefore, the relationship between them must be of the concrete variety described by choices (A), (B), or (C), not of the ambiguous nature described by choice (D). In such a case, you could always eliminate choice (D) and guess from the remaining choices. Here's another guessing tip. Say you find that Column A may be greater on a particular question, but you don't have time to determine whether this is always the case. The fact that Column A may sometimes be greater tells you that Column B can't always be greater and that the columns can't always be equal. In such a case, you could safely eliminate choices (B) and (C) and have a 50 percent chance of guessing correctly between choices (A) and (D).

VALUES FOR VARIABLES

The strategy used in the preceding Quantitative Comparison—selecting values for variables—is especially useful on Quantitative Comparisons. However it's important to try a variety of numbers in addition to positive integers. In some cases, the centered information places limits on the value(s) of the variable(s), but you should generally try 0, 1, a negative, and a fraction between 0 and 1. These numbers don't always behave in the same ways that positive integers do, and that's often the key to solving. If you had simply stopped after trying $n = 2$ above, you would have come to the faulty conclusion that choice (B) was correct. The goal is to see if the relationship is independent of the particular values involved or whether a specific kind of number could alter it. So, after finding that $n = 2$ made Column B greater, you'd want to try another value that you thought might make the columns equal or make the value in Column A greater. If the relationship remains constant despite trying these different kinds of values, you've found the answer. But as soon as you find that more than one relationship exists, you know that choice (D) must be correct.

THE USUAL SUSPECTS

When using values for variables on Quantitative Comparisons, remember to try 0, 1, a negative, a fraction between 0 and 1, and a positive number greater than 1.

SIX OF ONE, HALF A DOZEN OF THE OTHER

You might have two equal quantities right under your nose and not realize it because they're expressed in different forms. There could be a fraction in one column, a decimal in the other; a measurement given in inches in one, a measurement given in feet in the other; a factored expression in one column, and one that's multiplied through in the other, etc. Sometimes making a comparison is as easy as just putting the columns in the same form.

Column A	Column B
$\dfrac{x^2 - 1}{x + 1}$	$x - 1$

In this question, you have a fraction in Column A; see if you can get rid of it. Notice that its numerator is a common factorable: $x^2 - 1$ factors to $(x + 1)(x - 1)$, making the fraction $\dfrac{(x + 1)(x - 1)}{(x + 1)}$. Cancel out a factor of $(x + 1)$ from the numerator and denominator and you're left with $(x - 1)$, making the columns equal.

REFERENCE POINT

Common Factorables

$$a^2 - 1 = (a + 1)(a - 1)$$
$$a^2 - b^2 = (a + b)(a - b)$$
$$a^2 - 2ab + b^2 = (a - b)^2$$
$$a^2 + 2ab + b^2 = (a + b)^2$$
(See p. 93)

TREAT QUANTITATIVE COMPARISONS LIKE EQUATIONS/INEQUALITIES

This question type is all about comparing quantities, so the concepts of equalities and inequalities can help you out. Think of a Quantitative Comparison as an equation or an inequality: in general, doing the same thing to both columns won't change their relationship. However, you can't multiply or divide by a negative since that could potentially reverse the relationship. And you can only square both sides if you know they are positive; squaring a negative would throw the relationship off as well.

Column A	Column B

$$x + 5 = 2y + 4$$

$3x + 15$	$6y + 9$

Is there a way to simplify the columns? Since all of the terms are multiples of 3, divide both columns by 3. That leaves you with $x + 5$ in Column A and $2y + 3$ in Column B. You know that $x + 5 = 2y + 4$; therefore, $2y + 3$ must be less than $x + 5$, and Column A is greater.

CALCULATOR TIP

Since Quantitative Comparisons focus more on reasoning than computing, you'll use your calculator less on this question type than the other two.

FOCUS ON REASONING, NOT COMPUTING

Since Quantitative Comparisons are not about performing rote computation, there's often a way to compare the two columns without finding exact values for them. Not only does this save you time, but it also lowers your chances of making computational errors.

Column A	Column B
300^{150}	150^{300}

You might think that your calculator will save the day on this one, but most calculators can't display values this large in a way that will allow you to compare them. And you certainly don't want to try multiplying these values out on your own. What makes this problem difficult is that you're comparing powers with different bases. Is there a way to change that? There sure is. Since $300 = 150 \times 2$, you can rewrite Column A as $(150 \times 2)^{150}$ or $150^{150} \times 2^{150}$. To make the columns even easier to compare, factor out 150^{150} in Column B to get $150^{150} \times 150^{150}$. Now the first terms in each column are equal, but, since $150^{150} > 2^{150}$, Column B is greater. You still don't know the exact value of either column, but you have found their relationship.

REFERENCE POINT

When multiplying powers with the same base, add the exponents. *(See p. 93)*

Sometimes you can determine a definite relationship between the columns even though you can't find a definite value for either of them.

Column A   **Column B**

Line x is parallel to line y.

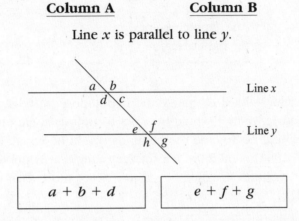

| $a + b + d$ | $e + f + g$ |

You can't determine the measures of the individual angles, but you do know something about their relative values. When two parallel lines are crossed by a transversal, all the acute angles formed are equal to each other, and all the obtuse angles formed are equal to each other. Looking at the diagram you can see that a, c, e, and g are acute, while b, d, f, and h are obtuse. Since in Column A you have two obtuse angles and in Column B you have only one obtuse angle, Column A must be greater. Unless you're told otherwise, diagrams on the SAT are drawn to scale. While that won't necessarily enable you to determine a particular measurement, it can give you a sense of the relative sizes of the measurements involved.

Assumptions Can Be Costly

Sometimes the relationship between the columns seems obvious at a first glance. In such cases, always examine the relationship to verify it. Making assumptions on Quantitative Comparisons, especially later ones, can lead to costly mistakes.

Column A	Column B

A right triangle has one side of length 6 and one side of length 8.

The hypotenuse of the right triangle	10

A triangle with sides of 6 and 8—well of course the hypotenuse is 10, right? Maybe, maybe not. If 6 and 8 were legs of the triangle, then it would be a 6-8-10 right triangle (a multiple of the 3-4-5 right triangle). Its hypotenuse would be 10, and the columns would be equal. However, since the centered information doesn't specify that 6 and 8 are legs of the triangle, it is possible that 8 is the hypotenuse. If that were the case, then Column B would be greater. Since more than one possibility exists, the answer must be choice (D).

REFERENCE POINT

Special Right Triangles: 3-4-5 (and its multiples);
5-12-13 (and its multiples);
30-60-90, and 45-45-90.
(See p. 101)

Help With Grid-ins

Grid-ins are like the questions that you're used to getting on high school math tests: you have to find the solution to a question without a selection of answers from which to choose. What's different about them is that instead of just writing down your answer, you have to represent it on a special grid. There are 10 Grid-ins on the SAT, so they account for a sixth of all the math questions. They turn up as questions 16–25 on the 30-minute math section that contains the Quantitative Comparisons. Try to allow yourself about 20 minutes for the 10 Grid-ins, as they are generally more time-consuming than Quantitative Comparisons. That's partly because without answer choices, you'll want to double check your work and also because it takes more time to grid an answer than it does to just bubble in an oval. Since you don't have the luxury of answer choices, you won't be penalized for incorrect responses. A wrong answer will be treated as an omission, and you will neither receive nor lose any points. Therefore, if you have any idea of the answer, grid it in. You've got nothing to lose.

The Grid

The directions below approximate those that you'll see on the test. We'll discuss the idiosyncrasies of the grid and what they mean for you, so that on test day you can focus on answering questions instead of worrying about how to grid in your responses.

Directions for Student-Produced Response Questions

Enter your responses to questions 16–25 in the special grids provided on your answer sheet. Input your answers as indicated in the directions below.

Answer: $\frac{4}{9}$ or 4/9

Answer: 1.4
Either position is correct.

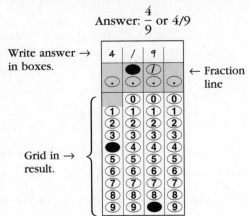

Write answer → in boxes.

← Fraction line

Grid in → result.

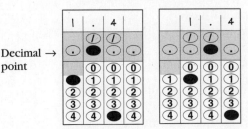

Decimal → point

Note: You may begin your answer in any column, space permitting. Leave blank any columns not needed.

- Writing your answer in the boxes at the top of the columns will help you accurately grid your answer, but it is not required. **You will only receive credit for an answer if the ovals are filled in properly.**

- Only fill in one oval in each column.

- If a problem has several correct answers, just grid in one of them.

- There are no negative answers.

- **Never grid in mixed numbers.** The answer $3\frac{1}{5}$ must be gridded as 16/5 or 3.2.

If 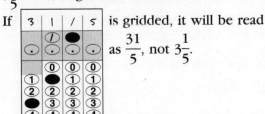 is gridded, it will be read as $\frac{31}{5}$, not $3\frac{1}{5}$.

Decimal Accuracy

Decimal answers must be gridded as accurately as possible. The answer 0.3333 . . . must be gridded as .333 or .334.
Less accurate values, such as .33 or .34, are not acceptable.

Acceptable ways to grid $\frac{1}{3}$ = .3333 . . .

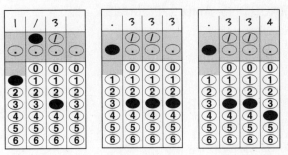

CALCULATOR TIP

Since you don't have answer choices on Grid-ins, you need to be especially careful to avoid computational errors. Your calculator can help you perform and check your calculations.

On multiple-choice math questions you can scan the choices to get a scope of what the answer may be. While you can't do that on Grid-ins, the grid itself places some limitations on the kinds of answers these questions can have. The grid cannot accommodate:

- negatives
- variables
- radicals
- pi
- numbers greater than 9,999

Therefore, these can never be part of the correct answer to a Grid-in. If you come up with an answer that includes any of them, you'll know you've made a mistake and need to check your work.

When you're ready to grid an answer, write it in the row of squares across the top of the grid, then darken the corresponding oval in each column. The scoring computer reads only the darkened ovals, so be careful to fill them in correctly. Don't try to save a few seconds by not writing the answer in the top row, though. This could lead to gridding errors that would cost you points in the end.

FRACTIONS AND DECIMALS

The grid contains fraction bars (represented by back-slashes "/") as well as decimal points, so fractions and decimals are both possible answers for Grid-ins. However, there are some rules you must follow when gridding them in. A particular answer may be gridded in as a fraction or a decimal. If the answer to a question is $\frac{1}{4}$, then either $\frac{1}{4}$ or .25 would be an acceptable answer.

It's not necessary to reduce a fraction unless it won't fit on the grid without being simplified. The fraction $\frac{18}{40}$ is too big for the grid, so you'd need to reduce it to $\frac{9}{20}$ or express it as the decimal .45.

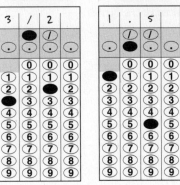

Decimals must be gridded in as completely as possible. If the answer is a long or repeating decimal, you must grid in as much of it as will fit. If the answer to a question is .54321, you'd have to grid .543 to get credit. If the answer is the repeating decimal .$\overline{77}$, you'd have to grid either .777 or .778. You wouldn't get any credit for gridding .77. Rounding is acceptable but not necessary, so don't worry about doing it.

INCORRECT   **CORRECT**   **CORRECT**

Never grid a mixed number; convert to a decimal or improper fraction instead. If the answer to a question is $1\frac{1}{2}$ and you grid in 1 1/2, your answer will be interpreted as $\frac{11}{2}$ and be marked incorrect.

This answer must be gridded as either $\frac{3}{2}$ or 1.5.

ABSOLUTE GRIDDING

NEVER grid mixed numbers. ALWAYS grid as much of a decimal as will fit. It's UNNECESSARY to reduce fractions or round decimals.

MORE THAN ONE ANSWER

Another peculiarity of Grid-ins is that there is not always just one correct answer. Sometimes the answer to a question is a range of values, and sometimes there are several correct responses. Say that you're asked for the value of x and find that $5 < x < 8$. While you'd get credit for gridding 5.1, 7.99, or any number of other values, make it easy on yourself and grid something simple, like 6. And for a question with many possible answers, as soon as you find one solution to the problem, grid it in and move on. You won't get any extra points for coming up with every possibility, and you'll waste time you could use to answer more questions and get more points.

GUESSING ON GRID-INS

There is no wrong answer penalty on Grid-ins, so there's no reason not to fill in an answer for every question. That doesn't mean that you waste lots of time trying to come up with a guess if you have no idea of the range of the correct answer or how to solve. This time would be better spent working on problems you actually have a shot at solving. There are some cases, however, when the possibilities are limited enough to make guessing a good idea.

GUESSING ADVICE

If you have any idea of the correct answer on a Grid-in, take a shot—you've got nothing to lose. Don't spend lots of time trying to pull an answer out of thin air, though, or you'll lose precious time.

$$\begin{array}{r} ABC \\ + \; CBA \\ \hline DDD \end{array}$$

$A, B, C,$ and $D \neq 0$

In the correctly worked addition problem above, if A, B, C, and D represent distinct digits, what is one possible value for B?

In the question above, you're told that the variables represent distinct digits. Therefore, the only possible values for B are 1, 2, 3, 4, 5, 6, 7, 8, and 9. Since there are multiple values for B, your chances of guessing correctly are already greater than 1 in 9, and you haven't done any work yet. If you think about the question a little, you'll notice that since nothing carries over in any of the columns, the sum of each pair of variables must be less than 10. That means that $2B$ must be less than 10 and B must be less than 5. Now you've further reduced the possible values of B to 1, 2, 3, or 4. With this extra insight, you've drastically increased your chances of guessing one of the correct values of B. (In fact, B can be either 2, 3, or 4.)

GRIDDING PRACTICE

Try gridding the following answers on the blank grids below, according to the rules and guidelines prevously discussed. *(See page 76 to check your work against the completed grids.)*

$\frac{2}{3}$ 132   5.37   1

$\frac{19}{38}$ $5\frac{1}{2}$ $\overline{.27}$ $\frac{11}{4}$

GRIDDING PRACTICE—COMPLETED GRIDS

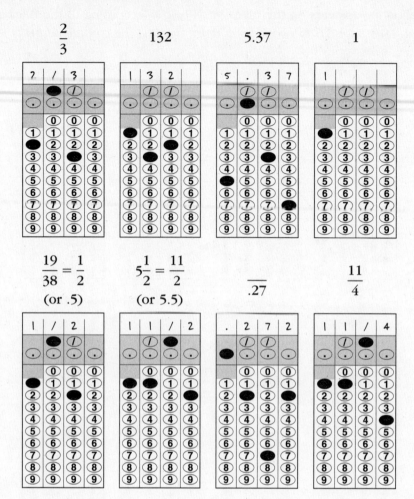

$\dfrac{2}{3}$ 132   5.37   1

$\dfrac{19}{38} = \dfrac{1}{2}$ $5\dfrac{1}{2} = \dfrac{11}{2}$ $\overline{.27}$ $\dfrac{11}{4}$

(or .5)   (or 5.5)

Math Reference Unit

Facts and Figures

Part of what's predictable about the SAT is the math content that's tested and the content that's *not* tested (e.g. trigonometry). The following section contains facts, formulas, and figures that are fair game on the test. Read through this list to get a sense of the scope of the test, stopping to spend more time on concepts that are unfamiliar or that give you trouble. Refer back to this section whenever you need to brush up on math definitions or concepts. In the Math Teaching Unit, you'll see how to apply the strategic insights from the Red Alert to this content on test-like questions.

Arithmetic

Integers

Integers are whole numbers and can be either positive or negative. Although 0 is neither positive nor negative, it is an integer.

Integers: $-5, 0, 4, 512$

Non-integers: $-12.5, 5\frac{1}{2}, 2\sqrt{3}$

Digits

Digits are the ten integers 0 through 9 of which other numbers are comprised.

Distinct

Distinct means different. The number 522 contains three digits (5, 2, and 2) but only two distinct digits (5 and 2).

Consecutive

Consecutive means following in order, without any omissions. The set of consecutive integers from 4 through 7 is 4, 5, 6, and 7. To find the number of consecutive integers in a set, subtract the smallest from the largest and then add one. In the set above, there are $(7 - 4) + 1 = 4$ consecutive integers. You can have sets of specific kinds of consecutive numbers, like consecutive even integers (2, 4, 6, 8 . . .) or consecutive multiples of 5 (5, 10, 15, 20 . . .).

Inclusive

Inclusive means "including." Describing the set of numbers "1 through 5 inclusive" means that both 1 and 5 are included in the set.

Even and Odd

Even numbers are divisible by 2; odd numbers are not. Zero is considered an even number. Check the last digit of any number to determine whether it's even or odd; if the last digit is odd, the entire number is odd, and if it's even, the entire number is even.

Even numbers: $-14, 0, 6,$ and $1,352$

Odd numbers: $-11, 5,$ and $2,469$

Positive and Negative

Positive numbers are greater than 0; negative numbers are less than 0. Zero itself is neither positive nor negative. Positive numbers get larger the farther away they are from 0, while negative numbers get smaller the farther away they are from 0: $25 > 20$, but $-25 < -20$.

Adding/Subtracting Signed Numbers

To add a positive and a negative, ignore the signs and subtract the smaller number from the larger. Then apply the sign of the larger number to this result.

$$-5 + 2 = -3 \qquad\qquad 5 + (-2) = 3$$

Subtracting a negative is the same as adding a positive.

$$5 - (-2) = 5 + 2 = 7 \qquad\qquad -5 - (-2) = -5 + 2 = -3$$

Multiplying/Dividing Signed Numbers

Multiply and divide as usual, attaching a positive sign to the result if there were originally an even number of negative terms or a negative sign if there were an odd number of negative terms.

$$3 \times -6 = -18 \qquad\qquad -18 \div 3 = -6$$
$$-3 \times -6 = 18 \qquad\qquad 18 \div -6 = -3$$
$$-3 \times -6 \times -1 = -18 \qquad\qquad -18 \div -6 = 3$$

Order of Operations

When you have to perform a string of calculations, remember PEMDAS to determine the order in which to compute. It stands for Parentheses, Exponents, Multiplication and Division (from left to right), and Addition and Subtraction (from left to right).

In the expression $1 + (2 + 3)^2 \div 4 - 5$, start with parentheses: $2 + 3 = 5$. Next, do exponents: $5^2 = 25$. Now you have $1 + 25 \div 4 - 5$. Do the division: $25 \div 4 = 6.25$. Finish with addition and subtraction: $1 + 6.25 - 5 = 2.25$.

Distributive Law

In essence, this law states that $a(b + c) = ab + ac$. You won't be called on to define this, but understanding the principle can help you save time on some arithmetic questions and is vital for questions involving factoring.

Commutative Law

In expressions involving addition or multiplication, order doesn't matter. In other words, $5 + 4 + 3 = 3 + 5 + 4$ and $(12)(15)(18) = (15)(18)(12)$. The commutative law does not apply to subtraction or division, because order does matter with these operations ($12 - 5 \neq 5 - 12$; $40 \div 2 \neq 2 \div 40$).

Factor

A factor of a number divides evenly into that number. The factors of 12 are 1, 2, 3, 4, 6, and 12, because none of these numbers leaves a remainder when divided into 12.

Multiple

A multiple of a number is evenly divisible by that number. Multiples of 12 include 12, 24, 48, and 120, because all of these numbers are divisible by 12.

Remainder

The remainder is the integer left over when a number is divided by a non-factor. Thirteen is not divisible by 5; 5 goes into 13 two times with 3 left over, so 3 is the remainder.

Prime

A prime number is one that has no factors other than 1 and itself. The number 1 itself is not prime. The smallest, and only even, prime number is 2. Other primes include 3, 17, and 41.

Prime Factorization

The prime factorization of a number is that number expressed as the product of its prime factors. Find it by expressing the number as the product of two factors, and then break down each of those factors until all of the factors are prime. Since $20 = 4 \times 5$, the prime factorization of 20 is $2 \times 2 \times 5$.

Common Multiple

A common multiple of two numbers is one that is evenly divisible by both of those numbers. Three and 15 share a common multiple of 30 since 30 is divisible by both 3 and 5.

Least Common Multiple (LCM)

The LCM is the smallest shared multiple of two numbers. Find it by listing multiples of the larger number until you find one that's also a multiple of the smaller number. To find the LCM of 9 and 15, list the multiples of 15: 15, 30, 45. Since 45 is also divisible by 9, it is the LCM.

Greatest Common Factor (GCF)

The GCF is the largest factor shared by two numbers and is actually the product of their common prime factors. To find the GCF of 24 and 90, first find the prime factorization of each: $24 = 2 \times 2 \times 2 \times 3$ and $90 = 2 \times 3 \times 3 \times 5$. They share a factor of 2 and a factor of 3, so the GCF is $2 \times 3 = 6$.

Divisibility Rules

Here are some rules to help you tell at a glance whether one number is divisible by another.

A number is divisible by 2 if its last digit is even: 7,534 is divisible by 2 since 4 is even.

A number is divisible by 3 if the sum of its digits is divisible by 3: 222 is divisible by 3 since $2 + 2 + 2 = 6$ is divisible by 3.

A number is divisible by 4 if its last two digits represent a number divisible by 4: 920 is divisible by 4 since 20 is divisible by 4.

A number is divisible by 5 if its last digit is either 0 or 5: 2,460 is divisible by 5 since it ends in 0

A number is divisible by 6 if it meets the rules for 2 and 3: 720 is divisible by 6 since 0 is even and $7 + 2 + 0 = 9$ is divisible by 3.

A number is divisible by 9 if the sum of its digits is divisible by 9: 333 is divisible by 9 since $3 + 3 + 3 = 9$ is divisible by 9.

A number is divisible by 10 if its last digit is 0: 970 is divisible by 10 since its last digit is 0.

Fraction

A fraction is another way of expressing division. The top number, or numerator, is being divided by the bottom number, or denominator. Since you can't divide by zero, the denominator of a fraction can never be zero. In the fraction $\frac{3}{4}$, 3 is the numerator and 4 the denominator.

Reducing Fractions

A fraction is in lowest terms when the numerator and denominator have no common factor (other than 1). To reduce a fraction to lowest terms, cancel out all common factors. $\frac{3}{5}$ is in simplest terms, since 3 and 5 have no common factor. $\frac{4}{6}$ can be reduced since 2 is a factor of both 4 and 6: $\frac{4}{6} = \frac{2 \times 2}{2 \times 3} = \frac{2}{3}$.

Adding/Subtracting Fractions

To add or subtract fractions, they must have a common denominator. A common denominator is simply a common multiple of the current denominators. Remember to multiply both the top and bottom of each fraction when finding the common denominator. For example,

$$\frac{2}{3} + \frac{1}{4} = \frac{4}{4}\left(\frac{2}{3}\right) + \frac{3}{3}\left(\frac{1}{4}\right) = \frac{8}{12} + \frac{3}{12} = \frac{11}{12}.$$

Peterson's SAT Success

Multiplying Fractions

To multiply fractions, simply multiply their numerators and their denominators:

$$\frac{1}{2} \times \frac{3}{5} = \frac{1 \times 3}{2 \times 5} = \frac{3}{10}$$

Dividing Fractions

Dividing by a fraction is the same as multiplying by its inverse:

$$\frac{5}{11} \div \frac{1}{2} = \frac{5}{11} \times \frac{2}{1} = \frac{10}{11}$$

Mixed Number

A mixed number is a number consisting of an integer and a fraction; for example, $5\frac{3}{8}$. To convert a mixed number into an improper fraction, multiply the integer by the denominator of the fraction; put the sum of this and the original numerator over the denominator:

$$\frac{(5 \times 8) + 3}{8} = \frac{43}{8}$$

Improper Fraction

An improper fraction is one in which the numerator is greater than the denominator; for example, $\frac{7}{2}$. To convert an improper fraction to a mixed number, divide the denominator into the numerator, making the quotient into the integer part of the mixed number and the remainder into the numerator of the fractional part of the mixed number: $7 \div 2 = 3$ remainder 1, so $\frac{7}{2} = 3\frac{1}{2}$

Complex Fraction

A complex fraction is one in which the numerator, denominator, or both are fractions themselves; for example, $\frac{\frac{3}{4}}{\frac{5}{6}}$. Since a fraction represents division, the complex fraction can be rewritten as

$$\frac{3}{4} \div \frac{5}{6} \text{ or } \frac{3}{4} \times \frac{6}{5} = \frac{18}{20} = \frac{9}{10}.$$

Reciprocal

The reciprocal of a number is the number that, when multiplied by the number itself, produces 1. To find the reciprocal of a number, express it as a fraction and flip its numerator and denominator. For example, the reciprocal of 5 or $\frac{5}{1} = \frac{1}{5}$.

Squares of Fractions

When a positive fraction less than 1 is squared, the result is smaller than the original number. For example, $\left(\frac{1}{2}\right)^2 = \frac{1}{2} \times \frac{1}{2} = \frac{1}{4}$ and $\frac{1}{4} < \frac{1}{2}$.

Comparing Fractions

If two fractions have the same numerator, the one with the smaller denominator is greater: $\frac{5}{15} < \frac{5}{6}$. If two fractions have the same denominator, the one with the larger numerator is greater: $\frac{6}{7} > \frac{1}{7}$.

You can also use your calculator to convert each fraction to a decimal and compare them.

Decimal

A decimal is another way of expressing a fraction and is actually a fraction with a power of ten in the denominator:

$$.3 = \frac{3}{10} \text{ and } .467 = \frac{467}{1,000}$$

Converting Fractions to Decimals

To convert a fraction to a decimal, divide the numerator by the denominator:

$$\frac{4}{5} = 4 \div 5 = .8$$

Converting Decimals to Fractions

To convert a decimal to a fraction, count the number of digits to the right of the decimal point and call this number n. The numerator of the fraction is the decimal number without the decimal point and the denominator is 10^n; reduce if necessary:

$$.125 = \frac{125}{10^3} = \frac{125}{1,000} = \frac{1}{8}$$

Comparing Decimals

Compare decimals by lining up the decimal points and comparing each place, from left to right: $.008 < .01$, because while the decimals both have zeros in the tenths place, in the hundredths place $0 < 1$.

Moving the Decimal Point

Moving the decimal point in a number one place to the right is the same as multiplying the number by 10; moving the decimal point one place to the left is the same as dividing the number by 10:

$$1.234 \times 10 = 12.34 \text{ and } 12.34 \div 100 = .1234$$

Percent

A percent is an implied fraction with a denominator of 100. The fraction represented by x percent is $\dfrac{x}{100}$. The word percent literally means "per 100," or "out of 100."

Percent Formula

The following formula can be used to solve for the percent, part or whole:

$$\text{Percent} = \frac{\text{Part}}{\text{Whole}} \times 100\%$$

Percent Increase/Decrease

Multiply the percent by the whole, and then either add or subtract the result from the original whole. Finding the increase or decrease can be easier if you convert the percent to a fraction or a decimal. Increasing 30 by 50% means adding $\dfrac{1}{2}$ of 30 or 15 to 30, for a total of 45.

Converting a Percent to a Fraction or Decimal

To convert a percent to a fraction, place the percent over 100 and then reduce: $35\% = \dfrac{35}{100} = \dfrac{7}{20}$. To convert a percent to a decimal, move the decimal point two places to the left: $35\% = .35$

Converting a Fraction or a Decimal to a Percent

To convert a fraction to a percent, divide the numerator by the denominator, and then move the decimal point two places to the right: $\dfrac{2}{5} = .4 = 40\%$. To convert a decimal to a percent, move the decimal point two places to the right: $.4 = 40\%$.

Equivalencies

Remembering the following equivalencies can save you time:

$$\frac{1}{5} = .2 = 20\% \qquad\qquad \frac{1}{2} = .5 = 50\%$$

$$\frac{1}{4} = .25 = 25\% \qquad\qquad \frac{2}{3} = .\overline{66} = 66\%$$

$$\frac{1}{3} = .\overline{33} = 33\frac{1}{3}\% \qquad\qquad \frac{3}{4} = .75 = 75\%$$

Average (Arithmetic Mean)

The average or mean value of a group of quantities is defined as

$$\text{Average} = \frac{\text{Sum of the Quantities}}{\text{Number of Quantities}}$$

The average of 5, -1, and 2 is $\dfrac{5 + (-1) + 2}{3} = \dfrac{6}{3} = 2$.

Median

The median is the middle value in a set of ascending or descending quantities. In the set {1, 1, 5, 11, 15}, 5 is the median. If there are an even number of values in the set, the median is the average (arithmetic mean) of the two middle values. In the set {1, 1, 5, 11}, the median is $\dfrac{1 + 5}{2} = \dfrac{6}{2} = 3$.

Mode

The mode is the value that appears most often in a set of quantities. In the set {2, 11, 14, 2, 17}, 2 is the mode because it appears twice, while all the other terms appear only once. If all the values in the set appear the same number of times, the set has no mode. A set may have multiple modes; in the set {2, 4, 6, 6, 8, 8, 10, 12}, there are two modes: 6 and 8.

Finding and Using the Sum

If you know the average of a group of quantities, as well as the number of quantities in that group, you can find the sum of those quantities. If the average of 3 numbers is 21, you know that the sum of those numbers must be $3 \times 21 = 63$. If you also know the values of some of the quantities, you can subtract them from the sum to find the others. If you knew that two of the three numbers were 30 and 5, you could find that the third must be $63 - (30 + 5) = 28$.

Weighted Average

A weighted average is the average of two or more groups in which there are different numbers of terms in each group. If Joan has an average of 90 on her first three tests and an average of 100 on her next two tests, you can't simply average 90 and 100 to find her average on all five tests. You need to "weight" the averages to account for the different numbers of tests each represents:

$$\frac{3(90) + 2(100)}{3 + 2} = \frac{270 + 200}{5} = 94$$

Average of Consecutive Numbers

There are two shortcuts for finding the average of a group of consecutive numbers. One is to average the first and the last terms of the group. The average of the group {1, 2, 3, 4, 5, 6, 7} is $\frac{1+7}{2} = \frac{8}{2} = 4$. The second shortcut is to simply take the middle value, which in the set above is again equal to 4.

Ratio

A ratio is a comparison between the different elements within a group or between one element and the group as a whole. If there are 5 boys and 3 girls in a class, we can say that the ratio of boys to girls is 5 to 3 or that the ratio of boys to all students is 5 to 8. The first type of ratio is a part-to-part ratio, and the second is a part-to-whole ratio. Ratios can be expressed in several different ways: stated as words, as fractions, or with a colon. The ratio of 5 to 3 is the same as $\frac{5}{3}$ or 5:3.

Using a Ratio to Solve for an Actual Number

If you are given a part-to-part ratio and the actual number of items in the group it describes, you can solve for the actual number of each part. You're given that there are a total of 30 red and green marbles and that the ratio of red to green marbles is 1 to 5. Since the marbles are 1 part red and 5 parts green, there are a total of 6 parts, with each part representing $\frac{30}{6} = 5$ marbles. Therefore, there are $1 \times 5 = 5$ red marbles and $5 \times 5 = 25$ green marbles.

Proportion

A proportion is two ratios set equal to each other. Express each ratio as a fraction, set them equal, and then cross-multiply to solve for the missing piece of information. If 2 bags of sugar weigh 5 pounds, how much do 5 bags of sugar weigh? $\frac{2}{5} = \frac{5}{x}$, $2x = 25$, $x = 12.5$. When working with proportions, make sure that all the units are consistent, converting if necessary. If a yard of ribbon costs $9, how much does 5 feet cost? It doesn't matter whether you convert yards to feet or vice versa, as long as you're consistent.

$$\frac{3 \text{ feet}}{\$9} = \frac{5 \text{ feet}}{x}, 3x = \$45, x = \$15$$

Rates

Remember the formula Rate × Time = Distance. If you have two pieces of the formula, you can always solve for the third. If Greg drives 40 miles per hour for 110 miles, how long does he drive?

$40T = 110$, $T = \dfrac{110}{40}$, $T = 2\dfrac{3}{4}$ hours.

Average Rates

You can't just average two speeds to find the average speed for a particular trip. You must use the formula $\dfrac{\text{Total Distance}}{\text{Total Time}}$. Say Maureen travels for 60 miles at 20 miles per hour and returns home at 30 miles per hour. That means that she spent $\dfrac{60}{20} = 3$ hours traveling at 20 mph and $\dfrac{60}{30} = 2$ hours traveling at 30 mph, making her average speed for the $60 + 60 = 120$ mile trip $\dfrac{120}{3+2} = \dfrac{120}{5} = 24$ miles per hour.

Probability

The probability of a particular event occurring is equal to

$$\dfrac{\text{Number of Desired Outcomes}}{\text{Number of Total Possible Outcomes}}$$

If a fair six-sided die with faces numbered 1 through 6 is rolled once, what is the probability that a 5 is rolled? There are a total of 6 sides and only one is marked 5, so the probability of rolling a 5 is $\dfrac{1}{6}$.

Fundamental Counting Principle

This principle helps you determine how many possibilities there are for combinations of items. If one event can occur x ways and another event can occur y ways, then the total number of ways the two events can occur is xy. If 4 different cars are available in 5 different colors, then there are $4 \times 5 = 20$ different vehicles available.

ALGEBRA

Variable

A variable is a letter used to represent an unknown quantity. Even though you don't know the value of the variable, you can essentially treat it as a number and add to it, subtract from it, and multiply or divide it following some basic rules.

Coefficient

The coefficient is the numerical part of an algebraic term. In the monomial $3ab$, 3 is the coefficient. In the expression $6x^2 + 5x + 4$, the coefficients are 6, 5, and 4.

Monomial

A monomial is an algebraic expression made up of only one term. Some examples of monomials are 4, x, and $3ab$.

Adding and Subtracting Monomials

Combine only "like terms." Add or subtract the coefficients of each term, leaving the variables unchanged:

$$5x + 2x = (5 + 2)x = 7x$$

Multiplying Monomials

Multiply the coefficients and variables separately:

$$3x \times 4y = (3 \times 4)(x \times y) = 12xy$$

Binomial

A binomial is an algebraic expression made up of two terms separated by a plus or minus sign. Some examples of binomials are $x + 5$, $a + ab$, and $y^2 + y$.

FOIL

FOIL is an acronym standing for the order in which you multiply the terms of binomials: First, Outside, Inside, Last. That is, you multiply the first terms of the binomials together, then the outer two, then the inner two, and finally the last two. Finish by combining any like terms. Use FOIL to find the product of $(n + 5)$ and $(n + 3)$:

First: n^2
Outside: $3n$
Inside: $5n$
Last: 15

So the product is $n^2 + 8n + 15$.

Polynomial

A polynomial is an algebraic expression made up of two or more terms separated by plus or minus signs. Some examples of polynomials are $x^2 - 4$, $4n^4 + 3n^3 + n$, and $a + b + c + d$.

Adding and Subtracting Polynomials

As with monomials, combine only "like terms".

$$5p + 2q + pq + 2pq + p = 6p + 2q + 3pq.$$

Note that neither $3ab + 2a$ nor $2y + y^2$ can be combined.

Multiplying Polynomials

Multiply each term in the first polynomial by each term in the second polynomial, then combine like terms:

$$(a^2 + 2a + 3)(a + 3) = a^2(a) + a^2(3) + 2a(a) + 2a(3) + 3(a) + 3(3)$$
$$= a^3 + 3a^2 + 2a^2 + 6a + 3a + 9$$
$$= a^3 + 5a^2 + 9a + 9$$

Evaluate an Expression

Plug in the values given for the variables and calculate, following PEMDAS. When $y = 3$, $y^2 - y + 5 = 3^2 - 3 + 5 = 9 - 3 + 5 = 11$.

Equation

An equation is a statement of equality between two algebraic expressions. Some examples of equations are $5x = 20 + x$ and $a^2 - a = 6$. As long as you do the same thing to both sides of the equation, the equation remains the same. This means you can add to, subtract from, and multiply and divide both sides of the equation by the same number without changing the relationship.

Solving a Linear Equation

A linear equation is one in which the variables are only raised to the first power. Do the same thing to both sides of the equation until you've isolated the variable you want to solve for on one side of the equation. Solve for x: $4x - 5 = 7$, $4x = 12$, $x = 3$. To solve for x you first had to add 5 to both sides, then divide both sides by 4.

Solving for One Variable in Terms of Another

Isolate the variable you are solving for on one side of the equation. This will leave you with an expression containing the other variable(s) on the other side: $5p + q = 7$, $5p = 7 - q$, $p = \dfrac{7 - q}{5}$. To solve for p, in terms of q you first had to subtract q from both sides, and then divide both sides by 5.

Systems of Equations

To solve for two variables, you need two distinct equations involving those variables. When you're given systems of equations on the SAT, there's usually some way you can combine them to solve, instead of having to solve for one variable in terms of the other and substituting. Say you're given $3x + 2y = 5$ and $x - 2y = 3$ and are asked to solve for y. If you add the equations, the ys cancel out:

$$3x + 2y = 5$$
$$\underline{+\ x - 2y = 3}$$
$$4x = 8$$

So, $x = 2$, and plugging that into one of the original equations, you find that $y = -\dfrac{1}{2}$.

Quadratic Equation

A quadratic equation involves variables that are squared but none that are raised to a higher power. You will never need to use the quadratic formula on the SAT. To solve a quadratic equation, put it in standard form ($ax^2 + bx + c = 0$), factor the left side, and set each factor equal to 0 to find each root. Solve $x^2 + x - 6$:

$$(x + 3)(x - 2) = 0$$
$$x + 3 = 0 \quad \text{or } x - 2 = 0$$
$$x = -3 \quad \text{or} \quad x = 2$$

Inequality

An inequality is a statement that two algebraic expressions are not equal or that one is greater than or equal to or less than or equal to another. The symbols used to demonstrate inequality are:

$>$ is greater than $\geq$ is greater than or equal to

$<$ is less than $\leq$ is less than or equal to

Solving an Inequality

Solve an inequality as you would an equation, but remember that if you multiply or divide both sides by a negative number, you must reverse the direction of the inequality sign:

$$5x + 10 < 3x$$
$$10 < -2x$$
$$-5 > x$$

Finding Common Factors

If a factor is common to every term in an expression, it can be factored out. In the expression $2c^4 - 4c^2 + 6c$, every term contains a factor of $2c$, so it can be rewritten as $2c(c^3 - 2c + 3)$.

Factoring A Quadratic

To factor a quadratic, try to determine which two binomials, when multiplied together, will produce that quadratic. First, get the quadratic in standard form ($ax^2 + bx + c = 0$). Then, write two sets of parentheses and select first terms whose product is ax^2. Fill in the remaining two terms by figuring out which last terms will produce c and which outer and inner terms will produce bx. For example,

$$x^2 + x - 6 = (x \quad)(x \quad)$$
$$= (x + 3)(x - 2).$$

Simplifying Fractions with Algebraic Expressions

If you have fractions with algebraic expressions in them, factor before you reduce. To reduce $\dfrac{x^2 - 1}{x^2 + 2x + 1}$, factor its numerator and denominator, $\dfrac{(x + 1)(x - 1)}{(x + 1)(x + 1)}$, and then cancel common factors: $\dfrac{(x - 1)}{(x + 1)}$.

Common Factorables

The key to many SAT questions is factoring or unfactoring expressions, so recognizing the following factorables could score you some points:

$$a^2 - 1 = (a + 1)(a - 1)$$
$$a^2 - b^2 = (a + b)(a - b)$$
$$a^2 - 2ab + b^2 = (a - b)^2$$
$$a^2 + 2ab + b^2 = (a + b)^2$$

Exponent

An exponent tells you how many times a number (or "base") is to be multiplied by itself. Five raised to the third power is expressed algebraically as 5^3, where 5 is the base and 3 is the exponent: $5^3 = 5 \times 5 \times 5$. A number raised to the zero power is equal to 1: $1^0 = 5^0 = 100^0 = -3^0 = 1$.

Multiplying/Dividing with Exponents

To multiply expressions with the same base, add the exponents:

$$a^2 \times a^5 = a^{2+5} = a^7$$

To divide expressions with the same base, subtract the exponents:

$$b^6 \div b^2 = b^{6-2} = b^4$$

Raising Exponents to Exponents

When raising a power to a power, add the exponents:

$$(c^3)^4 = c^{3 \times 4} = c^{12}$$

Negative Exponent

A base raised to a negative exponent is equal to a fraction whose numerator is 1 and whose denominator is the base raised to the positive value of that exponent. For example, $4^{-3} = \dfrac{1}{4^3} = \dfrac{1}{64}$.

Exponential Oddities

If you raise a positive number greater than 1 to a power, it becomes larger: $4^2 = 16$. However, if you raise a positive fraction less than 1 to a power, it becomes smaller:

$$\left(\frac{1}{4}\right)^2 = \frac{1}{16}$$

Raising a negative number to an even power will yield a positive result: $-3^2 = 9$. Raising a negative number to an odd power will yield a negative result: $-3^3 = -27$.

Radical

If $a^2 = b$, then a is the square root of b. The radical sign ($\sqrt{}$) indicates that the square root of a number is to be taken. By convention, this symbol denotes only the positive square root of a number. Therefore, $\sqrt{36} = 6$ even though $(-6)^2$ equals 36 as well.

Reducing Radicals

To reduce a radical, express it as the product of two factors, one of which is a perfect square. Then, extract the square root of the perfect square and place it in front of the remaining radical:

$$\sqrt{24} = \sqrt{4 \times 6} = \sqrt{4} \times \sqrt{6} = 2\sqrt{6}.$$

Adding/Subtracting Radicals

Radicals can only be added and subtracted when the part under the radical sign is the same:

$$6\sqrt{7} - \sqrt{7} = 5\sqrt{7}.$$

Multiplying/Dividing Radicals

The product of square roots is equal to the square root of the product:

$$\sqrt{6} \times \sqrt{8} = \sqrt{6 \times 8} = \sqrt{48}.$$

Reduce if necessary:

$$\sqrt{48} = \sqrt{16} \times \sqrt{3} = 4\sqrt{3}.$$

Likewise, the quotient of the square roots is equal to the square root of the quotient:

$$\sqrt{20} \div \sqrt{2} = \sqrt{20 \div 2} = \sqrt{10}.$$

Word Problems

To solve a word problem, you need to translate a given situation into mathematical language. Don't get overwhelmed, just translate piece by piece and then solve the math problem you've uncovered. The translation table below includes some of the more common terms and their mathematical translations:

Words	Symbol	Example	Translation
What, a number	x, n, etc	"A number is equal to itself squared."	$n = n^2$
Is, was, has, equal to	$=$	"x is equal to $2y$"	$x = 2y$
Sum of, more than, received, increased by	$+$	"Liza has five more books than Joe." "The sum of two numbers is half their product."	$L = 5 + J$ $x + y = \dfrac{xy}{2}$
Difference, less than, fewer, decreased by	$-$	"A number is decreased by 4." "Cole has 2 fewer toys than Henry."	$n - 4$ $C = H - 2$ (**Not** $C = 2 - H$)
Of, product, times	$\times$	"x is 45% of y." "Tony has 5 times as many CDs as Sal."	$x = .45y$ $T = 5S$
For, per	$\div$	"Carol reads 3 books per week." "For every 2 trips that Larry makes, Julie makes 5."	3 books/week $L{:}J = 2{:}5$ or $\dfrac{L}{J} = \dfrac{2}{5}$

Geometry

Complementary/Supplementary

Two angles are complementary if their measures sum to 90°. Two angles are supplementary if their measures sum to 180°. Adjacent angles are supplementary. In the figures below, angles *a* and *b* are complementary, and angles *x* and *y* are supplementary.

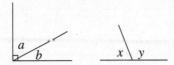

Acute/Obtuse/Right Angle

An acute angle is an angle whose measure is less than 90°. An obtuse angle is an angle whose measure is greater than 90° but less than 180°. A right angle is an angle whose measure is exactly 90°. In the figures below, *a* is an acute angle, *b* a right angle, and *c* an obtuse angle.

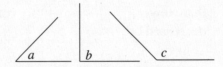

Vertical Angles

Two pairs of vertical angles are formed when two lines intersect. Vertical angles are equal. In the figure below, angles *w* and *y* are equal, as are angles *x* and *z*.

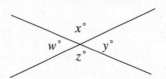

Parallel Lines

Lines that are parallel extend in the same direction and are the same distance apart at every point, so as never to intersect. The symbol "//" signifies that lines are parallel. When parallel lines are hit by a transversal, all of the acute angles formed are equal to each other, all the obtuse angles formed are equal to each other, and every acute angle is supplementary to every obtuse angle. In the figure below, angles a, c, e, and g are acute and equal to one another; angles b, d, f, and h are obtuse and equal to one another.

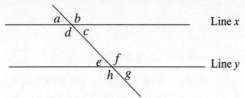

Perpendicular Lines

Perpendicular lines intersect such that they form 90° or right angles. The symbol "⊥" signifies that lines are perpendicular.

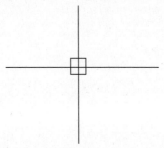

Triangle

A triangle is a three-sided figure whose three angles sum to 180°. In a triangle, sides opposite equal angles are also equal. Sides are related to each other in the same way that the angles opposite them are related; the greatest angle is opposite the greatest side, etc. In triangle ABC, if $x = z$, then $BC = AB$. If $y > x$, then $AC > BC$.

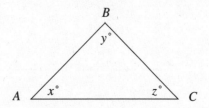

Exterior Angle

The exterior angle of a triangle is equal to the sum of the measures of its two remote interior angles. In the figure below, $n = 90 + 40 = 130$.

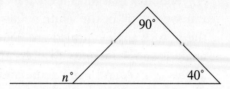

Perimeter and Area

The perimeter of a triangle is equal to the sum of its three sides. The area of a triangle is equal to $\frac{1}{2}$ (base × height). Every triangle has 3 bases, since any of its three sides can be considered base. The height of a triangle is the perpendicular distance from the base to the vertex opposite it. Regardless of which side you consider as the base, the area will always be the same. In the figure below, the perimeter of the triangle is $12 + 13 + 5 = 30$, and its area is $\frac{1}{2}(5 \times 12) = 30$.

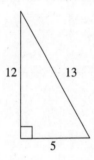

Inequality Theorem

The three sides of a triangle are related such that the third side must be greater than the positive difference of the other two sides and less than their sum. In the figure below, you know that $6 - 3 < x < 6 + 3$ or $3 < x < 9$.

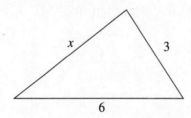

Similar Triangles

Similar triangles are triangles with equal angles and proportional sides. In the figure below, the triangles are similar because their angles are equal, and their sides are related in a ratio of 1:2. The ratio of the areas of similar figures is equal to the square of the ratio of their corresponding linear measurements. Therefore, the ratio of the area of the smaller triangle to the larger is $1^2:2^2 = 1:4$.

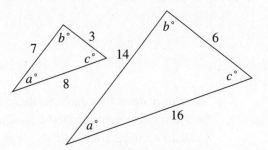

Isosceles Triangle

An isosceles triangle has two equal sides. The angles opposite these sides are also equal.

Equilateral Triangle

In an equilateral triangle, all three sides are equal. The three angles are also equal, each with a measure of 60°.

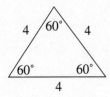

Right Triangle

A right triangle has one right angle and two acute angles. The side opposite the right angle, the hypotenuse, is the longest side. The other two sides of a right triangle are called the legs.

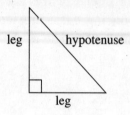

Pythagorean Theorem

The three sides of a right triangle are related by the Pythagorean theorem, which states that the square of the hypotenuse is equal to the sum of the squares of the legs ($a^2 + b^2 = c^2$, where a and b are the legs and c is the hypotenuse). In the right triangle below, $6^2 + 5^2 = h^2$, $36 + 25 = h^2$, and $\sqrt{61} = h$.

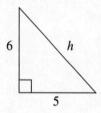

Special Right Triangles

Some special right triangles, whose sides or angles are related in specific ways, turn up with frequency on the SAT. If you recognize them, you won't need to use the Pythagorean theorem to find unknown measurements. In a 3-4-5 right triangle, the sides are related in the ratio of 3:4:5 (see Triangle *A*). In a 5-12-13 right triangle, the sides are related in the ratio of 5:12:13 (see Triangle *B*). In a 30-60-90 triangle, the sides are in a ratio of $1:\sqrt{3}:2$ (see Triangle *C*). In a 45-45-90 or isosecles right triangle, the sides are related in a ratio of $1:1:\sqrt{2}$ (see Triangle *D*).

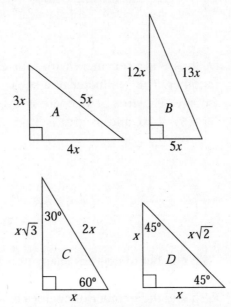

Quadrilateral

A quadrilateral is a four-sided polygon whose four angles sum to 360°. Parallelograms, rectangles, and squares are all quadrilaterals.

Parallelogram

A parallelogram is a quadrilateral whose two pairs of opposite sides are parallel and equal. Opposite angles are equal and consecutive angles are supplementary. The diagonals of a parallelogram bisect each other. The area of a parallelogram is *bh*, where *b* is its base and *h* its height. In the figure below, the area of the parallelogram is $10 \times 4 = 40$.

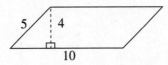

Rectangle

A rectangle is a parallelogram with four 90° angles. Its opposite sides are equal, and its diagonals bisect one another. The perimeter of a rectangle is equal to $2(l + w)$, where l is its length and w is its width. The area of a rectangle is lw. The perimeter of the rectangle below is $2(8 + 5) = 26$, and its area is $8 \times 5 = 40$.

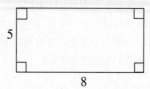

Square

A square is a rectangle with four equal sides. Its diagonals bisect one another. The perimeter of a square is $4s$, where s is a side of the square. The area of a square is s^2. The perimeter of the square below is $4(5) = 20$, and its area is $5^2 = 25$.

Angles in a Polygon

The number of degrees in any polygon is determined by the formula $180(n - 2)$, where n is the number of sides in the polygon. You can also find the number of degrees in a polygon by dividing it into triangles and multiplying the total by 180. Either way, you find the number of degrees in the hexagon shown is $180(6 - 2) = 180(4) = 720$.

Volume

The volume of a rectangular solid is determined by the formula lwh, where l is its length, w its width, and h its height. The volume of the rectangular solid shown is $3 \times 4 \times 7 = 84$.

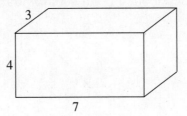

Surface Area

The surface area of a rectangular solid is equal to the sum of the areas of its six faces, or $2(lw + wh + lh)$. The volume of the rectangular solid shown in the preceding diagram is $2[(7 \times 3) + (3 \times 4) + (7 \times 4)] = 2(61) = 122$.

Cube

A cube is a rectangular solid whose length, width, and height are equal. The volume of a cube is e^3, where e is an edge of the cube. The surface area of a cube is $6e^2$. The area of the cube below is $3^3 = 27$, and its surface area is $6(3^2) = 54$.

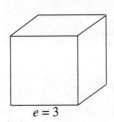

$e = 3$

Cylinder

The volume of a cylinder is $\pi r^2 h$, where r is its radius and h its height.

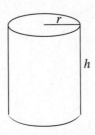

Circle

A circle is the complete set of points a given distance from a fixed point called its center. The distance from the center to any point on the circle is called a radius. All radii of a circle are equal. Since the angles about a point sum to 360°, a circle contains 360°.

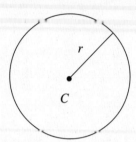

Diameter

A chord of a circle is a line segment whose endpoints are on the circle. The diameter is a chord that passes through the center of the circle. The diameter is twice the length of a radius and is the longest chord that can be drawn in the circle. In the circle below, *WX* is the diameter and *YZ* is a chord.

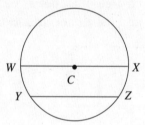

Circumference

The circumference of a circle is equal to $2\pi r$ or πd, where r is its radius and d its diameter. The circumference of the circle with radius 5 is $2\pi(5) = 10\pi$.

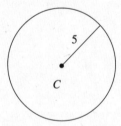

Area

The area of a circle is equal to πr^2, where r is its radius. The area of the circle with radius 5 is $\pi(5^2) = 25\pi$.

Tangent

A tangent to a circle is a line that touches the circumference of the circle at only one point. In the circle below, *AB* is a tangent.

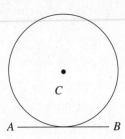

Arc Length

An arc is a fractional part of a circle's circumference. To find the length of an arc, use the formula

$$\frac{\text{length of arc}}{\text{circumference}} = \frac{\text{measure of central } \angle}{360°}$$

Since the central angle that defines arc *QRS* is 90°, the arc represents $\frac{90°}{360°} = \frac{1}{4}$ of the circle's circumference or $\frac{1}{4} \times 10\pi = 2\frac{1}{2}\pi$.

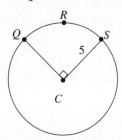

Sector Area

A sector is a fractional part of a circle's area. To find the area of a sector, use the formula:

$$\frac{\text{area of sector}}{\text{area of circle}} = \frac{\text{measure of central } \angle}{360°}$$

Since the central angle that defines the sector is 90°, the sector represents $\frac{90°}{360°} = \frac{1}{4}$ of the circle's area or $\frac{1}{4} \times 25\pi = 6\frac{1}{4}\pi$.

Coordinate Axes

The coordinate axes are formed by a horizontal number line, the x-axis, and a vertical number line, the y-axis. The axes are perpendicular to one another, and the point at which they intersect is called the origin.

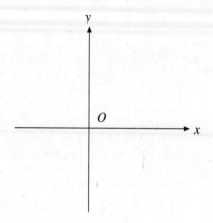

Quadrants

The coordinate axes are divided into four quadrants, which are numbered as shown in the figure below. The coordinates x and y are positive and negative in the quadrants as indicated on the graph.

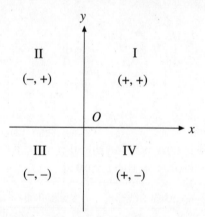

Points

Points on the coordinate plane are located by their x- and y-coordinates. The x-coordinate tells you how far to the right or left the point is located, and the y-coordinate tells you how far up or down the point is located. The coordinates of the origin are (0,0). All points on a horizontal line parallel to the x-axis have the same y-coordinate; all points on a vertical line parallel to the y-axis have the same x-coordinate.

Distance

To find the distance between two points on a line that is parallel to either axis, simply find the positive difference between their endpoints. If a line is not parallel to either axis, construct a right triangle whose hypotenuse is the length that you're trying to find. Each leg of this right triangle will be parallel to one of the axes, so once you find their lengths, you can use the Pythagorean theorem to solve for the hypotenuse. Alternately, you could use the distance formula:

$$d = \sqrt{(x_2 - x_1)^2 + (y_2 - y_1)^2}$$

In the figure below, since AB is the hypotenuse of a 3-4-5 right triangle, its length is 5.

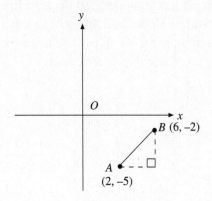

Slope

The slope of a line is its rise over its run, or its vertical change divided by its horizontal change. A line parallel to the *x*-axis is said to have a slope of 0. A line parallel to the *y*-axis is said to have an undefined slope (since a fraction with a denominator of 0 is undefined). Parallel lines have equal slopes. Perpendicular lines have slopes that are negative reciprocals. A line that rises from left to right has a positive slope, a line that rises from right to left has a negative slope. In the figure below, line 1 has an undefined slope, while line 3 has slope of 0. Line 5 has a positive slope, and line 4 has a negative slope; since these lines are perpendicular their slopes are negative reciprocals. Lines 2 and 5 are parallel, so their slopes are equal.

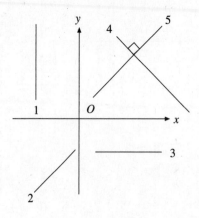

Slope Formula

To calculate the slope of a line, plug the coordinates of two points on the line into the formula $\dfrac{(y_2 - y_1)}{(x_2 - x_1)}$. The line with points $(0, -1)$ and $(3, 4)$ has a slope of $\dfrac{4 - (-1)}{3 - 0} = \dfrac{5}{3}$.

Slope-Intercept Equation

A line is defined by the equation $y = mx + b$, where *x* is its slope and *b* its *y*-intercept (the point where the line crosses the *y*-axis). The line $y = \dfrac{x}{2} - 5$ has a slope of $\dfrac{1}{2}$ and a *y*-intercept of -5.

Math Teaching Unit

Strategic Approaches

In the previous sections you were introduced to the different math question types and content that form the basis of the SAT math sections. Now you'll see specific ways that these concepts are tested on the SAT, along with the best approaches for handling them. Following are problems that turn up with frequency and require skills and strategies useful for solving an array of questions. Problems of the most basic nature aren't included, since the skills needed to solve them are necessary steps in the solutions to these more involved, less accessible problems. The problems are organized as Arithmetic, Algebra, and Geometry, although many include multiple concepts and could be categorized under more than one heading. More examples for study are available in the Practice Sets at the end of each content section. The third practice set in each group is made up of real SAT questions that appeared on previous administrations of the test.

Arithmetic

ODDS AND EVENS

If x is an even integer and y is an odd integer, which of the following must be odd?

  I. x^y
  II. $x + y$
  III. $xy - 1$

(A) II only
(B) III only
(C) I and II only
(D) II and III only
(E) I, II and III

This is an example of a Roman Numerals problem. While these questions can be a little time consuming, they don't have to be confusing. Just evaluate each statement in turn, eliminating choices as you go along. If, for example, you found that statement I satisfied the question, you'd be able to eliminate choices (A), (B), and (D) for not including it. Without even looking at either of the other two statements you would have narrowed it down to two choices. If you got hung up on the other statements or didn't have time to evaluate them, you'd still have a fifty-fifty shot at selecting the right answer. You don't have to evaluate the statements in the order in which they are given. Start with whichever one seems easiest. Then, if you get stuck or run out of time, you'll have eliminated some choices and be in a position to make an educated guess.

    This question deals with odd and even numbers. You're told that x is even and y is odd, and are asked which of the expressions that follow must produce an odd number. There are some rules governing operations with odd and even numbers, but it's not necessary to memorize them. The easiest way to approach such questions is to try valucs for the variables. And remember, you're not just looking for expressions that can be odd, but ones that *must* be odd, so test the statements accordingly.

Odds and Evens

$odd + even = odd$
$odd + odd = even$
$even + even = even$
$odd \times even = even$
$odd \times odd = odd$
$even \times even = even$

Statement I

If $x = 2$ and $y = 1$, then $x^y = 2^1 = 2$, which is even. If $x = 4$ and $y = 3$, then $4^3 = 64$ which is also even. In fact, for whatever values you choose, the result will be an even integer. Since a number is even if it has at least one even factor, multiplying a bunch of even factors together will certainly produce an even result. Since statement I does not produce an odd number, eliminate choices (C) and (E) for including it.

Statement II

If $x = 2$ and $y = 1$ then $x + y = 2 + 1 = 3$, which is odd. If $x = 4$ and $y = 3$, then $x + y = 4 + 3 = 7$ which is also odd. In fact, for whatever values you choose, adding an even and an odd will always result in an odd number. Since statement II must produce an odd number, eliminate choice (B) for not including it.

Statement III

If $x = 2$ and $y = ,1$ then $xy - 1 = (2)(1) - 1 = 1$ which is odd. If $x = 4$ and $y = 3$ then $(4)(3) - 1 = 11$, which is also odd. In fact, this statement will always produce an odd result. Since a number with at least one even factor is even, xy will always be even. One less than an even number will always be odd, so $xy - 1$ will always be odd. Since statement III must produce an odd number, eliminate choice (A) for not including it. Therefore, the answer is choice (D), II and III.

REMAINDERS

If the remainder when a is divided by 7 is 3, what is the remainder when $3a$ is divided by 7?

(A) 0
(B) 1
(C) 2
(D) 3
(E) 6

Remainder Questions

The best value to use for the variable is the divisor plus the remainder.

Remainder questions like this turn up on the SAT with frequency. While their abstract, algebraic nature might be a little intimidating, use values for variables and they're a piece of cake. What value should you pick? You're told that when a is divided by 7 the remainder is 3. Therefore, the best number to pick for a is $7 + 3 = 10$. To find the remainder when $3a$ is divided by 7 simply plug in: $3(10) \div 7 = 30 \div 7 = 4$, remainder 2. Therefore, choice (C) is correct.

CONSECUTIVE INTEGERS

If the sum of 5 consecutive even integers is 90, what is the greatest of these integers?

There aren't any answer choices here, so you can't work backward. You have to solve this problem head on. You could do so by setting up an equation representing the largest integer as x. You'd have to express the other 4 numbers in terms of x, being sure to account for the fact that they're consecutive *even* integers. In other words, the second largest number would be $x - 2$, not $x - 1$, and so on. This route would take a bit of time, and you'd have to be very careful as you solved the equation. Remember, the more work you do the more room you have to make a careless error.

There's a quicker, easier way to solve this problem. The average of consecutive integers is equal to the middle term. The sum of these five integers is 90, so their average is $\frac{90}{5} = 18$. If the third integer is 18, the fourth is 20 and the fifth and largest is 22. It's important to check your work on Grid-ins so see if this answer makes sense. If the 3 largest numbers are 22, 20, and 18, the other two must be 16 and 14: $22 + 20 + 18 + 16 + 14 = 90$, so you've got the right answer.

PATTERN RECOGNITION

Tatiana strings beads onto a necklace in the following order: red, blue, green, silver, purple, pink, gold. What is the color of the 82nd bead she strings onto the necklace?

(A) Red
(B) Blue
(C) Silver
(D) Purple
(E) Pink

Pattern Problems

1. *Isolate pattern*
2. *ID last term* n
3. *Find place number divisible by* n *near one in question*
4. *Count off to the place in question*

Whether you're asked for the color of the 82nd bead on a necklace or the 111th digit in a repeating decimal, you're working on a pattern question. The first step is to isolate the pattern. In this case it's clear that it's the colors of the beads in the order that they're strung on the necklace. In the case of a numerical pattern you'd probably have to do a little more work to recognize the pattern. Next identify the number of the last element in the pattern. In this case it's 7, since gold is the seventh and last bead strung. Any place number divisible by 7 will be occupied by a gold bead. Find a place number divisible by 7 near the one you're asked to find, then count off until you reach the place in question. In this case, since 84 is divisible by 7, the 84th bead will be gold. Therefore, the 83rd bead must be pink and the 82nd, purple, choice (D).

Averages

The average (arithmetic mean) of a, b, c, d, and e is 40. The average of a and e is 50.

The average of b, c, and d	-10

$$\text{Average (arithmetic mean)} = \frac{Sum\ of\ Quantities}{Number\ of\ Quantities}$$

Median = Middle Quantity

Mode = Most Frequent Quantity

Average questions turn up with great frequency on the SAT and in many different guises. On one test you may be asked to find the mean of x, $x + 5$, and $x - 11$ while on another you may be asked to find the median score from among 5 grades, but it's a pretty safe bet that there will be some kind of question(s) testing the concept of averages on your exam.

Although you'll rarely be given a question that simply asks you to plug into the average formula, you'll find many that require you to manipulate that formula in some way. You're given that the average of 5 variables is 40 and that the average of 2 of those variables is 50. Well, since you know the averages and the number of terms each represents, you can find their respective sums. Since

$$\frac{\text{Sum of Quantities}}{\text{Number of Quantities}} = \text{Averages, Average} \times \text{Number} = \text{Sum}.$$

Summing Up

When you know the average and the number of terms it represents, using the sum is often the key to solving the problem.

Therefore, the sum of a, b, c, d, and e is $40 \times 5 = 200$ and the sum of a and e is $50 \times 2 = 100$. Since the sum of all 5 variables is 200 and the sum of a and e is 100, the sum of b, c, and d is $200 - 100 = 100$. Therefore, the average of b, c, and d is $\frac{100}{3} = 33\frac{1}{3}$, which is certainly greater than -10 in Column B.

Rachael's average monthly sales commission for January through October is $400. Due to increased business during the holiday season, her average monthly sales commission for November and December is $1,000. What is her average monthly sales commission for the entire year?

(A) $500
(B) $600
(C) $700
(D) $800
(E) $1,200

When you come across a question that asks you for the average of two averages, check to see how many terms each represents. If they're not the same, you must "weight" each average accordingly.

Here's a particular kind of average question that often trips up test takers. Many students would simply average $400 and $1,000 to come up with choice (C), $700, as the answer. Many students would be wrong. You can't just average the two averages since each represents a different number of months. $400 is the average monthly commission for January through October, a total of 10 months. $1,000 is the average monthly commission for November and December, only 2 months. Each of these individual averages must be "weighted" accordingly to find the total average. Plugging into the average formula:

$$\frac{10(\$400) + 2(\$1,000)}{12} = \frac{\$6,000}{12} = \$500, \text{ choice (A).}$$

PERCENTS

A team won 55 percent of the games it played this season. If it lost 9 games, how many games did it win?

Percents is another topic that turns up all over the SAT, so you'll likely see one or more questions involving its concepts on your exam. As with averages, you'll need to know and be able to manipulate the standard formula, in this case, $\text{Percent} = \frac{\text{Part}}{\text{Whole}}$. You're asked for the number of games that the team won (the part). You can't just plug into the formula because although you know the percent of games won, you don't know the total number of games played (the whole). Unless you know 2 of the 3 pieces you can't use the formula.

What do you know? You know that the team lost 9 games. You also know that since it won 55 percent of its games, it must have lost $100 - 55 = 45$ percent of its games. Now that you have a percent and a part you can work with the formula to solve for the whole. Let the whole $= x$: $\frac{45}{100}$ or $\frac{9}{20} = \frac{9}{x}$ and $x = 20$. Don't grid in 20 and move on, though; 20 is the total number of games the team played but the question asks for the number it won. Since the team lost 9 games it must have won $20 - 9 = 11$. It's always a good idea to check your work, especially on Grid-ins, so see if this answer makes sense. Since $\frac{55}{100} \times 20 = 11$ you know you've found the correct answer.

Column A	Column B

The price of a sweater after a 20 percent reduction is x.

The original price of the sweater.	$1.2x$

This is a tough question and would turn up as one of the last few Quantitative Comparisons. If the price of the sweater after the reduction is x, its original price must be greater than x. You might think that since the original price was decreased by 20 percent that increasing x by 20 percent (120% of x or $1.2x$) would equal the original price. You'd be wrong, though. Remember, you can't combine percent increases or decreases that are made on different wholes. The 20 percent reduction is made on the original price, so it isn't equal to 20 percent of the reduced price x. To see this more clearly, try a value for the variable. The best number to use on percent problems is 100, so let the original price be 100. Decreasing the original price by 20 percent results in x, so $x = 80$. This means you're comparing 100 in Column A with $1.2(80) = 96$ in Column B, so Column A is greater.

AVERAGE RATES

Kecia drives from San Rafael to San Francisco at 40 miles per hour, and then returns to San Rafael at 60 miles per hour. What was her average speed for the entire trip?

(A) 48 miles per hour
(B) 50 miles per hour
(C) 55 miles per hour
(D) 57 miles per hour
(E) It cannot be determined from the information given.

Here's another tough question, and another one that could trip you up if you're not careful. The obvious answer here is choice (B), 50 miles per hour, which is the result of simply averaging 40 and 60. Unfortunately it's wrong. You can't just average two speeds; you need to use the formula:

$$\text{Average Rate} = \frac{\text{Total Distance}}{\text{Total Time}}.$$

The reasoning behind this is similar to that with a weighted average; since one speed is driven for a longer amount of time it must count more toward the total average.

However, you're not given any information about Kecia's trip other than the fact that it's a round trip. Perhaps choice (E) is correct? Not so fast—there is a way to solve this question. Since this is a round trip, the distance traveled at each speed is the same. Pick a value for that distance. Try a number that will be easy to work with, in this case, one that's divisible by both 40 and 60. Let the distance for each leg of the trip be 120 miles, making the total distance 240 miles. Now you need to find the total time. Leaning toward choice (E) again? No, you can find the amount of time that each leg took. Since you know the distance of each leg and the rate of speed it was traveled at, you can use the formula Rate × Time = Distance. Traveling 120 miles at 40 miles an hour would take 3 hours; traveling 120 miles at 60 miles an hour would take 2 hours. Therefore, the average rate is $\frac{240}{5} = 48$, choice (A).

PROPORTION

In each box of 12 donuts exactly 3 are lemon-filled. If there are 64 boxes of donuts in each case, how many lemon-filled donuts are there in 10 cases?

(A)   40
(B)   160
(C)   192
(D) 1,920
(E) 7,680

Units To Watch For

seconds & minutes
inches & feet
ounces & pounds

In a proportion, two ratios are set equal to each other. Just express each ratio, set them equal, and cross-multiply to solve for the unknown quantity. However, be careful on SAT proportion questions to make sure that the ratios are expressed in the same units. In the question above you need to determine how many lemon-filled donuts there are in 10 cases of donuts. You know that 3 donuts in every box of 12 are lemon-filled, or $\frac{3 \text{ lemon}}{12 \text{ donuts}}$. You need to know how many lemon donuts there are in 10 cases, or $\frac{x}{10 \text{ cases}}$. You can't solve for x until the denominators of each fraction are in the same unit. You know that there are 64 boxes of donuts in a case, so in 10 cases there are 640 boxes. In each box there are 12 donuts, so $\frac{x \text{ lemon}}{12(640) \text{ donuts}}$. Now you're ready to solve: $\frac{3}{12} = \frac{x}{12(640)}$, $3(640) = x$ and $1,920 = x$, choice (D).

WORD PROBLEM

If it takes Patricia x hours to complete a job by herself and it takes Jennifer y hours to complete the same job by herself, how long would it take for Patricia and Jennifer to complete the job together?

(A) $\dfrac{x+y}{2}$

(B) $\dfrac{1}{2}xy$

(C) $\dfrac{1}{x}+\dfrac{1}{y}$

(D) $\dfrac{x-y}{y-x}$

(E) $\dfrac{xy}{x+y}$

As soon as you find that they do $\dfrac{5}{6}$ of the job each hour, you know that the total job takes $\dfrac{6}{5}$ hours; since the reciprocal of the total amount of time to do the job equals the hourly rate, the reciprocal of the hourly rate equals the total amount of time to do the job.

This is the kind of problem you might opt to skip on a first go round. It's a tough question, and the variables make it even more intimidating. The main idea to keep in mind on work problems is that if x is the amount of time that it takes to complete a job, in each hour, $\dfrac{1}{x}$ of the job is done. You could use this fact to help you solve the problem algebraically, but you can also use it to help you use values for variables. Say that Patricia could do the job in 2 hours ($x = 2$); then each hour she does $\dfrac{1}{2}$ of the job. Say that Jennifer could do the job in 3 hours ($y = 3$); then each hour she does $\dfrac{1}{3}$ of the job.

Together they would do $\dfrac{1}{2} + \dfrac{1}{3} = \dfrac{5}{6}$ of the job each hour. For the job to be completed, the total amount of work must equal 1. Let n be the number of hours it will take to finish the job: $\dfrac{5}{6}n = 1$ so $n = \dfrac{6}{5}$.

Plugging into the answer choices, only choice (E) gives you $\dfrac{6}{5}$, so it is correct.

PROBABILITY

For a certain raffle, the winning ticket was selected at random from the total of 300 tickets sold. If Matt sold tickets numbered 83 through 118, what is the probability that he sold the winning ticket?

$$\text{Probability is equal to } \frac{\text{Number of desired outcomes}}{\text{Total number of possible outcomes}}.$$

The probability that Matt sold the winning ticket is equal to the number of tickets he sold, divided by the total number of tickets. Since 300 raffle tickets were sold, it's clear that 300 is the denominator of the fraction. All you need to figure out is how many tickets Matt sold.

You know he sold tickets numbered 83 through 118, so how do you find out how many tickets that totals? Counting them off isn't really an option; it'd take a lot of time and you'd likely lose track at some point and come up with the wrong total. To find the number of items in a consecutively numbered set, subtract the smallest from the largest and then add one: $118 - 83 = 35 + 1 = 36$. Be sure to remember to add one when you know the set is inclusive. It's easy to see this in a smaller situation: If Matt had sold tickets 1 through 4 it's clear that he'd have sold 4 tickets, not 3. So the probability that Matt sold the winner is $\frac{36}{300}$, which must be gridded as the decimal .12 or reduced to $\frac{3}{25}$ to fit on the grid.

COMBINATIONS

In how many different ways can 6 people arrange themselves in a row of 6 seats if 2 people insist on sitting in an end seat?

(A) 24
(B) 36
(C) 48
(D) 120
(E) 720

Think of this situation visually. Say that the people who want to sit in the end seats are *A* and *B*. That means you'd have a situation like this:

That leaves you 4 empty seats and 4 people to fill them. You have 4 choices for whom to put in the first empty seat. After placing one of the 4 in the first empty seat, you're left with 3 choices for the second, then 2 for the third and 1 for the last. This gives you a total of $4 \times 3 \times 2 \times 1 = 24$ possibilities. But that's not all. *A* and *B* could very well switch places like so:

Again, there'd be 24 possibilities for seating the other 4 people, for a total of $2(24) = 48$ possibilities, choice (C).

PRACTICE SETS

Answers for the following practice sets can be found on page 442.

Arithmetic Practice Set I

1. The number of boys attending Union High School is twice the number of girls. If $\frac{1}{6}$ of the girls and $\frac{1}{4}$ of the boys play soccer, what fraction of the students at Union play soccer?

   (A) $\frac{1}{24}$

   (B) $\frac{5}{24}$

   (C) $\frac{2}{9}$

   (D) $\frac{1}{3}$

   (E) $\frac{5}{12}$

2. If $\frac{N}{8}$ and $\frac{N}{36}$ are both integers, which of the following could be the value of N?

   I.   4
   II. 64
   III. 72

   (A) I only
   (B) II only
   (C) III only
   (D) II and III only
   (E) I, II and III

3. 25% of 72 is equal to 150% of what number?

   (A)   12
   (B)   18
   (C)   27
   (D)   36
   (E)   108

4. Carol's average score on her first 3 tests is 90. If her average on her last 2 tests is 80, what is her average score for all 5 tests?

   (A)   85
   (B)   86
   (C)   87
   (D)   88
   (E)   89

Column A | **Column B**

5.

| The product of the distinct prime factors of 7 | The product of the distinct prime factors of 81 |

8. Snow is falling at a rate of $\frac{1}{3}$ inch per 24 minutes. How much snow will fall in 2 hours?

6.

| $\dfrac{1,001 - 26}{13}$ | $\dfrac{1,001}{13} - 26$ |

9. On a certain day in February, the low temperature in a town ranged from -12 degrees to 19 degrees. What is the difference between the high and low temperatures for the day?

7.

| The sum of n numbers divided by the average of n numbers | n |

10. As part of a special promotion, customers receive one free woozle with every five they buy. Kate buys only woozles and leaves the store with a total of 30 of them. If she spent $75.00, how many dollars does each woozle sell for? (Disregard the $ sign when gridding your answer.)

Arithmetic Practice Set II

1. Carmela drives 20 miles from her home to the store at a speed of 30 miles per hour. If she makes the return trip home at a speed of 40 miles per hour, what is the total amount of time she spent driving?

   (A) 35 minutes
   (B) 50 minutes
   (C) 1 hour and 10 minutes
   (D) 1 hour and 30 minutes
   (E) 1 hour and 50 minutes

2. Sixty percent of a class goes on a field trip. If twelve students don't go on the field trip, how many students are in the class?

   (A) 20
   (B) 24
   (C) 30
   (D) 36
   (E) 48

3. Phil bought everyone in the office either a burger or pizza for lunch. A burger costs $5.50 per person and pizza costs $4.00 per person. If 12 people ordered pizza and 18 people ordered burgers, what is the average amount of money Phil spent on each person for lunch?

   (A) $3.94
   (B) $4.75
   (C) $4.90
   (D) $5.10
   (E) $5.25

4. All of the following statements about the number 51 are true EXCEPT

   (A) It is an integer.
   (B) It is an odd number.
   (C) It is a positive number.
   (D) It is a two-digit number.
   (E) It is a prime number.

Column A	**Column B**

5.

The remainder when 2,345,678 is divided by 5	The remainder when 2,345,678 is divided by 10

$$37.25\% \text{ of } 89.36 = a$$
$$37.25\% \text{ of } 8.936 = b$$

6.

$10a$	b

7.

$\dfrac{\sqrt{5}}{3}$	$\dfrac{\sqrt{5}}{6}$

8. The average of 5 numbers is 17. If the average of 2 of those numbers is 20, what is the average of the other 3 numbers?

9. In how many different ways can 3 people arrange themselves in a row of 4 seats?

10. The ratio of flour to sugar in a certain recipe is 7:1. If 12 cups of flour are used, how many cups of sugar are needed?

Arithmetic Practice Set III
Real SAT Questions

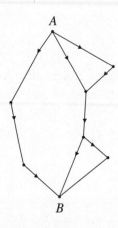

A

B

1. In the figure above, any path from *A* to *B* must follow the connected line segments in the direction shown by the arrows. How many different paths are there from *A* to *B*?

   (A) Five
   (B) Six
   (C) Seven
   (D) Eight
   (E) Nine

2. If *m* and *n* are both negative numbers, *m* is less than -1, and *n* is greater than -1, which of the following gives all possible values of the product *mn*?

   (A) All negative numbers
   (B) All negative numbers less than -1
   (C) All negative numbers greater than -1
   (D) All positive numbers
   (E) All positive numbers less than 1

3. Ms. Clark drove from her home to the museum at an average speed of 40 miles per hour and returned home along the same route at an average speed of 35 miles per hour. If her total driving time for the trip was 2 hours, how many <u>minutes</u> did it take Ms. Clark to drive from her home to the museum?

   (A) 70
   (B) 60
   (C) 56
   (D) 45
   (E) 40

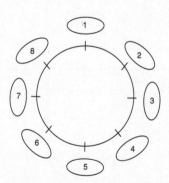

4. The figure above represents a circular table with 8 equally spaced chairs labeled 1 through 8. If two students are to sit directly opposite each other, leaving the other chairs empty, how many such arrangements of the two students are possible?

   (A) 4
   (B) 8
   (C) 16
   (D) 28
   (E) 56

126

5. A store charges $28.00 for a certain type of sweater. This price is 40 percent more than the amount it costs the store to buy one of these sweaters. At an end-of-season sale, store employees can purchase any remaining sweaters at 30 percent off the store's cost. How much would it cost an employee to purchase a sweater of this type at this sale?

(A) $8.40
(B) $14.00
(C) $19.00
(D) $20.00
(E) $25.20

Column A	Column B

−1, 1, 0, −1, 1, 0, . . .
In the pattern shown, the numbers −1, 1, 0 repeat indefinitely in the order shown.

6.

Column A	Column B
The 19th term in the pattern	The 17th term in the pattern

7.

Column A	Column B
The number of ways that 0 can be expressed as a product of two different one-digit integers	The number of ways that 12 can be expressed as a product of two different one-digit integers

8.

Column A	Column B
The sum of three different prime numbers if each number is less than 10	The sum of three different positive even integers if each integer is less than 10

9. Ten consecutive integers are arranged in order from least to greatest. If the sum of the first five integers is 200, what is the sum of the last five integers?

10. If the average (arithmetic mean) of three <u>different</u> positive integers is 70, what is the greatest possible value of one of the integers?

Algebra

SIMULTANEOUS EQUATIONS

If $3x - y = 9$ and $x + 5y = 19$, then $x + y =$

(A) 3
(B) 4
(C) 7
(D) 10
(E) 28

You likely learned how to solve a system of equations—two different equations containing two different variables—in algebra class. First, use one equation to solve for one variable in terms of the other. Then, plug this algebraic expression into the second equation to solve for the value of the other variable. Then, plug this value into either equation to solve for the remaining variable. While it's not a very difficult process, it is quite time consuming, which can be a problem on a timed test like the SAT. Also, with all the work that's involved in this method there are ample opportunities for errors. All the time you've invested in solving would be wasted if you made even a single careless mistake that throws off the solution. The good news is that there's often a better way to deal with simultaneous equations on the SAT. When you're given a question that asks you to solve not for one variable or the other, but some expression containing both of them, there's usually a way to combine the equations and solve for this expression (or some multiple of it).

Look at the two equations you're given. Notice what happens if you add them:

$$\begin{array}{r} 3x - y = 9 \\ + \ x + 5y = 19 \\ \hline 4x + 4y = 28 \end{array}$$

Factoring out a 4 you find that $4(x + y = 7)$, choice (C). This is a lot quicker and simpler than the by-the-book approach you learned in algebra class. It doesn't matter how you solve a problem on the SAT, as long as you solve it correctly.

INEQUALITY

Column A	Column B

$$12 + 3a < a$$

a	-6

The big thing to remember with inequalities is that if you multiply or divide by a negative you must change the direction of the inequality sign. Other than that, treat them as you would equations, doing the same thing to both sides to isolate the variable. To isolate a in the inequality above, first subtract $3a$ from both sides: $12 < -2a$. Now you must divide both sides by -2, being sure to flip the direction of the inequality sign: $-6 > a$. Since a is less than -6, Column B is greater. Not a very hard question, but one you could easily get wrong if you forgot to flip the sign.

EXPONENTS AND RADICALS

A lot of SAT questions will test the rules that govern exponents and radicals. On Quantitative Comparisons especially, make sure you're answering based on an understanding of the rules and not just on what seems or looks right.

Column A	Column B
$\sqrt{10} + \sqrt{17}$	$\sqrt{27}$

Remember, you don't necessarily need to find exact values to compare the columns.

If you were rushing, you might answer that the columns are equal. They're not. You can't add and subtract roots unless they have the same quantity under the radical sign. You could use your calculator to find the precise values of the columns, but you don't need to spend the time doing that to answer the question. It's enough to know that since $\sqrt{10}$ is a little more than 3 and $\sqrt{17}$ is a little more than 4, their sum will be a little more than 7. Since $\sqrt{27}$ is a just a little more than 5, Column A is greater.

Reference Point

When multiplying powers with the same base, add the exponents.

When dividing powers with the same base, subtract the exponents.

When raising a power to a power, multiply the exponents.

Column A	Column B
$\dfrac{a^{12}}{a^4}$	$(a^4)^2$

It's especially important to know the rules for multiplying, dividing and raising powers to powers. This information is necessary not only for answering questions like the one above, but in order to solve more complicated problems. In Column A you're dividing powers with the same base, so subtract the exponents: $a^{12} \div a^4 = a^{12-4} = a^8$. In Column B you're raising a power to a power so multiply the exponents: $(a^4)^2 = a^{4 \times 2} = a^8$. Therefore the columns are equal and choice (C) is correct.

Column A	Column B
$2^{99} + 2^{99}$	2^{100}

Even if you couldn't figure out how to answer this question, you could eliminate choice (D) and guess; you know choice (D) can't be correct since both columns contain only numbers.

In some questions it's a little less obvious what you're supposed to do. You're not asked to multiply, divide or raise powers here, so what should you do? It might help to make the columns look more alike. Both expressions involve powers of 2, but not the same powers of 2; in Column A, 2 is raised to the 99th power while in Column B, 2 is raised to the 100th power. See if you can rewrite Column B in terms of 2^{99}. When you multiply powers with the same base you add the exponents, so $2^{100} = 2^1 \times 2^{99}$, or simply 2×2^{99}. Since $2^{99} + 2^{99} = 2 \times 2^{99}$, the columns are equal, and choice (C) is correct.

RECOGNIZING COMMON FACTOTRABLES

If $x^2 + y^2 = 55$ and $xy = 3$, then which of the following could be the value of $x - y$?

(A)   4
(B)   7
(C)   49
(D)   52
(E)   None of the above.

Common Factorables

$a^2 - 1 = (a + 1)(a - 1)$

$a^2 - b^2 = (a + b)(a - b)$

$a^2 - 2ab + b^2 = (a - b)^2$

$a^2 + 2ab + b^2 = (a + b)^2$

When you approach SAT questions, there are certain things you should be on the lookout for. On geometry questions, for example, recognizing special triangles is often the key to solving a problem. On algebra questions, recognizing common factorables can break the question wide open. Here you're told that $x^2 + y^2 = 55$ and that $xy = 3$, and you're asked for the value of $x - y$. Remember that $(x - y)^2 = x^2 - 2xy + y^2$ and this question is a snap. Rewrite $x^2 - 2xy + y^2$ as $x^2 + y^2 - 2xy$ and you're ready to plug in: $(x - y)^2 = 55 - 2(3) = 49$. Therefore, $x - y$ must be either 7 or -7. Since choice (B) is 7, it is correct.

SYMBOLISM

A number is said to be "unbalanced" if the product of its digits is greater than the sum of its digits. Which of the following numbers is unbalanced?

(A)   1,111
(B)   505
(C)   132
(D)   42
(E)   22

Some questions on the SAT may throw you by using an odd term you've never heard before or some unusual symbol you'd swear you've never seen in a math text book. Don't get hung up on the weirdness, just follow the directions that accompany each term or symbol. Beneath their strange veneer these questions are really quite straightforward. The question above talks about an unbalanced number. In such a number the product of its digits is greater than their sum. It doesn't matter that you've never heard this term before, just see which of the answer choices fits its conditions.

(A)   1,111: product $1 <$ sum 4
(B)   505: product $0 <$ sum 10
(C)   132: product $6 =$ sum 6
(D)   42: product $8 >$ sum 6
(E)   22: product $4 =$ sum 4

It shouldn't take you too long to see that choice (D), 42, is the only unbalanced choice, since $4 \times 2 > 4 + 2$.

ALGEBRA

The following questions refer to the definition below:

For all integers x and y, let $x \bigstar y = x^2 + y$ and $x \, \bigodot \, y = x + y^2$

What is the value of $-3 \bigstar 5$?

(A) -4
(B) 4
(C) 14
(D) 22
(E) 34

What is the value of $6 \bigstar (4 \bigodot 2)$?

(A) 18
(B) 44
(C) 54
(D) 70
(E) 330

If $6 \bigstar a = a \bigodot b$, which of the following MUST be true?

(A) $b = 6$
(B) $a = b$
(C) $\dfrac{a}{b} = \dfrac{1}{6}$
(D) $b^2 = 36$
(E) None of the above.

Sometimes several questions refer to the same symbol or definition. In such cases the first question is usually quite easy, often requiring nothing more than plugging into the expression that defines the symbol. The subsequent questions tend to be more involved and more difficult. If you came across a set of these questions and were pressed for time, you might do well to answer only the first and scoop up some easy points. If you had time, you could return to the more difficult questions later.

So the first question in this set should be simple as long as you follow the directions and plug in carefully. Since $x \bigstar y = x^2 + y$, $-3 \bigstar 5 = (-3)^2 + 5 = 9 + 5 = 14$, choice (C). Unless you mistakenly followed the directions for $\bigodot$ instead of $\bigstar$, or made a computational error, it's a pretty safe bet you'd get this question right.

Now look at the second question. In this one you have to deal with both symbols, so be careful to keep them straight. Even though you're working with strange symbols, you're still doing computation and need to follow the order of operations, so start with the parentheses first. $4 \bigodot 2 = 4 + 2^2 = 4 + 4 = 8$. Now you're left with $6 \bigstar 8$. Just work it through, making sure to plug into the right expression: $6 \bigstar 8 = 6^2 + 8 = 36 + 8 = 44$, choice (B). This was a little tougher, but as long as you remembered to start with the parentheses and didn't mix up $\bigodot$ and $\bigstar$, you should have been all right.

Be careful when you see words like MUST, NEVER and ALWAYS. Make sure you test the situations carefully to make sure they satisfy the "absoluteness" these terms demand.

Now for the last question. If $6 \bigstar a = a \, \textcircled{O} \, b$, which of the following must be true? Already the problem is more intimidating since you're not asked to find a value, but to evaluate five statements. Plug the values you are given into the expressions that define each symbol: $6 \bigstar a = a \, \textcircled{O} \, b$ so $6^2 + a = a + b^2$. Subtracting a from both sides of the equation, you find that $36 = b^2$, choice (D). Watch out for choice (A) on this one. The question asks which statement MUST be true. While b could equal 6, it could also equal -6, since $(-6)^2 = 36$. If you were hasty and jumped at choice (A) you'd have lost out on a question you deserved to get right.

WORD PROBLEMS

If five less than three times a number is two more than half the number, which of the following equations could be used to solve for that number?

(A) $5 - 3n = \dfrac{n}{2} + 2$

(B) $5 - 3n = n + \dfrac{1}{2}$

(C) $3n - 5 = \dfrac{n}{2} + 2$

(D) $3n - 5 = n + \dfrac{1}{2}$

(E) $3(n - 5) = \dfrac{1}{2}(n + 2)$

"Five less than three times a number" = 3n − 5, NOT 5 −3n

There are lots of word problems on the SAT. Some simply require you to translate English into algebra. For these questions, just read the question carefully, translating each bit as you go along. Start with "five less than three times a number is." Let the number be n. Three times the number is $3n$. Five less than that is $3n - 5$. Be careful not to mistranslate this as $5 - 3n$; you must pay special attention to order when dealing with subtraction or division.

"Is" means equal, so you've got $3n - 5 =$, and you're halfway there. Finish translating "two more than half the number." Half the number is $\dfrac{n}{2}$. Two more than half the number is $\dfrac{n}{2} + 2$. So the entire equation is translated as $3n - 5 = \dfrac{n}{2} + 2$, choice (C).

Reference Point

English ⇒ Algebra
Less than ⇒ subtraction
Times ⇒ multiplication
Is ⇒ equals
Half ⇒ divide by 2
More than ⇒ addition

In a certain game, c chips are worth p points. How many points would $c + 1$ chips be worth?

(A) $p + 1$

(B) $\dfrac{p}{c} + 1$

(C) $\dfrac{cp + p}{c}$

(D) $\dfrac{p}{c + 1}$

(E) $\dfrac{c^2 + c}{p}$

Word problems like this require some sophisticated translating. Because of this they scare off a lot of students whose English to Algebra skills are less than stellar. So what should you do if faced with this question? Don't translate it. Use values for variables to make this abstract question more concrete.

When you're using values for variables, pick numbers that are easy to work with. Don't worry if they don't make any sense for the situation. For this question, let's say that 5 chips are worth 10 points ($c = 5$ and $p = 10$). That means each chip is worth $\dfrac{10}{5} = 2$ points. So 6 chips would therefore be worth 12 points. Plug $c = 5$ and $p = 10$ into the answer choices; whichever gives you 12 is correct.

(A) $p + 1 = 10 + 1 = 11$

(B) $\dfrac{p}{c} + 1 = \dfrac{10}{5} + 1 = 3$

(C) $\dfrac{cp + p}{c} = \dfrac{(5)(10) + 10}{5} = 12$ CORRECT

(D) $\dfrac{p}{c + 1} = \dfrac{10}{5 + 1} = \dfrac{10}{6}$

(E) $\dfrac{c^2 + c}{p} = \dfrac{5^2 + 5}{10} = 3$

What if more than one choice gives you the result you're looking for? Try new values for the variables in only the choices that matched your result, until just one matches. If you don't have time to try another set of numbers, you could guess from among the matching choices.

At a certain high school, 60% of the student body is female and $\frac{1}{3}$ of the student government is male. If 15% of the student body participate in student government and there are 900 female students who do not participate in student government, what is the total number of students in the school?

Some word problems don't involve translating into algebraic expressions. They give you a lot of information about a situation that you need to digest and organize to find the solution. Just take these problems one step at a time, keeping focused on what you're asked to find.

You're told that 60 percent or $\frac{3}{5}$ of the student body is female and that 15 percent or $\frac{3}{20}$ of the student body participates in student government. You're also told that $\frac{1}{3}$ of the student government is male, which means that the remaining $\frac{2}{3}$ must be female. You know that the number of female students that don't participate in student government is 900. If you knew what percent of the student body this number represented, you could solve for the value of the student body.

Let the student body equal x. You know the total number of female students is $\frac{3}{5}x$. You also know that female students make up $\frac{2}{3}$ of the student government. Since $\frac{3}{20}x$ of all students participate in government, $\frac{2}{3} \times \frac{3}{20}x = \frac{1}{10}x$ is the number of females who participate in student government. The total number of female students must be equal to the females who participate in student government plus the females who do not participate in student government. Therefore, you can solve for the number of female students not in government: $\frac{3}{5}x - \frac{1}{10}x = \frac{1}{2}x$. You know that there are 900 female students not in government, and now you know that this represents half of the student body, so there must be a total of $2(900) = 1800$ students.

Since this is a Grid-in, it's a good idea to check your work. Plug 1,800 in as the size of the student body and see if it all makes sense.

PRACTICE SETS

Answers for the following practice sets can be found on page 446.

Algebra Practice Set I

1. If $8x + 8y = 64$, what is the average of x and y?

   (A) 16
   (B) 8
   (C) 4
   (D) 2
   (E) It cannot be determined from the information given.

2. Which of the following statements MUST be true?

   I.   If n^2 is even, then n^3 is even.
   II. If $2n$ is even, then n is odd.
   III. If n is even, then $2n - 1$ is odd.

   (A) I only
   (B) II only
   (C) III only
   (D) I and II only
   (E) I and III only

3. The greatest of five consecutive odd integers is x. Which of the following represents the smallest of the five integers?

   (A) $\dfrac{x}{5}$
   (B) $x - 10$
   (C) $x - 8$
   (D) $x - 5$
   (E) $x - 4$

4. If b baubles cost d dollars, how much do $b - 1$ baubles cost?

   (A) $d - 1$
   (B) $d(b - 1)$
   (C) $\dfrac{d}{b - 1}$
   (D) $\dfrac{d(b - 1)}{b}$
   (E) $\dfrac{bd}{b - 1}$

Column A	Column B

$$\frac{1}{x} + \frac{1}{y} = \frac{1}{z}$$

$$xy = z$$

5.

$x + y$	1

$$a + 2 = b$$
$$b - 1 = c$$

6.

a	c

7.

$\dfrac{\sqrt{14}}{7}$	$\sqrt{2}$

8. A woman goes to the bank to get change for \$20.00 and receives an equal number each of quarters, dimes and nickels. How many coins did she receive in total?

$$1 \le x \le 5$$
$$6 \le y \le 10$$

9. What is the maximum value of $\dfrac{x}{y}$?

10. If $a^2 - b^2 = 5$ and $a - b = 1$, what is the value of $a + b$?

Algebra Practice Set II

1. If $\dfrac{p+q+r}{3} = \dfrac{p+q}{2}$, then $r =$

   (A) $2(p+q)$

   (B) $p+q$

   (C) $\dfrac{p+q}{2}$

   (D) p

   (E) q

2. If $x^2 + y^2 = 15$ and $xy = 5$, then which of the following could be the value of $x + y$?

   (A) -5
   (B)   3
   (C) 10
   (D) 15
   (E) 75

3. Ed and Lori go shopping. Ed spends $30 more than Lori in the first store and Lori spends $12 less than Ed in the second store. Which of the following must be true about Lori's total spending in the two stores compared to Ed's?

   (A) Lori spent $\dfrac{2}{5}$ of what Ed spent.

   (B) Lori spent $18 less than Ed.

   (C) Lori spent $21 less than Ed.

   (D) Lori spent $42 less than Ed.

   (E) Lori spent $42 more than Ed.

4. Thad bikes m miles every h hours. At this rate, how many miles would he bike in 45 minutes?

   (A) mh

   (B) $\dfrac{3m}{4h}$

   (C) $\dfrac{m}{h}$

   -15

   (D) $\dfrac{m}{60h}$

   (E) $\dfrac{h}{45m}$

Column A	Column B
5. The number of 33-cent stamps that can be bought with d dollars.	$\dfrac{d}{33}$

$$x > y$$
$$xy \neq 0$$

6. $\dfrac{x}{y}$	$\dfrac{y}{x}$

7. $\dfrac{\sqrt{75}}{\sqrt{3}}$	25

8. If 3 is subtracted from a certain number, the result is 5 less than twice the number. What is the number?

9. If $\dfrac{a}{b} = \dfrac{3}{4}$ and $\dfrac{b}{c} = \dfrac{5}{6}$, what is the value of $\dfrac{a}{c}$?

$$7a - 3b = 9$$
$$3a + b = 1$$

10. What is the value of $a - b$?

Algebra Practice Set III
Real SAT Questions

1. If $10x + y = 8$ and $7x - y = 9$, what is the value of $3x + 2y$?

   (A) -2
   (B) -1
   (C) $\dfrac{8}{9}$
   (D) 1
   (E) 17

Questions 2–3 refer to the following definitions for integers n greater than 1.

$$\triangle{n} = n^2 + n$$
$$\boxed{n} = n^2 - n$$

2. $\triangle{5} - \boxed{4} =$

   (A) 0
   (B) 8
   (C) 10
   (D) 18
   (E) 32

3. If m is an integer greater than 1, then $\boxed{m + 1} =$

   (A) $\triangle{m}$
   (B) $\triangle{m} + 1$
   (C) $\triangle{m} - 1$
   (D) $\boxed{m} + 1$
   (E) $\boxed{m} - 1$

4. Pat has s grams of strawberries and uses 40 percent of the strawberries to make pies, each of which requires p grams. The rest of the strawberries are used to make pints of jam, each of which requires j grams. Which of the following gives the number of pints of jam Pat can make?

   (A) $\dfrac{2s}{5p}$
   (B) $\dfrac{2s}{5j}$
   (C) $\dfrac{3s}{5j}$
   (D) $\dfrac{3p}{5s}$
   (E) $\dfrac{3sj}{5}$

5. A business is owned by 3 men and 1 woman, each of whom has an equal share. If one of the men sells $\frac{1}{2}$ of his share to the woman, and another of the men keeps $\frac{2}{3}$ of his share and sells the rest to the woman, what fraction of the business will the woman own?

(A) $\frac{5}{24}$

(B) $\frac{11}{24}$

(C) $\frac{1}{2}$

(D) $\frac{13}{24}$

(E) $\frac{11}{6}$

6. The price of ground coffee beans is d dollars for 8 ounces and each ounce makes c cups of brewed coffee. In terms of c and d, what is the dollar cost of the ground coffee beans required to make 1 cup of brewed coffee?

(A) $\frac{d}{8c}$

(B) $\frac{cd}{8}$

(C) $\frac{8c}{d}$

(D) $\frac{8d}{c}$

(E) $8cd$

Column A	Column B
7. The value of x when $3x + 6 = 15$	The value of y when $3(y + 2) = 15$
8. $(a^5)^6(a^6)^6$	$(a^{11})^6$

9. If x and y are each different positive integers and $x + y = 5$, what is one possible value of $4x + 9y$?

10. If $x^2 - y^2 = 10$ and $x + y = 5$, what is the value of $x - y$?

Geometry

SPECIAL TRIANGLES

Column A   Column B

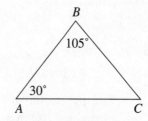

Note: Figure not drawn to scale.

$$BC = 8$$

AB	16

Figures on the SAT are drawn to scale, unless otherwise noted. When they are drawn to scale, you can rely on your eyes to judge the relative sizes of angles and line segments. In some cases this can even enable you to eliminate choices that are obviously too big or too small to be correct. However, the figure in the problem above is not drawn to scale, so you can't rely on the fact that *AB* certainly doesn't look twice as large as *BC* to determine its length.

When you're stumped on a geometry problem, always do what you can. While it might not be obvious at first why you're doing it, it can often lead you in the right direction. Since you know that the three angles of a triangle sum to 180° and you're given the measures of two of them, you can certainly find the measure of the third angle: $\angle BCA = 180° - 30° - 105° = 45°$. When you're working with triangles, you should always be on the lookout for special triangles. In this case you've got a 30° angle and a 45° angle, which should put you in mind of 30-60-90 and 45-45-90 triangles. Look what happens if you drop a perpendicular from point *B* to *AC*:

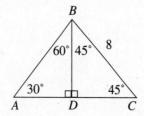

Since *BD* is perpendicular to *AC* it forms two right angles and consequently, two right triangles. The third angle in $\triangle ABD$ must be 60° and the third angle in $\triangle BCD$ must be 45°. In a 45-45-90 triangle, sides are in a ratio of 1:1 $\sqrt{2}$; since the hypotenuse of $\triangle BCD$ is 8, legs *BD* and *CD* must each be $4\sqrt{2}$ (since $4\sqrt{2} \times \sqrt{2} = 8$). In a 30-60-90 triangle, sides are in a ratio of 1:$\sqrt{3}$:2; since the side opposite the 30° angle, *BD*, is $4\sqrt{2}$, the hypotenuse *AB* must be twice that, or $8\sqrt{2}$. Since $8\sqrt{2} < 8 \times 2$, *AB* < 16 and Column B is greater.

AREAS OF SIMILAR FIGURES

Column A	Column B

The perimeter of Square *A* is 16 and the perimeter of Square *B* is 32.

Twice the area of Square *A*	The area of Square *B*

At a quick glance you might think that the columns are equal. Since the perimeter of Square *A* is half that of Square *B*, its area must be half as well; therefore, twice the area of Square *A* must be the same as the area of Square *B*, right? Wrong. This is the kind of assumption you might make if you're nervous or running out of time, so stay alert. You could sketch a diagram, but you won't have to if you remember the following fact: the ratio of the areas of proportional figures is equal to the square of the ratio of their corresponding linear measurements. Since the ratio of the linear measurements of *A* to *B* is 1:2, the ratio of their areas is $1^2:2^2 = 1:4$. In other words, since the perimeter of Square *B* is twice as large as that of Square *A*, its area is four times as big. Therefore, Column B is greater.

You could also work the problem through to come to this conclusion. Perimeter of a square is equal to $4s$ where *s* is a side of the square. Therefore a side of Square *A* is 4 and a side of Square *B* is 8. Area of a square is s^2, so the area of Square *A* is $4^2 = 16$ and the area of Square *B* is $8^2 = 64$. Twice the area of Square *A* is 32, which is still less than the area of Square *B*.

COMBINED FIGURES

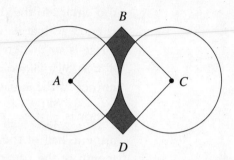

In the figure above, circles with centers *A* and *C* are tangent to each other and are intersected by square *ABCD*. If the circles are equal and the circumference of each is 16π, what is the area of the shaded region?

(A) $32(4 - 2\pi)$

(B) $32(4 - \pi)$

(C) $32\left(4 - \dfrac{\pi}{2}\right)$

(D) $32\left(2 - \dfrac{\pi}{2}\right)$

(E) $32\left(1 - \dfrac{\pi}{4}\right)$

The answer choices give you a hint to this effect, since each consists of a quantity minus another quantity including π.

In this question you need to find the area of the oddly shaped shaded region. Don't comb your brain for a formula to find the area of this strange shape, because there isn't one. So how do you find it? When you're dealing with combined figures, look for pieces the figures have in common and find the measurements of oddly shaped regions by considering them as the sum (or difference) of more ordinary shapes. In this question, try to see how the circles and square interact to form this region. You can see that the shaded region is inside of the square. You can also see that the unshaded parts of the square are sectors of the two circles. So the area of the shaded region is equal to the area of the square minus the areas of the two sectors. If you find the area of the square and subtract from it the area of the two sectors, you'll be left with the area of the shaded region.

You have a game plan, now you have to execute it. To find the area of a square you must know its side length. To find the area of a sector of a circle to need to know the measure of its central angle and the area of the entire circle. To find the area of the circle you need to know its radius. Work backwards from the information you're given to deduce these measurements.

You're told that the circumference of each circle is 16π. Circumference of a circle is equal to πd where d is the diameter of the circle, so the diameter of each circle is 16. The radius of a circle is equal to half its diameter, so the radius of each circle is 8. Area of a circle is πr^2 where r is a radius, so the area of each circle is $8^2\pi = 64\pi$. Since each sector has a central angle that is equal to a corner of the square, each is 90°. A circle contains 360°, so each sector is $\frac{90}{360} = \frac{1}{4}$ of the circle's area. There are two, so together they are one half of the circle's area or 32π. Now you just need the side length of the square, but how can you find it? You have plenty of information about the circle, so see if there's a way any of it is related to the square.

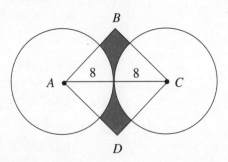

If you draw a line connecting the centers of the circles you'll see that this is also a diagonal of the square. Since this segment AC is composed of a radius of circle A and a radius of circle B, it has a length of $2(8) = 16$. A diagonal of a square is equal to a side length times $\sqrt{2}$ (which is easy to remember if you think of the square as two isosceles right triangles with sides in a ratio of $1:1\sqrt{2}$). Therefore, the side of the square is equal to $8\sqrt{2}$, since $(\sqrt{2})(8\sqrt{2}) = (8)(2) = 16$. Area of a square is equal to s^2 where s is a side of the square, so the area is $(8\sqrt{2})^2 = 8^2 \times (\sqrt{2})^2 = 64 \times 2 = 128$.

Don't despair if you don't immediately recognize your answer among the choices; check to see if it can be expressed in another way.

So the area of the shaded region is $128 - 32\pi$. However, this isn't one of the choices. Don't worry though—all the choices have 32 factored out, so your answer can be expressed as $32(4 - \pi)$, choice (B). That was a bit of work, but it really wasn't all that difficult. Once you recognized the relationships between the figures, it was simply a matter of working with the standard formulas for circle and squares. Also note that if you were running out of time or got stuck part way through the problem, you could have eliminated some choices.

Peterson's SAT Success

Right off the bat, choice (A) could be crossed off. Since 2π is a little more than 6, $4 - 2\pi$ will be negative as will $32(4 - 2\pi)$. Since you can't have a negative area, this choice simply isn't possible. Once you had figured out that the area of the square was 128, you could have eliminated choices (D) and (E), which start with 64 and 32 respectively. Once you find that the combined area of the sectors is 32π, you could have eliminated all the choices except (B), since it's the only one that subtracts this amount from the area of the square.

SIMILAR FIGURES

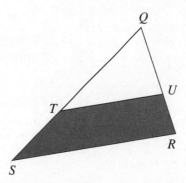

Note: Figure not drawn to scale.

In the figure above, SR is parallel to TU and $QT = \dfrac{TS}{2}$. If the area of triangle QTU is 1, what is the area of shaded region $STUR$?

Similar Thinking

- *Look for clues that the triangles are similar (2 equal angles, proportional sides)*
- *Infer from that (determine measurements of one figure from those given for the other figure)*
- *Avoid the length/area ratio trap (ratio of areas is the SQUARE of the ratio of corresponding linear measurements)*

Here's another figure that's not drawn to scale, so you can't trust your impression of the size of the shaded region. Consider what you're told and think about why. If you're given information, it's there for a reason; SAT questions rarely include unnecessary data. You're told that SR is parallel to TU. Think about your store of math knowledge concerning parallel lines. You know that when parallel lines are cut by a transversal all the acute angles formed are equal to each other and all the obtuse formed are equal. What does that mean for this figure? Since QS can be thought of as a transversal intersecting the parallel lines, angles QTU and QSR are equal. Likewise, considering QR as a transversal, angles QUT and QRS are equal. Since triangle QSR and triangle QTU have angle Q in common, all three of their angles are equal and the triangles are similar.

So now you know that the triangles are similar, but how does that help? Looking at the figure you can see that the shaded area is the difference between the area of the large triangle and the area of the small triangle. You're given that the area of triangle QTU is 1, so you just have to find the area of triangle QSR. Since you're told that

$QT = \dfrac{TS}{2}$, $2QT = TS$. Since $QS = QT + TS$, $QS = 3QT$. Therefore, the sides of $\triangle QSR$ are 3 times as large as those of $\triangle QTU$, or the ratio of their linear measurements is 3:1. Remember, the ratio of the areas of proportional figures is equal to the square of the ratio of their corresponding linear measurements. That means that the ratio of the areas of $\triangle QSR$ and QTU is 9:1. Since the area of $\triangle QTU = 1$, the area of $\triangle QSR = 9(1) = 9$. So the area of shaded region $STUR$ is $9 - 1 = 8$.

DIAGRAM-LESS

A circle is circumscribed about a square and another circle is inscribed within the square. What is the ratio of the area of the circumscribed circle to the area of the inscribed circle?

(A) 4:1

(B) 3:1

(C) 2:1

(D) $\sqrt{2}$:1

(E) It cannot be determined from the information given.

While you might think that a diagram not drawn to scale isn't much help, some geometry problems don't even give you a diagram at all. Although it's not always necessary to sketch one, doing so can be a great help in organizing the information you're given. You're not out to win any art prizes though, so don't worry about making a perfect diagram. You just want to accurately depict the information you're given so that it's easier to visualize the situation and the road to the solution.

While all the talk about inscribing and circumscribing may sound a little intimidating, it's really not that bad. To inscribe just means to draw within, and to circumscribe just means to draw around. So the question above is talking about a circle around a square that has another circle inside it. Make a sketch:

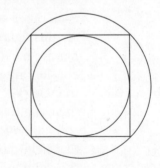

You're asked about the ratio of the area of the larger circle to the area of the smaller, but you're not given any information about any of the figures. Choice (E), "It cannot be determined . . ." is starting to look pretty good, huh? Not so fast. When you're dealing with combined figures, look for pieces that the figures have in common. If you sketch in a diameter of the smaller circle, you'll see that it's also a side of the square. Sketch in a diagonal of the square, and you'll see that it's also a diameter of the larger circle.

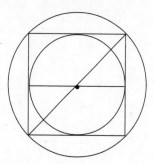

So while you still don't know any particular measurements, you know something about the way the three figures are related. If you pick some values for the linear measurements involved you can calculate the areas of the circles and determine their ratio. It doesn't matter what values you pick; their relative sizes will always be the same. Therefore pick numbers that are easy to work with. Start with the smallest measurement and work your way out. Set the radius of the smaller circle equal to 1. Since area of a circle is πr^2 where r is the radius of the circle, the area of the smaller circle is π. A side of the square is equal to the diameter of the smaller circle or $2(1) = 2$. The diagonal of a square is equal to a side times $\sqrt{2}$, so the diagonal is $2\sqrt{2}$. The diameter of the larger circle is therefore $2\sqrt{2}$ and its radius is $\sqrt{2}$. That means the area of the larger circle is $(\sqrt{2})^2 \pi = 2\pi$. Therefore, the ratio of the area of the larger circle to the area of the smaller circle is $2\pi{:}\pi = 2{:}1$, and choice (C) is correct.

PRACTICE SETS

Answers for the following practice sets can be found on page 450.

Geometry Practice Set I

1. A circle with diameter d has area A. What is the area of a circle with diameter $2d$?

   (A) $\dfrac{A}{2}$

   (B) A

   (C) $2A$

   (D) $4A$

   (E) $6A$

2. In triangle ABC, $AB = AC$. What is the measure of angle BAC?

   (A) $x°$
   (B) $2x°$
   (C) $x° + 90°$
   (D) $180° - 2x°$
   (E) $90° - x°$

3. A cylindrical roller 12 inches long is dipped into blue paint, and then rolled for one complete revolution over a white wall. If the area of the blue region is 48 square inches, what is the radius, in inches, of the roller?

   (A) $\dfrac{2}{\pi}$

   (B) $\dfrac{4}{\pi}$

   (C) 2

   (D) 4

   (E) 2π

4. A circle is inscribed within a square whose side length is 5. What is the area of the circle?

   (A) 5π
   (B) 6.25π
   (C) 10π
   (D) 25π
   (E) 100π

Column A   **Column B**

Line *m* is defined by the equation
$y + 2x = 5$.

5.
| The slope of line *m* | 2 |

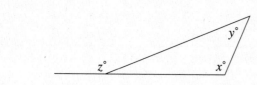

6.
| *y* | $z - x$ |

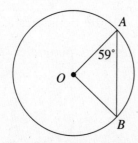

Note: Figure not drawn to scale.

A and *B* are points on the circle with center *O*.

7.
| *OA* | *AB* |

8. The angles in a triangle are in the ratio of 2:3:5. What is the number of degrees in the smallest angle of the triangle?

9. What is the slope of a line passing through the origin and the point with coordinates (2, 7)?

10. A rectangular solid with dimensions 12, 2 and *h* has the same volume as a cube with an edge length of 6. What is the value of *h*?

Geometry Practice Set II

1. What is the slope of the line that passes through points $(3, -3)$ and $(5, 0)$?

   (A) $-\dfrac{3}{2}$

   (B) $-\dfrac{2}{3}$

   (C) $\dfrac{3}{5}$

   (D) $\dfrac{2}{3}$

   (E) $\dfrac{3}{2}$

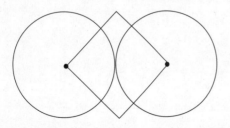

2. The figure above is formed of two equal circles and a square. If each circle has an area of 18π, what is the perimeter of the square?

   (A) 9
   (B) 12
   (C) 18
   (D) 24
   (E) 36

3. The area of a rectangle is 64. If its length is 16, what is its perimeter?

   (A) 48
   (B) 40
   (C) 20
   (D) 8
   (E) 4

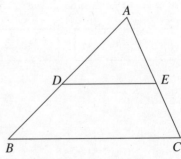

Note: Figure not drawn to scale.

4. In the figure above, DE is parallel to BC and $AD = \dfrac{DB}{2}$. If the perimeter of triangle ABC is 24, what is the perimeter of triangle ADE?

   (A) 6
   (B) 8
   (C) 12
   (D) 16
   (E) 48

Column A	Column B

An isosceles triangle has one side of length 3 and one side of length 7.

5.

The length of the triangle's third side	3

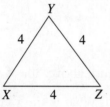

6.

The area of triangle *XYZ*	8

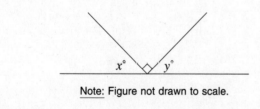

Note: Figure not drawn to scale.

7.

x	*y*

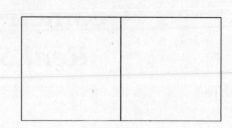

8. The rectangle above is composed of 2 equal squares, each with an area of 25. What is the perimeter of the rectangle?

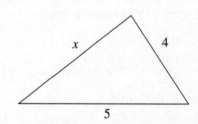

Note: Figure not drawn to scale.

9. Grid in a possible value for the perimeter of the triangle above.

10. Points *W*, *X*, *Y*, and *Z* lie on a line in that order. If *X* is the midpoint of *WY* and *Y* is the midpoint of *WZ*, what is the value of $\dfrac{XY}{XZ}$?

Geometry Practice Set III
Real SAT Questions

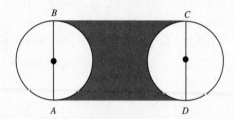

1. In rectangle *ABCD* shown above, sides *AB* and *CD* pass through the centers of the two circles. If *AB* = 12 and *AD* = 16, what is the area of the shaded region?

   (A) 120
   (B) 156
   (C) 192
   (D) 192 − 36π
   (E) 192 − 72π

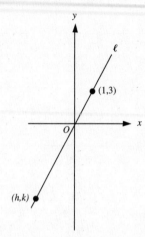

2. In the figure above, line ℓ passes through the origin. What is the value of $\dfrac{k}{h}$?

   (A) 3
   (B) 2
   (C) $\dfrac{3}{2}$
   (D) $-\dfrac{3}{2}$
   (E) −3

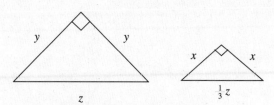

Note: Figures not drawn to scale.

3. In the figures above, what is the value of y in terms of x?

(A) $\sqrt{2}x$ (approximately 1.41x)

(B) $2x$

(C) $2\sqrt{2}x$ (approximately 2.83x)

(D) $3x$

(E) $3\sqrt{2}x$ (approximately 4.24x)

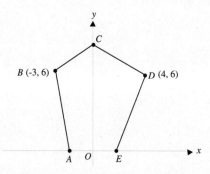

4. In pentagon *ABCDE* above, how many diagonals with positive slope can be drawn?

(A) None

(B) One

(C) Two

(D) Three

(E) Four

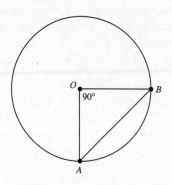

5. In the figure above, *O* is the center of the circle of radius 10. What is the area of $\triangle AOB$?

(A) 25

(B) 50

(C) $\dfrac{25}{2}\pi$

(D) 20π

(E) 25π

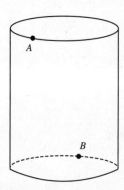

6. The figure above shows a cylinder with radius 2 and height 5. If points *A* and *B* lie on the circumference of the top and bottom of the cylinder, respectively, what is the greatest possible straight line distance between *A* and *B*?

(A) 3

(B) 5

(C) 7

(D) $\sqrt{29}$

(E) $\sqrt{41}$

Column A	**Column B**

7.

The increase in the area of circle *A* when its radius is increased by 1 inch	The increase in the area of circle *B* when its radius is increased by 1 inch

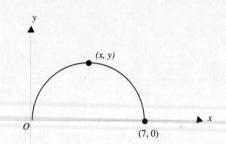

10. In the figure above, what is the *y*-coordinate of the point on the semicircle that is the farthest from the *x*-axis?

8.

The length of a side of a square whose perimeter is 12	The length of one side of a rectangle whose perimeter is 12

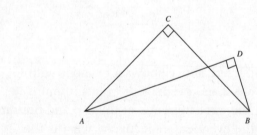

9.

$(AC)^2 + (BC)^2$	$(AD)^2 + (BD)^2$

RED ALERT

OVERVIEW

The verbal part of the SAT consists of three sections. Two of these sections are 30 minutes long, and the other is 15 minutes long. In total, these three sections contain 19 sentence completion questions, 19 analogy questions, and 40 critical reading questions, which means that you'll have 78 questions to answer in an hour and 15 minutes.

VERBAL QUESTIONS

19 sentence completions
19 analogies
40 critical reading

Remember that in addition to the usual math and verbal sections, you'll get an extra section–the experimental. It won't count toward your score. Even if you think you can tell which section is the experimental, don't blow it off because you don't know for sure and it's not worth the risk.

HELP WITH ANALOGIES

An analogy is a word problem that asks you to understand the relationship between two words. You'll be given one pair of words and then asked to choose the pair with the same relationship. You'll see a set of analogy questions in each of the two 30-minute verbal sections (and possibly an extra if your experimental section is verbal). In each set of analogy questions, the first third of the set is the easiest, the middle problems are more difficult, and the problems in the last third of the set are quite tricky.

An analogy question looks like this:

OAK : TREE ::

(A) forest : land
(B) lion : tiger
(C) branch : limb
(D) tulip : flower
(E) wave : ocean

TEST TIP

**Analogies generally show up on the SAT in one set of
13 questions and another set of 6 questions.**

Read the colon in an analogy question as the phrase "is to" and the double colon as the word "as."
The question then becomes

OAK is to TREE as

(A) forest is to land
(B) lion is to tiger
(C) branch is to limb
(D) tulip is to flower
(E) wave is to ocean

STRATEGY

Your job is to figure out how OAK and TREE are related and then pick the answer choice with the
same relationship. Your first step is to create a sentence that links the two capitalized words. In this
case, a good link would be

An OAK is a kind of TREE.

Keep in mind that the link between the two question words is going to be clear, simple, and definite—not ambiguous or vague. In fact, there are several links that show up year after year on the SAT,
and you can count on seeing them again in the future. Knowing these common links will give you a
big boost in the analogy sections.

Your second step is to test each answer choice in your link sentence.

(A) Is a forest a kind of land? No.
(B) Is a lion a kind of tiger? No.
(C) Is a branch a kind of limb? Maybe.
(D) Is a tulip a kind of flower? Yes.
(E) Is a wave a kind of ocean? No.

If your first link wasn't specific enough—if, for example, there are two answers that seem possible—
you need to move on to your third step: edit your link. In this case, you're debating between choices
(C) and (D). Rework your link to make it more specific: An OAK is a species of TREE. Now retest
your two possible answers.

A branch is a species of limb? No.
A tulip is a species of flower? Yes!

SOLVING ANALOGIES

1. **Create a link**
2. **Test each choice**
3. **If necessary, edit your link to make it more specific**

LINKS TO LOOK FOR

Link	Example
Part of a category	An OAK is a type of TREE.
Part of a whole	A SHEEP is part of a FLOCK.
Degree	BIG is a smaller degree of HUGE.
Trait by definition	A LIAR is by definition DISHONEST.
Lack by definition	A LIAR by definition lacks HONESTY.
Object and its function	A COMB is used to DETANGLE.
Person and his or her job	A PREACHER's job is to ORATE.
Usual location	A FISH is found in the SEA.

MATCHING PARTS

The parts of speech in the answer choices will always match the parts of speech in the question pair. In other words, if your question pair compares a noun to an adverb, all the answer choices will do the same. Some words are tricky because they can mean two different things depending on how they're used. For example, the word *rail* can be a noun, meaning the thing you hold onto when you climb stairs, or it can be a verb, meaning to complain. The SAT often uses common words in uncommon ways. You can avoid getting tripped up if you think about what part of spech the word has to be.

THE POWER OF POSITIVE AND NEGATIVE THINKING

If one of the words in the question pair has a positive meaning, such as one having to do with helping, liking, or making better, then you can bet the correct answer is also going to have a positive word in that slot. The same holds true for negative words.

WHEN THE GOING GETS TOUGH

What happens when the words in the question pair are unfamiliar or you can't figure out a link between them? Increase your odds of picking a correct answer through the process of elimination. You can eliminate any answer choices that have a weak or vague link because the correct answer will have a clear link. Also eliminate two or more answer choices with the same link because there can only be one correct answer choice.

SMART GUESSING

BLAH : BLAH ::

(A) dog : cat
(B) grass : tree
(C) calf : cow
(D) furnace : heat
(E) tadpole : frog

Which answers can you eliminate even without understanding the question pair? Well, choices (A) and (B) have weak links, so eliminate them. Choices (C) and (E) have the same link, so eliminate them—there can't be two right answers. That leaves (D) as your correct answer.

GUESS WHAT?

Even if you can only eliminate one or two choices, you boost your chances of guessing correctly.

HELP WITH SENTENCE COMPLETIONS

Sentence completion questions are sentences that contain one or two blanks. Your job is to figure out which answer choice offers the words that best fill in the blanks. Sentence completions test a combination of vocabulary and logic. You'll see one set of sentence completions in each of the two 30-minute verbal sections (and possibly an extra set if your experimental section is verbal.) As with the analogy questions, each set of sentence completions goes from easy to hard.

A one-blank sentence completion looks like this:

Despite the forecast for a sunny day, the sky looked quite _____.

(A) bright
(B) shady
(C) visible
(D) inviting
(E) menacing

TEST TIP

Sentence completions generally show up in one set of 9 questions and another set of 10 questions.

STRATEGY

You might be tempted to just reread the sentence five times, sticking in each of the answer choices. That eats up a lot of time, though, especially as the sentences get more complicated. Instead, read the sentence and figure out a general idea of what the answer should be. Only then should you scan your answer choices and pick out the ones that match your prediction.

SOLVING SENTENCE COMPLETIONS

1. **Read the sentence and make a prediction.**
2. **Find the answer choice that best matches your prediction.**
3. **Reread the sentence with your answer choice.**

The key to solving sentence completions is finding the clue words in each sentence. In the sample problem, the clue word is "despite." That tells that the sentence contains a contrast: despite the forecast for sun, something else happened. Even before you look at your answer choices, you can figure out that the correct answer is going to be something along the lines of "threatening." Sure enough, the correct answer is choice (E), "menacing." Always reread the sentence with your answer choice, just to make sure it makes sense: Despite the forecast for a sunny day, the sky looked quite menacing. Perfect!

GET A CLUE

While sentence completions are largely a test of vocabulary, they also require you to understand the logic of a sentence. Words and punctuation can let you know if the sentence is setting up a contrast or if it is continuing a single idea.

Here are some words that signal a change is coming in the sentence:

despite, although, since, unlike, but, however, in spite of, in contrast to

Here are some words that signal the sentence is continuing along with the same idea:

and, too, similarly, along with, just as, for example

A semicolon (;) is used between two halves of a sentence and is a signal that each half will be similar in meaning.

Owls are nocturnal creatures; they are rarely seen in daylight.

Watch out for a semicolon followed by a clue word that indicates a shift in meaning.

Expecting heavy traffic, we left early in the morning; however, we were pleased to find the roads nearly empty.

STANDARD SENTENCES

Here are some sentence types you can expect to see in the sentence completion sections.

Contrast Sentences

Although we had a heavy rain last night, the soil is still too _____ to plant crops.

The answer will be a contrast to heavy rain; look for something like *dry* or *arid*.

Cause and Effect Sentences

Because Shawna had prepared so _____, nobody was surprised when she won the debate.

The answer will be something like *well* or *thoroughly*.

Comparison Sentences

Like human babies, infant chimpanzees must not only be fed and protected, but _____ as well.

The answer will be something like *nurtured*.

Definition Sentences

His prose was intricate and _____, filled with long words and _____ phrases.

All this sentence does is describe intricate prose. The first blank will have a meaning similar to *intricate*, like *detailed*, and the second blank will be similar to *long*, something like *wordy*.

TWICE THE FUN

A two-blank sentence completion looks like this:

> Many viewers _____ the movie for its excessive use of violence, but other people believed that the violent scenes were _____.
>
> (A) praised..outrageous
> (B) criticized..justified
> (C) enjoyed..important
> (D) censored..gruesome
> (F) disliked..unbearable

Remember, your first step is to read the sentence, paying attention to the clues, and make a prediction. In this case, the word "but" signals a change coming. Many viewers felt one way about the movie's use of violence, *but* other people felt differently. Because the first part of the sentence mentions the movie's *excessive* use of violence, you can guess that those people thought it was too much—they didn't like it. The second part of the sentence is going to have a contrast, so you can predict that other people believed the violent scenes were okay. Your prediction is that the words will be something like *disliked* and *okay*.

DOUBLE CHECK

Reread your answer choice to make sure both words work in the sentence.

Now take a look at your choices. In a two-blank sentence completion, both words have to fit in order for the choice to be the right answer. That means you can immediately eliminate any answer choice with one word that doesn't fit. Choices (A) and (C) are out because they describe positive responses to the excessive violence, and you're looking for a negative one. Of the remaining choices, which one has a second word that means "okay"? Eliminate choice (D), gruesome, and choice (E), unbearable. Choice (B), justified, sounds good—if the violence was justified, that means it had a right to be there. Reread the sentence with the words from choice (B):

> Many viewers criticized the movie for its excessive use of violence, but other viewers believed that the violent scenes were justified.

It works!

SOLVING CRITICAL READING QUESTIONS

1. **Read the passage (or pair of passages) quickly, making a mental map of where the important parts are.**

2. **Simplify each question in your head before trying to solve it.**

3. **Go back to the passage to find the answers.**

4. **Select the best answer choice.**

WHEN THE GOING GETS TOUGH

Remember that in a two-blank sentence completion question, both words have to make sense. If you can tell that one of the words doesn't work, cross out the entire choice and don't look back.

HELP WITH CRICITAL READING

The critical reading parts of the test give you a passage or a pair of passages to read and then ask multiple choice questions about the passages. The questions are always about the material in the passage and do not require outside knowledge of the passage topic. You'll find critical reading passages in all three verbal sections. These questions account for about half of the points you can score in the verbal section of the SAT. Luckily, the critical reading part of the test is fairly predictable. In general, you'll see the same kinds of passages from test to test and you'll be asked the same kinds of questions. A little strategy can go a long way toward earning you points.

TEST TIP

You'll find 40 critical reading questions on the SAT—that's about half your total verbal points.

QUESTIONABLE ADVICE

Should you read the questions *before* you look at the passage? It's really a matter of personal preference. Some people find that quickly skimming the questions before looking at the passage helps them know what to read for. Other people find it a time-drain and not particularly helpful. Do what feels most comfortable to you.

KINDS OF PASSAGES

You'll be given four reading passages on the SAT. One of the passages is usually a fiction passage, meaning it comes from a story. The other passages will come from the following subject areas: science, social science (such as psychology), the arts, and humanities (literature, history, and philosophy). Each test will have one set of questions based on a pair of passages. Also, each test will have a passage that features a traditionally underrepresented group of people, such as women and minorities.

KINDS OF QUESTIONS

The questions you'll see in the critical reading section fall into three basic categories: main idea questions, detail questions, and vocabulary-in-context questions.

Main Idea Questions

Main idea questions ask you to take a broad look at the material in the passage. Typical main idea questions ask about the author's overall tone, the general theme of the passage, and the main topics covered in the passage.

Detail Questions

Detail questions ask you to take a closer look at the text, often providing you with the specific line number. (Every fifth line of the passage is numbered, to make finding a specific line easier.) Some detail questions are very straightforward, requiring you to find basic facts in the passage. Others ask you to do a little more work. Some detail questions, for example, ask you to *infer* information from the passage—that is, to use the information in front of you to figure out something that the author didn't say outright. Other detail questions test to see if you understand the logic of the passage. These questions may refer to a specific detail in the passage and ask why the author put it there or what main point it's supporting.

Vocabulary-In-Context

Vocabulary-in-context questions ask you to figure out the meaning of a word based on the surrounding parts of the passage. Unlike analogy and sentence completion questions, the critical reading questions won't test you on straight vocabulary. In fact, some passages provide footnotes with the definitions of difficult words. Vocabulary-in-context questions are designed to test your ability to use the context of the passage to figure out the meaning of a word. Even if the vocabulary word is familiar, *always* go back to the passage and read a few lines surrounding the word. Many vocabulary-in-context words are familiar words used in a slightly unusual way, and your job is to pick the answer choice that is closest to the way the word is used in the passage.

DO YOUR RESEARCH

The answer to a question is rarely in the exact line that the question cites. Always read a little before and a little past the line in order to understand it.

NARROW YOUR CHOICES

When you see answers that are way off base or extreme, eliminate them.

KINDS OF ANSWERS

Just like passage topics and question types, answer choices for the critical reading sections are quite predictable. You can expect to see the following kinds of wrong answer choices:

Too Broad

This choice goes too far, encompassing far more information than the question asks about.

Too Narrow

This choice doesn't go far enough. It covers only part of the question.

Too Extreme

This choice usually shows up as a wrong answer to questions about the author's tone or attitude toward his or her subject. You can usually—not *always*, but usually—eliminate answer choices that are extremely positive or extremely negative. SAT passages tend to be middle-of-the-road in tone. In addition, you can be pretty sure that the SAT isn't going to insult any group of people, so you can safely eliminate negative answers to questions about the author's attitude toward traditionally under-represented groups.

Very Close (the next-to-best answer)

This is a tricky one. It may be a fact from the text, but one that doesn't answer the question. Or it may be an answer that is almost correct, but isn't quite as good as the best answer. When you come across one of these answers, ask yourself if it's too broad or too narrow.

Completely Off The Mark

This one's easy to spot and eliminate.

STRATEGY

In critical reading sections, timing is everything. It's important *not* to try to read the passage (or pair of passages) as if you were studying for a test. Remember, most of your questions are either going to be about general ideas or are going to include the line numbers where you can find the specific word or detail about which they're asking. Begin the critical reading section by reading the passage quickly—you're just skimming for the gist of it. As you read, make a sort of mental map of where the main points are so you can find them later.

Don't get hung up trying to remember all the details or figure out all the scientific jargon. As long as you have a general grasp of the passage, you'll be able to find answers to the questions.

Look for the following as you read the passage (if it helps you, mark the passage with your pencil as you go, but keep your notations quick and simple):

The Main Idea

The Author's Tone
(or the narrator's tone if it's a fiction passage)

The Locations of the Important Points
If you're working on the paired passages, read for the main similarities and differences between the passages

Once you've read the passage or pair of passages, it's time to face the questions. Unlike analogies and sentence completions, critical reading questions do not appear in increasing order of difficulty. The order of the questions corresponds with the organization of the passage; early questions deal with the early part of the passage, and so on. Paired passage questions will first ask about each of the individual passages and then will require you to compare or contrast the passages.

If you're in a section that has more than one critical reading segment, you can start with the one that feels easiest to you. Just make sure you enter your answers in the correct spaces.

Remember that easy questions earn you the same amount of points as hard questions. If you're completely stumped by a question, move on to an easier one and go back later if you have time.

Sometimes questions are overly wordy and appear complicated. Ignore the extras and figure out in the simplest terms what it's asking you.

WHEN THE GOING GETS TOUGH

What do you do when time is running out? First, answer vocabulary-in-context questions. Remember, the question will tell you the line in which the vocabulary word appears. Even if you don't have time to read the passage, you can read the lines right around the word and get its meaning. Next, take a look at other questions that ask about a detail in a specific line. You might be able to solve them by reading quickly around the line even if you can't read the whole paragraph.

Verbal Reference Unit

Root and Prefix Teams

One of the best things you can do to build your vocabulary in preparation for the SAT is to become familiar with word roots. These are the parts of words that are the building blocks of the English language. They come mostly from the Latin, Greek, and Anglo Saxon languages. If you have a good grasp of word roots, you can often recognize one inside a long, unfamiliar word. Remember, though, that recognizing a root isn't a sure thing. Some words appear to contain a familiar root, but mean something entirely different. Still, roots can help you memorize clumps of words with similar meanings, and they can help you decode words you don't know.

Prefixes are the groups of letters at the beginning of a word that have a particular meaning. Like roots, they can help you decode a difficult word, or at least get a general idea of its meaning.

Don't try to memorize the roots and prefixes by themselves-pair them in your mind with words that use them. These roots and prefixes have been unscientifically organized by theme into "teams," to help you remember them. Remember, even recognizing if a word has a positive or negative meaning can add points on test day.

POSITIVE

Root	Meaning	Examples
am, amic	love, friend	amity—friendship amicable—friendly
ben, bon	well, good	benefactor—person who does good bonus—added reward benign—harmless beneficent—doing good
fid	faith, trust	affidavit—written oath perfidious—faithless, untrue
pac	peace	pacify—to soothe, calm pacifist—person opposed to war
sacr, sanct	sacred, holy	sanctify—to make holy sacrosanct—holy, most sacred desecrate—to profane or foul something sacred
soph	wise, wisdom	sophist—one who sounds clever but whose reasoning is faulty philosophy—search for wisdom; set of conduct
vit, viv	life, lively	vitality—animation, liveliness vivacious—sprightly, lively

Prefix	Meaning	Examples
eu	good, well	euphony—having a pleasant sound euphemism—a pleasant word or phrase used in place of a less pleasant word or phrase eulogy—written or spoken words in praise of a person

NEGATIVE

Root	Meaning	Examples
bel, bell	war	belligerent—looking for a fight bellicose—having a hostile, fighting nature
err	wander, mistake	errant—wandering; truant erroneous—full of mistakes
fall, fals	false, untrue	fallacious—faulty, wrong falsify—to lie; to make untrue infallible—without fault, perfect
ira	anger, rage	ire—anger irritate—to annoy, make angry irascible—easily angered
mal	bad	malignant—promising harm, virulent malediction—evil saying, curse dismal—gloomy, depressing
mor, mort	die, death	moribund—dying morbid—abnormally gloomy mortal—one who must die; something that causes death
turb	agitate	turbulence—agitation, roiling perturb—to annoy, irritate

Prefix	Meaning	Examples
a, an	lacking, not, without	atypical—not typical, unusual amoral—without morals
anti	against, opposing	antithesis—opposite antisocial—not sociable, against society antiseptic—sterile, free from infection
contra, counter	against, opposing	contradict—to say the opposite of something; to deny the truth of a statement counterproductive—bringing about effects that are the opposite of productive
mis	amiss, bad	misuse—to use incorrectly misfortune—bad luck misnomer—wrong name
non	not	nondescript—uninteresting, lacking describable qualities nonentity—person of no importance

PEOPLE

Root	Meaning	Examples
agog	lead, leader	pedagogue—teacher demagogue—leader of people
anthrop	man, mankind	anthropology—study of humans misanthrope—one who hates people
auto	self	automatic—self-acting, able to act autobiography—self-written life story
dem	people	democracy—rule by the people epidemic—disease widespread among people
ego	self	egoist—self—centered person
gen	kind, origin, birth, race	genus—kind or class; closely related species engender—to found; begin generic—characteristic of a class, universal
hom, homo	man	homage—honor, tribute homogenous—of the same kind

TIME AND PLACE

Root	Meaning	Examples
aev, ev	age, era, time	primeval—of ancient times medieval—of the Middle Ages
agri	field, land, farm	agriculture—science of farming agrarian—having to do with farming
annu, enni	year	annuity—yearly pay biennial—occurring every two years
brev	short, brief	brevity—briefness abbreviate—to make shorter
chrono	time	chronology—order in time synchronize—to cause to take place at the same time anachronism—something out of time sequence
medi	middle	mediocre—only half, inferior mediate—to interpose, go between
tempor	time	temporize—to stall, delay extemporaneous—impromptu, immediate
terr	land, earth	terrestrial—of the land subterranean—underground
urb	city	urban—of the city urbane—polished, citified

Prefix	Meaning	Examples
ante, anti	before, previous	antecedent—something that occurs before something else antebellum—before the war (commonly used in reference to the American Civil War) anticipate—to expect
fore	before	forecast—to predict in advance foresee—to know in advance
neo	new, latest of a period	neophyte—beginner, person starting at something neologism—new word; new meaning for an existing word
post	after, following	posthumous—after death postpone—to put off until a later time
pre	before	prevent—to keep from happening predict—to say in advance what will occur
pro	before, forward	produce—to bring forth progress—to move forward; forward movement

MIND AND BODY

Root	Meaning	Examples
anim	mind, spirit, soul	animated—full of life magnanimity—generosity of spirit
capit	head	capital—major city decapitate—to cut the head off
corp	body	corpse—dead body corpulent—fat
derm	skin	dermatology—study of skin epidermis—outer layer of skin
hem	blood	hemorrhage—to bleed profusely
man, manu	hand	manacle—restraint, handcuff manuscript—something written (origin., by hand)
morph	form	metamorphosis—change of form amorphous—formless
oss, oste	bone	ossify—to change into or form bone
ped, pod	foot	pedal—lever for a foot quadruped—four-footed animal
psych	mind	psychosomatic—relationship between mind and body
sci	know	conscious—aware, knowing omniscient—knowing all

SENSES

Root	Meaning	Examples
acer	sharp	acrid—bitter, sharply noticeable to taste or smell acute—pointed; keenly perceptive exacerbate—to make more severe, aggravate
aud, audit	hear, listen to	auditory—having to do with hearing inaudible—unable to be heard
chrom	color	monochromatic—of one color chromogen—substance that can become a pigment
cogno, cognit	notice, become acquainted with	cognizant—aware cognitive—known through awareness
path, pass	feeling, suffering	apathy—lack of feeling empathy—feeling that is like another's passionate—with deep feeling
phon	sound	phonograph—record player phonetics—speech sounds as elements of language
sent, sens	think, feel	resent—feel anger, indignation sentient—feeling, conscious
spec, spic, spect	see, look	specimen—sample perspicacious—cautious, observant spectator—one who watches, observes
tang, ting, tact, tig	touch, border on	tangible—touchable, perceptible contingent—dependent on tactile—concerning the sense of touch contiguous—touching, adjacent

MOVEMENT

Root	Meaning	Examples
ag, act	do, drive, impel	agitate—to stir up enact—decree, as a law; perform
cap, capt, cept, cip	take	captive—someone or something taken anticipate—to foresee
ced, cede, cess	yield, go	antecedent—something going before concede—to yield, agree with recession—act of going back, receding
cur, curr, curs	run, course	excursion—journey, trip concurrent—occurring at the same time cursory—done quickly
fac, fict, fect, fy	do, make	manufacture—to make fiction—made-up story affect—to influence, make a difference testify—to make a statement of witness
fer	carry, bear, yield	transfer—to carry across inference—conclusion; assumption
flect, flex	bend, turn, curve	inflection—turns of the voice flexible—changeable, bendable
flu, fluct	flow	influx—a flow coming in effluvium—outflow of vapor; bad smell fluctuate—to move up or down
her, hes	cling, stick	adhere—to stick coherence—quality of sticking together adhesive—sticking, clinging
it	go	exit—way out; to go out circuit—that which goes around initiate—to start in, begin
mob, mot, mov	move	mobility—ability to move remote—far removed, at a distance
vad, vas	go	invade—to go in (usually by force) pervasive—spreading throughout
vert, vers	turn	invert—to turn upside down convert—to turn from one belief to another; a person who changes beliefs aversion—turning against, dislike

COMMUNICATION

Root	Meaning	Examples
clam, claim	cry out	clamor—outcry, shouting acclaim—noisy approval
dict	speak, say, words	diction—speech verdict—statement from a jury
graph, gram	write, writing	graphic—clearly described epigram—brief, meaningful statement
leg, lect, lig	read, choose, select	legible—able to be read negligible—not worthy of being noticed election—choice
log, loqu, locut	speech, study, word, talk	epilogue—words at end of book or play elocution—effective speech soliloquy—speech by one person
ora	speak, pray	oration—formal speech oral—referring to speech oracle—prophet
quer, quir, quis	ask, seek	query—question inquire—to ask about quizzical—questioning (as a look) inquisition—official questioning or examination
rog	ask	interrogate—to question abrogate—to nullify, abolish derogatory—overly critical, disparaging
scrib, script	write	scribble—to write carelessly transcript—letter, document; record
voc, vok	call	vocation—life's work, job invoke—to call upon

DIRECTIONS

Prefix	Meaning	Examples
a	on, in, of, up, to	aboard—on board astride—with a leg on either side; extending across
ab, abs	from, away	absent—not present abdicate—to give up, renounce
circum	around	circumference—the distance around a circle circumnavigate—travel around (a specific area)
de	away, from, off, down	destruct—to destroy degrade—to bring down, lower
dia	across, apart, through, between	diagnose—to decide something through examination dialogue—conversation diameter—the distance across the center of a circle
di, dif, dis	away, down, off, opposing	digress—to go off the subject dissent—to disagree; disagreement diverse—varying
en, em	in, among, within	enliven—to make more lively
epi	on, outside, over, outer	epidermis—outer layer of skin epitaph—tomb inscription
ex, e, ef	from, out, away	expel—to force out emit—to send out
extra, exter, extro	outside, beyond	extrovert—outgoing person external—outside
hyp, hypo	under, beneath	hypodermic—of the area beneath the skin; going beneath the skin hypocrite—pretender, person claiming to be something he or she is not
inter	among, between	intervene—to come between interact—to react with something else
intro, intra	inwardly, within	introvert—to turn attention inward; one whose attention is turned inward intramural—within the limits of an organization
ob, oc, of, op	over, against, toward	obtuse—not sharp; blunt oppose—to place opposite to
sub, suc, suf, sug, sum, sup, sus	under, beneath	subzero—below zero supposition—the act of supposing, something supposed
super	over, above, extra	superimpose—to put on top of supervise—to oversee
tra, trans	across, beyond	transfer—to carry from one place to another transgress—to go beyond transitory—passing through

Word Teams

Each of these "word teams" lists words that are similar or the same in meaning to the title word. It's easier to learn words in groups, so use these lists as a jumping-off point for adding to your vocabulary. Remember, the more words you know, the more points you rack up on test day.

FRIENDLY

affable
amiable
avuncular
benign
blithe
congenial
convivial
cordial
felicitous
genial
gregarious
jocular
philanthropic
sanguine
winsome

UNFRIENDLY

abrasive
aloof
bellicose
brusque
cantankerous
combative
contemptuous
dour
fractious
haughty
incorrigible
malevolent
nefarious
odious
pernicious
petulant
pugnacious
querulous
truculent

SAD

dismal
doleful
funereal
lugubrious
maudlin
melancholy
mournful
poignant
somber

SHARP OR UNPLEASANT

acerbic
acidic
brackish
caustic
fetid
noisome
odious
pungent
rancid
scathing
vitriolic

LAZY, SLOW, INACTIVE

dilatory
dormant
flaccid
indolent
inert
lackadaisical
languorous
phlegmatic
quiescent
slothful
torpid
viscous

SORRY

apologetic
chagrined
contrite
penitent
remorseful
repentant
regretful
rueful

TALKATIVE

declamatory
garrulous
loquacious
verbose
vociferous
voluble

OPPOSITE OF TALKATIVE

brusque
concise
curt
laconic
reserved
reticent
retiring
succinct

taciturn
terse

TOO MUCH

excess
flood
glut
overabundance
plethora
preponderance
proliferation
surfeit
surplus

TOO LITTLE

dearth
deficit
deficiency
lack
paucity
scarcity
shortage

TO MOTIVATE, TO CAUSE

agitate
arouse
cajole
coerce
conscript
ignite
incite
engender
enjoin
goad
precipitate
prod
provoke

TO STOP, TO GIVE UP, TO GET IN THE WAY OF

abdicate
abort
capitulate
cease
curtail
daunt
debilitate
desist
halt
hinder
recant

TO CALM

allay
alleviate
appease
assuage
ease
mollify
pacify
palliate
placate
relieve
soothe

SMART, CLEVER

adroit
astute
cunning
ingenious
perceptive
precocious
proficient
shrewd

GREEDY

avaricious
avid
covetous
desirous
gluttonous
rapacious
ravenous
voracious

UNTRUSTWORTHY

biased
capricious
conniving
deceitful
deceptive
dubious
fallacious
furtive
mendacious
nefarious
pernicious
precarious
specious
spurious
surreptitious
traitorous
treacherous
underhanded
unscrupulous

Word List

A large part of your SAT verbal score depends on your vocabulary. You don't need to memorize this entire word list, but the more words you know, the better you'll do on test day. Learn as many new words as possible by making up flashcards, using the words in sentences, and making up your own word teams like the ones in this book.

If you're very short on time, learn as many words as you can from the Word Teams section. At the same time, study the Root Teams section. Keep your own list of difficult words you come across, and learn their meanings.

ABBREVIATIONS

n = noun   v = verb   adj = adjective   adv = adverb

abate (v) to become less in intensity; to subside, slacken, wane, or decrease
When the hurricane winds finally abated, we went outside to assess the damage to our house and garage.

abdicate (v) to give up, renounce, relinquish (often formally)
Henry abdicated his title of checkers champ when his younger brother won a game against him.

aberration (n) straying from what is right, normal, or expected; a mental straying that is strange or deviate
Uncle Harvey's burst of temper was an aberration from his usual calm demeanor.

abet (v) to help or encourage a bad act; to egg on, foment, instigate
The law has penalties for those who aid and abet a criminal.

abeyance (n) a condition of suspended activity or development (use after *in*) *"We'll hold the plans for our class trip in abeyance until we have voted on the budget," said our class president.*

abhor (v) to hate or loathe; to dislike strongly; to reject
Jill has abhorred snakes ever since she was scared by one in her sleeping bag last summer at camp.

aborigine (n) original person in a place (as a native)
The Australian aborigines have a unique musical culture.

abort (v) to fail to go forward or develop as expected; to miscarry; to terminate early
The mission of Columbia had to be aborted for several reasons, one of which was bad weather.

abrasive (adj) causing bad feelings of irritation or annoyance
The last thing a salesperson should have is an abrasive personality that sends customers hurrying away.

abscond (v) to run off in secret (usually because of bad actions or feelings/knowledge of guilt)
After absconding with the money, the thief moved frequently to avoid being caught.

absolve (v) to free of guilt or blame; to exonerate, exculpate
The witness's testimony absolved Harold of any wrongdoing.

abstemious (adj) restrained in consuming strong drink or food; moderate, restrained
A careful man concerned about his health, Gregory has always been abstemious in his habits.

abstract (adj) not concrete or definite, thus hard to grasp or understand; impersonal or detached in attitude
Brett had trouble as soon as he left the definite, concrete problems of math and moved on to abstract principles.

abstruse (adj) extremely difficult to understand; erudite, recondite
The abstruse calculations necessary to locate distant stars are mind-boggling.

accolade (n) verbal praise; award; recognition of accomplishment
Merry bowed to the cheering audience and basked in their accolades backstage after her performance.

accrue (v) to accumulate, pile up, collect; to grow (as a bank account)
I wish the interest on my bank account would accrue at a faster rate.

acerbity (n) bitterness, acrimony; having a biting, acidic nature, mood, or quality
Her acerbic remarks often hurt the feelings of the people at whom they were aimed.

acme (n) the highest point or peak of achievement; zenith
"I think," the mountain climber reflected, "that the acme of my career came when we conquered Everest."

acquiesce (v) to give in and agree without a fuss; to comply, assent
Privately, we hated Grandfather's rules; publicly, we acquiesced to avoid awkward scenes that would have embarrassed everyone involved.

acronym (n) word formed from the initial letter(s) of a longer term
The word sonar is an acronym for sound navigation ranging.

acumen (n) keen perception, shrewdness, and discernment
We studied industrial leaders who were famous for their business acumen.

adamant (adj) firm and unyielding; inflexible even when opposed
Fred adamantly refused to leave the house in bad weather.

adjudicate (v) to act as a judge or determiner
We will adjudicate the matter as soon as all of the jurors arrive.

admonish (v) to warn strongly or show disapproval; to reprove
My parents admonished me not to talk to strangers.

adulation (n) praise, flattery, worship
Hero worship is one form of adulation.

advocate (n) a person who pleads a case (as a lawyer)
advocate (v) to talk in favor of; to support, recommend
Dwayne advocates swift justice and the availability of a professional advocate for needy people.

aesthetic (adj) referring to a sense of beauty; artistic
A visit to an art museum might awaken aesthetic senses you didn't know you had.

affable (adj) easy to get along with; genial, friendly, warm
Her affable personality made her a natural candidate for public office.

affinity (n) natural inclination or tendency; attraction to or kinship with
Because they are nocturnal creatures, cats have a natural affinity with the night.

affluent (adj)   wealthy, rich
Between the affluent haves and the indigent have-nots lies a gulf in understanding that makes communication difficult.

aggravate (v)   to make worse; to exacerbate, burden, intensify, or irritate
You will aggravate your swollen ankle if you go hiking.

aggregate (adj)   total or combined amount of
The aggregate earnings at our class flea market set a school record for fund-raisers.

agnostic (n)   a person who thinks that God is unknown, probably unknowable; one who doubts and questions

agnostic (adj)   doubting or questioning regarding God and his nature
Frank, an agnostic, has spent a great deal of time pondering the mysteries of the universe.

agrarian (adj)   referring to fields, lands, and their crops
Iowa State University in Ames has long been a Midwestern center for agrarian research.

alacrity (n)   eagerness, willingness, or liveliness; celerity
Hal accepted the invitation with alacrity; he'd been hoping for it.

allay (v)   to lower in intensity or severity (as fears); to assuage, relieve, calm, alleviate
The veterinarian allayed our fears about our dog's sickness, saying that Chumley would be his old, spaniel self in a few days.

allegory (n)   a story using figurative language and characters; a symbolic portrayal
Animal Farm, by George Orwell, is an allegory in which animals represent different human types and political figures.

allocate (v)   to portion out or allot; to distribute, designate
Jason allocated the west side of the barn to us for our 4-H project this spring.

allude (v)   to hint at or refer to indirectly, without specific mention
My sister and I alluded to Aunt Molly's dyed-orange hair, but Mom gave us a dirty look and sent us outside before we got into real trouble.

aloof (adj)   reserved or cool in manner; apart because of lack of involvement, thus removed
Our older brother remained aloof as we planned how to turn the neighborhood empty lot into a health spa.

altercation (n)   noisy fight or quarrel; angry dispute
The debate, which had started peaceably enough, soon turned into an altercation that left bitter feelings behind.

altruism (n)   unselfish giving of time, money, interest, or support to others
Many revered saints lived lives of unusual altruism.

ambiguous (adj) not clear or definite; obscure, uncertain
His answer was ambiguous, so now I don't know any more than I did before.

ameliorate (v) to make better or to improve
Historically, we have tried to ameliorate the desperate conditions of developing countries.

amiable (adj) warm, friendly, easy to get along with; congenial, sociable
Her amiable manner made her well-liked among her peers.

amnesty (n) pardon or acceptance (by government) of some group behavior
The country granted amnesty to the refugees.

anachronism (n) a thing out of place in time; thus a chronological error
A horse-drawn fruit and vegetable cart on suburban streets today would be an interesting anachronism for shoppers.

anarchy (n) absence of government, often resulting in lawlessness and disorder
The tiny island was plunged into anarchy when its king fled north and took his ruling cabinet with him.

anathema (n) curse or formal ban; something or someone denounced in a strongly disapproving manner
To the werewolf, wolfsbane and a cross are anathema.

animosity (n) strong dislike, even hate; enmity, hostility
We quarreled so much as children that some of the old animosity still flares up when my sister and I get together.

animus (n) basic spirit, attitude, or intention; also a spiteful feeling of ill will
Rob questioned the animus of his drill sergeant, wondering if Sergeant Jones wanted all of the recruits to drop out of basic training.

annals (n) historical records; chronicles
In the annals of our town are accounts of early hand-to-hand combat among settlers.

annihilate (v) to wipe out, to destroy almost entirely; to vanquish, abolish
If humans continue to destroy natural habitats, more and more animal species will be annihilated.

anomaly (n) something different from the norm; irregularity or paradox
The dog's owner assured us that Rex's growling was an anomaly; usually he was calm and gentle.

antipathy (n) extreme dislike or aversion; distaste, enmity
Fred likes people, but shows his antipathy for dogs by arching his back and glaring balefully at any canine.

antithesis (n) a direct opposite
That program is the antithesis of everything I enjoy watching and listening to, so I am turning off the TV set.

apathy (n)   lack of feeling; indifference, impassiveness
Uncle Bert's indifference to oatmeal is matched only by his apathy toward tapioca.

aphorism (n)   short statement of principle, belief; adage, proverb
Ben Franklin wrote many famous aphorisms that school children still learn today.

aplomb (n)   absolute cool; complete poise and self-confidence
Everyone envied Jenny's aplomb as she sang and danced in our school musical.

apostate (n)   person who renounces a faith or a commitment to a previous loyalty
Having lost a great deal of weight on the diet, Arthur became an apostate of his old, unhealthy habits.

appalling (adj)   shocking or dismaying; causing fear, disgust, or even horror
The senator attacked his opponent's tax plan as an appalling misuse of money.

appease (v)   to quiet, calm, allay, soothe, pacify, or conciliate
His hunger and weariness somewhat appeased by a meal, the pony express rider leaped on a fresh horse and was gone.

apprehension (n)   the fear of evil, thus a foreboding; conception or comprehension of someone or something
The elderly couple viewed winter's approach with apprehension, dreading the ice storms and snow-covered streets.

arable (adj)   suited to cultivation or the growing of crops; tillable
The rocky soil was barely arable; it was no wonder that the farm failed.

arbitrary (adj)   according to wish or desire, decided by choice rather than merit; in a despotic or tyrannical way
Almost everyone respects a fair decision and loathes an arbitrary or capricious one.

arcane (adj)   known only to a select few people, therefore mysterious or secret
Currently lost in the darkness of time, the arcane folklore of Stonehenge would be a fascinating discovery.

archives (n)   place for public records; the records themselves
The establishment of a town as a national historic district requires researchers to spend many hours with local, county, and state archives.

arduous (adj)   demanding, difficult, and hard to achieve; strenuous, hard
Careful polishing of a car may be arduous, but the resulting shine is a terrific reward.

arrogance (n)   the feeling of superiority shown by an overbearing manner; excess pride
Even his superior skill and knowledge did not justify his arrogance toward his coworkers.

articulate (adj)	clearly spoken, intelligible and coherent (as *an articulate person*)
articulate (v)	to speak distinctly and clearly; to enunciate; to put into a logical whole or group
	Melinda's school articulated a music program that began in kindergarten and continued through high school.
askance (adv)	in a disapproving manner; scornfully
	The old woman, set in her ways, looked askance upon modern culture.
askew (adj)	out of line or place; awry
	His logic was so askew that no one could possibly accept his arguments.
asperity (n)	roughness or harshness of manner; acrimony
	Whoever plays the part of Cinderella's irritable stepmother must speak with asperity to portray the character correctly.
assiduous (adj)	marked by careful, diligent attention; persistent
	Michael's assiduous attention to the harder math problems paid a big dividend last week when he helped the school math team score a major victory.
astute (adj)	wise, shrewd, and perceptive; perspicacious
	Making astute decisions about investments is a skill everyone would like to cultivate.
atavism (n)	harking back to a form of an earlier time
	Ben's insistence upon using a typewriter made him an atavism among his more technically inclined friends.
atheist (n)	person who believes that there is no God
	Although he was an atheist, Stan attended religious services because he enjoyed the music and the company.
atrophy (v)	to waste away (as muscles) from a debilitating illness; to degenerate, wither
	Anna had to exercise regularly to make sure that her injured leg muscles didn't atrophy.
attest (v)	to affirm or authenticate; to prove, testify, verify
	We can attest to the raccoon's ingenuity; he figured out how to open the contraption Dad made for our garbage can.
audacious (adj)	adventurous and bold; intrepid, daring
	The audacious student told the teacher straight out that she was wrong.
augment (v)	to increase; to make something greater or larger
	Every few days we augment the supplies in our refrigerator by going to the supermarket.
augur (v)	to foretell, presage (as from omens); to predict

augur (n)	person who foretells events *The augur told our futures in such vague terms that we doubted his authenticity.*
auspices (n)	sponsorship or patronage; also favorable or prophetic signs (as *the auspices look good*)
auspicious (adj)	favorable, promising, of good omen *Although the business has a new name, it still operates under the auspices of the original owner.*
austere (adj)	reserved, somber, or grave in manner; unadorned; also abstemious or ascetic; restrained *As children, we were put off by Aunt Dorothea's reserved, austere manner, but as adults we've learned to admire her strength.*
autocratic (adj)	absolute, in the sense of final; dictatorial, despotic *A poor quality for a judge would be a tendency toward whimsical or autocratic decisions.*
avid (adj)	extremely eager or very greedy; fond of or devoted to *Jim is an avid bread baker and spends every Saturday morning creating a variety of treats for his friends.*
bailiwick (n)	distinct area; a person's normal territory or jurisdiction *The congresswoman had no decision-making power outside of her bailiwick.*
balm (n)	anything that soothes or makes you feel better *After running several miles, Tim reached for his water bottle, balm for his parched throat.*
banal (adj)	stale from overuse; trite, insipid, commonplace *The comedian's banal jokes bored the audience, who wanted to hear something more cutting edge.*
bane (n)	source of bad luck or harm; curse, destruction *The bane of John's college existence was the professor who insisted on correcting every tiny error in John's lab technique.*
baroque (adj)	extravagant, elaborate style of decoration or presentation; ornate, as music or literature *We are fascinated by Melissa's absolutely baroque life; her huge Victorian house, complex career, and elaborate clothing intrigue us.*
bellicose (adj)	looking for a fight; aggressive, feisty, warlike *One bellicose person can create unrest among a normally peaceful group.*
bellwether (n)	a leader, one who will take charge *Surviving from the Middle Ages, the word* bellwether *once meant the leading sheep of the flock who wore a bell round his neck.*

benign (adj)   gentle, gracious, kind; mild or favorable, not malignant
The queen was a benign leader, generally liked by all of her subjects.

beset (v)   to trouble, harass, or hem in
The exhausted fox, beset by eager hounds, looked frantically for a way to escape pursuit or a place to hide.

bias (n)   diagonal line; prejudice or personal outlook; bent, tendency
Unfortunately, a person's bias on a given subject may prevent him from ever hearing the facts on that subject.

bicker (v)   to quarrel over little things; quibble, argue
If the twins ever stop bickering, maybe they'll notice that they actually agree more than they realize.

bigot (n)   biased, narrow-minded person
The bigot was thoroughly disliked for his hate-filled opinions.

bilk (v)   to cheat or defraud
The traveling magicians managed to bilk our townspeople thoroughly, absconding with several hundred dollars after their single night performance.

blasphemy (n)   profanity; swearing about something sacred
Our father, who was very conservative, considered our liberal views blasphemy.

blatant (adj)   embarrassingly obvious, loud, or showy; brazen, tasteless
We stayed out late in blatant violation of our curfew.

blithe (adj)   cheerful, merry, and lighthearted; casual, heedless
He blithely ignored the warning and swam out far from shore.

boor (n)   person lacking manners or sensitivity
Jerry's boorish manners made him an unpopular dinner guest.

bourgeois (adj)   middle class, thus common
Tired of her bourgeois life, Emily sold all of her possessions and traveled the world in search of meaning.

bovine (adj)   cow-like; patient and slow-moving; dull or placid
His bovine expression revealed his dull-wittedness.

brackish (adj)   rather salty; unappealing
Though the water in those marshes is brackish and foul-smelling to us, the birds seem to like it.

brandish (v)   to wave about in a threatening way; to swing (a weapon) back and forth; to flourish with a flair
We thought we'd have to do without beverages until Mike brandished a bottle of sparkling water he'd brought.

brigand (n)   bandit or thief
Often in literature, a pirate or murderer is shown as a charming, devil-may-care brigand.

brusque (adj)   abrupt, short, or blunt, usually unpleasant in effect; curt
The team was put off by the brusque manner of the new lacrosse coach, but after a few days we realized it masked a warm heart.

bucolic (adj)   referring to the country; rustic, rural, pastoral
The bucolic setting, with its rolling hills and pastures, was the perfect vacation from city life.

bumptious (adj)   egotistic, often irritatingly self-assured; pushy, arrogant
Often, the first impression Trevor makes is that of a bumptious teenager, but that's deceiving because he's really thoughtful and intelligent.

buoyant (adj)   lighthearted, cheerful, upbeat; also able to float (as, *a buoyant raft*)
The long trek westward to settle the plains and Western states of America required people of strong wills and buoyant spirits.

burlesque (n)   a literary or dramatic work making fun or ridiculing by comic exaggeration; a mockery or caricature
The performance was a burlesque, our paper reported, a mere mockery of what was originally a fine stage play.

buttress (n)   a support that gives stability and strength
buttress (v)   to shore up, support, or strengthen
A good report states its thesis clearly, then buttresses that thesis with examples and facts as proof.

cacophony (n)   horrible sound; harsh, displeasing noise
Not all music strikes us as being worth listening to; some of it is cacophony making war on our eardrums.

cajole (v)   to beg, wheedle, or coax
I practiced first in front of my mirror and then went downstairs to cajole my parents into letting me have a Halloween party.

caliber (n)   moral or mental worth; quality; diameter of a projectile or bore of the gun
The general caliber of our employees is the envy of our competition.

calumny (n)   malicious, damaging talk about another; slander
The office was torn apart by calumny; soon nobody trusted anybody else.

candid (adj)   open and honest; fair or free of bias; frank, even to bluntness
One of the joys—although occasionally painful—of a close friendship is that you can depend on your friend's candid answers to your important questions.

cant (n)   hypocritical talk; dialect of a particular group; jargon; trite talk
The cant of careless tongues should be dismissed.

cant (v)	to tilt or slant at an angle
	I made that table in shop class, and I don't care if it cants off at a funny angle—I'm still proud of it.
cantankerous (adj)	grumpy, testy, bad-tempered and quarrelsome
	The older some people get, the more demanding and cantankerous they seem to become.
canvass (v)	to do a survey; solicit votes, opinions, or orders
	Mother said we should canvass the neighborhood to see if all of the families want to share in our Fourth of July block picnic.
capitulate (v)	to give in, surrender, or acquiesce
	Jess and I argued about our chem lab results until finally I capitulated and admitted that he was right.
capricious (adj)	not steady or constant; changing at a whim
	Darting in what seemed to be a capricious manner, the hummingbird flitted from flower to flower.
captious (adj)	overly critical, thus finding fault easily
	Teresa says that her boyfriend's mother is a captious person, always looking for faults in her son.
carnage (n)	slaughter or massacre (as in a war)
	The invention of television brought the carnage of war to the homes of the viewing public.
carp (v)	to nitpick; find fault in a petty manner
	Nancy's carping ruined the movie for Jeanine, who wouldn't otherwise have noticed the small flaws.
cathartic (n)	something that cleans or purges; a purifier
	A brisk walk can be a cathartic that wakes and cheers you up after hours of desk work.
caustic (adj)	biting or corrosive; incisive, cutting
	Ambrose Bierce, nicknamed Bitter Bierce, was known for his caustic wit and revealing satire.
cavil (v)	to object in a trivial or unimportant way; to find fault in a captious way
	I know that painting the fence is not your idea of a great afternoon, but caviling won't get the job done.
chagrin (n)	embarrassment; unhappiness brought on by humiliation
	Much to my chagrin, I discovered that the car I'd hit in the parking lot belonged to my prospective boss.
chaos (n)	extreme disorder, confusion
	The home stands were in absolute chaos after the football game as we noisily celebrated our victory.

192

charlatan (n)   quack or fraud who pretends knowledge; cheat, impostor
At the time of the California gold rush, clever charlatans thrived by selling fake maps showing the way to lodes of gold.

chaste (adj)   pure and innocent; modest; clean or simple in design
The chaste designs of classic Greek architecture appeal to many people because of their simplicity and cleanness of line.

chastise (v)   to scold severely or punish; to castigate, censure
The kids were chastised for picking their neighbors' flowers and had to promise to replant them.

chicanery (n)   deceit, trickery, or deception by clever means
Laws requiring truth in advertising limit the outright chicanery that was common decades ago.

circumspect (adj)   cautiously watchful, prudent, or careful
The forecaster looked with a circumspect eye at the storm that had begun to form.

citadel (n)   fortress; removed place of safety; stronghold
Above the town, on a high, steep peak, the citadel called Mountjoy looked out upon the world below.

cite (v)   to refer to officially (as *citing a reference*); to call to court; to commend in a formal manner
We're expected to two biographies, one live interview, and four other sources in our term paper for current events class.

civility (n)   good manners, politeness, or courtesy
The stereotype of an English butler includes a noticeably British accent, formal attire, and unfailing civility even in exasperating circumstances.

clandestine (adj)   secret, surreptitious
Because we didn't want Lucy to find out about the surprise party we were planning for her, we held clandestine meetings.

clarity (n)   clearness, lucidity
The speech teacher said she'd judge our next speeches on clarity and organization, so I made a careful outline of my speech.

clement (adj)   lenient or merciful; mild (as *clement weather*)
If the weather is clement, we will eat lunch outside today.

coerce (v)   to force or compel (*someone* or *something*)
Coercing people to help you and having them volunteer to help are two different experiences indeed.

cogent (adj)   convincing, persuasive, or valid (as *reasons*)
The experienced lawyer warned his new associate to use only well-organized, cogent arguments when presenting a case in court for their law firm.

cognate (n)	relation
cognate (adj)	related, or alike generically
	English and French are cognate languages, and both derive much from their Latin and Greek heritage.
coherent (adj)	logically arranged or ordered (as *a coherent speech*)
	It was difficult to turn the scraps of evidence into a coherent case, but we managed to prove our innocence.
cognizant (adj)	aware, conscious (followed by *of*)
	Julie was not cognizant of the problems she might have gathering eggs in her aunt's henhouse, so she allowed only 5 minutes for the task on her first afternoon of vacation.
colloquy (n)	fairly serious conversation, dialogue, or conference
	Juan burst into the house eager to tell his good news, but, noticing that his parents were engaged in quiet colloquy, he decided to wait.
comely (adj)	attractive to look at; pretty, appealing
	Despite her grandmother's pleas that she keep a comely appearance, Anita preferred to wear old, comfortable clothing.
commensurate (adj)	in proportion to; corresponding to size, type, abilities, etc.
	Your payment will be commensurate with the amount of experience you bring to the job.
compassion (n)	awareness and caring for others; sympathy for others' misfortunes
	Appalled by the speed and viciousness of the hen's attack, Emily hastily withdrew her hand and ran for the compassion her aunt and uncle would provide.
compatible (adj)	well suited or fit; adaptable, consonant, related
	Sometimes two people who seem to be compatible are actually nothing alike.
compunction (n)	misgiving or guilt feeling; qualm, scruple
	I have no compunction whatsoever about reporting your misconduct to the proper authorities.
conclave (n)	private, secret meeting; convention
	The cabinet spent most of the day deep in a conclave, debating who should be the next foreign minister of the new republic.
concur (v)	to agree, assent; approve; coincide
	After serious debate, all concurred that the most qualified candidate was a retired defense secretary.
condescend (v)	to come down in level; to unbend or stoop
	You don't need to condescend to me; I understand you perfectly.

condone (v) to overlook (an offense) or to pardon; to excuse
I can't condone your behavior, which sets a bad example for your younger sisters.

conducive (adj) promoting, furthering, or aiding; contributive
The study carrels in the library are conducive to progress, since they are private and quiet places to work.

congenital (adj) occurring during pregnancy or at birth; inherent, innate
The speech therapist felt that a congenital defect of the patient's palate made formation of certain sounds very difficult.

conjecture (n) a guess or supposition; inference, conclusion

conjecture (v) to guess or suppose; to infer or conclude
It is my conjecture that those clouds will bring us some rain later.

connive (v) to conspire, intrigue, or plot secretly
Although she tried to appear honest and trustworthy, she was a conniving person who wasn't above trickery.

connoisseur (n) expert or professional; a competent critic in an art, skill, or profession
An antiques connoisseur would be able to tell you the value of that painting you found in your attic.

connotation (n) the various implied meanings of a word, act, or event; what is suggested rather than actually stated
His actual words were innocent enough, but their connotation was accusing and unkind.

conscript (v) to draft or enlist (a person) by law or force
My mother conscripted the entire family last fall to help her mulch the gardens for winter.

consort (n) associate; your other half; conjunction or tandem (as in *consort with local groups*)
Because my consort was absent, I was unable to make the presentation that we'd planned.

consort (v) to run around with or associate with (followed by *with*)
People may judge you by the people with whom you consort.

consternation (n) worry or concern; dismay or astonishment
He was unable to mask his fear; his face betrayed his consternation.

construe (v) to interpret, analyze, decipher
I will construe your remarks to mean that you haven't completed your homework assignment.

consummate (adj) developed to a high degree; perfect, skilled, accomplished
His consummate skill in handling that quarter horse throughout the rodeo earned him applause and enough points to win first place.

consummate (v)
to bring to completion; perfect; or achieve
The two partners consummated a business deal with another firm that would augment their earnings considerably within the first year after signing the contract.

contaminate (v)
to infect or in some way ruin; pollute, taint, defile
Businesses that contaminate their local streams with waste products will anger residents and endanger the environment.

contemplate (v)
to mull over, think about; meditate, consider
Jane contemplated the virtues and drawbacks of several colleges before she finally chose one.

contiguous (adj)
bordering or adjacent; nearby as neighbors
Contiguous backyards often share things like swing sets, ball games, leaves, and crabgrass.

contingent (adj)
dependent on; by chance or accident (with *on* or *upon*)
My attendance at the office party was contingent upon my finishing the work due Friday by five o'clock.

contingent (n)
group or body
Bruce said that a contingent from the hospital staff would be joining our after-work party.

contrite (adj)
sorrowful or repentant for some wrong; regretful
Her set, contrite face told him more about her misery than words could have expressed.

contumely (n)
rude talk or behavior resulting from feelings of superiority or contempt; disdain
In Hamlet's famous soliloquy, he says how terrible it is to "bear the whips and scorns of time, The oppressor's wrong, the proud man's contumely."

convivial (adj)
lively or spirited; congenial, sociable
My old Uncle Charlie is loved by many for his cheerful outlook and convivial, warmhearted ways.

copious (adj)
superabundant; in plentiful supply
I took copious notes so that I would have enough material for my term paper.

corollary (n)
the natural result or logical follow-up; a normal parallel
We tend to believe that success is the corollary to hard work and initiative.

corporeal (adj)
of the physical, not spiritual, body; material, substantial
Ghosts and spirits have no corporeal presence.

corroborate (v)
to confirm or substantiate (by evidence or from an official position); to support
The evidence I found corroborates your story, so I'm certain the judge will believe you.

coterie (n) a distinct group of people with common interests; a set, clique, faction
A distinguished coterie from the local art association represented our city at the state annual arts convention.

covenant (n) a serious agreement, promise, or contract; pledge
The congresswoman made a covenant with the people who had elected her; she would do her best to protect natural resources.

cower (v) to cringe in fear
The dog, normally fearless, cowered in the corner when he saw his previous, abusive owner.

craven (adj) cowardly to a strong degree; chickenhearted
Most of us hope we will be brave in tough circumstances, not craven.

credence (n) believing acceptance; credentials (*letters of credence*)
You don't expect me to give credence to such a wild story.

crony (n) friend of long standing; pal, buddy, chum
Uncle Jack spent a lot of time hanging around with his old cronies, trading war stories.

crux (n) central or pivotal point; essential or main item
The crux of the matter, said our play director, was whether or not we could afford the royalty payments on the play we had chosen.

culinary (adj) of the kitchen or cooking
Last year, Jamal could barely heat a can of soup; look how remarkably his culinary skills have improved.

culmination (n) the highest point or summit; climax, zenith
Winning the school's spring decathlon was the culmination of Rob's dedicated training efforts.

culpable (adj) guilty; at fault
Our society puts those culpable of serious crimes in jail, with the desperate hope that some may be rehabilitated.

cumbrous (adj) heavy, bulky, therefore often unwieldy; cumbersome
The camping equipment was more cumbrous than I'd expected, so we would not reach our campsite soon.

cursory (adj) sketchy, as opposed to thorough; hasty, superficial
After only cursory study, Miho could summarize the main idea of the paragraph.

curtail (v) to cut short, as an activity; to shorten, abbreviate
My sister, who always studies till midnight before an exam, was forced to curtail her studying when our lights went out in the ice storm.

cynic (n) a person who thinks others act only in self-interest
Joel and his friends are such cynics that they make me feel like a starry-eyed idealist.

daunt (v)   to dismay or take away the courage of; to cow or subdue
Don't be daunted by the exam—it isn't as hard as you think.

dawdle (v)   to waste time or spend it fruitlessly; to delay
The toddler dawdled through his lunch, much to his mother's impatience.

dearth (n)   scarcity or lack; paucity
A dearth of rain will leave the river at a dangerously low level.

debility (n)   weakness, esp. after illness; infirmity, lack of strength
The crippling debility in Leon's right leg after his auto accident made him grit his teeth in pain and frustration.

decorum (n)   correct or expected behavior; politeness, propriety, fitness
We struggled to maintain decorum, but it was impossible not to laugh at the large wad of spinach that was caught in the lecturer's teeth.

decrepit (adj)   worn out from age or overuse; weak, dilapidated, run-down
All the kids on our block ride to school in Dan's decrepit station wagon, but we think we'll end up pushing the car home one day soon.

deference (n)   honor or respect due an older or more experienced person; esteem
Priscilla's father said, "I wish you would show deference to older people and to those in positions of authority."

degenerate (v)   to sink into a lower or less useful state
"Mom's worried I'll degenerate into a party-loving nonstudent when I go away to college," Sam told his friend.

delineate (v)   to show, outline, portray accurately
We sat for hours with the architect as she delineated each aspect of our proposed office complex.

demeanor (n)   manner of handling yourself; comportment, bearing
Our cat has a regal demeanor as he approaches any guest; then he sits down to survey the newcomer through slitted eyes.

denotation (n)   the absolute literal meaning (as opposed to what a word brings to mind)
The strict, biological denotation of the word mother is very different from its vast array of connotative meanings.

deplore (v)   to regret exceedingly; to lament, bemoan
Dermatologists deplore our habit of cultivating a deep suntan, because the sun's rays are harmful to skin.

deploy (v)   to arrange in an advantageous way (as *military troops are deployed in battle*)
"If I ever learn how to deploy these chess pieces properly," Margo sighed, "I might have some hope of beating my sister."

depraved (adj)   sinful or evil; perverted (morals)
Behavior that seems perfectly moral to me may seem depraved to you.

derelict (n)	abandoned or neglected possession
derelict (v)	neglected or abandoned *The street was strewn with bits of paper and derelict objects.*
derision (n)	scorn or ridicule; literally laughing down *Sophie's theory was met with derision until they rest of the team began to see how much sense it made.*
derogatory (adj)	negatively critical, disparaging; literally talking down *Writers usually welcome helpful criticism, but derogatory remarks tend to put them on the defensive.*
desecrate (v)	to defile or profane something sacred or very special *To write on the sacred text would be to desecrate it.*
desiccate (v)	to dry up, dehydrate; to wither away by dryness *After an apple has desiccated and is no longer moist, you can apply fake hair, eyes, and ears to make it resemble a shrunken head.*
desist (v)	to cease or stop (doing something) *Please desist from running in the store, before you break something by mistake!*
desolate (adj)	alone or deserted; downcast or sad; barren, lifeless *The desolate stretches of seaside beach early in the morning offer a perfect place for walking and thinking.*
despondent (adj)	downcast, dejected, depressed *Don't be despondent; there's still hope that you will meet your deadline.*
destitute (adj)	experiencing extreme need (of vital necessities); indigent, poverty-stricken *Pictures of destitute children always tug at our heartstrings.*
desultory (adj)	without set plan or purpose; random; haphazard, casual *"A desultory approach to research is not what I call the scientific method," said the physics teacher.*
deviate (v)	to vary from the normal or standard way; to digress, change course; swerve *Made wary by the swollen river, we deviated from the original plan and paddled the canoes down a side stream instead.*
deviate (n)	someone who is noticeably different from the norm *In a higher-level psychology course, we will study various deviates who have been unable to adjust to normal society.*
devious (adj)	at odds with the normal, accepted course; off the beaten path in the sense of remote; roundabout (as *a devious path*) *We knew from Greg's devious behavior that he was planning a surprise.*
dexterous (adj)	skilled with mind/hands; adroit, artful, expert, deft *You need to be dexterous to build this model; it is quite difficult.*

dichotomy (n)   division into two groups or ideas at odds with one another; literally cut in two
Many women today are faced with a dichotomy; they want a demanding job and career yet feel an equally strong pull toward a traditional home and family life.

didactic (adj)   instructive, designed to teach; offering moral preachments; pedantic
Even when he wasn't in front of the classroom, the professor spoke in a didactic tone.

diffident (adj)   lacking self-confidence; unassertive and shy
Connie's new employer was upset by Connie's diffident manner her first morning on the job, but by afternoon she was pleased to see her growing in self-confidence.

dilatory (adj)   causing delay; tardy; putting off (as in procrastinating)
A dilatory student may have trouble catching up at the end of the semester.

dilemma (n)   problem lacking a good solution; quandary in which the only two alternatives are equally unsatisfactory
Jill had a dilemma; should she stay home and study, like she'd promised to do, or should she go out with her friends?

dilettante (n)   a dabbler of superficial knowledge/interest
The dilettante may wish he had the expertise of a professional, but just as often he lacks the dedication necessary to achieve greater status.

discernment (n)   ability to fully understand; discrimination and penetrating insight; acumen
His discernment in selecting young horses that would mature into winning racers gave Charles an edge over other trainers.

discomfiture (n)   state of confusion and embarrassment; act of thwarting or state of being thwarted
Jeri's discomfiture was plain to see as she lost to her old chess rival from East High.

discord (n)   tension, strife, or lack of agreement and harmony; dissonance in music; conflict
Composers of twentieth-century classical music often used discordant sounds that were jarring to the ears of traditionalists.

discrepancy (n)   a difference
When I see a discrepancy between my checking account balance and the bank records, I hope that the error will be settled in my favor.

discriminate (v)   to notice differences; to distinguish between; to differentiate; to treat differently
Being color blind, Jon could not discriminate one hue from another.

discursive (adj)	moving from one topic to another; digressive *Miss Wilson's presentation was discursive, yet highly interesting, and we enjoyed her digressions into humor.*
disparage (v)	to belittle, downgrade, or decry *Leah refused to let her teacher's disparaging comments discourage her from becoming a professional dancer.*
disparity (n)	difference in type or quality *Will and Troy are identical twins, even though the disparity in their interests might suggest otherwise.*
disseminate (v)	to disperse or spread all over (knowledge, ideas) almost as though sowing seeds *The school paper was founded to disseminate information about students and school activities.*
dissipate (v)	to thin out or to drive away to the point that almost nothing is left (as *a mob is dissipated*); to use up in a worthless, foolish way (as *an inheritance*); to waste *By late spring, our fervent journalistic efforts are sadly dissipated, and the paper we put out in June is usually pretty embarrassing.*
divulge (v)	to make known, reveal *My desk could divulge secrets about me that I'd prefer no one knew, such as my tendency to stuff unwanted papers into bottom drawers.*
docile (adj)	easily managed; compliant, tractable, amenable, obedient *One kindergarten teacher said to another, "If I ever had a docile student, I'd think he was ill and send him to the nurse!"*
doctrinaire (adj)	dictatorial and autocratic in manner, usually dogmatic and stubborn as well *I prefer a professor who is less doctrinaire and more open to debate.*
dogmatic (adj)	strongly opinionated; dictatorial *It is difficult to discuss new ideas with a very dogmatic person.*
dormant (adj)	temporarily inactive, asleep; latent *One of the most exciting aspects of life is that each person has talents and abilities lying dormant, just waiting to be discovered.*
dour (adj)	harsh or stubborn; sometimes gloomy, even sullen *The cold, rainy weather contributed to her dour mood.*
drastic (adj)	radical or severe *Drastic surgical procedures were necessary to save the boy's life after the accident.*
drivel (n)	foolish, witless talk; as a verb, to talk like an idiot *"This poetry is absolute drivel," Mel complained. "If I wrote poetry, it would be profound and meaningful."*

droll (adj) humorous; distinct in an appealing way
After the first speaker's dry remarks, we welcomed the droll style of the second speaker.

dubious (adj) doubtful or undecided; equivocal; questionable
Sara's tone was dubious as she reluctantly agreed to take on extra work.

duplicity (n) double-dealing in a contradictory way; deception
Shelley told us that she hadn't revealed our place in the woods, but when half of her friends marched into our hideout, we were sure of her duplicity.

duress (n) restraint by force, forcing by threat (follows *under*)
Back home, under duress, Shelley finally confessed that she'd given away our secret.

dynamic (adj) energetic, forceful; unusually active
Although dynamic on stage, the performer is shy and soft-spoken in person.

eclectic (adj) carefully selected; chosen from the best or from various sources
Marcia reads an eclectic array of books and can always suggest a good title.

edification (n) act or process of instruction, enlightening, or improving
Here, for your edification, is a glossary of vocabulary words.

efface (v) to erase or obliterate; to wear away (as *by time*)
Wise campers carefully efface all traces of their habitation in wilderness areas.

effete (adj) no longer useful, nonproductive; outmoded (as a law)
Doom prophets warn us of what happens to effete cultures, pointing to the fall of Rome as a classic example.

efficacious (adj) capable of producing the effect wanted; effective, potent
For years, people hoped that someone would discover an efficacious treatment for polio; Dr. Salk's vaccine was the preventative they'd awaited.

effigy (n) likeness or image of a person (often a disliked person)
The angry crowd hanged their political leader in effigy to demonstrate their bitterness toward his cruel policies.

effluvium (n) unpleasant odor or exhalation; waste by-products
Neighbors concerned about the effluvium in nearby streams and rivers have begun a clean-water campaign to help enforce our antipollution laws.

effrontery (n) unlimited boldness; insolence, temerity
Did she have the effrontery to ask for a raise after working here only three days?

egregious (adj) profoundly noticeable in a negative way; flagrant; outstandingly bad
Over the years, their egregious errors in management and public relations have cost that company the goodwill of everyone in town.

elicit (v) to draw forth
When newspaper reporters have tried to elicit the truth from company representatives, they have been given devious answers.

elixir (n)   liquid to give eternal life; a cure-all
This magical elixir guarantees eternal youth.

eloquent (adj)   moving and forcefully phrased; memorable because of verbal skill
Martin Luther King, Jr.'s "I Have a Dream" speech is widely considered to be one of the most eloquent and effective speeches in American history.

emaciated (adj)   extremely thin; gaunt
Is it necessary to look emaciated in order to be a fashion model?

emanate (v)   to seep forth (as smells or ideas); to emit
The smell of warm cookies emanated from the kitchen.

eminence (n)   importance or prominence; lofty station
It would be difficult for those in positions of eminence to comprehend the lives of those who lack life's most basic necessities.

emolument (n)   salary, wages; compensation for work
Hannah's emolument as a grocery store checkout clerk is generous, and she saves half of every paycheck for college expenses.

empirical (adj)   experimental (as data from experience or observation)
The chemistry teacher described the difference between empirical evidence and that which is obtained by deductive reasoning.

emulate (v)   to try to equal (or even exceed) an example; to imitate
My little brother is always emulating the older boys next door, trying to rival their feats on our backyard climber.

enervate (v)   to diminish the strength of (either mind or body); to rob of energy
At the end of exam week, my friends and I were totally enervated physically and mentally.

engender (v)   to cause to exist, sponsor; to beget (a child or an idea); to produce, originate
The record of our varsity basketball team engenders respect and envy in the younger junior varsity team.

enhance (v)   to make better or more desirable in some way; to intensify
The summer Brent spent at music camp enhanced his value to the orchestra, and now he plays the cello as well as the bass.

enigma (n)   a thing hard to understand or fathom; conundrum, riddle, mystery
The wind instruments remained an enigma to Brent, who couldn't understand how musicians produced sound from them.

enjoin (v)   to order or direct officially; to prohibit, forbid (with *from*)
Our crowd was enjoined from loitering in front of the drug store after school.

enthralling (adj)   charming; entrancing or spellbinding
The performance was so enthralling that we couldn't believe three hours had passed by the time it was over.

ephemeral (adj) of brief duration, therefore fleeting, transient, short-lived
The joy of an ice cream cone on a hot day is an ephemeral one.

epicure (n) person of discriminating taste; a perfectionist regarding food and drink; gourmet
Epicures and gourmets are typically persnickety eaters, but a gourmand usually eats lots of whatever is served.

epitaph (n) writing on a tomb, or at the gravesite (in commemoration)
Legend has it that W. C. Fields wanted his epitaph to read: On the whole I would rather be in Philadelphia.

epithet (n) an expression representative of a person or place; also a disparaging phrase about someone or something
The little boys hurled cruel epithets at the awkward newcomer who had hoped to join their game.

epitome (n) summary; a typical example representative of a type
Every item in his house is the epitome of good taste.

equivocal (adj) open to two interpretations, therefore unclear and often misleading; undecided, obscure, evasive
The witness was asked to answer the question a second time because his first answer was equivocal and might have misled the jury.

eradicate (v) to wipe out, exterminate; to pull up as if by the roots; also extirpate, to eradicate, root out
Through careful, persistent use of the smallpox vaccine, smallpox has been eradicated in the United States.

erratic (adj) on no set course; wandering or nomadic; devious
We had to laugh at the erratic flight of the rabbit as he zigged and zagged ahead of us down the path.

erudite (adj) possessing great knowledge, therefore learned
The erudite scholar knew a great deal about ancient history but very little about current events.

esoteric (adj) of knowledge belonging to certain initiated people only
The old Druidic priests guarded their esoteric knowledge so carefully that archaeologists and historians fear their information may be lost forever.

essence (n) the very core or most vital aspect of a thing; its very nature; essential, basic thing
We have only physical remains like Stonehenge to help us understand the essence of the ancient culture of Britain.

estrange (v) to set apart or at odds that which had been closely attuned; to alienate
Sometimes new students in school feel estranged from society because they lack the close friendships they had in their former schools.

eulogy (n) great praise (often in a formal way, as at a funeral); encomium; literally *good words* in Greek
An apt eulogy for Mark Twain could have included his famous quote "When in doubt, tell the truth," since he always told it as he saw it.

euphemism (n) use of carefully chosen acceptable words in place of those that may insult, offend, or be too honest
Our language is crammed with euphemisms that let us say in public what would otherwise be upsetting words, such as "passed away" instead of "died."

euphony (n) pleasing, agreeable sound; literally *good sound* in Greek
Edgar Allan Poe, who wrote many horror stories and detective mysteries, is also remembered for the euphony of his poetry.

execration (n) swear or curse; the thing cursed or reviled
Jean spent the last 3 miles of the race muttering execrations at her injured knee, which threatened to give out at any minute.

exigency (n) an urgently demanding time or state of affairs; what is absolutely needed for a particular circumstance (usually used in the plural: exigencies)
The exigencies of racing, Mickey explained, are such that athletes must train carefully for marathons if they expect to finish with a good time.

exonerate (v) to free from blame or guilt; to exculpate, absolve
We felt certain that when all of the evidence was revealed, Sophie would be exonerated from the accusation that she stole a cupcake.

exorcise (v) to get rid of something terrible (as an evil spirit) by formal prayer, order, etc.
A modern horror fantasy, The Exorcist tells the story of a girl who was possessed by the devil and exorcised by a courageous priest.

exotic (adj) foreign, strange, different
Maureen disliked any food that seemed unfamiliar or exotic to her.

expatiate (v) to write or speak lengthily, with detail; to expound
While the lecturer expatiated about the need for greater community involvement, the audience struggled to stay awake.

expatriate (n) one living outside his or her native country, often voluntarily

expatriate (v) to order out of the country; to leave one's native country or renounce it; literally, out of the fatherland
Certain crimes against the government call for the guilty to be expatriated, often for the rest of their lives.

expedient (adj) suitable, practical; advisable, opportunistic
Doing what is merely expedient rather than what is right can be a strong temptation, but it may lead to a regrettable end.

expedite (v)
to cause to move along at a desirable rate; facilitate
In order to expedite this shipment of oranges, we will send them with the fastest carrier available.

expiate (v)
to make up for, in the sense of atoning; to make amends
Seeing the mouse in the trap made me feel so awful that I expiated part of my guilt by burying him in our backyard pet cemetery.

explicit (adj)
absolutely clear and definite; precise; specific, express
Although the directions on the package of hair dye were explicit, Bonnie did it her own way, and the result was orange hair.

expunge (v)
to obliterate, erase, efface totally; to destroy
Even good behavior cannot expunge wrong-doing from your file.

extant (adj)
in actual experience; intact (as opposed to lost or ruined)
Many old, original manuscripts are extant, carefully preserved in the rare book rooms of libraries.

extemporize (v)
to speak without formal preparation; to improvise on the spur of the moment
Using small note cards, with only a phrase on them for suggestions, each person in our speech class had to extemporize for 3 minutes.

extenuate (v)
to reduce the severity or importance of; to mitigate (a crime, an illness, etc.)
Jill sat down after only 2 minutes of her extemporaneous speech, saying that her sore throat ought to extenuate her crime of being too brief.

extraneous (adj)
of extra, nonessential parts; irrelevant; extrinsic as opposed to intrinsic
"What is all this extraneous information about mice doing in a term paper on feline intelligence?" asked the biology teacher.

facade (n)
front or outward appearance of a building or a person; the face you show to the world
Despite his brave façade, Jim was shy and frightened any time he had to speak publicly.

facetious (adj)
humorous, but sometimes awkwardly so; jocose, witty
Although she tried to be serious, Ava couldn't help making a few facetious remarks at the meeting.

facile (adj)
easily done, therefore maybe done superficially; ready, fluent
Joleen told our committee that a facile solution would not suffice in place of a solid plan.

fallacious (adj)
false or deceptive; tending to delude or mislead
Angry consumers sued the company for making fallacious claims about its products.

fastidious (adj)   demanding the utmost, persnickety; showing meticulous workmanship or care
True science is exact, requiring that experiments be performed with fastidious care under strict guidelines.

feasible (adj)   capable of being accomplished; reasonable or possible; likely
If it's feasible to eat dinner early, we could go to the first movie showing and still be home by nine-thirty.

felicitous (adj)   fortunate or apt (as a remark); pleasant, fit, suitable
The entire family enjoys Clare because her felicitous comments and ever-pleasant manner put each one of us at ease.

feral (adj)   fierce, wild, savage; returning to the wild after being domesticated
Feral dogs roam in packs throughout Africa, hunting for food, which is often hard to find.

fervent (adj)   full of strong, sincere emotion; impassioned
In some West Coast suburbs, occasional coyote raids on young children and pets have inspired fervent pleas for action from local governments.

festoon (n)   a draped garland
festoon (v)   to drape or hang into festoon shapes
The prom committee was allowed to festoon the hotel ballroom with flower garlands before the dance.

fetid (adj)   stinking, malodorous
As the water level dropped to lower and lower depths in the canal, nearby residents noticed a fetid odor from that region.

fetish (n)   something of personal—possibly irrational—significance; charm, talisman, or amulet
That old, chewed-up square of blanket is our dog's fetish.

fiasco (n)   a total flop, complete failure
"No more fiascoes like last time," my sister announced. "This time we'll plan the party so that people don't sit around and yawn."

filch (v)   to steal in a sneaky way (usually something of minor value)
Don't filch any of those cookies before they've had time to cool.

flaccid (adj)   without customary firmness, flabby, limp
The elderly dog was flaccid from lack of exercise and an abundance of dog food.

flagrant (adj)   conspicuous in a highly negative way; glaring, gross
In flagrant disobedience of house rules, our cat Fred crouches atop the television set and gazes longingly down into the gerbils' cage.

flaunt (v)   to show off; display in a superior, objectionable manner
You can flaunt your knowledge by using long vocabulary words in everyday speech.

florid (adj)	very flowery (as writing style); high-colored, ruddy (of complexion) *Modern editors generally avoid a florid literary style, deleting extraneous words and sentences whenever feasible.*
fluctuate (v)	to come and go, as waves; to shift up and down (as *the stock market fluctuates daily*) *Temperatures in a Florida winter may fluctuate greatly, a fact that gives citrus growers many headaches.*
foible (n)	a minor fault or shortcoming; weakness *It's strangely comforting to know that others are as full of foibles as we are.*
forensic (adj)	of law or public debate; argumentative (as in a case in court) *The forensic scientist reconstructed the scene of the accident to prove her client's innocence.*
formidable (adj)	arousing fear or worry; fostering respect or awe *Those dark clouds indicate that a formidable storm is on its way.*
forte (n)	special strength or skill; what you're known for *Ali's forte was belly dancing, but she was also an excellent ballerina.*
fortuitous (adj)	happening by chance; accidental *How fortuitous that airline fares went down just before you planned your trip.*
fractious (adj)	difficult to discipline; unruly, troublesome *The toddler became fractious when she was hungry or needed a nap.*
frugal (adj)	careful about how money or goods are used; carefully economical; sparing *Cara says she has enough money to last through the month, but only if she is frugal in her spending.*
fulsome (adj)	overabundant; flattering to the point of annoyance or embarrassment; overdone; obsequious or servile *The professional golfer was embarrassed to read the newspaper's fulsome praise of his achievements on the tour.*
furtive (adj)	of sly or secretive behavior; surreptitious, even stolen (as furtive goods) *The furtive movements of the fox in the henhouse went unnoticed until it was too late for one sleepy hen.*
futile (adj)	without use or purpose; ineffectual; vain, fruitless *The noisy and futile efforts of the hen to escape the fox aroused all of the other chickens and eventually the entire farm.*
gambol (v)	to frolic about like lambs in a pasture; to frisk about *The young children gamboled over the soccer field, learning the skills of the game.*

Peterson's SAT Success

gamut (n)	a range (as *scales run the gamut from high to low notes*)
	As he watched the birth of his first child, the father's emotions ran the gamut from fear to exment to awe.
garrulous (adj)	extremely talkative; loquacious, gabby, verbose
	After his daughter's birth, the normally shy father became garrulous, telling everyone he saw about his new and perfect child.
gelid (adj)	very cold; icy (said of people's attitudes as well as of substances)
	The haughty old queen gave her subjects a brief, gelid smile as she informed them that their audience was over.
generic (adj)	of a type or class (not a brand name, for example); universal
	Generic products appear regularly as merchants try to offer lower prices and a variety of products to their customers.
gentility (n)	referring to the upper class or gentry; courtesy
	Ashamed of his background, he wove an elaborate lie about the gentility of his ancestors.
germane (adj)	fitting and appropriate; pertinent, relevant
	The example in the textbook was not at all germane to a real-life situation.
gibe (v)	to make fun of or tease with rude remarks; to scoff, deride
	The comedian hit his mark with the deadly accuracy of a clever jibe.
girth (n)	a measurement around; strap or band that encircles
	A good diet should improve a person's overall health, not just reduce his or her girth.
goad (n)	an instrument or prod used to stimulate action
goad (v)	to urge onward; to spur
	My cousin goaded my normally considerate, polite aunt into remarks that I was sure she would later regret.
gossamer (n)	anything delicate, as a spider's web
gossamer (adj)	filmy, insubstantial
	The women stood about in the summer evening, their gossamer dresses stirring in the breeze.
gratuitous (adj)	offered freely; not necessary under the circumstances, and therefore unwanted; unasked for; unwarranted
	Many parents dislike the gratuitous violence in children's cartoons.
gregarious (adj)	fond of groups; social and sociable, convivial
	Like people, elephants are gregarious and enjoy the company of family groups.
grueling (adj)	demanding, exhausting, tiring; punishing
	"Sitting for Harold is a grueling job," his mother admitted, "because you have to keep your eyes on him every minute."

guile (n)   trickery or cunning; duplicity
One of his greatest qualities was his complete lack of guile; he never lied or manipulated the truth.

gullible (adj)   easy to fool or deceive; ingenuous
Do you think I'm gullible enough to believe that crazy story?

hackneyed (adj)   without originality; trite, banal, overused
The book reviewer criticized the author for his use of hackneyed phrases and his cliché ending.

haggard (adj)   appearing drawn, gaunt, and exhausted
After hours of dragging the river for bodies from the capsized boat, the rescuers were haggard and distraught.

hapless (adj)   unlucky, unfortunate
The hapless boat crew, unused to the whims of the river, had run aground and capsized their craft during the night.

harass (v)   to irritate or annoy repeatedly
Although they seem to be harassing us, people who call on the phone trying to sell things are usually just trying to make a living.

harbinger (n)   forerunner; something that foreshadows the future; precursor
If robins are the harbingers of spring, then dandelions are never far behind as precursors of summer.

haughty (adj)   unbecomingly proud, disdainful
Normally a laughing, friendly girl, Ellen had to act haughty and reserved for her role in the school play.

hedonist (n)   someone who lives for pleasure or happiness
The billionaire was a notorious hedonist, spending enormous amounts of money on luxuries.

heed (v)   to pay attention to or notice; be mindful of
Physicians caution patients to heed the advice printed on all medicine bottles.

heinous (adj)   absolutely hateful; abominable, outrageous
Newspapers seem to concentrate on reporting heinous crimes, knowing that gory news sells papers.

heresy (n)   belief that is against church teachings; any strong dissent from accepted belief or theory
Margot's refusal to put her research before her teaching was considered heresy by the other faculty members.

heyday (n)   the best period in performance, prosperity, health, etc.
In his heyday, Fred Astaire was film's most polished dancer.

hiatus (n) a gap or lapse in action; a break
The vacation provided a welcome hiatus for students who needed a holiday from books.

hirsute (adj) noticeably hairy; bristly
The carpet had a hirsute quality that made sitting on it uncomfortable.

histrionic (adj) of acting or drama; sometimes, overly dramatic; theatrical
His histrionic manner was not surprising, considering the fact that he was an actor.

hoax (v) to deceive, dupe
hoax (n) a trick or deception
The photograph of a flying saucer turned out to be a clever hoax.

homily (n) a lecture or sermon on being good
We sat impatiently through the homily, all the while planning what our next prank would be.

hoodwink (v) to fool by false appearances; to dupe or hoax
The false photograph hoodwinked the newspaper editor, who printed it immediately.

humane (adj) demonstrating kindness, understanding, and compassion for other human beings or for animals
Humane zookeepers create animal habitats that are as close as possible to natural ones.

husbandry (n) careful use of resources; conservation; also the care and growth of plants and animals; agriculture
The bounty of their vegetable garden and the beauty of their property testify to the careful husbandry that Jan and Frank have practiced over the years.

hyperbole (n) wild exaggeration, often deliberate (for effect)
Despite its hyperbole, the article made a good point about the need for people to limit their use of fossil fuels.

hypocrite (n) someone who pretends to hold beliefs or virtues that he or she really doesn't have; a dissembler; a fake (in a sense)
Only a hypocrite would loudly proclaim the need to preserve the environment while supporting companies that actively destroy it.

hypothetical (adj) depending on conditions; based on a hypothesis or supposition
Our premise is purely hypothetical so far, but once we test it we'll have some concrete facts.

iconoclast (n) a person who criticizes established ideas or traditions
Besides being something of an iconoclast, John Lennon is remembered for his musical talents.

idiom (n)   a language (or phrases) distinct for a locale or set of people; dialect; a common, well-known expression of a specific person, place, or time
Certain idioms make sense only in their native language; translated, they sound absurd.

idiosyncrasy (n)   a peculiarity that sets someone apart; eccentricity
My grandfather had many lovable idiosyncrasies, one being his insistence that dessert be eaten after every meal, even after breakfast.

ignominy (n)   profound disgrace or humiliation; dishonor; infamy
The mayor fled town in ignominy, leaving behind a tangled financial mess.

imbroglio (n)   an awkward, embarrassing, often confusing situation; embroilment or altercation
The game ended, as usual, in an imbroglio that included tears and name-calling.

immutable (adj)   unchangeable, unalterable; eternal
Survival of the fittest is one of nature's immutable laws.

impale (v)   to stab with a pointed instrument
She impaled a piece of potato with her skewer and cooked it on the grill.

impalpable (adj)   not able to be felt, therefore intangible; also not easily discernible to the mind
Certain feelings, like lifting of the spirits, are nearly impalpable, yet highly significant to each of us.

impart (v)   to give information, communicate; to give as from an abundance
The company was reluctant to impart too much information about its strategy.

impasse (n)   point at which no way out can be seen; a dead end or cul-de-sac; a deadlock
Negotiations have reached an impasse, reported the mediator, with both sides refusing to budge an inch.

impeccable (adj)   flawless or perfect; free from blame or sin; immaculate
Although our French instructor was English, his French accent was impeccable.

impecunious (adj)   without money; penniless; poor; indigent
Having grown up in poverty, she vowed never again to lead an impecunious life.

impediment (n)   something that gets in your way and impedes progress or speech; a hindrance
Dave's broken leg was more of an impediment than he had ever believed possible.

imperturbable (adj)	being unusually calm and serene; cool or unflappable *We tried to rile Joe by teasing him, but he was imperturbable.*
impervious (adj)	not capable of being penetrated or harmed; impenetrable; unaffected *The raincoat formed an impervious layer between the weather and my clothes.*
impetus (n)	the stimulus that gets something going; impulse, incentive *Was kindness the impetus for this good deed, or was there another motive?*
implacable (adj)	not able to be appeased or soothed *After another car hit his vehicle, Jack was implacable; he hadn't finished paying for the car, and already it was dented.*
implicit (adj)	implied though not stated; suggested *Dad didn't actually say we had to be home by 12, but it was implicit when he urged us to be in on time, which has always meant midnight in our family.*
importunate (adj)	being persistent in demands or requests; troublesome *Our dog was importunate in his insistence upon being fed at exactly the same time every day.*
imprecation (n)	curse; denunciation; execration *Checking his watch, he muttered an imprecation at the enormous snarl of traffic.*
impunity (n)	freedom from punishment or penalty *Maria is so well-respected that, unlike many newer employees at the firm, she can speak her mind with impunity.*
inadvertent (adj)	not on purpose; unintentional; accidental *My inadvertent gesture knocked my glass of soda to the floor.*
inane (adj)	empty, silly, and foolish; insipid, fatuous *After several minutes of inane chatter, they finally began discussing the real agenda of the day.*
incandescence (n)	noticeable brightness or clarity; glowing *Mary's incandescence on stage lights up not only her performance but that of the other cast members too.*
incantation (n)	a written or spoken spell with the hope of invoking magic; any special group of repeated words *Entering the temple, he lit a candle and spoke the incantation.*
incarcerate (v)	to lock up or confine against a person's will; to imprison *The judge determined that the young offender should do community service rather than be incarcerated.*
incendiary (n)	a person who sets fires; a bomb

incendiary (adj)
of deliberate burning (of property); tending to start fires, either literally or figuratively; inflammatory
The rebel's incendiary pamphlets were circulated among the people, who were then inflamed by the revolutionary words and ideas.

incessant (adj)
going on without interruption; ceaseless, continuous
Our science field trip had to be canceled because the incessant spring rains had flooded the road that led to the wildlife refuge.

inchoate (adj)
not well formed or formulated; embryonic, in a sense; vague
The principal's inchoate suspicions that the seniors were up to another prank were proved accurate when a mooing cow met him at the door to the gym on Monday morning.

incipient (adj)
just beginning or apparent; commencing, burgeoning
"I think," Kay said as she scratched discreetly, "that these little bumps are an incipient case of poison ivy."

in (v)
to stir or spur on to action; to foment, instigate, abet
The citizens were angry and restless, and the slightest incident could in a riot.

incognito (adj or adv)
with a hidden identity
Famous stars prefer traveling incognito to avoid being mobbed for autographs.

incongruous (adj)
seeming out of place or unsuited; incompatible
Her formal dress was incongruous in the casual setting.

incorrigible (adj)
extremely difficult to manage or control (of people or animals); delinquent, recalcitrant
Despite our threats to punish him, our little brother's behavior was incorrigible.

increment (n)
an increase, as in salary or worth; one of a series of regular enlargements
A regular cost-of-living pay raise provides salary increments based on rising costs.

incriminate (v)
to accuse of blame or implicate as blameworthy
The incriminating footprints confirmed my suspicion that someone had walked through my flower garden.

incubus (n)
evil spirit; any depressing weight (as worry) or burden
The decision of whether or not to move pressed upon our family like an incubus as the days wore on without a conclusion.

indifferent (adj)
neutral or unbiased; impartial; sometimes apathetic
Molly said she was indifferent to where we pitched camp, since she planned to stay near the tent and read every day.

Peterson's SAT Success

indolent (adj)   naturally lazy or idle
We accused Molly of being indolent, but she retorted that vacations were supposed to be a change, and relaxation was the change she had in mind.

indomitable (adj)   unconquerable; dauntless
Molly proved indomitable as our vacation days slid by and she continued to read contentedly near the tent.

ineffable (adj)   indescribable; difficult to express in words
As we tired of the constant swimming, boating, and hiking, we noticed the ineffable expression of peace that had settled on Molly's face.

inept (adj)   lacking competence or fitness; not suited to the place, time, or job; awkward, bungling
We had to laugh with Molly over her dedicated yet inept attempts to build a campfire.

inert (adj)   exceedingly slow to move or act; sluggish, inactive
One late afternoon we returned to camp to find Molly inert, dozing on her air mattress.

inevitable (adj)   not avoidable by any means
I suppose it was inevitable that the end of our camping trip found everyone in a state of sunburned exhaustion.

inexorable (adj)   not movable by any means; relentless, inflexible
The storm's path was inexorable; the best we could do was to prepare for the worst and stay inside until it passed.

inference (n)   something deduced or concluded from evidence; a proposition gained from available data; a conclusion
Even though the dancer did not tell us she was from Mexico, we made that inference from the style of dance that she performed.

infidel (n)   a religious unbeliever in respect to a particular religion; a disbeliever in some specific sense
"Infidel!" roared the editor. "Anyone who thinks he can publish without careful research and editing will never write for me!"

ingratiate (v)   to work your way into someone's good graces (use with *with*)
Cowed by the editor's anger, the new writer spent the rest of the week ingratiating himself with all of the other editors on the staff.

inherent (adj)   natural, inborn; of essential nature, given the subject; innate
Her inherent stubbornness made her an excellent trial lawyer.

iniquity (n)   wickedness, sin; also grave injustice
The iniquity of the trial's outcome stunned onlookers, who were convinced that the jury was in grave error.

innocuous (adj)
not offensive or harmful; also dull or insipid
Cedric had thought Constance was annoyed with him, but her innocuous letter gave no hint of anger.

inordinate (adj)
beyond normal limits; unreasonable, excessive, immoderate
We had to do an inordinate amount of work, but finally we finished our project with a week to spare.

inscrutable (adj)
difficult to understand or interpret; mysterious
His inscrutable stare betrayed no emotion.

insidious (adj)
alluring but dangerous; treacherous or deceitfully damaging
Even though Ben's roommate was sick with the flu, Ben had thought he was safe until the insidious virus sent him to bed, too.

insipid (adj)
lacking interest or stimulation; flat, dull
The dialogue in the movie was as insipid as the frilly costumes.

insolvent (adj)
lacking money; impoverished, broke; the opposite is solvent
In a typical cartoon gesture, Wally pulled out his pants pockets to illustrate that he was insolvent after buying Christmas gifts.

insular (adj)
set apart; isolated (as an island);
"The students at our school lead rather insular lives," explained the headmaster, "because we are so far outside the town."

interpolate (v)
to add by insertion (words or ideas); to insert (something) between other things
The story was vague, but by interpolating the missing details we were able to make some sense of it.

intone (v)
to say something in a ritualistic or singsong way; to chant
After intoning the traditional prayers, we ate our meal.

intrinsic (adj)
referring to the essential nature of a thing; innate
We all like to be judged for our intrinsic worth and not for extrinsic things like money or position.

intuition (n)
natural, quick understanding or perception
Many new parents hesitate to rely on their intuition about infants, preferring to consult books and doctors.

inundate (v)
to overwhelm or flow over, as with a flood
Near the end of the year, the seniors were inundated with commitments and work at school.

inure (v)
to adjust to something basically unpleasant; to habituate or accustom
After basic training, recruits are inured to long hours and inclement weather—the harsh demands of army life.

invective (n)
verbal abuse or insult; vituperation
We would have been far more motivated by kind, encouraging words than we were by invective.

inveigh (v) to object with bitterness; to complain forcefully, maybe lengthily; to rail
The lawyer inveighed against the unnecessarily strict sentence given to his client.

inveigle (v) to convince or persuade by cleverness or flattery; to entice, cajole, wheedle
We at last inveigled Dad into lending us the car keys by promising to drive carefully and to call home as soon as we got to the party.

inveterate (adj) well established over time (as a habit); confirmed; chronic
An inveterate liar, Mike seemed not to know the difference between the truth and fiction.

irascible (adj) easily angered; testy, touchy; cross, choleric
Be careful around that fat, gray cat; he looks calm, but he is irascible and might bite at any time.

irony (n) the unexpected, when it is the opposite of what you expected; humor based on incongruity; deliberate use of words so that the meaning construed is the opposite of what was actually said
Zack was so angry about failing his test that nobody pointed out the irony of the fact that he would have passed if he hadn't cheated.

iterate (v) to repeat over and over; to reiterate
There's no need for you to iterate the point; I heard you the first three times.

itinerary (n) travel route or guide; guidebook
We planned an itinerary for our trip that takes us through seven Southern states.

jargon (n) special language or terminology; a dialect or hybrid language
The advertising jargon confused Suzanne for days until she learned all the terms in her new profession.

jaundice (n) disease characterized by yellowness of skin; an attitude of unfriendliness, envy, or boredom

jaundiced (adj) revealing an attitude of unpleasantness or distaste
The neighbors regarded our noisy, late party with jaundiced eyes.

jaunty (adj) lively and cheerful in manner; sprightly
Our mountain guide had a jaunty air about him as we set off on our trek up the slopes of White Mountain.

jeopardize (v) to put in danger; to risk, imperil
Mike's guidance counselor warned him not to jeopardize his high standing in his class by goofing off during his final semester.

jingoism (n) strongly partisan nationalism, usually accompanied by an aggressive foreign policy; a jingoist may be termed a hawk in modern slang
The leader's jingoism made him unpopular among many peace-loving constituents.

jocular (adj) naturally cheerful and playful; witty, jocose
Bima's jocular manner hid a more serious side of her personality.

judicious (adj) showing sound judgment; wise, discreet
At my first job interview, I was very nervous and hoped my prospective employer would give my resume a judicious appraisal.

juxtapose (v) to arrange side by side, one thing next to another
We watched as the artist skillfully juxtaposed colors and shapes on his canvas.

kaleidoscopic (adj) like a kaleidoscope, in a variety of different patterns
In the autumn, the trees around the lake are kaleidoscopic in their brilliant and changing colors.

ken (n) sight or range of sight; knowledge, understanding
ken (v) to know or recognize
This math problem is difficult, but it is not beyond my ken.

labyrinth (n) any maze or complex arrangement difficult to figure out; intricacy; perplexity
Trying to find our way around the corridors and rooms in the ancient castle was like puzzling through a labyrinth.

lacerate (v) to rip, rend, or tear in a harsh way; to distress emotionally
As a result of his serious car accident, Phil was lacerated and bruised but fortunately escaped more serious injury.

laconic (adj) sparing or terse in speech; concise almost to the point of rudeness
Although his brother enjoyed talking to a crowd of people, Chris was withdrawn and laconic.

laity (n) church congregation, not the ministers (clergy); the masses, as opposed to those with special skills
Some congregations distribute responsibilities among the laity.

lampoon (n) satire aimed at a person or persons
lampoon (v) to ridicule or make fun of, to satirize
The play lampooned a traditional, serious drama.

languor (n) tiredness or weakness of body or mind; indolence, dreaminess; lassitude
Pat was so used to the snapping cold of the far north that she was surprised by her languor when she first moved to New Orleans.

latent (adj) hidden or submerged, waiting to be aroused; dormant, quiescent
Since my uncle retired from law, his latent abilities as a chef have blossomed, and he now makes delicious soups and stews.

laudable (adj) deserving of praise; commendable
The committee's efforts to raise money for social programs were laudable.

levity (n)   lightness of approach or treatment; humor
Students recognize that a little levity in the classroom helps rather than hinders learning.

levy (n)   an assessment or tax

levy (v)   to take or require by legal means
The city council had to levy higher taxes to pay for road repairs.

lexicon (n)   a dictionary; vocabulary particular to a language or topic
Try browsing through a Greek lexicon sometime to see how many words you recognize as parents of today's English words.

linguistics (n)   study of speech; philology
The study of linguistics reveals how many English words are borrowed from other languages.

litany (n)   a chant, either musical or repetitive (or both); a prayer of entreaty with responses
Andy's litany of complaints seems to have no end.

litigation (n)   a lawsuit or legal dispute
We thought we held clear title to that land, but since another claim has been filed against it we will be in litigation for months.

lithe (adj)   flexible and graceful
We watched the lithe, beautiful motions of the dancers and were impressed with their outstanding physical condition as well as their grace.

livid (adj)   discolored, as by bruises; pale or ashen; also extremely angry, enraged
We were livid when we found out that all of our hard work was in vain.

loquacious (adj)   extremely talkative; gabby, garrulous
The loquacious teller held up the line with each customer, chatting about her day.

lucid (adj)   clear and distinct; being sane, in full possession of intelligence; intelligible
The salesman's forceful, lucid delivery convinced Carrie that he knew his product and the competitor's products well enough to be trusted.

lucrative (adj)   earning money or something valuable; profitable
My little brother says that, although weeding the neighbors' flower beds may be lucrative, it is also a rotten job.

ludicrous (adj)   appearing ridiculous or laughable; absurd
He knew he looked ludicrous in the costume, but he had agreed to wear it for the duration of the party.

lugubrious (adj)   looking or sounding profoundly sad, maybe for effect
The clown had an exaggerated, lugubrious frown painted on his face.

lurid (adj)   excessively pale-looking; red, as fire seen through smoke; provoking horror, gruesome
My brother insisted on relating the lurid details of a car accident he had witnessed.

machinations (n)   schemes or artful plots (usually toward bad ends)
The wily machinations of some government officials engender distrust of all who are in government.

magnanimous (adj)   noble and generous in victory as well as defeat; forgiving
Our class president is respected for her intelligence, but she is loved for her magnanimous nature and ready laughter.

malevolent (adj)   exuding evil or intense hatred
The character was not entirely malevolent; the author made a point of showing her good qualities as well as her bad ones.

malign (v)   to speak of in an evil, ill-willed manner; to defame or slander
People in high political positions realize that unscrupulous opponents may malign them in an effort to gain advantages.

manifest (adj)   readily understood or perceived; obvious, evident
manifest (v)   to show; to make certain and clear
Mozart manifested his incredible talents at the early age of 4, when he composed five piano pieces that are still performed by the world's great musicians.

manipulate (v)   to use skillfully or appropriately; to manage to your own benefit
After Art had manipulated the puzzle pieces for a time, he figured out the solution.

marauder (n)   seeker of goods; raider, pillager
The raccoon is a masked nighttime marauder who roots through garbage cans in search of a meal.

maudlin (adj)   overly sentimental
The greeting card had a syrupy picture and a maudlin verse.

maxim (n)   a proverb or repeated saying of truth
My dad's favorite maxim is "Early to bed, early to rise, makes a man healthy, wealthy, and wise."

melancholy (n)   abnormal depression; excessively low spirits; dejection
melancholy (adj)   depressed, blue; sorrowful; downcast
Don't be melancholy—things are bound to get better soon.

mendacious (adj)   lying, deceptive, dishonest
The advertisement made mendacious claims about a miracle weight-loss product.

mendicant (adj)   begging

mendicant (n)   beggar; occasionally, a monk or friar
The mendicant beagle found her reward when her owner fed her a cupcake.

menial (adj)   lowly or servile; humble, subservient
It's difficult to get excited about menial household tasks such as dishwashing, dusting, and vacuuming.

mercenary (adj)   working only with money or reward in mind; greedy

mercenary (n)   a person working only for money; also a hired soldier
Noblemen were accustomed to hiring mercenaries, who fulfilled their military obligations for them.

meretricious (adj)   glamorous in a cheap, showy way; gaudy; also rooted in bigotry or hypocritical views
The meretricious arguments of certain lobbyists were discounted by the more thoughtful legislators, who tried to examine proposals fairly.

metamorphosis (n)   unexplainable but usually very noticeable change of form or character
The family photographs showed the twins' metamorphosis from childhood to adulthood.

meticulous (adj)   showing extreme care in all respects
A copy editor must correct written materials with meticulous care so that published writing is as nearly perfect as possible.

mince (v)   to cut into tiny sections; to talk or walk in an affected or overly dainty manner; to hold back words discreetly
Do not mince words with me—tell me what you're thinking.

minion (n)   a minor official, sometimes a dependent servant
Outlaws of the old west had little use for the minions of the law.

mitigate (v)   to relieve or lighten or lessen (as *pain is mitigated by medication*); to mollify (as *anger is mitigated*); to alleviate
The knowledge that Joel's surgery had been successful mitigated his classmates' fears.

mollify (v)   to calm someone's temper or appease bad feelings, placate
We mollified Mom by promising to clean our rooms when we got home from school.

moot (adj)   something debatable or in dispute; also plainly abstract, strictly academic (in the sense that the outcome will not be affected)
Because the picnic had been cancelled, Jack's arguments as to why he should be allowed to go were moot.

morass (n)   a thing that entraps or restricts (as a marsh or swamp)
Bob felt he was drowning in the morass of legal questions he needed to answer before he could claim his inheritance.

mordant (adj)	biting or stinging in approach; cutting to the heart of the matter; incisive *The comedian's mordant wit struck at the heart of every issue.*
motley (n)	typical, multicolored garments of a court fool
motley (adj)	of different, oddly grouped parts *Despite our motley group, we managed to work together to finish the project.*
mundane (adj)	earthly as opposed to heavenly; worldly; ordinary or run-of-the-mill; also menial (as mundane chores) *The easiest time to let your imagination roam is when you're doing mundane jobs like mowing the lawn or cleaning up the kitchen.*
munificent (adj)	very liberal; generous in giving; lavish *Munificent contributions from some corporations make it possible for excellent programs to appear on public television.*
murky (adj)	heavy, foggy dark (as air); obscure or vague *Lloyd's bike light was a feeble glow in the murky night air and fog that enveloped the lane leading to his house.*
nadir (n)	the lowest point or absolute bottom; *Critics loathed the play, calling it the nadir of the director's career.*
naive (adj)	unworldly, unsophisticated, unaffected; ingenuous, innocent, natural *Although he appeared naive, Tim would not allow himself to be swindled.*
nebulous (adj)	vague and unformed (as a nebulous idea); indistinct *Our plan for touring the West had been so nebulous that every night on the trip we had to pore over guidebooks, deciding where to go next.*
nefarious (adj)	noticeably wicked, evil; vicious *The nefarious villain in the play led such an evil life that audiences cheered when he died.*
negligible (adj)	of little or no importance; inconsequential, trifling *Luckily, the accident wasn't serious, and the damage to the cars was negligible.*
negligence (n)	lack of proper care and attention *The death of her plant was not due to negligence; she watered it regularly and saw that it got proper sunlight.*
neophyte (n)	a convert or beginner *"We have several neophytes in our sales organization," the manager noted, "but their enthusiasm and zeal more than make up for their lack of experience."*
niggardly (adj)	very tight with money or means; stingy, penurious, parsimonious *The company's niggardly salaries discouraged many of its employees, who began to look elsewhere for better pay.*

nocturnal (adj)	referring to night *Nocturnal animals are adept at hunting in the dark.*
noisome (adj)	extremely unpleasant to the senses, especially the sense of smell; malodorous, noxious *As we drove by the sewer plant, we rolled up our car windows to block out the noisome vapors.*
nominal (adj)	referring to nouns; in name only; trifling, insignificant *The company president had only a nominal leadership position; all of the decisions were actually made by the staff.*
nuance (n)	a shade of difference or variation; subtlety, hint, trace *The artist reproduced every nuance of light and color in his paintings.*
nurture (n)	training or upbringing; education
nurture (v)	to feed, nourish, raise *When we find a wounded young rabbit, we nurture it carefully, intent on returning it to the wild as a healthy adult.*
obdurate (adj)	rigid or set in feelings or behavior; unyielding, inflexible, adamant *When you meet with obdurate resistance to your suggestions, even persuasive argument is usually wasted speech.*
obese (adj)	uncommonly fat *We tried not to overfeed our dog, for fear that she would become obese.*
obliterate (v)	to erase completely or wipe out; to efface, remove, cancel *A sandstorm swiftly obliterates any evidence of human or animal movement on the desert.*
obloquy (n)	strong verbal abuse; the state of being discredited (as a bad reputation) *Listening to the obloquy one candidate heaped upon the head of the other persuaded me not to vote for either one of them.*
obsequious (adj)	unusually servile or subservient; overly compliant, fawning *The waiter gave an obsequious bow before taking orders from the table.*
obsolete (adj)	out of style or no longer used; old, outmoded *Modern technology makes many older inventions obsolete.*
obtuse (adj)	slow to catch on; insensible or rather dull mentally *"Don't be deliberately obtuse," my brother John grumbled. "You know which ones are weeds and which are flowers, so lend a hand."*
odious (adj)	arousing hatred or disgust *Weeding the garden, out in the heat with bugs stinging, was a truly odious job.*
officious (adj)	butting in with advice where none is wanted; meddlesome *Although he had only been on the job for one month, Ron's officious attitude implied that he had been doing it for years.*

oligarchy (n)	government by a very few; the ruling group itself or group being ruled *At one time, Rome was governed by a triumvirate, an oligarchy of three.*
ominous (adj)	promising or foreshadowing something bad; inauspicious, portentous *The storm in the distance sounded ominous, causing us to worry about exposed livestock and young crops.*
omniscient (adj)	possessing complete awareness and understanding *As children we think that our parents are omniscient, a belief that gives both comfort and stability.*
onus (n)	any (disliked) chore, necessity, burden, or obligation *"The onus of proving this man's guilt lies with the prosecution," reiterated the judge.*
opprobrium (n)	public shame following bad conduct; disgrace, infamy *The politician's latest scandal brought on the opprobrium of his own party as well as that of the opposition.*
opulence (n)	wealth *Her extravagant jewelry matched the opulence of her clothing.*
oracular (adj)	as from the mouth of an oracle (a wise person, a seer), therefore solemn; sometimes, dictatorial *His oracular prediction of a coming flood proved to be untrue.*
orifice (n)	a mouth or opening *The mouth and nose are two orifices in the human body.*
ossify (v)	to become bone or like bone; to turn hardened and callous; set in one's ways, rigid *An elderly volunteer at the hospital told us she preferred activity and meeting people. "I don't want to ossify like so many old people do," she said.*
ostentatious (adj)	noticeably showy in display; pretentious *Having five cars seems ostentatious, Diane observed, when you consider that he can drive only one of them at a time.*
ostracize (v)	to exclude someone from society or from a group *The children had been taught not to ostracize anyone from their group; everyone could join their games.*
overt (adj)	easily seen because of being open to view; manifest *While she remained quiet about her personal life, her political views were quite overt.*
pacify (v)	to soothe or appease; to settle or calm down *One of the more difficult jobs a baby-sitter has is to pacify a fretful, crying infant.*
palatable (adj)	agreeing with your taste buds or your mind; appetizing, pleasing, agreeable *The food at that restaurant is more than palatable—it's delicious.*

pall (v)	to lessen in interest; to become boring; to grow weary because of overexposure *Perhaps I'm old and jaded, but TV has palled as far as I'm concerned, and I rarely watch it anymore.*
panacea (n)	a cure-all; the perfect remedy *There is no panacea for your condition; you'll need to eat right, exercise, and avoid stressful situations*
panache (n)	flair or flamboyance in style, behavior, speech, etc.; dash or verve *The actor was known for his quick wit and his panache.*
parable (n)	short tale pointing out a moral idea *The story wasn't really just about animals; it was a parable about an actual political situation.*
paradigm (n)	an extremely fine model or example of a type; archetype *Her work, well-researched and topical, was a paradigm of fine journalism.*
paradox (n)	a statement that appears to contradict itself but, even so, may be true; anything with apparent contradictions *Oscar Wilde, known for his ability to compose a memorable paradox, wrote: One's real life is so often the life that one does not lead.*
paragon (n)	a model, or anything that is perfect; the ideal *After hearing repeatedly that our cousin Amy was a paragon of virtue, we lost all interest in meeting her.*
paraphrase (v)	to reword written material in your own way to aid understanding or clarity; a free translation *Please paraphrase the article so that we don't have to read the whole thing.*
pariah (n)	an outcast of society *Emma worried that she would be a pariah if she didn't wear the right brand of shirt to school.*
pastoral (adj)	of the country; rural, rustic, bucolic; also referring to a member of the clergy and his or her job *The paintings depict beautiful pastoral settings that remind me of my childhood on the farm.*
patent (n)	referring to legal claim (as a patent on an invention)
patently (adv)	evidently; obviously *It is patently clear that I don't want to be disturbed, since I've locked my door and posted a Keep Away sign.*
pathos (n)	stirrings of pity; poignancy *Some clowns stir feelings of pathos rather than hilarity.*

paucity (n)	lack or scarcity; dearth *The paucity of volunteers meant that the soup kitchen was in danger of closing down.*
peccadillo (n)	a minor fault or flaw; small offense *It wasn't each peccadillo of his that I minded; it was the fact that there were so many of them.*
pedant (n)	someone who shows off his knowledge; a nitpicking type *In college, where students can often choose their professors, pedants may find their classrooms rather empty.*
pejorative (adj)	making something worse; disparaging (as *pejorative remarks*) *Receiving a term paper marked in red with only pejorative comments makes the writer less willing to write the next paper.*
perceptive (adj)	observant and aware; keenly discerning *Many of the student papers made interesting observations, but this one is even more perceptive than the others.*
peremptory (adj)	not allowing contradiction; showing need or urgency; haughty, masterful, dictatorial, autocratic *With a peremptory wave of his hand, the coach called all of the team into his office for a meeting.*
perfidy (n)	faithlessness, disloyalty, treachery *The double agent was punished for his perfidy.*
perfunctory (adj)	mechanical or routine, therefore not careful; without enthusiasm; apathetic *We could tell by his perfunctory nod that he did not wish to renew our acquaintance.*
pernicious (adj)	very destructive, even deadly; deleterious, noxious, baneful *The pernicious mushroom looked innocent enough, but if eaten it could be deadly.*
perquisite (n)	an extra, other than salary, that may accompany a job; special privilege; now called perks *The best perquisite I have in my job, other than my big office window, is the freedom to set my own hours.*
perspicacious (adj)	acutely shrewd or keen in understanding and perception, discerning *We think of the owl as a wise, perspicacious bird, one of many stereotypes in the animal world.*
pertinacity (n)	a stubborn persistence, sticking with ideas or purposes; obstinacy *Watching a well-trained Labrador retriever at work, I had to admire his pertinacity as he repeatedly located birds.*
perturb (v)	to bother greatly or annoy; to disquiet, discompose *Your shrill voice perturbs me; please go talk to someone else.*

pervade (v)	to become part of something else; to permeate (as *smoke pervaded the air*) *An air of expectation and holiday spirits pervaded the halls of our school the week before vacation.*
petulant (adj)	ill-humored and peevish; occasionally rude and ill-mannered *As she is normally warm and polite, her petulant reply to my question caught me off guard.*
philanthropy (n)	monetary or volunteer promotion of mankind's welfare; generous giving of self or resources *Your generous acts of philanthropy are greatly appreciated by the institutions to which you have donated money.*
phlegmatic (adj)	sluggish, slow, showing little emotion; impassive, stolid *My uncle's workhorses were phlegmatic types, plodding through the long day's routine without resistance.*
placate (v)	to calm, appease, particularly by offering to be good or to do a favor for someone *It's not always easy to placate an angry toddler with a toy.*
platitude (n)	an old, stale comment lacking originality or freshness; banality, trite remark *Guest speakers who mouth platitudes usually aren't invited to speak again.*
plausible (adj)	superficially believable, whether actually true or not *That story is barely plausible; next time make up one that is slightly more realistic.*
plebeian (adj, n)	concerning the common folk or masses (often used in a derogatory way); *Only somebody snobbish would call your taste plebeian.*
plethora (n)	a vast amount; great excess *Our neighboring physician owns a plethora of books on tropical diseases, which he lent me as references for my term paper on malaria.*
poignant (adj)	profoundly affecting feelings; highly emotional in effect; piercing *We hadn't expected to be touched by the story, but in fact it was extremely poignant.*
portly (adj)	round in shape, but not grossly fat; also dignified in manner *The portly gray cat enjoyed licking the inside of a tuna can.*
posthumous (adj)	occurring after death (as *posthumously published manuscripts*) *The government awarded several soldiers posthumous medals; the families of the men received the awards.*
postulate (n)	an axiom or assumed truth; a hypothesis, presupposition
postulate (v)	to accept as truth or to offer as truth; to presume *The thieves were first thought to be in the city, but now we're postulating that they escaped.*

potent (adj)   possessing strength or power; effective (as *a potent remedy*)
These medicines have been around so long that I doubt if they're still potent.

pragmatic (adj)   useful and practical; down-to-earth, sometimes excluding artistic or intellectual endeavors
We need to forget the elaborate plans we had and figure out a quick, pragmatic solution to this problem.

precarious (adj)   subject to chance or circumstances beyond control, therefore risky or hazardous
The road, which wound around a mountain, was particularly precarious when covered with snow.

precedent (n)   something occurring before that may serve as a model for subsequent, similar acts; antecedent
Before sentencing the convicted offender, the judge considered precedents set by similar cases in her state.

precipitate (adj)   unusually (maybe unwisely) fast; headlong, impetuous
precipitate (v)   to bring about in an abrupt manner; to fall suddenly or move unexpectedly
The strike precipitated changes in the working conditions of the transit workers.

preclude (v)   to make impossible or ineffectual by planning or acting in advance; to forestall, hinder, avert, prevent
Hoping to preclude any chance of failure when he folded his first parachute, Jesse memorized every step of the procedure until he thought he could fold a chute in his sleep.

precocious (adj)   having unusually early mental development
The precocious child could speak three languages by the time he was eight years old.

predatory (adj)   of plundering and preying
A predatory animal may stalk its prey by following a scent trail.

predilection (n)   positive feelings or opinion held beforehand; natural preference, prejudice
I have a predilection for Mexican food, whereas you prefer Japanese food.

prelude (n)   introduction to the main work, performance, or musical movement
The first two acts of the play were a mere prelude to the dramatic events of the third act.

prerogative (n)   special right or privilege
Off-campus housing is the prerogative of juniors and seniors.

presumptuous (adj)   presuming or assuming too much in an overbearing way; overweening, overstepping
If you assume that I will hire you for this position just because your aunt owns the company, you are being presumptuous.

prevaricate (v)   to stray from the truth; to lie or equivocate
Please don't prevaricate; I can always tell when you're not telling the truth.

probity (n)   sticking to noble ideals; uprightness
The mayor was long respected for her probity in the face of government corruption.

proclivity (n)   natural inclination or tendency toward; inherent leaning toward something objectionable
The proclivity of these mountain roads to turn icy every winter keeps most tourists away.

procrastinate (v)   to put off or delay until another time
If I procrastinate for too long, I won't have time to finish my project.

prodigious (adj)   inspiring awe; extremely large; enormous, monstrous
We had to cook an enormous meal in order to satisfy the prodigious appetites of our guests.

profess (v)   to declare or affirm (as *to profess faith in a religion*); also to pretend, to feign
Hoping to impress people, he frequently professed interest in their hobbies even if he'd never tried them.

proficient (adj)   skillful and advanced in knowledge, ability, performance; adept
You will have to practice hard to become proficient on the piano.

prolific (adj)   extremely fruitful or productive; fertile, fecund
Flannery O'Connor was not as prolific as some writers who turn out reams of material, but her stories are gems that live on after her early and tragic death.

propensity (n)   distinct, and sometimes strong, natural tendency or inclination; leaning
Some animals have a propensity for water; others prefer land.

propinquity (n)   proximity or nearness of relationship; contiguity
The propinquity of China to Japan has led to some interesting comparisons in cultures, as well as to contrasts worth noting.

propitiate (v)   to get into someone's good graces or to earn someone's goodwill; to appease, to gain favor; also propitious (adj), favorable, auspicious, of good omen
In ancient Greece and Rome, small and large animals were sacrificed to propitiate the gods.

propriety (n)   what is proper or customary; decorum; polite manners
In public she was the picture of propriety, but in private she had terrible manners and spoke coarsely.

prosaic (adj) of facts, therefore not imaginative or original; everyday, ordinary; also dull, banal
Josie's account of our trip to Mexico was a carefully prosaic recital tailored for our grandmother, who would have been appalled by some of our adventures there.

proscribe (v) to outlaw, forbid, prohibit
The school strictly proscribed behaviors that it considered unfitting for its students.

protuberant (adj) swelling or bulging out; obtrusive
The tree had one protuberant branch that threatened to break off in a strong storm.

provident (adj) providing for times ahead; saving, thrifty; prudent, frugal
The women, predicting hard times ahead, hoped their provident habits would see them through difficulty.

provoke (v) to stir up, spark; to pique
The advertisement, which depicted violence, provoked a great deal of controversy.

prowess (n) unusual skill or ability; military bravery and skills
Your prowess as a basketball player is impressive.

pseudonym (n) a pen name; any assumed name
Embarrassed about the contents of the article he had written, he considered using a pseudonym to hide his true identity.

puerile (adj) juvenile or immature; silly, inane
The assembly speaker bored all of us with his puerile remarks, which were an insult to our intelligence.

pugnacious (adj) spoiling for a fight; combative, belligerent, truculent
Some breeds of dogs are believed to be pugnacious, when in fact they are quiet friendly.

punctilious (adj) precise (or careful) about observing customs and rules; conventional, scrupulously exact
Julia was punctilious about following her daily routine, and any deviation from it upset her greatly.

pungent (adj) extremely painful or poignant (said of odors, tastes, or words); biting (of remarks); apropos or fitting (as pungent lines in a play); acrid, caustic
The pungent smell in the refrigerator let us know it was time to clean out the old food.

purge (n) an elimination

purge (v) to cleanse or rid yourself of something unwanted; to eliminate or free
With difficulty, he purged himself of his prejudices and started learning the truth about other people.

purport (n)	meaning that is open or suggested; the substance, gist, import
purport (v)	to appear to be something; to profess, intend *While you purport to be listening to me, I know that you're really watching television.*
pusillanimous (adj)	very timid, cowardly; lacking forcefulness *His pusillanimous argument was no match for the expert debater.*
quaff (v)	to take a long, deep drink *They clinked glasses, and then they quaffed their sodas.*
quell (v)	to put down completely or overwhelm (as quell an insurrection); to crush, squash; also to pacify or soothe *Military troops were ordered to quell the riot.*
querulous (adj)	complaining, faultfinding, and fretful (usually applied to tone of voice); petulant, captious *Querulous by nature, the ballet master seldom praised his students but instead complained about their performances.*
quiescent (adj)	resting, quiet; giving no trouble; inactive *Normally quiescent, Mount Saint Helens erupted violently and caught many area residents off guard.*
quietus (n)	permanent settlement (as of an obligation); end of any activity (as in death); anything that quiets or holds down in a repressive manner *The president's statement put the quietus on all rumors about her impending resignation.*
quintessence (n)	the core of a thing in its purest state; its essential part; also the model or typical example *"This painting," the art teacher explained, "represents the quintessence of cubist art."*
quizzical (adj)	teasing, yet often questioning at the same time; puzzled, yet with humor *I didn't say a word, but my quizzical expression betrayed my disbelief.*
rabid (adj)	incredibly furious; pursuing at length some opinion or interest; also referring to the disease rabies *She was rabid in her enthusiasm for the arts, speaking for hours about music and dance.*
raconteur (n)	a fine storyteller *Oscar Wilde, known for his plays, was also in demand as a gifted raconteur around the turn of the century.*
ramifications (n)	offshoots or outgrowths; also the implications or consequences (as of an act) *We need to consider all the ramifications of your problem before we can decide how to solve it.*

rancid (adj)   smelling or tasting strong, perhaps spoiled; malodorous and offensive to taste or smell
The odor of rancid fat permeated the entire restaurant.

rancor (n)   enmity or hatred built up over time; bitterness
As he denounced the government, we could hear the rancor behind every word.

rant (v)   to denounce in an angry way or to rave against noisily; also to talk pretentiously, in a dominating manner
When someone rants at length about a subject, I find myself ignoring the actual words and watching the display instead.

rapport (n)   a closeness (usually positive) of beliefs, interests; a good relationship of understanding and sympathy
The team had an unusually good rapport, which helped them to work together even under the most trying circumstances.

rational (adj)   open to logical reason or being reasonable; of sane mind
While the jewels seem to have vanished into thin air, there must be a more rational explanation for their disappearance.

raucous (adj)   sounding annoyingly loud or disagreeable; disorderly in a noisy way
Fans of Western movies revel in the raucous barroom brawls featuring hurled chairs, broken mirrors, and random gunshots.

ravenous (adj)   extremely hungry, for food or other satisfaction
"My goal is to develop ravenous readers," the librarian said with a smile.

raze (v)   to destroy totally, right down to the ground; demolish
Crowds of curious onlookers gathered to watch as a professional wrecking crew razed the old Paramount Theatre.

rebuttal (n)   denial or opposition to an argument; refutation; disproving response
Our debate team was demoralized by the strong rebuttal of their opponents at the state debate contest.

recalcitrant (adj)   tough to manage or control; strongly against authority; unruly, refractory
Cancer, if widespread, is a stubbornly recalcitrant disease.

recant (v)   to renounce (an opinion, belief, position); to confess error or wrongdoing
Although my opinion is unpopular, I refuse to recant it.

recapitulate (v)   to recap or restate the main points in discussions, papers, proposals, etc.
Before we continue, let's recapitulate our reasons for reading this book so that we keep our main goals in mind.

reciprocal (adj)   complementary, evident on both sides; often mutually beneficial
Reciprocal trade agreements are often canceled when two countries differ over foreign policy.

recluse (n)   anyone who lives mostly alone, or mainly secluded from others; a hermit
Thoreau lived as a recluse at Walden Pond in order to think about what he believed and why.

recollect (v)   to call back to mind in remembrance
Try, if you can, to recollect the events that led up to the accident.

redoubtable (adj)   inspiring fear or awe or both; formidable
William the Conqueror landed in England with a redoubtable force that won him control of the lands he coveted.

refute (v)   to show as wrong by giving evidence to the contrary; to disprove, rebut; to deny
She had no difficulty refuting the argument, which was full of holes.

relegate (v)   to put away or aside; to classify in a definite place or position by rank; to commit
The teddy bear, once our favorite childhood toy, was relegated to the back of a shelf.

relevant (adj)   important, significant (to whatever is being considered)
The facts have already been discussed; any other information is not relevant to the case.

remiss (adj)   failing to give care or attention, therefore negligent or neglectful; careless, lax
We'd be remiss in our duty if we didn't finish the job we agreed to do.

remonstrate (v)   to speak out strongly against something; to object or expostulate with feeling
Before he turned me loose with his car, Dad remonstrated at length about the price of cars, the dangers of driving, and the many worries parents have when kids begin to drive.

remorse (n)   an uneasy feeling derived from real or imagined guilt; self-reproach or regret
The criminal did not deny his behavior, and he showed no remorse for the pain he had caused.

remuneration (n)   payment for goods or services; recompense
I'll take the job if the remuneration is generous.

reprehensible (adj)   earning disapproval or blame; blameworthy
Your behavior is reprehensible and sets a bad example for everyone who observes it.

reprisal (n)   retaliation for wrongs suffered; taking something back; a reaction to another's behavior causing you to act (usually in a negative way)
Any action taken against us will be met with swift reprisal.

requisite (adj)   required, essential
As soon as all the requisite forms have been filled out, we will process your application.

rescind (v)	to cancel, annul (as *rescind a command*); to repeal or call back *If you continue to lose library books, we will rescind your right to borrow them.*
resonant (adj)	echoing, as sound; vibrating (as rich sound) *The sound of the French horn was rich and resonant in the concert hall.*
resourceful (adj)	showing intelligence and skill at meeting situations and dealing with them; capable *Although all of the books on his paper topic had been checked out of the library, Jose was resourceful enough to find alternative sources.*
respite (n)	a time of relief; a pause, rest from activity, lull *The eye of the storm provided respite from the pounding rain and heavy winds.*
reticent (adj)	not talkative by nature; naturally silent or reserved; also simple and restrained in manner *Because Angie was normally reticent, we were surprised when she volunteered to make a speech for our organization.*
retribution (n)	the payment of either reward or punishment *In retribution for the capture of one of their ships, the pirate band attacked and sank two valuable cargo ships.*
revere (v)	to respect and honor; venerate, worship *The leader was revered far and wide for his intelligence and his commitment to justice.*
rhetoric (n)	the skill of fine, meaningful speaking and writing; also pompous and hypocritical language; discourse *The art of rhetoric begins with a strong idea and good grammar.*
ribald (adj)	offensive, often because of crudeness (language or behavior); indecent or coarse (as ribald humor) *The program's humor was too ribald for network television.*
rococo (adj)	referring to elaborately detailed artistic or musical style; intricately ornate *The old painting was dull when compared to its gilt, rococo frame, which drew our immediate attention.*
rostrum (n)	a raised dais, stage, or platform for speaking or performing *The speaker on the rostrum is the man who spoke to us last year about animals that are nearly extinct.*
rotund (adj)	referring to any sound with notable rhythm or richness (as *a rotund phrase*); plump or chubby of body *He had grown a little bit grayer and more rotund, but all in all, he hadn't changed much since the last time I'd seen him.*
rue (n)	regret or sorrow

rue (v)   to regret exceedingly; to feel remorse or sorrow
You will rue the day you insulted me.

ruse (n)   a clever trick or deception; subterfuge
The students acted as though they were interested in their teacher's war stories, but it was merely a ruse to distract him from beginning the day's lesson.

sacrilegious (adj)   lack of deference, respect, or reverence for anything sacred or special
Carlton refused to add blueberries to cornbread, claiming that any deviation from the standard recipe was sacrilegious.

sagacity (n)   wisdom and discernment; keen perception, shrewdness
We admired our grandmother's sagacity and often asked for her advice and opinions.

salient (adj)   very noticeable or conspicuous; prominent
While he had many good qualities, his most salient feature was his honesty.

salubrious (adj)   giving a feeling of well-being or aiding in well-being; favorable to health; also salutary (adj), promoting good health
Members of the Polar Bear Club have tried to convince me that it's salubrious to plunge into icy winter waters, but I'm skeptical.

sanguine (adj)   high-colored (as of complexion); cheerful, confident
Despite the difficulty of the test, Janice emerged from the classroom appearing quite sanguine.

satiate (v)   to give complete satisfaction; surfeit
I was so hungry that it took three plates of food to satiate me.

scathing (adj)   harsh or severe to an extreme; strongly critical
Carlos wrote a scathing editorial for our school newspaper attacking those who pollute our local streams and waterways.

scourge (v)   to lash, whip, or flog; to make miserable

scourge (n)   any instrument—person or thing—used to punish; whip or lash; affliction
These rats are a scourge upon the city.

scrupulous (adj)   being punctilious and precisely correct; showing painstaking care and adherence to scruples or morals
I paid scrupulous attention to the recipe, but just look at this disaster of a cake!

sedulous (adj)   done with care and diligence; particular
Every day, several times a day, our cat washes his fur and paws with sedulous attention.

senile (adj)   showing advanced age or mental deterioration that may accompany old age
Some memory loss is normal with aging and not a sign that a person is completely senile.

serendipity (n) the finding of luck or good fortune when you're not even looking for it
Finding that parking space right in front of the museum was sheer serendipity.

serene (adj) calm, tranquil, peaceful; free from stress
In order to feel more serene, many people practice yoga or meditation.

servile (adj) subservient (as a slave or menial worker); overly submissive in an off-putting way
Sooner or later, people kept in a servile position will rebel.

shibboleth (n) a commonly accepted word or phrase that has become a byword or slogan; also old doctrine or beliefs of a group
The shibboleths of simpler times seem generally inadequate to the problems of today.

simulate (v) to approximate; to appear to be like something else in a superficial way; to assume or feign
"We can simulate flying conditions here on the ground in our trainer," the flying instructor told his class.

sinecure (n) any job or position that yields an income but demands little work, maybe none at all
Many of the higher-level jobs were sinecures passed down from one party member to another.

sinuous (adj) showing flexibility in the form of undulating, wavy motion
The sinuous movement of the snake propelled it through the desert sand.

skeptic (n) someone inclined to doubt or suspend judgment, to be disbelieving, uncertain, or frankly critical
Because Joe is a skeptic, he believes no story without proof of its validity.

slavish (adj) behaving as a slave; servile; also reproducing exactly in a manner lacking freshness or originality, therefore imitative
My earliest attempts at drawing cartoons were slavish imitations of my favorite cartoonists, but I later developed my own style.

slovenly (adj) sloppy and unkempt (in appearance); lazy and haphazard (in workmanship)
The store manager lectured his employees on the importance of neatness, warning them that a slovenly appearance was cause for dismissal.

solicitous (adj) concerned or worried; anxious; showing thoughtfulness or care; also very careful, meticulous
The salesperson was overly solicitous, plying us with samples when we wanted only to browse.

somber (adj) of dark or gloomy aspect; sober or grave in manner
What had been merely an overcast sky turned somber and forbidding as the storm approached our city.

sophisticated (adj) removed from original, natural simplicity, therefore complex (as *sophisticated machinery*); of persons, knowledgeable and often polished (mentally or socially); worldly, informed, highly aware
Our school band has progressed to several sophisticated musical arrangements, which we're practicing for the winter concert.

specious (adj) appearing legitimate on the surface but lacking truth or validity; plausible, but false underneath
Our debate coach warned us to be on the lookout for specious reasoning so that our rebuttal could poke holes in the argument of the opposition.

spectral (adj) referring to a specter or ghost; ghostly; also of a spectrum
In the dimness of nighttime hospital corridors, patients flapping down the halls in white gowns assume a spectral appearance.

speculate (v) to think or wonder about something; to guess or suppose; also to risk in business, hoping for profit
In current events class, we were asked to speculate on the future of the world twenty-five years from now.

splenetic (adj) easily irritated and grouchy; ill-tempered, spiteful
Normally sweet and kind, she had a splenetic side that occasionally showed itself.

sporadic (adj) not regular or predictable; infrequent, random
The snowfall was sporadic, not steady as had been predicted, so there was little accumulation.

spurious (adj) false or fake, though outwardly legitimate; forged (as spurious credentials)
After a famous millionaire died, several people submitted spurious inheritance claims that were easily disproved.

squalor (n) dirt, neglect, wretched conditions
After weeks of not cleaning my bathroom, I was overcome by the squalor and began scrubbing.

squander (v) to use in a silly or extravagant way; to waste or dissipate
It's better to save your money for when you really need it than to squander it.

stagnate (v) to be without movement or inactive; to be out of use, therefore stale
The green scum over the top of the pond indicated that the water had stagnated and was unsafe to drink.

static (adj) lacking change or movement; being quiet, at rest (as *a static pattern*); fixed or stationary; of electronic noise, as radio

static (n) colloquially: negative noises or disagreement
The population in our town has remained relatively static for a decade but now shows signs of declining.

status (n) the state or condition of someone or something; rank relative to others; a position in any hierarchy; situation
My status at the office increased tremendously when I brought in a box of doughnuts for my coworkers.

strident (adj) unpleasantly harsh; getting attention through persistence and loudness
The pleasure of public television is twofold: intelligent programming combined with the absence of strident commercials.

stringent (adj) showing strict and rigid compliance with accepted standards; also lacking money or credit
In spite of the rather stringent rules at camp, we enjoyed the activities, the other campers, and the counselors.

stupefy (v) to astonish or astound; to cause someone to be slow-witted or insensible
Stupefied by the number of items required for a lengthy canoe trip, I gritted my teeth and set about collecting the supplies.

subsistence (n) minimal standard of living; the necessities of existing or the minimum required to permit life; the source that allows life to exist
"We're managing a bare subsistence on this poor land," admitted the farmer, "but we plan to stick it out and maybe buy better acreage next year."

succinct (adj) brief and to the point; concise, pithy, terse, economical (word use)
Some words defy succinct definition and require a fairly lengthy explanation.

succulent (adj) juicy and very appealing to the taste
He finished every last succulent morsel in his dish.

sully (v) to make less appealing; to soil or defile (usually refers to persons' names, reputations, standings in the community)
Try not to sully your clothing before the photographer arrives to take the class picture.

supercilious (adj) excessively proud; disdainfully superior
The actress threw a brief, supercilious glance at her audience, then disappeared into her dressing room.

superficial (adj) on the surface (as a superficial cut); interested mainly in appearances, hence shallow in nature
Although we had important issues to debate, our conversation remained politely superficial.

surfeit (v) to feed too much; to cloy, satiate

surfeit (n) an extra amount or excess; a kind of gluttony regarding food and drink; the revulsion brought on by overindulgence
A surfeit of peaches this year means that their price will go down.

surpass (v)   to reach beyond or exceed expectations; to overstep
We didn't just reach our goal; to our delight, we surpassed it.

surreptitious (adj)   in a secretive, underhanded, or deceptive way; clandestine
The man next to me on the subway read my newspaper over my shoulder in a surreptitious manner.

tacit (adj)   understood or suggested but not actually stated
We had a tacit agreement that whoever woke up first would fix breakfast.

taciturn (adj)   untalkative by nature; silent, reticent
A naturally taciturn man, our father said little and encouraged us to do likewise.

tactile (adj)   felt, touchable; tangible
Learning how to read Braille, which uses a series of raised dots for letters, is a tactile skill taught in schools for the blind.

talisman (n)   a special, meaningful object thought to be lucky; an amulet
I keep this coin in my pocket as a talisman.

tautology (n)   needless repetition of words or ideas; redundancy
She tried to win the argument using tautology, but her opponent demanded that she back up her statement with evidence.

tedious (adj)   going on at length, often boring; tiresome
This book is particularly tedious in its descriptions, which go on for pages at a time.

temerity (n)   unwise boldness; reckless or rash behavior in the face of danger; effrontery
Do you have the temerity to tell me that you stayed out all night instead of writing your term paper?

tenet (n)   a basic belief or truth for a group of people; doctrine
One of the basic tenets of their religion is donating part of their income to charity.

tentative (adj)   incomplete or lacking development; hesitant or uncertain (as a tentative smile)
I dipped my toe tentatively in the water, debating whether or not to go swimming.

tenuous (adj)   slim or slender; flimsy; weak, barely perceptible
My grasp of the new algebra material was so tenuous I stayed after school for help.

terse (adj)   stripped of all but the essentials; concise, succinct (said of written or spoken words)
Willa had hoped for a comment about her term paper, but all she received was a letter grade—a terse response to all her hard work.

theology (n) religion and its accompanying theory; a set body of beliefs; literally, study of god

Many aspects of Russian and Greek Orthodox theology are illuminated by various icons, small paintings of exquisite beauty and deep significance.

thwart (v) to foil, baffle, or frustrate (someone's attempts)

Please don't thwart my efforts to keep the house neat.

tolerance (n) ability to withstand adverse conditions; understanding or acknowledgment of another's viewpoint or beliefs

At first we did not like our new neighbors, but as we got to know them better we had more tolerance for them.

tome (n) usually refers to a large volume or set of volumes; a weighty book, very scholarly or heavy or both

This enormous dictionary is a useful tome, but difficult to carry from place to place.

torpid (adj) motionless or lacking feeling (as numb); slow or sluggish in action; lethargic

The sloth is a torpid animal whose movements are very slow and deliberate.

toxic (adj) poisonous (as snake's venom may be toxic)

Across the country, we are building plants to treat toxic wastes safely in response to citizens' demands.

tractable (adj) obedient and docile; easy to teach, train, control

Killer whales, once presumed dangerous, are now known as tractable mammals.

transcend (v) to go above or beyond the known or accepted limits; to exceed expectations

While we expected the performance to be a good one, it transcended all of our expectations.

transient (adj) of extremely brief duration; short-lived, transitory, fleeting, ephemeral, evanescent

It's important to identify which problems are transient and which will have lasting effects.

trenchant (adj) highly effective and well-spoken, hence keenly perceptive; penetrating, even biting or caustic (of comments); incisive

Many times Mark Twain abandoned his lighter satire for the trenchant commentary of a bitterly disappointed idealist.

trepidation (n) fear, worry, or apprehension

We huddled behind the door, listening with trepidation to the approaching footsteps.

trite (adj)	worn-out and ineffective from overuse; hackneyed, banal, stale (applies to expressions and words) *The story would have been interesting enough if it weren't for the trite ending.*
truculent (adj)	showing a belligerent or cruel attitude; harsh or destructive *Normally a mild-tempered child, he became rather truculent when he was hungry.*
truncate (v)	to cut short; curtail *Due to the drought, the trees were thin and truncated.*
tumid (adj)	swollen or protuberant; enlarged, bulging; also bombastic or wordy, verbose (said of prose) *Bed rest proved a miserable experience for Ken, whose body felt tumid and sluggish from enforced idleness.*
turgid (adj)	distended by swelling; also ornate or verbose in language use; tumid *Readers fond of Hemingway's clean, lucid style may dislike authors of more turgid prose.*
ubiquitous (adj)	being everywhere at once; widespread *It seems that advertisements are ubiquitous, showing up on t-shirts, billboards, and television.*
unbridled (adj)	without restraint or confinement; uncontrolled *A temper tantrum is a display of unbridled rage.*
undulate (v)	to move in a wavy, rhythmic motion; to move sinuously; to swing *The Snake River undulates for a thousand miles through the Northwest from Idaho to Washington.*
unremitting (adj)	without pause or letting up; constant, incessant *Unremitting attention to detail is one mark of a thorough laboratory scientist.*
untenable (adj)	not possible to defend or uphold (as an untenable position) *"We have an untenable location in this remote outpost," reported the army captain, "and we must have additional troops."*
upbraid (v)	to scold in a severe manner; to criticize harshly for faults *The angry basketball coach upbraided his team after the game, listing each of the errors that had led to their defeat.*
usurp (v)	to take (a position or authority) forcefully and often without the right to do so *The army quickly usurped power over the small country.*
usury (n)	lending money at abnormally high (or illegal) interest rates *Laws against usury are intended to prevent people from charging outrageously high interest on loans.*

vacillate (v)
to move or sway back and forth; to fluctuate; to change from one opinion to another; also to hesitate
Dad vacillated from one day to the next, first saying we could go with the youth group on a canoe trip, then saying no.

vacuous (adj)
without content, empty; minus ideas or intelligence (as looks, words, the mind)
Beneath his good looks, he was completely vacuous.

vagary (n)
a whimsical, erratic, or unexpected occurrence or idea; caprice
Let's leave as little as possible to the vagaries of chance, and plan us well as we can.

validate (v)
to declare or make legally true or valid; to authenticate; to support, corroborate, affirm
Before Ralph could board his flight for Holland, he had to have his passport validated by airport officials.

vanguard (n)
the forward or first army troops; any forerunner
Jeb found himself almost paralyzed with fear in the vanguard of the troops that advanced into enemy territory.

vehement (adj)
fervent or strongly emotional; impassioned
Adam's vehement pleas to go along on our canoe trip were to no avail.

venerate (v)
to revere or admire deeply; to worship
The venerated elders gave advice to the younger members of their community.

veracity (n)
truthfulness or accuracy; honesty
A boy in our group professed to be an expert canoeist, but one look at his canoeing form made us doubt his veracity.

verbatim (adv)
repeated word for word, exactly
Our canoeing leader made us repeat verbatim the description of our first stop until he was sure everyone knew where to meet for that first lunch.

verbose (adj)
using more words than necessary; wordy
The writing in this story is rather verbose; I prefer cleaner, less wordy prose.

verify (v)
to confirm or make certain, leaving no doubt; to establish in a definite way
I think those figures are correct, but I will check my records to verify them.

vernal (adj)
of the springtime; also fresh, like spring; youthful
People rave about the beauty of the trees in the autumn, but I think the vernal foliage, too, is a sight to behold.

vestige (n)
the barest trace or amount
You know, I haven't a vestige of interest in what you're saying.

vicarious (adj)   felt or experienced through another person; in place of someone or something
Myra's description of her vacation to the mountains was so vivid that I felt like I experienced the trip vicariously.

vicissitudes (n)   changeability; mutability; movement or change in circumstances; fluctuations or difficulties
It is nearly impossible to plan for all the vicissitudes of life.

vilify (v)   to slander, malign, defame, or reduce someone's name or community standing
The candidate decided to focus on the issues of the election rather than on vilifying her opponent.

vindicate (v)   to free, clear of blame; to absolve, exonerate, or exculpate; to prove right, to justify
I know that it looks as though I am guilty, but when all of the facts come out I will be vindicated.

vindictive (adj)   seeking revenge; spiteful
Your vindictive behavior only makes you seem more guilty.

virtuoso (n)   any highly skilled person in the arts and sciences
To everyone's surprise, he turned out to be an absolute virtuoso on the guitar.

virulent (adj)   with fast, powerful, and often fatal progress (as a virulent disease); highly poisonous; noted for malignancy or evil intent
The disease, once a virulent threat to the community, has been virtually wiped out through vaccinations.

visage (n)   the appearance (often the face) of a person, animal, or place; aspect
We imaged we saw visages in the clouds as we stared up at them.

viscera (n)   the vital organs of the body; the guts
The athlete wore padding to prevent himself from injuring his viscera.

viscous (adj)   slow-flowing, like heavy oil, honey, or syrup
That viscous liquid leaking from your car is oil.

vitiate (v)   to cause imperfections or errors, sometimes by adding a substance that harms; to lower in status (esp. moral status); to debase or cause to lack effectiveness
The contamination vitiated the subject of the experiment, so we had to throw out what we'd done and start over.

vitriolic (adj)   of words or emotions akin to the biting effect of vitriol (a sulfate), therefore caustic, corrosive
Anna's vitriolic speech angrily decried everything that she felt was wrong with our town government.

vociferous (adj)
loudly vocal, and usually insistent; clamorous, boisterous
The speech was met with vociferous support from the crowd.

volatile (adj)
easily triggered or exploded (as a volatile chemical); quick to express emotion; explosive, changeable; easy to set off
We wanted a fireworks display for the Fourth of July but were told that all volatile and most flammable materials were prohibited in the woods.

voluble (adj)
extremely talkative; loquacious, garrulous, glib, fluent
For someone who was usually so voluble, he said very little last night.

voracious (adj)
incredibly hungry; ravenous; also showing a large appetite
By noon we were voracious, since we'd worked for five hours on almost no breakfast.

votary (n)
a devout admirer, a devotee; someone who worships, venerates; a believer, advocate, enthusiast
"I am a true votary of the wilderness," Larry said, as he gazed appreciatively at the vast pine woods.

vulnerable (adj)
open to harm or physical or emotional hurt; assailable, indefensible
The open fields were vulnerable to the strong winds that swept through them unchecked by trees.

wan (adj)
pale in appearance or sickly; also weak or feeble; faint, slight
The medical students looked wan after witnessing their first autopsy.

wane (v)
to dwindle or grow less (as *the moon wanes*); to dim, be less noticeable; to decline in power or influence
As the day wore on, the winds, which had been strong in the morning, began to wane.

wary (adj)
being aware and cautious regarding danger; prudent
You should be wary when somebody makes a promise that sounds too good to be true.

willful (adj)
showing a strong will to do as you like; headstrong, intentional; also stubborn, unruly
Paddling back upstream, we had to cope with a willful canoe that wanted to turn and head downstream.

winsome (adj)
very appealing and winning of personality; cheerful, in a childlike or innocent way; sweet
Several adults complimented the child's winsome personality.

wistful (adj)
showing much longing or desire; yearning; also sad, pensive, thoughtful
With a wistful look at the beautiful river and woods, Abby said she wished that our canoe trip could go on forever.

wizened (adj)
dried up, wrinkled, and shrunken; withered
The apple, once plump, had wizened with age.

Peterson's SAT Success

wont (n)	custom, use, habit
wont (adj)	used or accustomed; apt, inclined
	Robin did her grocery shopping on Thursday, as was her wont.
wraith (n)	a ghost or apparition of a person; shadow or vague human form
	It could have been a trick of the light, but we thought we saw a wraith flicker across the room.
wreak (v)	to inflict misery upon, punish, or avenge; to allow ill feelings free rein; to cause, bring about
	Those ghost stories wreaked havoc with my night's sleep.
wrest (v)	to bring about by forceful action or hard work; also to distort
	I had hoped to wrest a few hours of sleep from the night.
zealous (adj)	eager or determined in the pursuit of something; fervent, passionate
	My zealous efforts to finish the project finally paid off.
zephyr (n)	a typically gentle breeze, often from the west
	The zephyr cooled our brows and rustled the leaves in the trees as it drifted by.

Verbal Teaching Unit

How to Solve
Analogy Questions

Analogies are probably the most confusing-looking of the three types of verbal questions on the SAT. Don't worry, though. As strange as they may seem at first, analogy questions follow a specific logic that you'll learn in this section. Analogy questions test you on a combination of vocabulary and reasoning.

Analogies are word problems that require you to figure out the relationship between a pair of words and then identify another pair of words with that same relationship. That may sound complicated, but one of the basic rules of analogies is that the relationships are simple. In fact, there are several relationships that show up again and again on the test.

Analogies usually show up on the SAT in one set of 13 questions and another set of 6, for a total of 19 questions. That's about a quarter of your total verbal points. The first third of a set of analogies is the easiest. The second third is harder, and the last third is generally quite tricky.

TIMING TIP

Analogy questions will show up as 13 out of 35 questions in one 30-minute section and as 6 out of 30 questions in another. Your average time to solve each analogy question should be between 20 and 60 seconds. If you find yourself taking longer than a minute, move on.

STRATEGY OVERVIEW

Here's a typical easy-level analogy question.

FISH : SCHOOL ::

(A) whale : shark
(B) bird: sky
(C) mouse : mammal
(D) dog : pack
(E) bird : feather

The first thing you need to know is how to read an analogy question. Think of the colon (:) as the phrase "is to" and the double colon (::) as the word "as." The question then says,

FISH is to SCHOOL as

(A) whale is to shark
(B) bird is to sky
(C) mouse is to mammal
(D) dog is to pack
(E) bird is to feather

MAKING A LINK

Now you're ready to begin. You need to figure out the relationship, or link, between FISH and SCHOOL. The question pair—and therefore, the correct answer pair—always has a clear, specific link. To figure out the link, put both words in a sentence that specifically defines their relationship. In this case, you might try the following link: FISH are found in a SCHOOL.

Now you need to figure out which of the answer choices has the same relationship. Try putting each choice into your link.

Are whales found in a shark? No.

Are birds found in the sky? Yes—this could be an answer. Keep checking, though.

Are mice found in a mammal? No.

Are dogs found in a pack? Yes. Now there are two possible answers.

Are birds found in a feather? No.

When you have two possible answers, you need to move on to the next step of solving analogy questions: editing your link to make it more specific. Try this:

A group of FISH is called a SCHOOL

Are a group of birds called a sky? No.

Are a group of dogs called a pack? Yes. There's your correct answer.

SKILL DRILL: THINK OF A LINK

How would you link each of the following pairs?

mountain : chain

flammable : burn

plain : embellish

wood : sliver

eraser : clear

LINKS TO LOOK FOR

The same sorts of links show up regularly on SAT analogy questions. Here are some types of relationships you can expect to see on the test.

Link Type	Examples
Part of a category	SLEET is a type of PRECIPITATION. A CLOAK is a kind of GARMENT. A WAVE is a kind of GESTURE.
Part of a whole	A WEDGE is a piece of a PIE. A group of BIRDs is a FLOCK. A group of MOUNTAINS is called a CHAIN.
Degree	DRIZZLE is a smaller degree of POUR. FLOOD is a larger degree of TRICKLE. SCORCHING is a larger degree of WARM.
Trait or activity by definition	A BALM, by definition, SOOTHES. A MISER, by definition, HOARDs. A PREVARICATOR, by definition, LIES.
Lack by definition	A DROUGHT is a lack of WATER. Someone who is CRUDE lacks REFINEMENT. Something PALLID lacks COLOR.
Object and its function	A PEN is used to INSCRIBE. A SHED is used to STORE. A VEHICLE is used for TRANSPORTATION.
Person and his or her job	The job of a VENDOR is to SELL. The job of an ORACLE is to FORETELL. It is an AGENT's job to REPRESENT.
Usual location	A TRIAL takes place in a COURT. An ARENA is where a MATCH takes place. A FLOCK is found in a PASTURE.

SKILL DRILL: WHICH LINKS STINK?

Circle the word pairs with weak links.

grass : blade

costume : scary

snow : deep

burglar : steal

dislike : taste

itinerant : wander

STEPPING UP YOUR STRATEGY

Making a strong link between the question words is a crucial skill in solving analogies. But what happens when those words are tricky or downright unrecognizable?

Unusual Use

The SAT likes to use common words in uncommon ways. You might see an analogy question like this.

FLAG : STRENGTH ::

(A) infuriate : anger
(B) inspire : gall
(C) calm : boredom
(D) fail : attempt
(E) slip : footing

Your first thought when you see the word FLAG is probably the thing on a flagpole. There are two ways you can tell that you need to find an alternate meaning.

1. Parts of speech in the question pair and the answer choices always match. In other words, if the question pair compares a verb and a noun, so will all of the answer choices. And if all of the answer choices compare a verb and a noun, the question pair must, too.

2. There's no clear link between the noun FLAG and STRENGTH.

Think of a Link: Answers

Your links should be similar to these:

A group of *mountains* is called a *chain*.

Something *flammable*, by definition, *burns*.

Something *plain* is never *embellished*.

A small piece of *wood* is called a *sliver*.

The job of an *eraser* is to *clear*.

Turn it Around

Sometime it's a lot easier to make a link sentence if you reverse the order of the words in the question pair. That's fine—just remember to also reverse each answer choice as you test it.

You can tell from looking at the answer choices that FLAG has to be a verb. In fact, to FLAG is to weaken. Can you make a link now?

To FLAG is to lose STRENGTH.

Is to infuriate to lose anger? No.

Is to inspire to lose gall? No.

Is to calm to lose boredom? No.

Is to fail to lose attempt? No.

Is to slip to lose footing? Yes.

Weird Words

What if you're faced with one or even two question words that are completely foreign to you? Even when your vocabulary fails you, you can use strategy to narrow your answer choices.

PAREGORIC : ASSUAGE ::

(A) goal : achieve
(B) scale : measure
(C) balm : irritate
(D) flood : parch
(E) virus : infect

Let's say you don't recognize the question words. The next step is to take a look at the choices and see if you can eliminate any. You know that an SAT analogy will always have a clear, strong link. So you can eliminate any choices that have a weak link. You can also eliminate two or more answers with the same link, since there can't be more than one correct answer.

(A) A *goal* is something you may or may not *achieve*? Sounds weak. Eliminate it.
(B) A *scale* is something you use to *measure*? That works— it's an object and its function.
(C) A *balm* does the opposite of *irritate*? That's a possible link, too.
(D) A flood does the opposite of parch? Same link as choice (C). They can't both be right, so eliminate them.
(E) A *virus infects* a system. The words often go together, but it's hard to make a clear link between them.

Which Links Stink: Answers

The following are weak links:

costume: scary
snow: deep
taste: dislike

The best answer is choice (B). In fact, a PAREGORIC (medicine for pain) is something you use to ASSUAGE (soothe).

Even if you can only eliminate a couple of answers with weak links, you substantially increase your odds of correctly guessing.

Odd links

Sometimes, analogy questions will not have links that are similar to the most common ones. In fact, some question pairs even have what seems to be a weak link. Take a look at this question pair:

REMARK : ACERBIC ::

Looks like a weak link, one you'd cross out if you saw it as an answer choice. A REMARK may or may not be ACERBIC. But it's the question pair, so the words must have some kind of relationship. An ACERBIC REMARK is sharp or unpleasant. Take a look at your choices:

flavor : sour

behavior : acceptable

speech : oratory

dance : clumsy

rhetoric : dull

A REMARK that's sharp or unpleasant is ACERBIC, as a FLAVOR that is sharp or unpleasant is SOUR.

Think of this kind of link as a *transplanted idea*. It asks you to take the question pair and then place it in another situation: a remark that's sharp is acerbic. What if we were talking about something other than a remark? How would we describe that thing as sharp or unpleasant? The only choice that answers that question is choice (A).

WATCH OUT!

When you don't know the answer to an analogy question, it can be tempting to choose the answer with words that remind you of the question words. Remember that the correct answer has the same *relationship* as the question pair, not the same meaning. Often, a choice that is about the same subject as the question pair is a trap for the unwary test-taker. Not always, though. Don't automatically cross out any answer without testing it. The people who make the SAT like to throw in a little surprise now and then.

SUMMING UP

To solve analogy questions, follow these steps:

1. Create a link between the question pair.

2. Test each answer choice.

3. If necessary, edit your link to make it more specific.

PRACTICE SETS

Answers for the following practice sets can be found on page 455.

Analogy Practice Set I

1. METER : LENGTH ::

   (A) pound : weight
   (B) yard : stick
   (C) petal : flower
   (D) inch : mile
   (E) water : depth

2. RUTHLESS : PITY ::

   (A) merciful : kindness
   (B) ingenious : character
   (C) enamored : love
   (D) bewildered : comprehension
   (E) elderly : longevity

3. PHILOSOPHER : REASON ::

   (A) advocate : oppose
   (B) artist : dream
   (C) dancer : exercise
   (D) teacher : learn
   (E) speaker : orate

4. SCRIVENER : SCROLL ::

   (A) cartwright : tractor
   (B) sculptor : chisel
   (C) woodsman : forest
   (D) seamstress : garment
   (E) engraver : stamp

5. CHILD : MATURE ::

   (A) bud : burgeon
   (B) spine : flex
   (C) shrub : wither
   (D) stalk : support
   (E) youth : imitate

6. TORTUOUS : PATH ::

   (A) wretched : miscreant
   (B) worthless : solution
   (C) convoluted : prose
   (D) heinous : crime
   (E) ignominious : defeat

7. MENDICANT : WEALTHY ::

   (A) farmer : successful
   (B) expert : inept
   (C) strategist : masterful
   (D) soldier : mercenary
   (E) victor : courageous

8. EMOLLIENT : SOOTHE ::

   (A) glaze : finish
   (B) sheen : dull
   (C) hammer : secure
   (D) hinge : close
   (E) scaffold : cover

9. OBESE : HEAVY ::

   (A) distraught : sad
   (B) amused : bewildered
   (C) awake : asleep
   (D) pale : wan
   (E) intelligent : educated

10. TRITE : NOVELTY ::

    (A) opulent : wealth
    (B) new : interest
    (C) invisible : sight
    (D) trendy : future
    (E) torpid : energy

Analogy Practice Set II

1. BRANCH : TWIG ::

   (A) stem : flower
   (B) blade : knife
   (C) river : stream
   (D) sapling : bush
   (E) cave : rock

2. GRAM : WEIGHT ::

   (A) inch : length
   (B) pool : depth
   (C) circle : circumference
   (D) thermometer : temperature
   (E) ruler : height

3. ROSE : FLOWER ::

   (A) stem : thorn
   (B) elm : tree
   (C) tide : water
   (D) plant : shoot
   (E) dew : drop

4. GLADE : TREE ::

   (A) creek : water
   (B) blade : grass
   (C) mound : dirt
   (D) pass : mountain
   (E) paper : log

5. WAN : RUDDINESS ::

   (A) specific : guidelines
   (B) dour : gloom
   (C) vapid : depth
   (D) arid : sun
   (E) glass : clarity

6. MANNER : BRUSQUE ::

   (A) behavior : improved
   (B) clothing : ornate
   (C) comportment : stately
   (D) gait : hurried
   (E) speech : curt

7. ORACLE : FORESIGHT ::

   (A) sage : wisdom
   (B) pauper : wealth
   (C) neophyte : experience
   (D) athlete : speed
   (E) singer : talent

8. MUSEUM : DISPLAY ::

   (A) tier : soprano
   (B) theatre : performance
   (C) school : debate
   (D) hall : symphony
   (E) kitchen : table

9. FLAG : ENERGY ::

   (A) clog : sink
   (B) ail : illness
   (C) restore : health
   (D) wane : light
   (E) calm : nerves

10. MENDACIOUS : VERACITY ::

   (A) impaired : vision
   (B) inspired : direction
   (C) jaded : perspective
   (D) aged : longevity
   (E) conceited : humility

Analogy Practice Set III
Real SAT Questions

1. EXPOSITION : CLARIFY ::

   (A) rebuttal : humiliate
   (B) refutation : disprove
   (C) illumination : darken
   (D) allegation : verify
   (E) summary : end

2. PARODY : IMITATION ::

   (A) farce : laughter
   (B) caricature : likeness
   (C) mask : disguise
   (D) deviation : similarity
   (E) gem : embellishment

3. BULKY : VOLUME ::

   (A) straight : curvature
   (B) hollow : vastness
   (C) gouged : surface
   (D) hefty : weight
   (E) grisly : appearance

4. FORD : RIVER ::

   (A) basement : edifice
   (B) terminal : airport
   (C) dam : reservoir
   (D) crosswalk : road
   (E) gangplank : boat

5. PRECIPITATE : HASTE ::

   (A) withdrawn : interaction
   (B) preposterous : belief
   (C) vindictive : motive
   (D) hesitant : speed
   (E) overwrought : excitement

6. ASK : IMPORTUNE ::

   (A) begin : recommence
   (B) damage : restore
   (C) pursue : hound
   (D) misbehave : displease
   (E) stimulate : motivate

7. CONVALESCENCE : HEALTHY ::

   (A) contamination : purified
   (B) renovation : dilapidated
   (C) validation : unproven
   (D) isolation : uninhabited
   (E) reclamation : useful

8. BRUISE : SKIN ::

   (A) muscle : bone
   (B) smudge : blemish
   (C) rash : allergy
   (D) layer : veneer
   (E) stain : fabric

9. POISON : TOXIC ::

   (A) mixture : soluble
   (B) sugar : sweet
   (C) medicine : prescribed
   (D) milk : bottled
   (E) solid : liquid

10. POSTSCRIPT : LETTER ::

    (A) preamble : document
    (B) footnote : reference
    (C) epilogue : play
    (D) signature : name
    (E) index : page

How to Solve
Sentence Completion Questions

The sentence completion questions provide you with a sentence that has one or two blanks and five choices of words to complete the blanks. It's your job to pick the best answer, based on your knowledge of the vocabulary and your understanding of the sentence. Having a good vocabulary is one key to solving sentence completion questions. The other key is understanding the logic of the sentence.

Sentence completion questions usually show up in one set of 9 questions and another set of 10 questions. Like analogy question sets, the first few questions will be the easiest, the middle few will be harder, and the last questions in the set can be quite tricky. As a set of sentence completion questions progresses, the vocabulary gets more difficult. One-blank questions and two-blank questions can show up anywhere in the set, and a one-blank sentence isn't necessarily easier than a two-blank.

Timing Tip

Sentence completion questions show up as 9 out of 35 questions in one 30-minute set and as 10 out of 30 questions in another. Your average time to solve each sentence completion question should be between 20 and 60 seconds. If you find yourself taking longer than a minute, move on.

Strategy Overview

Here's what an easier-level one-blank question might look like.

Despite the _____ claims made by its proponents, the vitamin supplement has not been proven to be effective against any illnesses.

(A) careful
(B) vague
(C) grandiose
(D) harmful
(E) prosaic

Cross it out!

When you eliminate a choice, draw a line through it. That way, when you look back at your choices, you won't waste time rereading it.

The best way to go about solving a sentence completion question is to get an idea of the word or words you're looking for before you actually check out the choices. You might be tempted to just go through the sentence and stick in each of the choices. That might work, but it eats up a huge amount of time. If you know what you're looking for ahead of time, you can scan your choices, pick the one or two that seem the closest, and then test them out.

In this sentence, the word *despite* tells you that there's some kind of contrast. If it helps, you can rephrase the sentence in a simpler form.

Even though people made a certain kind of claim, the vitamin supplement has not been proven effective.

Whatever kind of claim people are making contrasts with the fact that the supplement hasn't been shown to do anything. Even if you don't know that *proponents* are supporters, you can still figure out that these people are making exaggerated claims. Choice (C), *grandiose,* is perfect. Always test your answer in the sentence to make sure it works.

Despite the grandiose claims made by its proponents, the vitamin supplement has not been proven to be effective against any illness.

A perfect fit!

Here's an easy, level 2, blank sentence completion question.

Even people who never thought they could _____ new technology are taking advantage of the _____ computers can provide.

(A) understand..hassles
(B) create..help
(C) forget..problems
(D) master..convenience
(E) unlearn..speed

All or Nothing At All

Remember, in a two-blank sentence completion, both words have to work. If you know one word can't work, eliminate the choice.

Again, begin solving the question by forming your own idea of what the correct answers will be. You might not have an idea yet of what kind of word should go in that first blank. In a two-blank sentence, you can start with whichever blank seems easier to you. In this sentence, the second blank is a little easier to figure out. If people are *taking advantage of* whatever goes in the blank, it must be something good. Scan the second-blank choices for something good, and eliminate any choices that won't work. Choice (A), *hassles,* and choice (C), *problems,* can't be anything good, so cross out those answers.

Now take another look at the first blank.

Even people who never thought they could *something* new technology are enjoying the good things about computers.

The word you're looking for probably means something like "use" or "understand." Of your remaining choices, which works the best in the first blank? The closest choice is (D), *master*. You may be tempted by choice (B)—after all, *help* makes sense. But people who never thought they could *create* new technology? It's close, but it doesn't quite make sense. Creating technology doesn't directly relate to using it.

Now test your choice in the sentence:

Even people who never thought they could master new technology are now taking advantage of the convenience computers can provide.

There's your answer.

Skill Drill: Guess the Rest

Read each sentence, and jot down the general meaning that you can expect the correct answer to have.

1. The volunteer crew, _____ to their work restoring houses in the community, toiled all afternoon despite the _____ weather conditions.

2. Once _____ by movie viewers all over the world, the actress had been forgotten by all but her most _____ fans.

3. Mayor Alvarez had to _____ attending the tree-planting ceremony, as she had already agreed to participate in a debate that afternoon.

4. In spite of his seemingly _____ manner, he is a solitary person who prefers quiet meditation to lively conversation.

5. Because of the _____ warnings forecast on the news, we were well-prepared for the _____ amount of snow that fell overnight.

Use the Clues

Guess the Rest: Answers

This was an exercise in estimation, so there are no exact answers. The words you chose should be similar in meaning to these suggested answers:

1. *dedicated..bad*
2. *loved..loyal*
3. *skip*
4. *outgoing*
5. *urgent..large*

Count on the Clues

Sentence Completion questions will never give you a sentence like this:

I wore a _____ shirt.

(A) gray
(B) wool
(C) large
(D) red
(E) striped

They always include enough information to point you toward a specific choice.

Now that you know how to approach sentence completion questions, it's time to take a look at more advanced strategy. You've already seen how important a strong vocabulary is in the Sentence Completion section of the SAT. But you need to do more than understand the meaning of the words—you need to understand the structure of the sentence. Is it telling you a fact and then providing an example? Is it setting up a contrast between two ideas? Understanding how a sentence works will help you make accurate answer predictions when you hit more complicated sentences.

Here's a sentence completion question of medium difficulty level.

> Although projections for voter turnout had been _____, many voters felt _____ about the issues on the ballot and didn't vote.
>
> (A) grim..excited
> (B) high..angry
> (C) optimistic..apathetic
> (D) uncanny..outraged
> (E) low..indifferent

What are your clues in this sentence? The word *although* lets you know that there's going to be a contrast: Although *something* was expected, *something else* happened. Right away, you can guess that either projections were high but turnout was low, or projections were low but turnout was high. At the end of the sentence, you learn that many voters didn't vote. So, voter turnout was low, meaning that projections must have been high. The correct answer for the first blank is going to mean something like *high*. Right away, you can go to your choices and cross out choice (A), *grim*, choice (D), *uncanny* (remarkable), and choice (E), *low*. The second blank is going to describe the reason why voters didn't vote, so it's got to mean something like uninterested. Scanning your remaining choices, you can eliminate choice (A), excited, and choice (D), outraged. Your best answer is choice (C). Optimistic means hopeful, and apathetic means not interested.

Check your answer choice in the following sentence.

> Although projections for voter turnout had been optimistic, many voters felt apathetic about the issues on the ballot and didn't vote.

It looks like the clues led to the correct answer.

SENTENCE COMPLETION CLUES

Certain words and punctuation can clue you in about how the sentence works. Look for these clues to help you figure out if a sentence is setting up a contrast or if it's continuing one idea. Understanding the logic of a sentence is the key to accurately predicting an answer choice.

Words That Signal A Change

despite, although, since, unlike, but, however, in spite of, in contrast to

You can tell from the clue words that these sentences are headed for a contrast:

Despite our intentions to finish construction this summer . . .

Although I promised that I'd remember your birthday . . .

Unlike the chimpanzee, which is a highly social animal, the goldfish . . .

Words That Tell You To Stay On Course

and, too, similarly, along with, just as, for example

The clue words tell you that these sentences are not heading for a contrast:

Just as the dire flood warnings had suggested, . . .

Last year, Elizabeth spent a week hiking, and this year, similarly, . . .

Just as people have changing moods, animals often . . .

Punctuation That Tells You To Stay On Course

A semicolon (;) is a type of punctuation that shows up between two halves of a sentence. It signals that each half of the sentence will be similar in meaning, often with the second half backing up the first half with an example:

Walker is a devoted musician; he would rather play his bass than do anything else.

Sometimes, trickier sentences will have a semicolon followed by a clue word for change. In a case like that, look out for a contrast between the first and second halves of the sentence:

Jon has been a musician for many years; however, it is only recently that he has begun learning to play the guitar.

The contrast is between *many years* and *only recently*.

SENTENCES YOU'LL SEE

There are certain kinds of questions that show up a lot in the SAT Sentence Completion sections. The more familiar they are to you, the faster you'll be able to solve them on test day.

Contrast Sentences

Contract Sentences contain a shift in direction. They usually contain words that signal change (see above) and describe opposite things or ideas.

> Unlike last spring, which was one of the rainiest on record, this spring has suffered a _____ of moisture.

The contrast is between last spring and this spring. Since last spring was rainy, this one must be *dry*.

Cause And Effect Sentences

Cause and effect sentences say that because of an event or circumstance, something happened. Look for clue words like *because* and *as a result of*.

> Due to the enormously _____ response to our new pizza toppings, we will be making them a regular part of our menu.

Your clue words are *due to*. Some kind of response made these people decide to make the toppings a regular part of their menu. It must have been an enormously favorable response.

Comparison Sentences

Comparison sentences, unlike contrast sentences, describe similarities. They contain such words as *similarly*, *like*, and *just as*.

> Just like last year's graduating class, which did a great deal of volunteer work in the community, this year's seniors are committed to _____ the _____ between the school and the town.

Your clue words are *just like*. This year's class is like last year's—interested in the community. So the seniors are probably committed to *improving* the *relations* or *bridging* the *divide* between the school and the town.

Extra Help

As you know, figuring out the gist of the correct answer isn't enough—you have to choose the vocabulary word that expresses it. Study the Word Teams (page 180) to learn different ways to express the same idea, and use the Word List to compose your own Word Teams.

Definition Sentences

Definition sentences describe or define something without a direction shift. Your job is usually to pick the word that is similar to the ones already in the sentence.

> The hot weather left us feeling _____ and dull, unwilling to _____ even enough energy to get an ice cream cone.

This sentence doesn't take any unexpected twists; it's all about feeling sapped of energy because of the heat. A good choice for the first blank would be *listless* or *lethargic*, and a the second blank must be something like *expend*.

FACING THE TOUGH STUFF

When you're looking at really difficult Sentence Completion questions, remember this: simplify. Don't get swamped in extra phrases and difficult vocabulary words. Read around them to get to the heart of the sentence. Chances are that even if you don't completely understand it, you can figure out a general idea of what's going on. Even if your idea is as vague as "something good is happening" or "this thing isn't as good as this other thing," you can eliminate one or more choices.

> In her effort to _____ a love of science to her students, Dr. Greene, a prominent chemist who abhorred the _____ jargon of traditional lectures, encouraged young scholars to spend more time in the laboratory and less in the lecture hall.
>
> (A) impart..abstruse
> (B) provoke..clear
> (C) promote..lucid
> (D) prevent..confusing
> (E) hinder..convoluted

OK—this sentence has a lot of long words in it, and some of the choices might be unfamiliar. But it's nothing you can't handle. Start by reading the sentence and looking for clue words to help you understand it. Then, predict what kind of words will fill the blanks.

What's the general idea of this sentence? Even if you don't know the words *prominent* (standing out, famous) and *abhorred* (hated), you can still boil it down to something like this: To make her students like science better, Dr. Greene has them spend more time in the lab instead of listening to lectures. So does Dr. Greene like lectures? No. Even if you don't know that *jargon* is difficult, highly specialized language, you can still figure out that the word in the second blank is going to be something negative. And the first blank must mean something like *give* or *provide*.

Move on to your choices, and start eliminating.

(A) *Impart* means to give, and *abstruse* means hard to understand. Even if you don't know that, keep it as a possibility.

(B) *Provoke* means to goad, and *clear* is a positive quality, not the negative one you're looking for, so eliminate.

(C) *Promote* works, but *lucid* means clear, so eliminate.

(D) Why would Dr. Greene want to *prevent* a love of science in her students? Eliminate.

(E) *Convoluted* (twisted) works in the second blank, but to *hinder* something is to hold it back, so eliminate.

Even if you couldn't eliminate all of the other answer choices, you probably knew enough to narrow them down significantly. The correct answer is choice (A). Reread your sentence, inserting the words from choice (A), and you'll see that it works.

SUMMING UP

To solve Sentence Completion questions, follow these steps:

1. Read the sentence, and make a prediction.

2. Find the answer that best matches your prediction.

3. Reread the sentence with your answer.

PRACTICE SETS

Answers to the following practice sets can be found on page 457.

Sentence Completion Practice Set I

1. The natural _____ of fish in our streams
   _____ our looking further afield for
   either sustenance or sporting entertainment.

   (A) paucity..discouraged
   (B) plethora..encouraged
   (C) absence..assisted
   (D) amount ..obviated
   (E) abundance ..forestalled

2. Although critics praised the play highly, few
   viewers went to see it, causing the play to
   have only a _____ run before closing.

   (A) modest
   (B) precise
   (C) maudlin
   (D) lengthy
   (E) special

3. Always a popular instrument, the clarinet
   becomes even more _____ when played
   by a _____ such as Pete Fountain, the
   New Orleans musician.

   (A) euphonious..novice
   (B) daunting..musician
   (C) appealing..virtuoso
   (D) eclectic..tyro
   (E) erudite..master

4. Modern scientists zealously study that
   _____ known as a living cell, even as
   they realize that its complexity may cause
   certain definitive relationships to _____
   description for years to come.

   (A) conundrum..defy
   (B) incongruity..entail
   (C) profundity..elude
   (D) enigma..promote
   (E) elaboration..promulgate

5. Even though certain forms of cancer now
   respond well to treatment, others have
   remained an _____ , continuing to
   puzzle physicians.

   (A) illusion
   (B) illustration
   (C) enmity
   (D) enigma
   (E) allusion

6. The park, once an _____ stretch of land
   with pristine streams and majestic trees, has
   seen its purity _____ by pollution and
   neglect.

   (A) ephemeral..enhanced
   (B) ugly..eroded
   (C) elaborate..unchanged
   (D) idyllic..compromised
   (E) excellent..renewed

7. Furniture made in the Shaker style has
   clean, simple lines; it lacks the _____
   embellishments found in some other styles.

   (A) severe
   (B) ornate
   (C) untoward
   (D) unadorned
   (E) understated

8. Dissension spread among the troops,
   _____ like a plague and equally _____
   in its grip.

   (A) unwelcome..corrosive
   (B) infamous..futile
   (C) virulent..tenacious
   (D) subtle..stubborn
   (E) contemptible..conspicuous

9. Sondra was a remarkably _____ worker, always thinking of new approaches to old problems; unfortunately, her employers _____ change in the work place.

(A) challenging..decried
(B) innovative..discouraged
(C) versatile..promoted
(D) efficient..attempted
(E) attentive..belittled

10. The museum has undergone _____ change in the last few years; where once there were staid, unmoving exhibits behind glass, there are now accessible, moveable exhibits that encourage viewer _____.

(A) increasing..frustration
(B) slight..interaction
(C) visible..interference
(D) little..reaction
(E) noticeable..participation

Sentence Completion Practice Set II

1. Although Michael is usually clear and direct in his speech, his remarks yesterday were uncharacteristically _____.

   (A) sprightly
   (B) lucid
   (C) superficial
   (D) obscure
   (E) servile

2. The textbook, with its _____ prose and difficult concepts, _____ students who had previously had no trouble in school.

   (A) lucid..enraged
   (B) dense..challenged
   (C) tricky..bored
   (D) twisted..enfeebled
   (E) clear..embarrassed

3. After spending weeks researching at the library, Christopher gleaned the _____ information from his notes and discarded the rest.

   (A) spurious
   (B) unusual
   (C) biased
   (D) relevant
   (E) subjective

4. Many critics _____ the music of Igor Stravinsky, claiming that it was _____ and atonal.

   (A) adored..melodic
   (B) admired..elusive
   (C) deplored..jarring
   (D) disliked..elaborate
   (E) embraced..rich

5. Although the trail was steep and winding, the hikers refused to be _____ by its difficulty.

   (A) daunted
   (B) threatened
   (C) relieved
   (D) enlivened
   (E) stifled

6. Despite her _____ as a public orator, in private, Sarah is _____, speaking rarely.

   (A) ineptitude..hesitant
   (B) prowess..taciturn
   (C) fame..loquacious
   (D) strength..remonstrative
   (E) competence..verbose

7. Until we can _____ the _____ of the witnesses' statement, we cannot ask him to testify at the trial.

   (A) confirm..ambiguity
   (B) discount..veracity
   (C) insure..mendacity
   (D) verify..accuracy
   (E) instill..truthfulness

8. The professor endeavored to prove that the epic story Beowolf was not merely a _____, as his colleagues believed, but that it was based on actual events.

   (A) representation
   (B) recollection
   (C) legend
   (D) falsehood
   (E) symbol

9. Unlike the present time, in which a huge variety of cars is available to consumers, in the early years of automobile manufacturing, car-buyers did not have a _____ of models from which to choose.

(A) dearth
(B) glut
(C) lack
(D) scarcity
(E) range

10. The benign personality of Dr. Jekyll underwent a total _____ as he became Mr. Hyde, a _____ character bent on evil.

(A) alteration..dubious
(B) refurbishing..masterful
(C) indoctrination..original
(D) advancement..different
(E) metamorphosis..ruthless

Sentence Completion Practice Set III
Real SAT Questions

1. By nature he was _____, usually confining his remarks to _____ expression.

   (A) acerbic..friendly
   (B) laconic..concise
   (C) garrulous..voluminous
   (D) shrill..complimentary
   (E) vague..emphatic

2. Many contemporary novelists have forsaken a traditional intricacy of plot and detailed depiction of character for a distinctly _____ presentation of both.

   (A) convoluted
   (B) derivative
   (C) conventional
   (D) conservative
   (E) unadorned

3. The film star conveys the wit and charm of the character she portrays, but, unfortunately, many of her most _____ lines have been cut.

   (A) tactless
   (B) sober
   (C) ingenious
   (D) unintelligible
   (E) unnecessary

4. His _____ maintained that Mr. Frank was constantly at odds with the corporate officers; the truth, on the contrary, was that his ideas were not at all _____ with the officers' reasonable goals.

   (A) detractors..in accord
   (B) supporters..at variance
   (C) advocates..harmonious
   (D) disparagers..incompatible
   (E) apologists..in conflict

5. The short story, with its _____, its pointed movement toward a single moment of discovery, can economically reveal the _____ of the illusions that somehow sustain most people's lives.

   (A) casualness..destructiveness
   (B) optimism..barrenness
   (C) capriciousness..rigidity
   (D) digressiveness..poignancy
   (E) compression..precariousness

6. The speaker asserted that humans have such a strong natural tendency toward self-deception that the moral imperative to _____ this drive with respect for _____ is becoming more critical than ever.

   (A) dignify..individuality
   (B) intensify..integrity
   (C) invalidate..treachery
   (D) counterbalance..truth
   (E) rationalize..privacy

7. Robert was the embodiment of amorality, capable of committing the most odious acts without ever _____ even a hint of _____.

   (A) suppressing..revulsion
   (B) betraying..reproof
   (C) inspiring..malice
   (D) evincing..compunction
   (E) condoning..indelicacy

8. Galloping technological progress has made consumers _____: advances undreamed of a generation ago are so common that they seem humdrum.

   (A) flabbergasted
   (B) miffed
   (C) jaded
   (D) wary
   (E) embittered

9. The unusually large herb *Gunnera* is difficult to study because it is found only in _____ areas.

   (A) fertile
   (B) hospitable
   (C) inaccessible
   (D) mundane
   (E) extensive

10. Ironically, the same executives who brought bankruptcy to the coal fields were _____ by their contemporaries, who _____ the notion that these people were industrial heroes.

    (A) celebrated..cherished
    (B) respected..doubted
    (C) ignored..belied
    (D) condemned..rejected
    (E) antagonized..enjoyed

How To Solve
Critical Reading Questions

GETTING STARTED

Half of your verbal points come from the 40 critical reading questions you'll find on the SAT. As you can figure out, these questions test your reading skills. However, they also test your strategy skills. Critical reading questions are all about knowing how to approach a reading passage, what to read for, and how to handle specific types of questions.

To start with, what *don't* you need to know in order to earn points in the critical reading section? Unlike analogies and sentence completions, critical reading questions don't require you to have an especially large vocabulary. The questions in this section will only test you on vocabulary words in terms of how they're used in the context of the passage, never on their general meaning.

You also don't need to have any outside knowledge on whatever subject the passage is about. You will only be asked questions about the content of the passage and what you can infer (figure out) from it.

Finally, you don't have to know how to memorize the details of a reading passage in record time. You just have to create a general mental map of where the important points are so that you can go back and find them later when you need them.

TIMING TIP

Critical reading questions will show up as 13 out of 35 questions in a 30-minute section, as 14 out of 30 questions in another 30-minute section, and as 13 out of 13 questions in a 15-minute section. You'll need to spend at least as much time reading the passages as you will answering the questions. If you find yourself taking more than half a minute on a question, move on.

STRATEGY OVERVIEW

Read the Blurb

Each passage begins with a short, italicized blurb that gives you a little bit of information about the passage. Always read it—it will help you understand what you're reading.

TIME TO JUMP IN

You have two jobs in the critical reading section: (1) to read and understand the passages, and (2) to correctly answer questions about the passages. In order to accomplish these tasks, you need to know how to approach reading passages and how to solve the specific types of questions you'll encounter.

1. Give the passage a quick read, making a mental map of where the important parts are and noting the tone and main idea of the passage.

2. Simplify each question so you know exactly what you're trying to solve.

3. Go back to the passage to find the answers.

4. Approach the choices with an idea of what you're looking for, and choose the best one.

Here's a typical SAT critical reading passage. Give it a quick read, noting main ideas and getting an idea of where important details are located.

The following passage was compiled from essays about the history of the skyscraper.

Line The industrial revolution changed more than just the way America worked; it changed the way America looked. As the country moved from an agrarian economy to a goods-producing economy, real estate began to literally move in new directions, and the American land-
(5) scape was forever changed. In a farm-based economy, of course, it was acreage—pure expanse—that people valued. In the late nineteenth century, changing technology and changing needs led to the construction of the first skyscrapers. Suddenly, in America's big cities, height was the defining characteristic of the landscape.
(10) At the heart of the redefinition of the urban landscape was the invention of the steel frame. The first building to be supported by a complete steel frame was the Home Insurance Building in Chicago, built between 1884 and 1885. In the 1870's, the Tribune Building and the Western Union building, both over ten stories tall, were built in
(15) New York. Later, in 1919, workers began construction of New York's Woolworth Building, which they completed in 1913. The Woolworth Building was a triumph of industrial-age technology, with its steel frame and its foundation on concrete piers. As remarkable as the building was for its height, 792 feet, it was equally remarkable for
(20) how far it extended beneath the earth, all the way to bedrock. The

concrete piers that support the building are themselves the result of an important technological innovation of the age: the caisson. Caissons are chambers that use air pressure to drive away water, allowing people to work below the water line.

(25)   The changing American urban landscape reflected the changing needs of American commerce. The geographic isolation of rural life was not feasible for the people who ran the country's bourgeoning industries. Mutually reliant businesses, such as fuel companies and transportation companies, needed to be in proximity to each other.

(30) Businesses needed space for their employees, as office jobs became a growing presence in the urban work force. Additionally, companies used their headquarter buildings as a means of establishing presence and identity in an increasingly competitive market. The Woolworth Building, and others like it, served as advertising for the companies

(35) they housed. City dwellers associated the regal, powerful buildings with the businesses for which they were named. Landscape, industry, and advertisement had begun to blend together in America's big cities.

WHAT DID YOU GET OUT OF IT?

You don't need to memorize details when you read a passage. In fact, reading too closely will just slow you down and ultimately cost you points. A quick read should give you an understanding of the main idea, the important points, the author's tone, and a good idea of where to find the details when you're asked about them.

NOW FOR THE QUESTIONS

Take a look at these questions, which are typical of what you'll find on the test. Notice that they fall into three basic types: main idea questions, detail questions, and vocabulary-in-context questions. Main idea questions test your overall understanding of the passage. Detail questions are more specific and usually provide you with a line reference for the detail about which they're asking. Vocabulary-in-context questions ask you to choose the closest definition of a vocabulary word taken from the passage. These always provide a line reference so you can find the word, and they always require you to read around the word to figure out how it's being used.

1.   A fitting title for this passage would be

   (A) The Effects of the Industrial Revolution in America
   (B) The Skyscraper: A Sign of the Times in Industrial America
   (C) From Farmland to Cities: America's Changing Economy
   (D) The History of the Industrial Revolution
   (E) The Effects of the Skyscraper on American Commerce

This is a main idea question, so you'll need to consider the passage as a whole and reject choices that are too broad, too narrow, or off the topic. Choice (A) is too broad—the passage is specifically about one effect—the skyscraper. Choice (B) looks good—keep it as a choice. Choice (C) is a possibility. The passage talks about the change from farming to industry, but economics isn't really the main focus. Choice (D) is much too broad in scope, covering far too much territory, and choice (E) is too narrow, ignoring the information about the role of technology in building skyscrapers. The correct answer is choice (B).

2. The author's purpose in this passage is to

   (A) show pride
   (B) persuade
   (C) entertain
   (D) inform
   (E) argue

This is another type of main idea question. Consider the passage as a whole. Does the author have a particular point to prove, or is she arguing for or against anything in particular? Is the language in the passage particularly emotional or showy? The language is clear and straight-forward and the author isn't speaking for or against anything. Rule out choice (A), since it seems far-fetched. Choice (B) isn't quite right—this passage is more factual than persuasive. Choice (C) feels wrong for a factual passage, and eliminate choice (E) because the author doesn't present an argument. The correct answer is choice (D).

3. You can infer from the statement "The Woolworth building, and others like it, served as advertising for the companies they housed" (lines 33–34) that

   (A) urban buildings used billboards for commercial messages
   (B) businesses were beginning to experiment with unusual forms of advertising
   (C) architecture and corporate identity were starting to merge
   (D) shoppers in cities preferred large businesses to small ones
   (E) the Woolworth Building was considered to be the finest skyscraper in New York

One kind of detail question that you'll see frequently in critical reading is the inference question. It asks you to use material in the passage to infer something—that is, to use the passage to draw a conclusion that isn't directly stated. To solve an inference question, you need to read carefully and try to take what you see to a logical next step. For this question, go back to the passage and reread the referenced line in context (that is, read a little bit before and after it).

What's this sentence really saying? Eliminate choices (A) and (B), because they take the words too literally. The buildings themselves served as advertising, not billboards or anything else. Choice (C) needs translating. Could "architecture" be a building? Yes—and if the building helps advertise a company, it must be part of the company's identity. Keep choice (C) as a possibility. There's no evidence to support choice (D); eliminate it. Choice (E) may have been true, but it doesn't have much to do with the line in the question. Eliminate it. The correct answer is choice (C).

4. The author mentions fuel companies and transportation companies (lines 28–29) in order to

   (A) show how technology created new types of business
   (B) illustrate the necessity of urban buildings
   (C) list industries that provided the technology used in skyscrapers
   (D) demonstrate the economic results of competition
   (E) compare urban industries to farming

This detail question requires you to look back in the passage and read the context in which fuel and transportation companies are mentioned. "Mutually reliant businesses . . . needed to be in proximity to each other." This sounds like a reason that skyscrapers were necessary. In fact, if you read further in that paragraph, you'll see that the mention of fuel and transportation companies is part of a list of reasons why skyscrapers (urban buildings) were necessary. The correct answer is choice (B).

5. In line 25, the word *reflected* most closely means

   (A) influenced
   (B) bent
   (C) expressed
   (D) imitated
   (E) considered

This is a vocabulary-in-context question. Always go back to the passage and reread before and after the word, so you understand how it's being used in the text. In this case, the sentence says that the changing landscape reflected the changing needs of commerce. You can guess that the correct answer will be something like *showed*. The closest answer is choice (C) *expressed*.

WHAT TO EXPECT ON TEST DAY: THE PASSAGES

You can expect to see four reading passages on the SAT—more if you have an experimental critical reading section. (Remember—never assume that you're working on an experimental section. You don't want to throw an entire test section by mistake.) Here is a breakdown of the types of critical reading passages that you're likely to see on test day.

Fiction or Personal Narrative

You'll be given an excerpt from a story or novel or from a personal narrative.

Science

This passage might cover biology, chemistry, physics, or any other branch of science.

Social Science

This covers topics like psychology, sociology, and anthropology.

Arts and Humanities

This category includes art, literature, history, and philosophy. One of these passages is often about a group that is typically underrepresented, such as women and minorities.

Passage Pairs

Each test contains a pair of passages on similar topics or offering two viewpoints on the same topic. They share a set of questions.

WHAT TO EXPECT ON TEST DAY: THE QUESTIONS

The questions you just looked at are typical critical reading questions—you'll see ones similar to them on test day. Following are the question types that you can expect to see.

Main Idea Questions

These test your overall understanding of the passage, including main ideas, the author's tone, and the author's reason for writing the passage, all of which you should be keeping in the back of your mind while you read. Don't worry about getting all the details—you can go back for those later, as you need them.

Detail Questions

These are the questions that require you to go back and take a close look at the text. You'll be well-prepared for them if you've understood the main ideas of the passage and if you have a general memory of where things are located. Many detail questions provide you with a specific line reference (every fifth line of critical reading passages is numbered) so you can easily go back into the passage and find the answer.

Some detail questions can be solved through straight research—the answers are right there on the page. All you have to do is go back and find them. Remember that you'll need to read a little bit before and after the detail in the question in order to understand what it means. The correct answer will use different wording to restate a fact or idea that is in the passage.

Other detail questions are less straight-forward. These are the questions that ask you to *infer*, to figure out something that is not directly stated in the passage. In order to solve these questions, you need to go back into the passage and read carefully. Then you have to go one step further and draw a logical conclusion based on what you've just read.

Some detail questions ask why the author included a particular detail in the passage. These questions require you to think about the logical structure of the passage. It's your job to go back to the passage and read before and after the detail and to figure out what its purpose is. Does it support the main idea? Disprove a theory? Give away the author's feelings toward a subject? These kinds of questions may be straight-forward, or they may require you to make an inference.

What's the Main Idea?

Some phrases that signal a main idea question are:

This passage might be called
The author's main point in this passage is
The author's purpose in writing this passage is

To Infer is Human

These words and phrases signal that a question is asking you to make an inference:

the author suggests that
the author implies
the author apparently believes
the author would most likely agree that
this statement most likely means
this example is most likely included to
this line can be interpreted as

Peterson's SAT Success

Vocabulary-In-Context Questions

Unlike analogy and sentence completion questions, critical reading questions don't test your actual vocabulary. Instead, they test your ability to figure out the meaning of a word based on context, or what's around it. Often, these questions use common words in uncommon ways. You always need to go back into the passage and read the sentence containing the word. Then pick the choice that describes that particular use.

SKILL DRILL: MAKING INFERENCES

Use the information in each passage to answer the questions.

Line   Harry stared up at the ceiling as his clock radio blared. In the 15 seconds since he'd been thrust from sleep, he had remembered in remarkable detail all of the reasons why he'd been dreading this day. The main reason, of course, was the meeting. Harry loathed nothing (5) more than confrontation. There was no avoiding it today; the day of his job performance evaluation. If his boss were a tactful person, a polite person, someone with the tiniest bit of sensitivity, that would be one thing. If that were the case, Harry would leap out of bed and greet the day joyfully. He would face the meeting with calm dignity. (10) But there was no chance of that. Harry's boss did not go in for sugar-coating the truth, and the truth, Harry had to admit, was not flattering.

Context is Crucial

Vocabulary-in-context questions test your reading comprehension, not your vocabulary, so never make a blind guess on one. Always go back into the passage and read around the word.

1. According to this passage, you can infer that

    (A) Harry plans to quit his job today
    (B) Harry's boss dislikes him
    (C) Harry expects a poor review of his job performance
    (D) Harry prefers to sleep late whenever possible
    (E) Harry would consider any work-related meeting an unnecessary confrontation

Line   Tornados, violent funnels of air, usually form during thunderstorms, although they can occur when lightening is not present. The United States has the highest occurrence of tornadoes worldwide; about 1,000 tornadoes are spawned in the U.S. each year. What causes all (5) these tornadoes? In short, geography. Polar air from Canada meets tropical air from the Gulf of Mexico and dry air from the Southwest region of the United States. These air masses meet in the middle of the country. Strong thunderstorms result, which can spawn single tornadoes or clusters of them. With wind speeds exceeding 200 miles (10) an hour, tornadoes can do deadly damage.

2. Which of the following can you infer from this passage?

(A) Areas in which air masses clash are prone to violent weather.

(B) Tornadoes occur only in the United States.

(C) Tornadoes occur as a direct result of thunder and lightening.

(D) Tornadoes are less violent if they occur when lightening is not present.

(E) The storms in the United States are more violent than storms in any other part of the world.

Line Kate Chopin's novel *The Awakening* shocked its audience when it was published in 1899. Readers of late-Victorian romantic fiction were unprepared for the story of a young wife who, unhappy in her marriage, sought fulfillment through infidelity. Chopin's work was
(5) considered scandalous, an affront to polite society and to the conventions of literature. It is only recently that Chopin's work has been recognized for its literary merits.

3. Which of the following is implied in the passage?

(A) Chopin deliberately alienated her readers by writing shocking material.

(B) Romantic fiction of the late-Victorian era avoided the subject of marriage.

(C) Chopin's novel would have been considered less shocking if it had been written by a man.

(D) Most romantic fiction of the late-Victorian era dealt less frankly with marriage than Chopin's book.

(E) Contemporary fiction rarely portrays marriage positively.

Skill Drill: Answers

1. **The correct answer is (E).** Harry clearly dreads hearing whatever it is his boss has to say to him, and Harry admits that the truth (about his job performance) is not flattering. You may have picked choice (B). While it's certainly possible that Harry's boss dislikes him, there is no evidence to support it. All you know is that he's going to be brutally honest about Harry's job performance.

Don't Go Too Far!

The correct choices to inference questions will be a short step away from what is actually written in the passage. Don't choose an answer that requires a great leap or elaborate reasoning.

2. **The correct answer is (A).** The passage tells you that the United States gets a lot of tornadoes because several air masses meet in the middle of the country, causing the storms that spawn tornadoes. You can logically conclude that areas where air masses meet are prone to very bad weather. If you chose choice (E), remember that the passage tells you that the United States gets the greatest number of tornadoes, but says nothing about where the world's most violent storms are located.

3. **The correct answer is (D).** If Chopin's book was considered scandalous and an affront to the conventions (rules) of litera-ture, you can infer that the other literature of the time was less frank (honest). There is no evidence in the passage to support the other answers. It is doubtful that Chopin would want to "deliberately alienate" her readers choice (A), and the passage doesn't imply that Victorians avoided the subject of marriage altogether, choice (B). Choices (C) and (E) are way off and can be immediately eliminated.

WHAT TO EXPECT ON TEST DAY: THE ANSWERS

As in the other sections of the SAT, knowing how to eliminate wrong answers is key to your success. Here are the types of wrong answers that show up as decoys again and again in the critical reading section.

Too Broad

These answers go way beyond the territory of the question. They may make a statement that is correct, but they don't address the specific idea in the question. If an answer seems vague or all-inclusive, regard it with suspicion.

Too Narrow

These answers zoom in too closely and leave out part of what the question asked.

Too Extreme

If an answer is extremely positive or extremely negative, you can usually eliminate it. Be suspicious if you see answers that contain words like *always*, *never*, *all*, or *none*. It's possible that they are correct, but it is not likely.

The rule of avoiding extremes also goes for author's tone questions. Critical reading passages tend to stick close to the middle of the road. You may have an author who is *mildly amused, reserv-edly critical, subtly sarcastic*, or even *enthusiastically admiring*, but it's very unlikely that an author will be *harshly denouncing, utterly adoring*, or *enraged*. In particular, the people who write the test don't want to insult any group of people. When you see a passage about a traditionally underrepresented group of people, you can bet the author's attitude toward them is not negative.

Very Close (next-to-best)

These are the answers to watch out for once you've eliminated most of the other choices. The next-to-best answer might be almost correct but not quite as good as the best answer. It may be a fact that comes straight from the text but doesn't answer the question. Ask yourself which choice is the most relevant to the question.

Completely Off The Mark

These answers are easy to spot and eliminate—cross them off right away so you don't keep rereading them as you look at the other choices.

GENERAL STRATEGIES FOR CRITICAL READING

There are a few different approaches that you can take in solving critical reading questions. You'll have to decide by practicing what works best for you. One person's sure-fire strategy is another person's time-waster.

Questions Now or Questions Later?

One approach to critical reading is to skim the questions before you even look at the passage, so you know what to read for. However, there might be as many as 10 questions, which is a lot to keep in mind, and some of them are quite complicated. You might be better off saving them until after you've quickly read the passage. After all, once you've read the passage, you should be prepared for main idea questions, and you are going to go back into the passage anyway for detail questions. Practice solving critical reading sections by reading the passage first and also by reading the questions first, and see which method works for you.

Take Notes or Not?

It's often helpful to make brief marks on your passage or in the margin. You might want to put a check in the margin next to main ideas and important-looking details that you don't have time to digest. You may find it helpful to jot down a brief note about the author's tone, especially in passage pair sections. In addition, you may want to make very brief margin notes about similarities and differences between passages in pairs.

That said, remember that you don't earn any points for your note-taking. Whatever marks you make, keep them brief and clear. The more passages you practice on, the better you'll get at figuring out what works for you.

Translation, Please

Sometimes questions look far more complicated than they actually are. If you're confused or overwhelmed by a question, don't hesitate to take your pen to it and cross out filler words. For example, consider this question: "Which of the following best describes the author's method of presenting the information in this passage?" You already know you're choosing from "the following," and you already know the question is about "this passage." Trim away the extra words and you have, "Which describes the author's method of presenting information?"

Always translate intimidating-looking questions into plain English, so you understand what you're looking for. For example, "The speaker primarily conveys which of the following sentiments" is a long, fancy way of saying, "What does the speaker think?" You don't have to write down your translation, as long as you have a clear idea of what you're trying to solve.

SPECIFIC STRATEGIES FOR CRITICAL READING

Passage Pairs

Shortcut

The question will tell you where to look for the answer. If it asks only about passage 1, that's where you should look! In fact, if you're running short of time, read only the first passage, and answer the questions that pertain to it. Then move on to passage 2, if you have time.

The questions for passage pairs are the same kinds of questions you'll see for the other passages. The only difference is that they usually ask you first about passage 1, then about passage 2, and then they will ask you to compare the passages. The test-makers want to see if you understand the similarities and differences between the passages. As you read, ask yourself what the two passages have in common and what their main differences are. The passages might disagree about a subject, or they might discuss two different issues related to the same subject. Sometimes, two people with different perspectives or occupations write about the same subject. Always start by reading the italicized blurb that comes before the passages; it will tell you who wrote each passage and will give you an idea of each author's relationship to the subject matter.

Take a look at this abbreviated pair of passages, and then try the questions.

These passages are about urban renewal, the process of restoring underresourced neighborhoods. Passage 1 was written by a newspaper journalist. Passage 2 is an excerpt from a speech given at a town meeting.

Passage 1

Line   The North Hills neighborhood, once written off by the rest of the city as a blight and an embarrassment, has undergone a remarkable turnaround in the last two years. The former haven for crime and violence has become a trendy home to upscale cafés and expensive
(5)   boutiques. Sky-rocketing rents are driving out many long-time residents as young, well-to-do professionals settle into renovated apartments. Plans are underway to convert the waterfront warehouse area into luxury condominiums, a move that has been met with controversy by the North Hills Neighborhood Association. According
(10)   to a spokesperson from the Association, "This is not the character of our neighborhood, these coffee shops and condominiums. These are not the kinds of changes we had hoped to see." Still, city officials cite North Hills as an urban success story: "Crime is down, housing code violations are down, there's a new energy in the air. How can we call
(15)   that anything but success?"

Passage 2

Line   I'm speaking to you today not about progress, not about improvement, but about the ruination of the North Hills Neighborhood. The city higher-ups promised us an active voice in the North Hills Renovation Project, a promise that they did not keep. I don't know
(5)   about you, but no one asked for my opinion before my rent was doubled. No one asked how I felt about it before they took away a third of our health clinic to make way for a shoe store. Nobody consulted me before I saw my friends and neighbors lose their businesses as they could no longer afford the property taxes. The
(10)   mayor is patting himself on the back for a job well done, but those of us who have lived in North Hills all our lives, who have worked here and raised our families here, are paying a terrible price for the city's triumph. We were promised safer streets and a better future; instead, we're being swept aside in the name of progress.

Peterson's SAT Success

1. The author's purpose in passage 1 is

   (A) to present a broad view of an issue
   (B) to express opposition to a city program
   (C) to provide a satirical look at a local problem
   (D) to express support for a positive change
   (E) to persuade the reader to take a stand

2. In Passage 2, the speaker feels

   (A) encouraged by the city's success
   (B) angry about the loss of his business
   (C) disbelieving about the plight of his neighbors
   (D) a sense of betrayal by the local government
   (E) a strong aversion to any kind of change

3. The author of passage 1 and the speaker in passage 2 would probably agree that

   (A) luxury apartments are a positive change in North Hills
   (B) North Hills has seen both positive and negative changes as a result of the North Hills Renovation Project
   (C) North Hills had a crime problem before the renovation program began
   (D) the rents in North Hills should be lowered
   (E) North Hills should have been kept as it was before the Renovation Project

As you read passage 1, you should have noticed that it was an informative look at the issue of urban renewal in North Hills. The author cited information and quotes both in favor of and against the project to revitalize the neighborhood. Passage 2, on the other hand, showed the point of view of a person who had been adversely affected by the project and was speaking out against it.

Here are the answers to the questions.

1. **The correct answer is (A).** This question deals only with the first passage. That passage was not argumentative or persuasive; it took a broad look at the issue.

2. **The correct answer is (D).** This questions deals only with the second passage, in which the speaker points out that the people in his neighborhood were promised positive changes, but has only been hurt by the Renewal Project.

3. **The correct answer is (C).** Now is the time to go back into both passages. Passage 1 clearly states that North Hills used to be a haven for crime. In Passage 2, the speaker says, "We were promised safer streets," from which you can infer that there was a problem with crime.

Science Passages

Critical reading science passages can be quite intimidating, as they are often filled with long, unfamiliar words and complicated details. When you're facing a science passage, it's important to remember the golden rule of critical reading: don't worry too much about the details. You're not studying for a science test. As with any other critical reading passage, you're looking for the main ideas and the layout of the passage. Any large words or confusing details you come across can wait until later—if you need them at all. As with all critical reading passages, you're not being tested on outside knowledge. All your answers will be in the text, and chances are that you'll even be told where to look for them.

Timing for Tough Spots

If a section offers you a choice of passages, start with the one with which you're most comfortable. The questions do not get harder as they go, so skim them for the easiest ones. If you get stuck, move on—you can always come back later if there's time. Save the difficult questions for last, particularly ones that require you to look for several different details in the passage. (For example, a question that says, "Which of the following ideas was NOT mentioned in the passage" requires you to go back and search for five different ideas, a big waste of time when you could be earning the same number of points on a simpler question.)

If time is running out, here are some quick ways to earn points:

1. If you don't have time to read both passages in a paired passage section, go straight to the questions and skim them. Read the passage which more questions are based on.

2. If you don't have time to read a passage, turn to the questions and look for vocabulary-in-context questions. You can go straight to the referenced line, read a little bit before and after it, and answer the question.

3. The same goes for detail questions that give a line number, although some of them will be too complicated to solve that way.

4. For a quick, last-resort way to figure out a main idea question in a hurry, read just the italicized blurb, the first line in each paragraph, and then the end of the last paragraph.

Summing Up

To solve critical reading questions, follow these steps:

1. Give the passage a quick read, noting main ideas.

2. Simplify each question.

3. Go back to the passage to find the answers.

4. Predict an answer choice, and choose the closest one.

Practice Sets

Answers to the following practice sets can be found on page 460.

Critical Reading Practice Set I

The following passage is an excerpt from a book about the nineteenth-century novelist Jane Austen.

Line   Everyone loves Jane Austen's novels—
scientists, feminists, college freshmen,
traditionalists, even readers who think they
don't like fiction. After Shakespeare and
(5)   perhaps Dickens, Austen is the most
universally admired writer in the English
language. Her popularity is extraordinary
when one considers that she deals with
neither death nor religion nor great mo-
(10)   ments in history. Her subject is courtship,
and her stories all end the same way—in
happy marriage. Yet no one has ever
accused Austen of being shallow or suggested that her novels appeal because of
(15)   their escapism. Quite the contrary—her
work is usually characterized as wise, witty,
and realistic.

In many ways, Austen's novels resemble
Shakespeare's comedies, which also end in
(20)   marriage. Both the novels and the comedies
demonstrate how much human nature may
be revealed within the confines of a circumscribed environment and a limited plot. Like
Shakespeare, Austen makes women her
(25)   central characters. By using their wits and
their moral sensibilities as a substitute for
the power they do not have, they bring
about a desired end. This element in
itself—the success of the weak over the
(30)   powerful—may account for some part of
Austen's popularity.

The greater part of Austen's appeal,
however, is rooted in her ability to combine
the seemingly incompatible qualities of
(35)   romance and irony, engagement and
detachment. Rational though she may
initially appear from the beauty of her

balanced sentences, there is much in
Austen's work that is firmly rooted in the
(40)   realm of the feelings. Despite her elevation
of civility, restraint, good manners, good
sense, and duty, Austen's novels are essentially fairy tales—fantasies. They are
grounded in realism and made credible by
(45)   careful observation and sound precepts of
moral behavior, but they are fantasies
nevertheless.

1. The author's attitude toward his or her
   subject can best be described as

   (A) moderately approving
   (B) enthusiastic and admiring
   (C) completely unbiased
   (D) a blend of approval and disapproval
   (E) blindly worshiping

2. We can infer from this passage that most
   literary critics would admire Austen's work
   for all of the following EXCEPT

   (A) her insights into human nature
   (B) her revelation of universal truths
   (C) her humor
   (D) the realism of her plots
   (E) the inventiveness of her heroines

3. The author compares Austen's novels to
   Shakespeare's comedies primarily in
   order to

   (A) establish Austen's literary stature
   (B) emphasize the wit that both authors
       displayed
   (C) discuss the role of women in literature
   (D) illustrate how each author developed
       characters
   (E) reiterate the undying popularity of
       both authors

4. The author of this passage appears to respect Jane Austen the most for

   (A) her universality of appeal

   (B) her gift in discussing even very painful subjects

   (C) her lack of irony

   (D) her treatment of important historic events

   (E) the great variety of her plots

5. In line 45, the word *sound* most closely means

   (A) based on truth

   (B) accurate

   (C) financially secure

   (D) free from decay

   (E) forceful

6. The author claims that Austen's work resembles Shakespeare's comedies in that both writers

   (A) placed stock characters in complex situations

   (B) placed more emphasis on setting than on plot

   (C) worked to create an awareness of women's political inequality

   (D) created complex characters within restricted plots

   (E) often wrote unhappy endings to demonstrate social injustice

7. The author mentions *the realm of the feelings* (line 40) to describe

   (A) the rational thoughts of Austen's character

   (B) the deep emotion that Austen's characters experience

   (C) one way in which Austen's work resembles that of Shakespeare

   (D) the fairy tale nature of Austen's plots

   (E) the realism that is the basis for Austen's novels

8. You can infer from the sentence that begins *This element in itself . . .* (lines 28–31) that the author believes which of the following

   (A) The strongest characters are those who start out poor and become rich.

   (B) The most popular literary characters are those who are the most powerful.

   (C) Readers dislike plots in which powerless characters increase their social rank by misrepresenting themselves.

   (D) Austen overcame powerlessness to become a novelist.

   (E) Readers like to identify with characters who overcome adversity.

9. According to the passage, Austen's main subject matter is

   (A) politics

   (B) relationships

   (C) adventure

   (D) historic events

   (E) feminism

Critical Reading Practice Set II

This passage is an excerpt from a NASA book about the Mercury Project, the United States' first manned space flight. The book was published in October 1963.

Line   On April 9, 1959, as a press conference in
Washington, a NASA Administrator introduced to the public the seven men chosen
to be this Nation's nominees for the first
(5)   human voyagers into space.

They were to be called "astronauts," as
the pioneers of ballooning had been called
"argonauts," for they were to sail into a new,
uncharted ocean. These personable pilots
(10)   were introduced in civilian dress; many
people in their audience forgot that they
were volunteer test subjects and military
officers. Their public comments did not class
them with any elite intelligencia. Rather,
(15)   they were a contingent of mature Americans, average in build and visage, family men
all, college-educated as engineers, possessing
excellent health, and professionally committed to flying advanced aircraft.

(20)   Despite the wishes of NASA headquar-
ters, the fame of the astronauts quickly grew
beyond all proportion to their current
activities and their preflight mission assign-
ments. Perhaps it was inevitable that the
(25)   astronauts were destined for premature
adulation, what with the enormous public
curiosity about them, the risk they would
take in space flight, and their exotic training
activities. But the power of commercial
(30)   competition for publicity and the pressure
for political prestige in the space race also
whetted an insatiable public appetite for this
new kind of celebrity.

The astronauts were first and foremost
(35)   test pilots, men accustomed to flying along
in the newest, most advanced, and most

powerful vehicles this civilization had
produced. They were talented specialists
who loved to fly high-performance aircraft
(40)   and who had survived the natural selection
process in their profession. The demand for
excellence in piloting skills, in physical
health, and psychological adaptability
becomes ever more stringent as one ascends
(45)   the ladder toward the elite among military
aviators, those senior pilots with upwards of
1,500 hours' total flying time.

Although the psychophysiological
criteria for the selection of the best possible
(50)   pilots for manned space flight had been
under discussion for several years, the actual
arrangement of the selection procedures for
Mercury was directed by a NASA selection
committee. Individually, each candidate
(55)   arrived at Albuquerque to undergo approximately a week of medical evaluations under
each of five different schedules. In this third
phase of the program, over 30 different
laboratory tests collected chemical, encepha-
(60)   lographic, and cardiographic data. X-ray
examinations thoroughly mapped each
man's body. In addition to pressure suit
tests, acceleration tests, vibration tests, heat
tests, and loud noise tests, each candidate
(65)   had to probe his physical endurance on
treadmills, title tables, with his feet in ice
water, and by blowing up balloons until
exhausted.

Two of the more interesting personality
(70)   and motivation studies seemed like parlor
games at first, until it became evident how
profound an exercise in Socratic introspec-
tion was implied by conscientious answers
to the test questions "Who am I?" and
(75)   "Whom would you assign to the mission if
you could not go yourself?" In the first case,
by requiring the subject to write down 20

definitional identifications of himself, ranked in order of significance and interpreted (80) projectively, the psychologists elicited information on identity and perception of social roles. In the peer ratings, each candidate was asked which of the other members of the group of five accompanying (85) him through this phase of the program he liked best, which one he would substitute for himself. Candidates who had proceeded this far in the selection process all agreed with one who complained, "Nothing is (90) sacred anymore."

1. The best title for this passage would be

   (A) The History of the Mercury Project
   (B) Psychological Testing in Space Exploration
   (C) Great American Astronauts
   (D) NASA's Role in Space Exploration
   (E) Choosing the First Space Voyagers

2. The passage compares *astronauts* to *argonauts* because both groups

   (A) explored the ocean
   (B) took great risks to benefit mankind
   (C) ventured into unknown territory
   (D) attempted to send men to the moon
   (E) earned degrees in engineering

3. The passage lists all of the following as reasons for the astronauts' popularity EXCEPT

   (A) the astronauts' appearance as an elite group
   (B) the interesting training regimen of the astronauts
   (C) political pressures
   (D) the public's curiosity about astronauts
   (E) the difficulty of the astronauts' job

4. The sentence "Rather, they were a contingent of mature Americans . . ." (lines 14–19)

   (A) describes what made the astronauts different from most Americans
   (B) shows how the astronauts differed from the public's expectations of military officers
   (C) explains the public's need to see the astronauts as heroes
   (D) compares the astronauts to earlier pioneers of ballooning
   (E) casts doubt on the ability and intelligence of the astronauts

5. You can infer from the description of "pressure suit tests, acceleration tests, vibration tests . . . and by blowing balloons until exhausted" (lines 62–68) that

   (A) NASA was experimenting with various kinds of tests
   (B) nobody know exactly what the astronauts would experience in space
   (C) the physical tests were not as important as the psychological tests
   (D) the public was curious to learn about the astronauts' physical conditions
   (E) the astronauts would face extremely challenging conditions in space

6. The word *whetted* (line 32) most nearly means

   (A) satisfied
   (B) lessened
   (C) hindered
   (D) stimulated
   (E) honed

7. "The natural selection process in their profession" (lines 40-41) refers to

(A) the high accident rate among test pilots
(B) the series of physical and psychological tests administered to prospective astronauts
(C) the highly competitive nature of the military
(D) the process by which better and faster aircraft are manufactured
(E) the relatively small number of pilots who advance to the highest ranks

8. The personality and motivation studies that "seemed like parlor games at first" (lines 70-71)

(A) were tools for understanding how the subjects viewed themselves
(B) served to test the subjects' psychological endurance
(C) revealed the personal philosophy of each subject
(D) were designed to make physical tests unnecessary
(E) allowed psychologists to judge how motivated each subject was to travel into space

9. Which of the following can you infer from the candidates' complaint that "Nothing is sacred anymore" (lines 89-90)?

(A) The candidates were disappointed with the lack of respect given to them.
(B) The selection process felt psychologically invasive to the candidates.
(C) The candidates felt violated by the public's excessive interest in them.
(D) The psychologists discouraged the candidates from practicing religion.
(E) The candidates preferred the physical tests to the psychological tests.

Critical Reading Practice Set III
Real SAT Questions

Questions 1–12 are based on the following passages.

Below are two excerpts that consider the relationship between works of literature and social conditions. The first is from a book published in 1974 and written by a Black male scholar about Black American literature. The second is from a book published in 1979 and written by two White female scholars about literature written by women in the nineteenth century.

Passage 1

Line   One of the most notable aspects of the Black narrative tradition is that at the beginning of the narrative the main character is usually in a state of bondage or imprisonment, either
(5)   physical or mental or both. The main action of the narrative involves the character's attempt to break out of this narrow arena. By the end of the narrative, however, the character has seldom achieved a state of
(10)   ideal freedom; often it is a mixture of hope and despair, madness and sanity, repleteness and longing. *The Narrative of the Life of Frederick Douglass, An American Slave, Written by Himself* (1845) offers a case in
(15)   point.

In his autobiography Douglass describes his journey from "the prison house of slavery" to the North and the abolitionist movement. As a slave he was in a condition
(20)   of bondage, deprivation, and injustice. The young Douglass does not know his father, sees his mother only two or three times before she dies, and is confronted early and often by the nakedness of the power
(25)   wielded by White people.

A climactic point in the *Narrative* occurs when Douglass complains to his White master about the brutal treatment he has received at the hands of another White
(30)   man to whom he has been consigned. He asks for just treatment, but is informed that he must go back tothe other man "come what might" and that he will be punished severely if he ever complains again. This
(35)   encounter, in which the only tribunal before which a slave can demand just consists of a slaveholder, who acts as both judge and jury, is representative of the patterns of justice that the book describes.

(40)   It is Douglass' expanding awareness of the exclusiveness of White justice that leads to subtle rebellion, physical revolt, and finally an escape from slavery. When he first arrives in New York, Douglass is still unsure
(45)   of himself and fearful of the omnipresent threat of capture. He changes his name in order to avoid the thoroughgoing "justice" of the White world. He moves to Massachusetts before he feels somewhat secure.
(50)   Douglass comes to feel, however, that the security offered by Massachusetts is not enough. He must join the abolitionist movement to find sanctuary: the entire system must change before he can be free.

(55)   The final positions of Frederick Douglass and the protagonists of other Black narratives carry us toward a more elevated conception of the human condition. We have not only the insights and the liberating
(60)   strategies that illuminate the course of the narration but also the honest complexity of endings that indicate no solution is final

until the basis of the White court's power has been destroyed. The Black narrative does
(65) not offer a comfortable majority report. It speaks of the enduring struggle of those who have been unjustly judged and restricted and yet have sought to evolve humane standards of existence. There is
(70) suffering involved, but ultimately the process augurs well for some essential human dignity.

Passage 2

Line Dramatizations of imprisonment and escape are so all-pervasive in nineteenth-century literature by women that we believe they represent a uniquely female tradition in this
(5)   period. Interestingly, though works in this tradition generally begin by using houses as primary symbols of female imprisonment, they also use much of the other paraphernalia of "woman's place" to enact their central
(10) symbolic drama of enclosure and escape. Ladylike veils and costumes, mirrors, paintings, statues, locked cabinets, drawers, trunks, strongboxes, and other domestic furnishings appear and reappear in women's
(15) novels and poems. They signify the woman writer's sense that, as Emily Dickenson put it, her "life" has been "shaven and fitted to a frame," a confinement she can tolerate only by believing that "the soul has moments of
(20) escapes / When bursting all the doors / She dances like a bomb abroad." Significantly, too, the explosive violence of these "moments of escape" that women writers continually imagine for themselves reminds
(25) us of the phenomenon of the mad double* that so many of these women have projected into their works. For it is, after all, through the violence of the double that the female author enacts her own raging desire
(30) to escape male houses and male constructs, while at the same time it is through the double's violence that the author articulates for herself the costly destructiveness of anger repressed until it can no longer be
(35) constrained.

1. Both passages are primarily concerned with the themes of

   (A) madness and sanity
   (B) rescue and deliverance
   (C) weakness and strength
   (D) captivity and escape
   (E) memory and forgetfulness

2. Passage 1 is developed primarily through

   (A) quotations from specific texts
   (B) references to the truths expressed by myths
   (C) the interpretation of symbols
   (D) extended treatment of a specific example
   (E) the presentation of abstract principles

3. How do the pairs of nouns in lines 10–12 of Passage 1 ("hope and . . . longing") support the author's generalization about the endings of Black narratives?

   (A) They convey the complex, unresolved nature of the endings.
   (B) They illustrate the contradictions that are explained in the endings.
   (C) They evoke the heightened sense of power expressed by the author.
   (D) They describe the extremes of emotions that the endings avoid.
   (E) They suggest that readers will find the endings climactic.

---

* mad double: a literary device in which a seemingly insane character represents certain aspects of a conventional character's personality.

4. When he first arrived in New York, Frederick Douglass behaved most like someone who

(A) acts more confident about his accomplishments than the facts warrant

(B) is aware of the tenuous nature of his freedom

(C) objects to being praised publicly, even though such praise is justified

(D) is constantly afraid of things that offer no real threat

(E) takes risks when the occasion seems to justify them

5. The word *thoroughgoing* (line 47) emphasizes Douglass' perception that the justice system is

(A) an efficient mechanism for protecting human rights

(B) a pervasive system of oppression

(C) a local, rather than a federal system

(D) a comprehensive set of abstract beliefs

(E) an inescapable pretext for violence

6. The statement in lines 64-65 ("The Black . . . report") suggests that the Black narrative

(A) offers a subjective, and therefore unrevealing, view of social reality

(B) delivers in a new way truths that are obvious to the unbiased

(C) reveals unpleasant truths that many would prefer not to face

(D) has important things to say, even though it is not read widely enough

(E) confirms discouraging facts already familiar to most readers

7. In Passage 2, the list of objects in lines 11-14 serves to suggest

(A) the lavishness of domestic furnishings

(B) the precarious economic position of women

(C) society's concern with surface rather than underlying truth

(D) the limitations placed on women

(E) the threat of violence in the home sometimes faced by women

8. In Passage 2, Dickinson's perception (lines 16-21) is similar to views expressed by other women writers of her era in that it

(A) hints at the intensity of the urge to be free

(B) asserts that only those who have experienced freedom directly can appreciate it

(C) conveys the impression of belonging to a larger whole

(D) affirms that there is but one correct way to behave

(E) suggests that only those who work well with others will be able to achieve freedom

9. In Passage 2, the inclusion of Dickinson's description of the soul (lines 19-21) reinforces the suggestion that women's desire for escape is

(A) a potentially violent longing

(B) suppressed during childhood

(C) not a common wish

(D) worth risking danger to achieve

(E) hardly ever realized

10. In Passage 2, the word *constructs* (line 30) refers to

(A) literature written by men

(B) definitions of masculinity

(C) physical objects men have created

(D) rules for building and architecture that men admire

(E) sets of ideas established by men

11. The central focus of the two passages suggests that Frederick Douglass and the women writers most significantly share a

(A) heightened awareness of the past
(B) feeling of optimism
(C) belief in the power of literature
(D) desire for freedom and power
(E) determination to improve their economic circumstances

12. Which statement most accurately describes a difference between the two passages?

(A) Passage 1 deals more with general cases than does Passage 2.
(B) Passage 1 is more concerned with the role of language in combating oppression
(C) Passage 1 ends with an expression of optimism, and Passage 2 does not.
(D) Passage 1 deals less directly with political and legal considerations than does Passage 2.
(E) Passage 1 mentions specifically the category of people who are the oppressors, and Passage 2 does not.

Practice Test 1

Section 1

Time—30 Minutes
25 Questions

Solve the following problems, select the best answer choice for each and fill in the corresponding oval on the answer sheet. Use your test booklet for scratchwork.

Notes:

1. You may use a calculator. All of the numbers used are real numbers.

2. Figures accompany some problems. Assume that each has been drawn accurately and lies in a plane, unless the instructions indicate otherwise.

Reference Information

  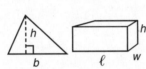

$A = \pi r^2$
$C = 2\pi r$ $\qquad$ $A = \ell w$ $\qquad$ $A = \frac{1}{2}bh$ $\qquad$ $V = \ell wh$ $\qquad$ $V = \pi r^2 h$ $\qquad$ $c^2 = a^2 + b^2$ $\qquad$ Special Right Triangles

The number of degrees of arc in a circle is 360.
The measure in degrees of a straight angle is 180.
The sum of the measures in degrees of the angles of a triangle is 180.

---

1. The cost of a 25-cent candy bar is raised 20 percent. What is the new cost of the candy bar?

   (A) 45¢
   (B) 40¢
   (C) 30¢
   (D) 25¢
   (E) 20¢

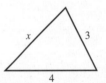

Note: Figure not drawn to scale

2. All of the following could be the value of x EXCEPT

   (A) 3
   (B) 4
   (C) 5
   (D) 6
   (E) 7

GO ON TO THE NEXT PAGE

3. A drawer contains 3 green socks, 6 black socks, and 9 white socks. If a sock is removed at random from the drawer, what is the probability that it will be green?

(A) $\dfrac{1}{2}$

(B) $\dfrac{1}{3}$

(C) $\dfrac{1}{5}$

(D) $\dfrac{1}{6}$

(E) $\dfrac{3}{17}$

4. If $\dfrac{1}{2} \cdot \dfrac{2}{4} \cdot \dfrac{4}{8} \cdot \dfrac{8}{16} = \dfrac{1}{y}$, then $y =$

(A) $\dfrac{1}{2}$

(B) 2

(C) 16

(D) 64

(E) 1,024

5. If each of the digits of 3,642 is increased by 1, the resulting number is then

(A) 1 more than 3,642
(B) 4 more than 3,642
(C) 1,000 more than 3,642
(D) 1,111 more than 3,642
(E) 4,753 more than 3,642

6. A textbook regularly sells for $9.89. When at least a dozen books are purchased, the price is discounted to $9.14 per book. A school purchases 12 dozen of these textbooks for a third-grade class. What is the total amount of money the school saves by buying the textbooks by the dozen instead of individually?

(A) $9.00
(B) $18.00
(C) $19.03
(D) $75.00
(E) $108.00

7. Point Y lies between points X and Z on a line, such that $XY = \dfrac{XZ}{3}$. In terms of XY, what is YZ?

(A) $\dfrac{XY}{3}$

(B) $\dfrac{XY}{2}$

(C) XY

(D) $2XY$

(E) $3XY$

8. A man leaves a $50,000 inheritance after his death. Before the inheritance can be distributed, $10,000 in outstanding debts must first be paid. Half of the remaining money is to be donated to charity, and the balance is to be equally divided among the man's four children. Which of the following expresses the amount to be received by each child?

(A) $\frac{1}{2}(\$50,000) - \$10,000 \div 4$

(B) $\left[\frac{1}{2}(\$50,000 - \$10,000)\right] \div 4$

(C) $\frac{1}{2}(\$50,000) - \$10,000 \div \frac{1}{4}$

(D) $\$50,000 - \$10,000 \times \frac{1}{2} \times \frac{1}{4}$

(E) $\frac{1}{2}(\$50,000 - \$10,000) \times 4$

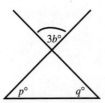

9. From the diagram above, the sum of p and q, in terms of b, equals

(A) $2b$
(B) $3b$
(C) $180 - b$
(D) $180 - 2b$
(E) $180 - 3b$

10. For which values of x is the statement $x^3 > x^2$ true?

(A) all x
(B) $x > 0$
(C) $x > 1$ or $x < -1$
(D) $-1 < x < 1$
(E) $x > 1$

11. If $y = \dfrac{1}{x + 1}$, then what is x in terms of y?

(A) $\dfrac{1}{1 + y}$

(B) $\dfrac{1}{y - 1}$

(C) $\dfrac{1}{y}$

(D) $\dfrac{1 - y}{y}$

(E) $\dfrac{1}{y} - y$

12. The instructions on a can of orange juice concentrate state that the water should be mixed with the concentrate in the ratio of 3 to 1. If 12 liters of orange juice are needed, how many liters of concentrate need to be bought?

(A) 3
(B) 4
(C) 6
(D) 36
(E) 48

GO ON TO THE NEXT PAGE

13. Vinny has an average grade of 88 after taking five tests. What must Vinny score on his sixth test to raise his overall average to 90?

(A) 89
(B) 92
(C) 96
(D) 98
(E) 100

14. $(a - b)^2 =$

(A) $a^2 - b^2$
(B) $a^2 + b^2$
(C) $b^2 - a^2$
(D) $(b - a)^2$
(E) $-(b - a)^2$

15. Mike has five fewer CDs than Greg. Greg has two more CDs than Thad. Which of the following could be the total number of CDs possessed by Mike, Greg, and Thad?

(A) 10
(B) 17
(C) 19
(D) 21
(E) 24

16. The points with coordinates $(-1, 0)$ and $(7, 4)$ lie on line m. Which of the following points also lies on line m?

(A) $(1, -3)$
(B) $(0, 0)$
(C) $(3, 2)$
(D) $(4, 5)$
(E) $(4, 7)$

17. In a certain state, a resident must pay a state income tax of 5 percent. The federal income tax instructions allow a deduction of 75 percent of the amount of state income tax paid. If Jessie was able to claim a deduction of $1,800 on her federal income taxes because of her state income tax, what was her income?

(A) $12,000
(B) $18,000
(C) $24,000
(D) $48,000
(E) $60,000

18. Margaret has n nickels and d dimes, totaling $3.00. If she has 40 coins altogether, which of the following pairs of equations could be used to solve for the number of each coin that Margaret has?

(A) $5n + 10d = 40$
     $n + d = 300$

(B) $5n + 10d = 300$
     $nd = 40$

(C) $5n + 10d = 300$
     $n + d = 40$

(D) $2n + d = 300$
     $n + d = 40$

(E) $n + 2d = 40$
     $nd = 300$

19. In a prehistoric village, rocks, stones, and pebbles were used as money. The relative values of the "coins" were:

    1 rock = 7 stones
    1 rock = 49 pebbles

    If a man used 6 rocks to purchase a hide that cost 5 rocks, 2 stones, and 3 pebbles, how much change was he owed?

    (A) 1 rock, 5 stones, 4 pebbles
    (B) 5 stones, 4 pebbles
    (C) 4 stones, 4 pebbles
    (D) 5 stones, 5 pebbles
    (E) 6 stones, 5 pebbles

20. All of the following are implied by the equation $\dfrac{a}{b} = \dfrac{c}{d}$ EXCEPT

    (A) $ad = bc$

    (B) $\dfrac{a}{c} = \dfrac{b}{d}$

    (C) $\dfrac{a - b}{b} = \dfrac{c - d}{d}$

    (D) $\dfrac{a + b}{a - b} = \dfrac{c + d}{c - d}$

    (E) $\dfrac{ad}{c} = \dfrac{bc}{d}$

21. In the figure above, a square has been circumscribed about a circle with a radius of 5. What is the area of the shaded region?

    (A) $25 - \dfrac{25\pi}{4}$

    (B) $100 - 10\pi$
    (C) $100 - 25\pi$
    (D) $125 - 25\pi$
    (E) $125 - 10\pi$

22. S is the sum of all the consecutive odd integers from 1 through 99 inclusive. T is the sum of all the consecutive even integers from 2 through 98 inclusive. What is the value of $S - T$?

    (A) -50
    (B) -49
    (C) $\quad 0$
    (D) $\quad 49$
    (E) $\quad 50$

GO ON TO THE NEXT PAGE

23. Four congruent equilateral triangles are arranged without overlapping to form one large equilateral triangle. If the perimeter of one of the small triangles is x, what is the perimeter of the large triangle, in terms of x?

    (A) $2x$
    (B) $3x$
    (C) $4x$
    (D) $6x$
    (E) $12x$

24. A 16-inch by 36-inch piece of material is to be cut into equal circles, with the least amount of material left over. What is the amount of material that remains if the largest possible circles are cut from the material?

    (A) $576(\pi - 1)$
    (B) $4(144 - \pi)$
    (C) 144π
    (D) $144 - \pi$
    (E) $144(4 - \pi)$

25. Office A has a staff of 6 people. A certain project will take the regular staff 24 hours to complete. Assuming that all of the workers will perform at this rate, how many additional workers must be employed to complete the job in 8 hours?

    (A)   4
    (B)   12
    (C)   18
    (D)   24
    (E)   48

S T O P   If you finish before time is called, you may check your work on this section only. Do not turn to any other section in the test.

[This page intentionally left blank]

Section 2

For each question below, choose the best answer from the choices given and fill in the corresponding oval on the answer sheet.

Each sentence below has either one or two blanks in it and is followed by five choices labeled (A) through (E). These choices represent words or phrases that have been left out. Choose the word or phrase that, if inserted into the sentence, would best fit the meaning of the sentence as a whole.

Example:

Canine massage is a veterinary technique for calming dogs that are extremely _____.

- (A) inept
- (B) disciplined
- (C) controlled
- (D) agitated
- (E) restrained

1. Although we've seen considerable _____ in the various media about political realignments and power shifts, no one has professed certain knowledge on these complex topics.

- (A) articles
- (B) coverage
- (C) essays
- (D) journalism
- (E) speculation

2. Most people are willing to accept just and well-considered decisions; it is the _____ ones that provoke dissent.

- (A) punitive
- (B) unpopular
- (C) negative
- (D) arbitrary
- (E) perturbing

3. The violation was so _____ that the camp counselor, who customarily overlooked harmless offenses, felt that the time had come to enforce the rule.

- (A) unintentional
- (B) flagrant
- (C) unusual
- (D) secretive
- (E) petty

4. Appalled by the nearly _____ conditions in the run-down tenement, the social worker wrote an _____ letter to the newspapers hoping to focus attention on the problem.

- (A) awful..entrancing
- (B) intolerable..impassioned
- (C) indescribable..upbeat
- (D) unique..irritable
- (E) unpleasant..angry

5. Unlike his early figures with _____ proportions that disturbed most viewers' sensibilities, Claude's later sculptures revealed an agreeable symmetry.

- (A) skewed
- (B) uneven
- (C) offbeat
- (D) surprising
- (E) astounding

Peterson's SAT Success

6. Fans of Gabriel García Márquez believe that the atypical _____ of fantasy and reality in his novels is a deliberate attempt to _____ the bizarre juxtaposition of those elements in real life.

(A) mixture..repudiate
(B) exposition..highlight
(C) blend..mirror
(D) occurrence..explain
(E) complexity..justify

7. Genetic researchers are interested in answering the question of whether certain human traits are _____, or if they arise only after birth, as a result of a person's _____.

(A) natural..culture
(B) innate..wishes
(C) learned..upbringing
(D) inherited..environment
(E) inborn..heritage

8. *The Autocrat of the Breakfast Table*, by Oliver Wendell Holmes, reflects not the _____ attitude suggested by its title but rather the _____ of an educated, witty man.

(A) lighthearted..novel insights
(B) frivolous..profound contemplations
(C) serious..jocularities
(D) doctrinaire..enlightened humor
(E) cavalier..sharp observations

9. While Janet enjoyed the challenge of plowing through dense, _____ passages of nineteenth-century prose, her students found the work _____.

(A) boring..interesting
(B) annoying..enervating
(C) terse..intensely profound
(D) formal..depressing
(E) verbose..convoluted

GO ON TO THE NEXT PAGE

Each question below consists of two words that are related to one another in some way. Following these words are five sets of two words each, labeled (A) through (E). From these, you must choose the set that denotes a relationship most similar to the relationship expressed in the original set.

Example:
RUNNER : SPEED::
(A) acrobat : height
(B) dancer : grace
(C) minister: holy book
(D) waiter : order
(E) landlord : rent

10. TIRED : EXHAUSTED ::

(A) free : democratic
(B) tidy : haphazard
(C) hungry : famished
(D) hesitant : weak
(E) innocent : savvy

11. CINNAMON : SPICE ::

(A) batter : cake
(B) lace : braid
(C) cider : beverage
(D) broccoli : condiment
(E) decoration : furniture

12. CHUCKLE : AMUSEMENT ::

(A) sorrow : misery
(B) comment : opinion
(C) tremor : glee
(D) whimper : fear
(E) titter : giggle

13. FOOD : EDIBLE ::

(A) rations : careful
(B) water : potable
(C) clothing : protective
(D) energy : swift
(E) glass : breakable

14. FALLACIOUS : TRUTH ::

(A) erroneous : fault
(B) anxious : perception
(C) ornery : scorn
(D) distraught : thought
(E) diminutive : bulk

15. JEOPARDIZE : DANGER ::

(A) legalize : threat
(B) lampoon : ridicule
(C) undermine : faith
(D) compose : harmony
(E) hypothesize : theory

Peterson's SAT Success

Read each of the passages carefully, then answer the questions that come after them. The answer to each question may be stated overtly or only implied. You will not have to use outside knowledge to answer the questions—all the material you will need will be in the passage itself.

Line There has been very little research on the relationship between economics and sociology. But even if many single pieces of knowledge are still missing, the main
(5) structure of the relationship can be discerned without too much difficulty. There are only a few different ways in which economics and sociology can be related to each other. One of the two disciplines can
(10) try to take over the subject matter of the other, which would constitute a case of "economic imperialism" or "sociological imperialism." Alternatively, they can each have their own distinct subject areas and
(15) ignore the other, as has been the case during the twentieth century. And finally, there can be open borders and free communication between economics and sociology, which it is hoped represents the direction in
(20) which things are currently moving.

The early economists, such as Adam Smith, Karl Marx, and John Stuart Mill, are generally considered to have struck a happy balance between economics and sociology.
(25) They wrote about economic theory as well as social institutions with both ease and insight. It is true that "economics" and "sociology" did not exist as two distinct academic disciplines at that time, but it was
(30) of course perfectly clear to these economistswhen they were dealing with economic topics as opposed to social topics.

What distinguished Smith, Marx, and Mill from many later sociologists and
(35) economists was their ambition to define economics in a broad manner and to be interested in the insights of the other social sciences. Mill said, "A person is not likely to be a good economist who is nothing else.
(40) Social phenomena acting and reacting on

one another, they cannot rightly be understood apart."

Mill's pragmatic attitude toward economic science was not popular in all
(45) circles, least of all with his colleague and one-time friend Auguste Comte. The thrust of Comte's argument (in *Cours de Philosophie Positive*) was that knowledge and society are going through an evolutionary
(50) development from lower to higher stages, and that "sociology" represents the highest stage of human knowledge. In Comte's scheme, "economics" had no independent place and his book actually contained a
(55) vitriolic attack on economics—that "alleged science" as he repeatedly referred to it. Apart from the work of Adam Smith, which Comte for some idiosyncratic reason exempted from his attack, he considered
(60) economics a thoroughly useless and metaphysical enterprise. The best one could do was give it up and replace it with sociology, the "queen of all sciences."

GO ON TO THE NEXT PAGE

16. With which of the following statements about economics and sociology would the author of the passage most likely agree?

   (A) Very little is understood about the difference between economics and sociology.
   (B) One discipline should simply blend with the other for the sake of unity.
   (C) Economics and sociology are separate but equal disciplines.
   (D) Economics is best understood separate from sociology altogether.
   (E) The metaphysical aspects of economics render it impossible to quantify.

17. The author uses the phrase "economic imperialism" (line 12) to describe

   (A) a discipline asserting authority over another discipline
   (B) the merging of two distinct disciplines
   (C) a discipline making amends for its shortcomings
   (D) the creation of a new and balanced philosophy
   (E) the destruction of an outdated philosophy

18. The passage presents Auguste Comte as

   (A) a close former associate of Adam Smith
   (B) an environmental evolutionist
   (C) the only former economist who understood the new discipline of sociology
   (D) a detractor of the study of economics
   (E) the most respectable sociologist since John Stuart Mill

19. According to the passage, John Stuart Mill was

   (A) regrettably in opposition to Auguste Comte
   (B) the only sensible economist of the early group
   (C) the only early economist worth quoting
   (D) more interested in sociology than in economics
   (E) both practical and broad-minded

20. The author of the passage believes that the difficulty with more recent professionals in economics and sociology is

   (A) their inattentiveness to earlier colleagues
   (B) their parochial interests
   (C) their absolute lack of pragmatism
   (D) an ignorance of the current global state
   (E) a lack of awareness of the historic contributions of colleagues even in their own fields

21. In line 33, "distinguished" most nearly means

   (A) eminent
   (B) set apart
   (C) dignified
   (D) discriminated
   (E) recognized

22. The primary purpose of the passage as a whole is to

   (A) suggest that the fields of economics and sociology should interact more closely than they do now
   (B) support Auguste Comte's assertion that sociology is the "queen of all sciences"
   (C) describe the primary differences between the disciplines of economics and sociology
   (D) trace the historical development of the fields of economics and sociology
   (E) contrast the views of Adam Smith, Karl Marx, and John Stuart Mill with those of Auguste Comte

Questions 23–30 refer to the following passage.

Line Several years ago, Ralph Nader sailed through our town knocking everyone flat with fear. His pronouncement? Hot dogs contain only 12 percent protein!

(5) What did this mean to a nation of weiner eaters? Was it much too little? How much harm does a 12 percent hot dog do? The panic eventually subsided, and we are now able to place the weiner in perspective.

(10) From a nutritional point of view, we should calculate protein as a proportion of the calories, rather than of the weight, in the food. In weiners, 16 percent of the calories are protein. The real reason for concern is

(15) not that hot dogs contain 16 percent protein calories, but that they contain 80 percent fat calories.

The protein content of a hot dog is actually quite respectable. There is no such

(20) thing as a 100 percent protein food. All protein sources contain large amounts of fats, carbohydrates, and water and probably quite a bit less protein than you have been led to believe. People on so-called high

(25) protein diets are advised to eat steak and cheddar cheese, for example. The proportion of calories from protein in round or T-bone steak is at most 50 percent (and 50 percent fat), cheddar cheese is 25 percent

(30) protein and 75 percent fat, while fillet of sole is almost 80 percent protein (with 20 percent fat). While all these foods are rich in protein, they (except for the sole) are even richer in fat. They contain no carbohydrates.

(35) There are rich sources of protein that contain no fat, but are high in carbohydrates. Take, for example, skim milk, with 40 percent of calories from protein and 60 percent from carbohydrates; cooked red

(40) kidney beans with 25 percent protein calories and 70 percent carbohydrate calories; whole wheat bread with 16 percent protein and almost 80 percent carbohydrate

calories; and oatmeal porridge with 15

(45) percent protein and 70 percent carbohydrate calories. This is why we need to eat a variety of sources of protein to ensure the right balance of fat and carbohydrates. Remember, we want our diets to have no

(50) less than 10 percent of the calories from protein, no more than 30 percent from fat, and the remaining 60 percent from carbohydrates.

Protein is necessary for the constant

(55) building and rebuilding of every cell in our bodies. It and other nutrients are used in the performance of the various functions of the body. Proteins produce enzymes that cause life-sustaining reactions in the body. There

(60) are enzymes to handle every nutrient in our food. For example, there are enzymes called amylases in the mouth and intestines that convert the starch in our foods to the sugar maltose. The enzyme maltase in the intestine

(65) converts it to glucose (blood sugar) which passes through the intestine wall into the blood to be distributed to various tissues such as muscle, brain, and liver. In every cell of these tissues there are about thirty

(70) enzymes involved in breaking down glucose to give the cell the energy it contains; about four calories for each gram of glucose. Without these enzymes, the body can't use the food it receives.

(75) We must have amino acids to make protein. Amino acids look like beads, and proteins are like long bead chains twisted together. The body breaks down the protein it receives from foods into amino acids,

(80) reorganizes them, and then forms its own protein. Of about twenty amino acids in all protein foods, only nine cannot be formed or transformed by our bodies and must be in the diet in the right amounts. These are

(85) called essential amino acids.

GO ON TO THE NEXT PAGE ▶

23. The passage suggests that one reason for not eating hot dogs is that
    (A) Ralph Nader finds them objectionable
    (B) 80 percent of their calories are fat calories
    (C) they are low in protein
    (D) their caloric value is unknown
    (E) our diets don't require fats

24. The author's tone in this passage can best be described as
    (A) instructive
    (B) philosophical
    (C) outraged
    (D) amused
    (E) rebellious

25. According to the passage, amino acids
    (A) produce enzymes that sustain life
    (B) manufacture maltase and convert it to glucose
    (C) are derived from carbohydrates
    (D) are used by the body to form proteins
    (E) are the source of our calories from protein

26. The author lists T-bone steak and cheddar cheese (lines 28–29) as
    (A) components of a diet that the author is endorsing
    (B) foods that should be replaced by lower-fat choices
    (C) examples of the link between fat and protein
    (D) foods whose nutritional value has been questioned by activists
    (E) healthier and more natural alternatives to hot dogs

27. The main purpose of this passage is to
    (A) provide the reader with a lesson
    (B) debunk a myth
    (C) change the reader's opinion
    (D) dispute the authority of a self-proclaimed expert
    (E) dispute conventional wisdom

28. The questions in lines 5–7 serve primarily to
    (A) highlight the author's doubt about the role of protein in the human diet
    (B) express the confusion with which the public greeted Ralph Nader's pronouncement about the protein in hot dogs
    (C) condemn Ralph Nader's inability to explain the significance of his finding about the protein content of hot dogs
    (D) outline the main points that the author will discuss in the rest of the passage
    (E) introduce the distinction between protein content as a proportion of weight and protein content as a proportion of calories

29. The passage suggests that the primary role proteins play in the body is to

(A) convert sugars into starches
(B) strengthen the muscles and bones
(C) break down and rearrange amino acids
(D) enable the body to convert food into energy
(E) rebuild the tissues of the liver and brain

30. The reference to "beads" in line 77 provides an analogy for the

(A) difference between amino acids and enzymes
(B) purposes for which the body uses amino acids
(C) importance of certain amino acids in the body
(D) functions of amino acids in the body
(E) way in which amino acids form proteins

STOP If you finish before time is called, you may check your work on this section only. Do not turn to any other section in the test.

Section 3

Reference Information

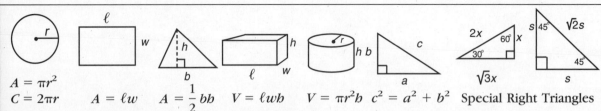

$A = \pi r^2$
$C = 2\pi r$ $A = \ell w$ $A = \dfrac{1}{2}bh$ $V = \ell wh$ $V = \pi r^2 h$ $c^2 = a^2 + b^2$ Special Right Triangles

The number of degrees of arc in a circle is 360.
The measure in degrees of a straight angle is 180.
The sum of the measures in degrees of the angles of a triangle is 180.

Directions for Quantitative Comparison Questions

Questions 1–15 each consist of two boxed quantities, one in Column A and one in Column B. Compare them and select:

   A if the quantity in Column A is greater;
   B if the quantity in Column B is greater;
   C if the two quantities are equal;
   D if the relationship cannot be determined from
      the information given.

A response of E will be considered an omission.

Notes:

1. Some questions provide information about one or both of the quantities to be compared. This information is unboxed and centered above the two columns.
2. A symbol that appears in both columns represents the same value in each.
3. Letters such as x, n, and k stand for real numbers.

EXAMPLES

	Column A	Column B	Answers
E1	$\dfrac{1}{2}$ of 50	$\dfrac{1}{4}$ of 25	● Ⓑ Ⓒ Ⓓ Ⓔ
E2	The number of degrees in a circle	The number of degrees in a square	Ⓐ Ⓑ ● Ⓓ Ⓔ
	$x > 0$		
E3	x	$\dfrac{1}{x}$	Ⓐ Ⓑ Ⓒ ● Ⓔ

Column A	**Column B**

1. $\dfrac{16 \times 10^6}{32 \times 10^4}$ 10^2

2. The number of seconds in x minutes   The number of minutes in x hours

3. 32 8.2×4.3

Column A	**Column B**

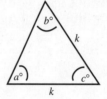

4. $a + c$ $b + c$

$z \neq 0$

5. $4z$ $(2z)^2$

6. $3^2 \cdot 2^3$ $2^2 \cdot 3^3$

GO ON TO THE NEXT PAGE

Column A | **Column B**

7.

| The perimeter of a square with area 64 | The perimeter of a rectangle with area 64 |

A coat is on sale for x dollars, which is 25% less than its original price.

8.

| The original price of the coat | $.75x$ |

9.

| Volume of a cylinder with a diameter of 2 and a height of 4 | Volume of a rectangular solid with dimensions $2 \times 2 \times 4$ |

Questions 10–11 refer to the following definition.

Column A   **Column B**

$$a!b = \frac{1}{a} + \frac{1}{b}$$
$$ab \neq 0$$

10.

| $a!b$ | $\dfrac{a+b}{ab}$ |

$$x!y + 9 = 0$$

11.

| 9 | $x!y$ |

Column A	**Column B**		**Column A**	**Column B**

12.

The distance from the point (a, a) to the point (p, q) on the coordinate axes	The distance from the point (a, a) to the point (q, p) on the coordinate axes

14.

$(x + y)^2 - (x - y)^2$	0

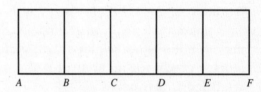

Note: Figure not drawn to scale.

A row of apartments is represented by the boxes above. A surveyor wants to measure the width of each apartment. He finds that:

$$AD = CF = 12 \text{ and } BD = CE = 8$$

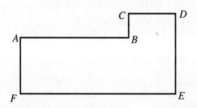

In the figure above, all segments intersect at right angles.

13.

$FA + AB + BC + CD$	$FB + BD$

15.

CD	4

GO ON TO THE NEXT PAGE

Directions for Student-Produced Response Questions

Enter your responses to questions 16–25 in the special grids provided on your answer sheet. Input your answers as indicated in the directions below.

Answer: $\frac{4}{9}$ or 4/9

Answer: 1.4
Either position is correct.

Write answer → in boxes.

← Fraction line

Grid in → result.

Decimal → point

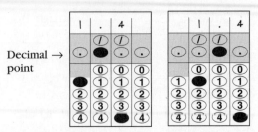

Note: You may begin your answer in any column, space permitting. Leave blank any columns not needed.

- Writing your answer in the boxes at the top of the columns will help you accurately grid your answer, but it is not required. **You will only receive credit for an answer if the ovals are filled in properly.**

- Only fill in one oval in each column.

- If a problem has several correct answers, just grid in one of them.

- There are no negative answers.

- **Never grid in mixed numbers.** The answer $3\frac{1}{5}$ must be gridded as 16/5 or 3.2.

If  is gridded, it will be read as $\frac{31}{5}$, not $3\frac{1}{5}$.

Decimal Accuracy

Decimal answers must be gridded as accurately as possible. The answer 0.3333 . . . must be gridded as .333 or .334. **Less accurate values, such as .33 or .34, are not acceptable.**

Acceptable ways to grid $\frac{1}{3}$ = .3333 . . .

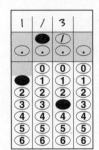

Peterson's SAT Success

16. If $a = b + 10$, $b = c + 15$, and $c = d + 25$, what is the value of $a - d$?

17. If Kelvin eats $\frac{1}{4}$ of a pie, Kirsty eats $\frac{1}{3}$ of what's left after Kelvin is done, and Kitty eats $\frac{1}{2}$ of what's left after Kirsty is done, then what part of the pie is left?

1 pound of turkey costs $0.85
2 pounds of chicken costs $1.30

18. What is the difference, in dollars, between the price of a 12-pound turkey and a 3-pound chicken? (Disregard the $ sign when gridding your answer.)

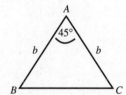

19. How many degrees greater is the measure of $\angle B$ than the measure of $\angle A$?

20. The average of three numbers is 67. The average of two of the numbers is 65. What is the third number?

$$4 \le a \le 14$$
$$7 \le b \le 12$$

21. What is the maximum value of $\frac{b}{a}$?

$$\begin{array}{r} X\,Y\,X \\ +\ Z\,Y\,Z \\ \hline W\,W\,W \end{array}$$

22. Grid in a possible value of Y in the correctly worked addition problem above.

23. The houses on Main Street are numbered in multiples in 6. That is, the first house has a street number of 6, the second 12, and so on. What is the sum of the last digits of the street numbers of the 83rd, 84th, and 85th houses?

GO ON TO THE NEXT PAGE

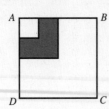

24. Each of the three squares in the figure above shares a common vertex at *A*. The shaded interior square has another vertex at the center of square *ABCD*, and the smallest square has another vertex at the center of the shaded square. What fractional part of square *ABCD* is shaded?

25. On a certain street corner there are two lights, a red one and a blue one, that flash at regular intervals. The red light flashes three times per minute and the blue light flashes once every minute and a half. If the lights have just flashed at the same time, the number of times the red light will flash alone before the two lights flash together again is how many times greater than the number of times the blue light will flash alone before the two lights flash together again?

S T O P If you finish before time is called, you may check your work on this section only. Do not turn to any other section in the test.

Peterson's SAT Success

[This page intentionally left blank]

Section 4

Time—30 Minutes
35 Questions

For each question below, choose the best answer from the choices given and fill in the corresponding oval on the answer sheet.

Each sentence below has either one or two blanks in it and is followed by five choices labeled (A) through (E). These choices represent words or phrases that have been left out. Choose the word or phrase that, if inserted into the sentence, would best fit the meaning of the sentence as a whole.

Example:

Canine massage is a veterinary technique for calming dogs that are extremely _____.

(A) inept
(B) disciplined
(C) controlled
(D) agitated
(E) restrained   Ⓐ Ⓑ Ⓒ ⬤ Ⓔ

1. Despite his blustery manner, Kevin was so _____ that he could not bear the sight of his own blood when he scraped his knee.

   (A) frightened
   (B) extroverted
   (C) foolish
   (D) squeamish
   (E) emotional

2. Long terms in prison can foster an odd duality for prisoners who regard their release date with both _____ and _____.

   (A) eagerness..excitement
   (B) fear..trepidation
   (C) anticipation..apprehension
   (D) antipathy..fear
   (E) pleasure..confusion

3. While the ancient Greek artists valued beauty, they were ultimately _____, who felt that function dictated form.

   (A) craftspeople
   (B) pragmatists
   (C) inventors
   (D) aesthetes
   (E) traditionalists

4. Doctors frequently warn dedicated runners that a(n) _____ return to training will only serve to _____ an injury.

   (A) failure to..prolong
   (B) hurried..exacerbate
   (C) impulsive..expedite
   (D) inevitable..extenuate
   (E) prompt..coddle

5. He was a truly _____ man, insistent upon _____ pronouncements at inopportune times, so that his family tended to leave the scene if his lips so much as parted.

   (A) misunderstood..deliberate
   (B) maligned..historic
   (C) loquacious..hearty
   (D) irascible..placid
   (E) tedious..oracular

6. Escaping a stormy, _____ career as head coach at a state university, Jeff gratefully accepted a more private position at a small college.

   (A) blustering
   (B) public
   (C) exciting
   (D) recent
   (E) impressive

7. The director allowed her younger dance troupe to embark on a world tour, but she _____ from committing them to a breakneck pace and _____ the right to cancel engagements if the toll of traveling proved too great.

   (A) abstained..anticipated
   (B) withheld..ignored
   (C) refrained..reserved
   (D) departed..observed
   (E) disembarked..embraced

8. Lawmakers eager to promote a piece of legislation no doubt feel _____ whenever their bill _____ in committee.

   (A) exhilaration..stalls
   (B) exasperation..passes
   (C) uplifted..falters
   (D) thwarted..languishes
   (E) satisfaction..idles

9. In a typical autocracy, _____ is held by one individual who may ignore public will in favor of a personally _____ course.

   (A) control..mandated
   (B) rule..sophisticated
   (C) triumph..gratifying
   (D) power..reviled
   (E) management..approved

10. The Berlin Wall, constructed between East and West Berlin after World War II, formed a visible political _____; even after the wall fell, cultural differences _____ the nation.

    (A) barrier..conquered
    (B) boundary..united
    (C) statement..separated
    (D) partition..democratized
    (E) demarcation..divided

GO ON TO THE NEXT PAGE

Each question below consists of two words that are related to one another in some way. Following these words are five sets of two words each, labeled (A) through (E). From these, you must choose the set that denotes a relationship most similar to the relationship expressed in the original set.

Example:
RUNNER : SPEED::
(A) acrobat : height
(B) dancer : grace
(C) minister: holy book
(D) waiter : order
(E) landlord : rent

11. PILOT : JET ::

(A) pharmacist : drugs
(B) chef : kitchen
(C) captain : ship
(D) guide : museum
(E) teacher : school

12. FURNACE : WARMTH ::

(A) vessel : space
(B) coffee : caffeine
(C) bicycle : trip
(D) thread : cloth
(E) wall : enclosure

13. SYLLABUS : COURSE ::

(A) synopsis : novel
(B) nave : church
(C) outback : territory
(D) introduction : lesson
(E) history : nation

14. REFEREE : GAME ::

(A) manager : sales
(B) dancer : technique
(C) arbiter : dispute
(D) coach : team
(E) consultant : recommendation

15. REASON : PLAUSIBLE ::

(A) welcome : cordial
(B) desire : fervent
(C) pursuit : vain
(D) defense : lackluster
(E) argument : cogent

16. DRIVER : MAP ::

(A) dancer : pirouette
(B) baker : salad
(C) author : novel
(D) builder : blueprint
(E) cartwright : shed

17. CANISTER : STORAGE ::

(A) attic : insulation
(B) vehicle : transporation
(C) wine : cask
(D) yoke : ox
(E) train : speed

18. VORACIOUS : HUNGER ::

(A) exhausted : sleepiness
(B) artless : guile
(C) massive : length
(D) small : frailty
(E) fanciful : exaggeration

19. SWEETEN : ACERBIC ::

(A) sugar : caloric
(B) anger : riled
(C) correct : accurate
(D) relax : rigid
(E) provoke : languid

20. VISION : GLASSES ::

(A) hearing : radio
(B) movement : limb
(C) sight : eyes
(D) limp : cane
(E) injury : helmet

Peterson's SAT Success

21. ATTITUDE : BROAD-MINDED ::

(A) education : catholic
(B) goal : elusive
(C) opinion : hidebound
(D) behavior : uninhibited
(E) business : international

22. SPREAD : PROLIFERATE ::

(A) plead : remonstrate
(B) goal : prod
(C) seep : pour
(D) preach : promote
(E) desist : commence

23. INDIFFERENT : PREJUDICE ::

(A) explicit : clarity
(B) timid : effrontery
(C) alluring : apparel
(D) elaborate : detail
(E) articulate : presentation

GO ON TO THE NEXT PAGE

Read this passage carefully, then answer the questions that come after it. The answer to each question may be stated overtly or only implied. You will not have to use outside knowledge to answer the questions—all the material you will need will be in the passage itself.

Questions 24–35 are based on the following passage.

The following passage is adapted from a short story, published in 1891.

Line Suddenly Lady Windermere looked eagerly round the room, and said, in her clear contralto voice, "Where is my chiromantist?"

"Your what, Gladys?" exclaimed the
(5) Duchess, trying to remember what a chiromantist really was, and hoping it was not the same as a chiropodist.

"My chiromantist, Duchess; I can't live without him at present. I must certainly
(10) introduce him to you."

"Introduce him!" cried the Duchess. "You don't mean to say he is here?" She began looking about for a small tortoise-shell fan and a very tattered lace shawl so as to be
(15) ready to go at a moment's notice.

"Of course he is here; I would not dream of giving a party without him. He tells me I have a pure psychic hand."

"Oh, I see!" said the Duchess, feeling very
(20) much relieved. "He tells fortunes, I suppose?"

"And misfortunes, too," answered Lady Windermere. "Any amount of them. Next year, for instance, I am in great danger, both by land and sea, so I am going to live in a
(25) balloon, and draw up my dinner in a basket every evening. It is all written down on my little finger, or on the palm of my hand. I forget which."

"But surely that is tempting Providence,
(30) Gladys."

"My dear Duchess, surely Providence can resist temptation by this time. Everyone should have their hands told once a month, so as to know what not to do. Of course,
(35) one does it all the same, but it is so pleasant to be warned. Ah, here is Mr. Podgers! Now, Mr. Podgers, I want you to tell the Duchess of Paisley's hand."

"Dear Gladys, I really don't think it is
(40) quite right," said the Duchess, feebly unbuttoning a rather soiled kid glove.

"Nothing interesting ever is," said Lady Windermere. "But I must introduce you. Duchess, this is Mr. Podgers, my pet
(45) chiromantist. Mr. Podgers, this is the Duchess of Paisley, and if you say that she has a larger mountain of the moon than I have, I will never believe in you again."

"I am sure, Gladys, there is nothing of
(50) the kind in my hand," said the Duchess gravely.

"Your Grace is quite right," said Mr. Podgers, glancing at the little fat hand. "The mountain of the moon is not developed. The
(55) line of life, however, is excellent. You will live to a great age, Duchess, and be extremely happy. Ambition—very moderate, line of intellect not exaggerated, line of heart—"

"Now, do be indiscreet, Mr. Podgers,"
(60) cried Lady Windermere.

"Nothing would give me greater pleasure," said Mr. Podgers, bowing, "if the Duchess ever had been, but I am sorry to say that I see great permanence of affection,
(65) combined with a strong sense of duty."

"Pray go on, Mr. Podgers," said the Duchess, looking quite pleased.

"Economy is not the least of your Grace's virtues," continued Mr. Podgers, and
(70) Lady Windermere went off into fits of laughter.

"Economy is a very good thing," remarked the Duchess complacently. "When I married Paisley he had eleven castles, and
(75) not a single house fit to live in."

"And now he has twelve houses, and not a single castle," cried Lady Windermere. "You have told the Duchess's character admirably, Mr. Podgers, and now you must
(80) tell Lady Flora's." In answer to a nod, a tall girl stepped awkwardly from behind the sofa and held out a long, bony hand.

"Ah, a pianist!" said Mr. Podgers. "Very reserved, very honest, and with a great love
(85) of animals."

"Quite true!" exclaimed the Duchess, turning to Lady Windermere. "Flora keeps two dozen collie dogs at Macloskie, and would turn our town house into a menag-
(90) erie if her father would let her."

"Well, that is just what I do with my house every Thursday evening," cried Lady Windermere, laughing. "Only I like lions better than collie dogs. But Mr. Podgers
(95) must read some more hands for us. Come, Lady Marvel, show him yours."

But Lady Marvel entirely declined to have her past or her future exposed. In fact, many people seemed afraid to face the odd
(100) little man with his stereotyped smile and his bright, beady eyes; and when he told poor Lady Fermor right out before everyone that she did not care a bit for music, but was extremely fond of musicians, it was generally
(105) felt that chiromancy was a most dangerous science, and one that ought not to be encouraged, except in private.

Lord Arthur Savile, however, who did not know anything about Lady Fermor's
(110) unfortunate story, was filled with curiosity to have his own hand read, and feeling somewhat shy about putting himself forward, crossed to where Lady Windermere was sitting and asked her if she thought Mr.
(115) Podgers would mind.

"Of course he won't mind," said Lady Windermere. "That is what he is here for. All my lions, Lord Arthur, are performing lions, and jump through hoops whenever I
(120) ask them."

24. Lady Windermere's attitude toward fortune telling can best be described as

(A) wistful
(B) reverent
(C) dismissive
(D) playful
(E) serious

25. The Duchess wants to "be ready to go at a moment's notice" (line 15) because she

(A) is afraid of chiropodists
(B) is tired of Lady Windermere
(C) is embarrassed at not being able to remember the difference between a chiropodist and a chiromantist
(D) thinks having her fortune told would be tempting Providence
(E) does not want to meet Mr. Podgers

26. The passage suggests that the Duchess wears a tattered shawl (line 14) and soiled gloves (line 41) because she

(A) likes to save money
(B) cannot afford to buy nicer ones
(C) cares little about her appearance
(D) prefers to buy nice things for her homes
(E) knew that this party would not require fancy dress

GO ON TO THE NEXT PAGE

27. Lady Windermere's plan to live in a balloon and draw up her dinner in a basket (lines 24–25) indicates her

(A) desire to impress the Duchess
(B) inability to separate reality from fantasy
(C) whimsical attitude toward fortune-telling
(D) fear of the danger Mr. Podgers has predicted
(E) respect for the accuracy of Mr. Podger's fortunes

28. Lady Windermere's speech in lines 31–36 shows that she

(A) likes to give advice to others
(B) dislikes knowing what is going to happen to her
(C) believes that Mr. Podgers has amazing and uncanny powers
(D) does not take either Providence or chiromancy very seriously
(E) makes a point of disagreeing with the Duchess whenever possible

29. The Duchess says, "I really don't think it is quite right" in lines 39–40 because she

(A) has philosophical and moral objections to fortunetelling
(B) thinks that trying to discern the future could be dangerous
(C) does not like to do what Lady Windermere tells her to do
(D) believes that Mr. Podgers is likely to predict bad events in her future
(E) is afraid that Mr. Podgers will reveal her secrets in front of Lady Windermere

30. Lady Windermere's use of the phrase "my pet chiromantist" (lines 44–45) suggests that Lady Windermere

(A) provides for Mr. Podgers's needs
(B) desires Mr. Podgers's companionship
(C) perceives Mr. Podgers's devotion to her
(D) feels possessive toward Mr. Podgers
(E) likes to belittle Mr. Podgers in front of her friends

31. By characterizing the Duchess's line of intellect as "not exaggerated" (line 58), Mr. Podgers shows himself to be

(A) tactful
(B) disdainful
(C) imaginative
(D) indifferent
(E) suspicious

32. The Duchess looks "quite pleased" (line 67) because

(A) her future is brighter than is Lady Windermere's
(B) she is relieved that Mr. Podgers is not a chiropodist
(C) her fears about tempting Providence have been allayed
(D) Mr. Podgers has not suggested any danger in her immediate future
(E) Mr. Podgers has described her characteristics positively

33. The word "reserved" in line 84 most nearly means

    (A) limited in scope
    (B) retained for oneself
    (C) characterized by reticence
    (D) set aside for a particular purpose
    (E) marked by lack of enthusiasm

34. In addition to telling people's fortunes, Mr. Podgers

    (A) describes their characteristics
    (B) describes their past endeavors
    (C) describes their present occupations
    (D) encourages their unspoken plans
    (E) tells them how to avoid the difficulties that he foresees

35. In line 97, the word "declined" most nearly means

    (A) failed
    (B) drooped
    (C) refused
    (D) descended
    (E) deteriorated

S T O P If you finish before time is called, you may check your work on this section only. Do not turn to any other section in the test.

Section 5

Time—15 Minutes
10 Questions

Solve the following problems, select the best answer choice for each and fill in the corresponding oval on the answer sheet. Use your test booklet for scratchwork.

Notes:

1. You may use a calculator. All of the numbers used are real numbers.

2. Figures accompany some problems. Assume that each has been drawn accurately and lies in a plane, unless the instructions indicate otherwise.

Reference Information

  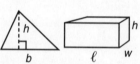

$A = \pi r^2$
$C = 2\pi r$ $\quad A = \ell w \quad A = \frac{1}{2} bh \quad V = \ell wh \quad V = \pi r^2 h \quad c^2 = a^2 + b^2$ Special Right Triangles

The number of degrees of arc in a circle is 360.
The measure in degrees of a straight angle is 180.
The sum of the measures in degrees of the angles of a triangle is 180.

1. If $1 + 2 + 3 + 4 + 5 + 6 = x + 7 + 11$,
then $x =$

   (A) 1
   (B) 2
   (C) 3
   (D) 4
   (E) 5

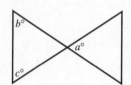

2. In the figure above, what is the value of $a + b + c$?

   (A)   270
   (B)   180
   (C)   120
   (D)   90
   (E)   45

3. At a dairy it takes 90 seconds to fill 30 one-gallon jugs of milk. How many minutes does it take to fill 90 jugs of milk?

   (A) 1
   (B) 3
   (C) 3.5
   (D) 4
   (E) 4.5

4. If the ratio of the altitude of ΔA to the altitude of ΔB is 2:1, then the ratio of the area of ΔA to the area of ΔB is

   (A) 1:1
   (B) 2:1
   (C) 4:1
   (D) 8:1
   (E) It cannot be determined from the information given.

5. A number that is divisible by both 6 and 8 is also divisible by

   (A) 5
   (B) 9
   (C) 11
   (D) 16
   (E) 24

6. What is the average (arithmetic mean) of $8x + 5$, $-3x + 9$, 0 and $7x - 2$?

   (A) $3x + 1$
   (B) $3x + 3$
   (C) $4x + 1$
   (D) $4x + 4$
   (E) $12x + 12$

7. If Elizabeth runs m miles in h hours, how many miles does she run in x hours, in terms of m, h, and x?

   (A) mhx
   (B) $mx + mh$
   (C) $\dfrac{mh}{x}$
   (D) $\dfrac{mx}{h}$
   (E) $\dfrac{m}{h + x}$

8. If a truck has a wheel with a radius of 2 feet, how many revolutions does the wheel make each time the truck is driven 1 mile? (5,280 feet = 1 mile)

   (A) $\dfrac{1,320}{\pi}$
   (B) $\dfrac{2,640}{\pi}$
   (C) $\dfrac{5,280}{\pi}$
   (D) 5,280
   (E) $5,280\pi$

GO ON TO THE NEXT PAGE

9. The operation $\boxed{x}$ indicates that one should subtract 2 from x and then multiply the result by 2. The operation $\textcircled{x}$ indicates that one should multiply x by 2 and then subtract 2 from the product.

$$\textcircled{x} - \boxed{x} =$$

(A) -2

(B) 0

(C) 2

(D) 4

(E) It cannot be determined from the information given.

10. A beaker contains x ounces of a solution composed entirely of equal parts of Liquid A and Liquid B. How many ounces of Liquid A, in terms of x, must be added to the beaker to result in a solution that is 40% Liquid B?

(A) $10x$

(B) $25x$

(C) $\dfrac{x}{2}$

(D) $\dfrac{x}{4}$

(E) $\dfrac{x + 25}{4}$

S T O P If you finish before time is called, you may check your work on this section only. Do not turn to any other section in the test.

[This page intentionally left blank]

Section 6

Time—15 Minutes
13 Questions

Select the best answer for each question in this section from the choices given, and fill in the corresponding ovals on the answer sheet.

Read each of the passages carefully, then answer the questions that come after them. The answer to each question may be stated overtly or only implied. You will not have to use outside knowledge to answer the questions—all the material you will need will be in the passage itself. In some cases, you will be asked to read two related passages and answer questions about their relationship to one another.

Questions 1–13 are based on the following passages.

These passages are adapted from opinions of the United States Supreme Court on a case in which the "petitioner" appealed his conviction on a charge of carrying a concealed weapon on the grounds that the search that revealed the weapon was unconstitutional. The Fourth Amendment to the U.S. Constitution holds that "the right of the people to be secure . . . against unreasonable searches and seizures, shall not be violated" and that search warrants may not be issued except on "probable cause." Passage 1 is the majority opinion, Passage 2 a dissenting opinion.

Passage 1

Line   We must first establish at what point in this encounter the Fourth Amendment becomes relevant: whether the police officer "seized" petitioner and conducted a "search" before
(5)   placing him under arrest. Using the terms "stop" and "frisk" may suggest that these police actions are outside the purview of the Fourth Amendment because neither action rises to the level of a "search" or "seizure."
(10)   We emphatically reject this notion. The Fourth Amendment clearly governs "sei-
zures" of a person that do not result in arrest. Whenever a police officer restrains an individual's freedom to walk away, the
(15)   officer has "seized" that person. And it is sheer torture of the English language to suggest that a careful exploration of a person's clothing in order to find weapons is not a "search."

(20)   The main governmental interest involved here is crime prevention; this interest authorizes police officers to approach individuals to investigate possibly criminal behavior even though there is no
(25)   "probable cause" for arrest. The arresting officer was discharging this legitimate function when he approached petitioner and his companions. He had observed them go through a series of acts, each perhaps
(30)   innocent in itself, but which taken together warranted investigation. There is nothing unusual in two men standing on a street corner, perhaps waiting for someone. Nor is there anything suspicious about people
(35)   strolling up and down the street. Store windows, moreover, are made to be looked in. But the story is quite different where, as here, two men hover about a street corner for an extended time, obviously not waiting
(40)   for anyone; where these men pace along an

334

identical route, pausing to stare in the same store window numerous times; where they confer on the corner after each completion of this route; and where they are joined in
(45) one such conference by a third man who leaves swiftly. For the officer to have failed to investigate would have been poor police work indeed.

At the time he seized and searched
(50) petitioner, the officer had reasonable suspicion that petitioner was armed and dangerous. Such a search is a reasonable search under the Fourth Amendment, and any weapons seized may properly be
(55) introduced in evidence against the person who carried them.

Passage 2

Line   I agree that petitioner was "seized" within the meaning of the Fourth Amendment, and that frisking petitioner for guns was clearly a
(60) "search." But it is a mystery how that "search" and that "seizure" can be constitutional by Fourth Amendment standards, unless there was "probable cause" to believe that a crime had been, was about to be, or
(65) was in the process of being committed.

The majority opinion does not claim the existence of "probable cause." If loitering were the offense charged, there would be "probable cause" shown. But the
(70) crime here is carrying concealed weapons; the officer had no "probable cause" for believing that this crime was being committed. Had a search warrant been sought, a judge would, therefore, have been unautho-
(75) rized to issue one, for judges can act only if "probable cause" is shown. The Court holds today that the police have greater authority to make a "seizure" and conduct a "search" than a judge has to authorize such action.
(80) To give the police greater power than judges have is to take a long step down the totalitarian path. Perhaps such a step is

desirable to cope with modern forms of lawlessness. But it should be taken only as
(85) the deliberate choice of the people through a constitutional amendment. Until the Fourth Amendment is rewritten, the person and his or her effects are beyond the reach of all governmental agencies until there are
(90) reasonable grounds to believe ("probable cause") that a criminal venture has been or is about to be launched.

There have been powerful pressures throughout our history that bear heavily on
(95) the Court to water down constitutional guarantees and give the police the upper hand. That pressure has probably never been greater than it is today.

Yet if the individual is no longer to be
(100) sovereign, if the police can pick someone up whenever they do not like the cut of his or her jib, if they can "seize" and "search" an individual in their discretion, we enter a new regime. The decision to enter it should
(105) be made only after a full debate by the people of this country.

1. The author of Passage 1 implies that the "point in this encounter" at which "the Fourth Amendment becomes relevant" (lines 1–3) is the point at which the police officer

    (A) noticed the suspicious behavior of petitioner
    (B) stopped petitioner and frisked him
    (C) found the concealed weapon in petitioner's clothing
    (D) arrested petitioner
    (E) placed the weapon he had found in evidence against petitioner

GO ON TO THE NEXT PAGE

2. With which of the following interpretations of the Fourth Amendment is the author of Passage 1 most likely to agree?

(A) The Fourth Amendment applies to "stop and frisk" actions only when there is "probable cause" to believe that a crime is taking place.

(B) The police may momentarily stop a person whose behavior seems suspicious without having engaged in a "seizure" as defined by the Fourth Amendment.

(C) Searches that result from a well-founded suspicion of criminal activity are not "unreasonable searches" under the Fourth Amendment.

(D) The requirement for "probable cause" applies only to judges issuing search warrants and not to police officers conducting a search at the scene of a possible crime.

(E) Fourth Amendment guarantees of individual rights must take second place to the duty of the police to protect public safety.

3. The word "discharging" in line 26 most nearly means

(A) performing
(B) unloading
(C) releasing
(D) dismissing
(E) setting aside

4. In concluding that the police officer had reason to believe petitioner was "armed and dangerous" (lines 51–52), the author of Passage 1 assumes that

(A) a person who carries a concealed weapon should be considered armed and dangerous

(B) a person whose actions seem to indicate an intention to rob a store is likely to be carrying a weapon

(C) the police officer conducted an unreasonable search under the Fourth Amendment

(D) actions that might otherwise seem innocent become suspicious when someone engages in them repeatedly

(E) police officers have the duty to investigate all unusual behavior

5. The word "properly" in line 54 most nearly means

(A) strictly
(B) suitably
(C) validly
(D) decorously
(E) characteristically

6. In line 68, "loitering" is presented as an example of the crime

(A) that is less likely to endanger public safety than is the crime of carrying a concealed weapon

(B) that requires grounds of "probable cause" before a search can be conducted

(C) for which the police officer in the case should have arrested petitioner

(D) in which petitioner appeared to be engaged at the time he was accosted by the police officer

(E) to which "probable cause" applies more directly than it does to the crime of carrying a concealed weapon

7. The author of Passage 2 believes that the police

   (A)   may stop and frisk a person only if they have a search warrant issued by a judge

   (B)   should not be allowed to conduct searches that a judge would be unable to authorize

   (C)   should have proof that a crime is under way or being planned before they can search or seize an individual

   (D)   have as their primary responsibility the protection of individuals' Fourth Amendment rights

   (E)   must be given considerable leeway in investigating possible criminal behavior

8. In Passage 2, the author's attitude toward the ruling allowing a police officer to frisk an individual whose behavior the officer finds suspicious is most clearly indicated in which of the following phrases?

   (A)   "a long step down the totalitarian path" (lines 81–82)

   (B)   "desirable to cope with modern forms of lawlessness" (lines 83–84)

   (C)   "the deliberate choice of the people" (line 85)

   (D)   "beyond the reach of all governmental agencies" (lines 88–89)

   (E)   "powerful pressures throughout our history" (lines 93–94)

9. The author mentions "modern forms of lawlessness" (lines 83–84) primarily in order to provide

   (A)   a reason for accepting his argument

   (B)   an illustration to support his argument

   (C)   a rebuttal of a point made against his argument

   (D)   a modification of the position taken earlier

   (E)   a concession to the opposing viewpoint

10. By insisting that this Fourth Amendment issue should be put before the people of the United States, the author of Passage 2 suggests that

   (A)   public trust in the police would increase if the people were allowed to decide the limits of police power

   (B)   a guarantee of Fourth Amendment rights is no longer necessary in modern society

   (C)   the interpretation of the Constitution should be determined by the public rather than by the courts

   (D)   the people are not likely to choose to rewrite the Fourth Amendment because recent increases in crime rates have made them fearful of criminal activity

   (E)   the majority opinion has taken over a right reserved to the people by effectively overthrowing the Fourth Amendment

11. The author of Passage 2 believes that the majority opinion in Passage 1 does not meet Fourth Amendment standards because the majority opinion

   (A)   replaces the term "unreasonable searches" with the term "probable cause"

   (B)   holds that frisking a person before arresting that person is a "search"

   (C)   ignores the need to show "probable cause" before conducting a search

   (D)   places too much emphasis on the "governmental interest" (line 20) of preventing crime

   (E)   rejects the necessity of obtaining a warrant from a judge before conducting a search

GO ON TO THE NEXT PAGE ➤

12. The basic disagreement between the author of Passage 1 and the author of Passage 2 is over the issue of whether

(A) the Fourth Amendment should be rewritten

(B) Fourth Amendment standards are relevant to this case

(C) the Fourth Amendment required the police officer to obtain a warrant for the arrest of petitioner before searching him

(D) the search and seizure of petitioner was a reasonable search as required by the Fourth Amendment

(E) a search and seizure, as defined in the Fourth Amendment, had occurred prior to petitioner's arrest by the police officer

13. The author of Passage 2 uses the phrase "it is a mystery" in line 60 to express which of the following reactions to the majority opinion in Passage 1?

(A) His admission that defining the terms "search" and "seizure" can be difficult

(B) His doubt that the Fourth Amendment applies to this particular search and seizure

(C) His disapproval of the way the majority opinion defined "search" and "seizure"

(D) His rejection of the assertion that this particular search and seizure meets Fourth Amendment standards

(E) His opposing argument that the Fourth Amendment should be revised

S T O P If you finish before time is called, you may check your work on this section only. Do not turn to any other section in the test.

Peterson's SAT Success

Quick-Score Answers

Practice Test 2					
Math			**Verbal**		
Section 1	**Section 3**	**Section 5**	**Section 2**	**Section 4**	**Section 6**
1. C	1. B	1. C	1. E	1. D	1. B
2. E	2. C	2. B	2. D	2. C	2. C
3. D	3. B	3. E	3. B	3. B	3. A
4. C	4. C	4. E	4. B	4. B	4. B
5. D	5. D	5. E	5. A	5. E	5. C
6. E	6. B	6. B	6. C	6. B	6. D
7. D	7. D	7. D	7. D	7. C	7. B
8. B	8. A	8. A	8. D	8. D	8. A
9. E	9. B	9. C	9. E	9. A	9. E
10. E	10. C	10. D	10. C	10. E	10. E
11. D	11. A		11. C	11. C	11. C
12. A	12. C		12. D	12. E	12. D
13. E	13. A		13. B	13. A	13. D
14. D	14. D		14. E	14. C	
15. B	15. D		15. B	15. E	
16. C	16. 50		16. C	16. D	
17. D	17. 1/4 or .25		17. A	17. B	
18. C	18. 8.25		18. D	18. A	
19. C	19. 22.5 or 45/2		19. E	19. D	
20. E	20. 71		20. B	20. D	
21. C	21. 3		21. B	21. A	
22. E	22. 1, 2, 3, or 4		22. A	22. C	
23. A	23. 12		23. B	23. B	
24. E	24. 3/16, or .187,		24. A	24. D	
25. B	or .188		25. D	25. E	
	25. 8		26. C	26. A	
			27. A	27. C	
			28. B	28. D	
			29. D	29. B	
			30. E	30. D	
				31. A	
				32. E	
				33. C	
				34. A	
				35. C	

Detailed explanations can be found on page 407.

Scoring the Test

Check your answers to the math sections against the answer key, and record the number of correct and incorrect answers for each section in the spaces provided. For sections 1 and 5, multiply the number of incorrect answers by .25, and subtract this from the number correct. This gives you your raw scores for sections 1 and 5. For questions 1–15 in section 3, multiply the number of incorrect answers by .33, and subtract this from the number correct. For questions 16–25 in section 3, simply record the number of correct answers; these questions are Grid-ins and have no wrong answer penalty. Adding these two numbers gives you your total for section 3. Now sum the raw scores of each math section, and round the total to the nearest whole number. This is your math raw score.

Check your answers to the verbal sections against the answer key, and record the number of correct and incorrect answers in the spaces provided. Multiply the number of incorrect answers by .25, and subtract this from the number correct. Round the result to the nearest whole number. This is your verbal raw score.

Use the score chart to translate your raw scores into scaled scores. However, remember that these scores are only approximations of how you might do on the real test. Lots of factors will affect your actual SAT scores: taking the test under controlled conditions, your preparation between now and test day, etc. Use these scores to get a rough idea of your score range on the exam and to decide how to focus your SAT preparation.

Scoring Worksheet

MATH				
	Number Correct	**Number Incorrect**	**=**	**Raw Score**
Section 1	_____	− (.25 × _____)	=	_____
Section 3				
1–15	_____	− (.33 × _____)	=	_____
16–25	_____	(no wrong answer penalty)	=	_____
Section 5	_____	− (.25 × _____)	=	_____
		Total Rounded Raw Score		_____
VERBAL				
Sections 2, 4, and 6	_____	− (.25 × _____)	=	_____
		Total Rounded Raw Score		_____

Score Charts

Math			
Raw Score	**Math Scaled Score**	**Raw Score**	**Math Scaled Score**
60	800	28	500
59	800	27	490
58	790	26	490
57	770	25	480
56	760	24	470
55	740	23	460
54	720	22	460
53	710	21	450
52	700	20	440
51	690	19	430
50	680	18	420
49	670	17	420
48	660	16	410
47	650	15	410
46	640	14	400
45	630	13	390
44	620	12	380
43	610	11	370
42	600	10	360
41	600	9	350
40	590	8	340
39	580	7	330
38	570	6	320
37	560	5	310
36	560	4	300
35	550	3	280
34	540	2	270
33	540	1	250
32	530	0	240
31	520	−1	220
30	510	−2	210
29	510	−3 and below	200

Verbal			
Raw Score	**Verbal Scaled Score**	**Raw Score**	**Verbal Scaled Score**
78	800	37	510
77	800	36	510
76	800	35	500
75	790	34	500
74	780	33	490
73	770	32	490
72	760	31	480
71	750	30	480
70	740	29	470
69	730	28	460
68	720	27	460
67	710	26	450
66	700	25	450
65	700	24	440
64	690	23	440
63	680	22	430
62	670	21	420
61	670	20	410
60	660	19	410
59	650	18	400
58	640	17	390
57	640	16	380
56	630	15	380
55	620	14	370
54	610	13	360
53	610	12	360
52	600	11	350
51	600	10	340
50	590	9	330
49	590	8	320
48	580	7	310
47	570	6	300
46	570	5	290
45	560	4	270
44	550	3	260
43	550	2	250
42	540	1	240
41	540	0	230
40	530	−1	220
39	520	−2	210
38	520	−3 and below	200

Practice Test 2

Section 1

Time—30 Minutes	Solve the following problems, select the best answer
25 Questions	choice for each and fill in the corresponding oval on the
	answer sheet. Use your test booklet for scratchwork.

Notes:

1. You may use a calculator. All of the numbers used are real numbers.

2. Figures accompany some problems. Assume that each has been drawn accurately and lies in a plane, unless the instructions indicate otherwise.

Reference Information

$A = \pi r^2$
$C = 2\pi r$ $A = \ell w$ $A = \frac{1}{2} bh$ $V = \ell wh$ $V = \pi r^2 h$ $c^2 = a^2 + b^2$ Special Right Triangles

The number of degrees of arc in a circle is 360.
The measure in degrees of a straight angle is 180.
The sum of the measures in degrees of the angles of a triangle is 180.

---

1. For which of the following values of n is $\frac{30}{n}$ NOT an integer?

    (A) 2
    (B) 3
    (C) 4
    (D) 5
    (E) 6

---

2. If $A + B = 7$ and $C + D = 5$, then $A + B - C - D =$

    (A) −4
    (B) −2
    (C) 1
    (D) 2
    (E) 4

---

3. What is the slope of the line defined by the equation $y = 3x - \frac{1}{2}$?

    (A) 3
    (B) $\frac{1}{2}$
    (C) $\frac{1}{3}$
    (D) $-\frac{1}{2}$
    (E) −3

GO ON TO THE NEXT PAGE

4. When z is divided by 6, the remainder is 4. What is the remainder when $2z$ is divided by 6?

(A) 1
(B) 2
(C) 3
(D) 4
(E) 8

5. It takes 2 hours to drive from City A to City B at 50 miles per hour. How much less time would it take to drive from City A to City B at 60 miles per hour?

(A) 1 hour and 40 minutes
(B) 1 hour
(C) 20 minutes
(D) 10 minutes
(E) 5 minutes

6. If today is Saturday, what day of the week will it be 365 days from now?

(A) Thursday
(B) Friday
(C) Saturday
(D) Sunday
(E) Monday

7. All of the following are equal EXCEPT

(A) 1.6
(B) $\dfrac{8}{5}$
(C) $1 + \dfrac{3}{5}$
(D) 160%
(E) $\dfrac{16}{100}$

$$A + B + C = 21$$
$$C + D + E = 7$$

8. If A, B, C, D, and E represent distinct digits between 1 and 9 inclusive, then $C =$

(A) 3
(B) 4
(C) 5
(D) 6
(E) 7

9. Four cups of coffee and a bagel cost $4.50, and one cup of coffee and four bagels cost $3.00. How much does a cup of coffee and a bagel cost?

(A) $0.50
(B) $1.00
(C) $1.50
(D) $1.75
(E) $2.00

10. Twenty percent of 75 is 50 percent of what number?

(A) 7.5
(B) 15
(C) 30
(D) 37.5
(E) 125

$$X = \{2, 4, 6, \ldots\}$$
$$Y = \{5, 10, 15, \ldots\}$$

11. X is the set of all positive even integers. Y is the set of all positive multiples of 5. How many elements whose values are less than 100 do the sets have in common?

(A) 0
(B) 9
(C) 10
(D) 20
(E) 99

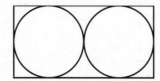

12. In the figure above, two circles are inscribed within a rectangle and are tangent to each other at only one point. If the rectangle's area is 18, what is the radius of a circle?

(A) 6
(B) 4.5
(C) 3
(D) 2
(E) 1.5

13. The post office charges a cents for the first ounce a package weighs and b cents for each additional ounce or part thereof. Which of the following expressions represents the cost to ship a package that weighs 4 pounds and 5 ounces?

(A) $4a + b$
(B) $a + 9b$
(C) $16(a + 9b)$
(D) $a + 68b$
(E) $a + 69b$

14. A star is formed with twelve equilateral triangles, as shown above. If the perimeter of one of the triangles is $2\frac{1}{2}$ centimeters, what is the perimeter of the star in centimeters?

(A) 10
(B) 15
(C) 20
(D) 22.5
(E) 30

15. A candy factory produces only 2 kinds of candy, chocolate-covered pretzels and licorice sticks. If these confections are produced in a ratio of 3:1, licorice sticks represent what percent of the factory's total production?

(A) 25%
(B) 31%
(C) $33\frac{1}{3}\%$
(D) $66\frac{2}{3}\%$
(E) 75%

GO ON TO THE NEXT PAGE

16. The positive product of three consecutive integers is the same as their sum. What is the middle number?

(A) −2
(B)   0
(C)   1
(D)   2
(E)   6

17. For a pizza party, *p* pizzas that cost *d* dollars each were ordered. If the total cost is shared evenly among *b* boys and *g* girls, which expression represents how much the girls paid?

(A) *gpd*

(B) $\dfrac{pd}{g}$

(C) $\dfrac{pd}{b + g}$

(D) $\dfrac{(b + g)pd}{g}$

(E) $\dfrac{gpd}{b + g}$

18. The ratio of the perimeter of Square *A* to the perimeter of Square *B* is 1 to 4. What is the ratio of the area of Square *A* to Square *B*?

(A) 1:2
(B) 1:4
(C) 1:5
(D) 1:8
(E) 1:16

19. If $4^{x + 2} = 8^{2x}$, then *x* =

(A) −1
(B) $\dfrac{1}{2}$
(C) 1
(D) 2
(E) 4

20. Line *m* lies in the coordinate plane and contains points with coordinates (*R*, *S*) and (*S*, *R*). What is the slope of line *m*?

(A) −1

(B) $-\dfrac{S}{R}$

(C) *S* − *R*

(D) $\dfrac{R}{S}$

(E) 1

21. Eileen has 8 fewer Beanie Babies than Brenna, who has one-third as many Beanie Babies as Ryan. Which of the following could be the total number of Beanie Babies that the three have?

(A) 22
(B) 38
(C) 45
(D) 53
(E) 67

22. A shelf is attached to a wall such that it extends 12 inches perpendicularly. It is supported by a rod that makes a 30° angle with the wall and reaches the edge of the shelf. How long is the rod?

(A) 6 inches
(B) $6\sqrt{3}$ inches
(C) 12 inches
(D) $12\sqrt{3}$ inches
(E) 24 inches

23. The cube root c of positive integer n is equal to half the square root of n. Which of the following could be c?

(A) 1
(B) 2
(C) 4
(D) 16
(E) 64

24. If n is a positive number, which of the following is equivalent to decreasing n by 25% and then increasing the result by 20%?

(A) Decreasing n by 5%
(B) Decreasing n by 10%
(C) Decreasing n by 22.5%
(D) Increasing n by 5%
(E) Increasing n by 90%

25. A 54-inch by 117-inch piece of material is to be cut into equal squares, each of which must have an area greater than 6. If the squares are to be cut so that no material remains, what is the positive difference between the number of the smallest squares that can be cut and the number of the largest squares that can be cut?

(A) 72
(B) 78
(C) 81
(D) 624
(E) 702

STOP If you finish before time is called, you may check your work on this section only. Do not turn to any other section in the test.

Section 2

Time—30 Minutes
31 Questions

For each question below, choose the best answer from the choices given and fill in the corresponding oval on the answer sheet.

Each sentence below has either one or two blanks in it and is followed by five choices labeled (A) through (E). These choices represent words or phrases that have been omitted. Choose the word or phrase that, if inserted into the sentence, would best fit the meaning of the sentence as a whole.

Example:

Canine massage is a veterinary technique for calming dogs that are extremely _____.

(A) inept
(B) disciplined
(C) controlled
(D) agitated
(E) restrained   (A) (B) (C) ● (E)

1. Having been damaged by acquaintances who told her what they thought she wanted to hear, Lisa now looks for friends who will be totally _____ with her.

   (A) patient
   (B) gregarious
   (C) candid
   (D) affectionate
   (E) confidential

2. The house's _____ exterior _____ the impression of conspicuous wealth created by the sumptuous furnishings on the inside.

   (A) opulent..contrasted
   (B) Spartan..suggested
   (C) austere..belied
   (D) rugged..denied
   (E) handsome..eroded

3. The identification of the new insect species can only be described as _____; the entomologists were studying the mating habits of known species rather than looking for new ones.

   (A) superlative
   (B) erudite
   (C) serendipitous
   (D) incomprehensible
   (E) preposterous

4. Flannery O'Connor's exploration of religious themes in *The Violent Bear It Away*, far from yielding a dry, _____ story, instead puts her characters in _____ situations where they seem completely, and ludicrously, out of place.

   (A) intense..bizarre
   (B) pedantic..incongruous
   (C) conventional..familiar
   (D) enticing..uncomfortable
   (E) ethical..customary

5. In contrast to the durability of the old classic movies, many of today's movies seem designed to have only _____ appeal.

   (A) sensual
   (B) mundane
   (C) ephemeral
   (D) ambiguous
   (E) superficial

Peterson's SAT Success

6. The notion that remaining competitive requires businesses to continually replace people with technology has as its natural _____ the idea that machines are more important than people.

(A) epitome
(B) corollary
(C) covenant
(D) resolution
(E) admonition

7. Because they are made of cloth and often portray _____ subjects, Faith Ringgold's quilts are an _____ in an art world where painterly abstractions are the norm.

(A) earthy..accomplishment
(B) idealized..ambiguity
(C) tangible..equivalency
(D) aesthetic..enigma
(E) identifiable..aberration

8. At the beginning of the course, we were _____ novices at the mercy of an _____ subject, but by the end of the semester, we had mastered the rigors of trigonometry.

(A) insipid..abstruse
(B) diligent..enigmatic
(C) rank..immaculate
(D) perfidious..exacting
(E) uncomprehending..inscrutable

9. He impersonated a sheriff's deputy in an attempt to _____ the _____ duties of a sworn officer of the law.

(A) usurp..licit
(B) expropriate..dominant
(C) undermine..characteristic
(D) discharge..legitimate
(E) supervise..essential

GO ON TO THE NEXT PAGE

Each question below consists of two words that are related to one another in some way. Following these words are five sets of two words each, labeled (A) through (E). From these, you must choose the set that denotes a relationship most similar to the relationship expressed in the original set.

Example:
RUNNER : SPEED::
(A) acrobat : height
(B) dancer : grace
(C) minister: holy book
(D) waiter : order
(E) landlord : rent

10. WORSHIPPER : CONGREGATION ::

   (A) leader : seminar
   (B) cast : ensemble
   (C) reader : poem
   (D) pupil : class
   (E) choir : anthem

11. SURFEIT : SCARCITY ::

   (A) haze : clarity
   (B) dearth : lack
   (C) flood : water
   (D) eclipse : sunlight
   (E) muckraker : trouble

12. PURGATIVE : PURIFY ::

   (A) cohesive : separate
   (B) painful : assuage
   (C) explicit : paraphrase
   (D) opaque : illumine
   (E) incendiary : ignite

13. RUSE : SUBTERFUGE ::

   (A) swindle : fraud
   (B) catalyze : experiment
   (C) alienate : negotiation
   (D) beautify : landscape
   (E) doubt : veracity

14. VOTARY : VENERATION ::

   (A) charlatan : integrity
   (B) skeptic : incredulity
   (C) coward : flight
   (D) director : management
   (E) priest : religion

15. PINE : LONG ::

   (A) wave : well
   (B) land : roll
   (C) unearth : bury
   (D) low : moo
   (E) wheel : float

Read each of the passages carefully, then answer the questions that come after them. The answer to each question may be stated overtly or only implied. You will not have to use outside knowledge to answer the questions—all the material you will need will be in the passage itself.

Questions 16–22 are based on the following passage.

The following is an excerpt from an autobiographical essay about the author's childhood.

Line   On a July evening in the middle of a drought, my father took us for a drive through our California town. I remember pointing out the back seat window of our station wagon, to
(5)   the sky. "Look, a helicopter." An airplane followed not far behind, then another helicopter. We pulled back into our driveway just in time to see a helicopter dump a load of water onto a nearby mountain top. Smoke rose from
(10)   the peak, unnaturally darkening the evening. The mountain, called Mt. Diablo, was burning. In the late afternoon a storm had gathered across the hills. There had been wind, heavy clouds, and even lightning, but no rain.
(15)   When lightning struck the mountain top, like a spark in a tinderbox, the peak caught fire. The sage, border oaks and grasses, dead-dry from the lack of rain, carried the flames across the mountain.
(20)   The old saying about nature being "in your own backyard" sounds trite, but there it was, an uncontrollable wildfire, and we watched it from the comfort of our patio chairs. As the sun set, the flames on the
(25)   mountain top became more visible. Neighbors gathered with coolers of soda, my father made popcorn, and my mother let me stay up late to watch the swaying, dancing light on top of the mountain.
(30)   About a week after the fire, my family piled back into the big green station wagon, and we drove up to the Mt. Diablo state park, or what was left of it. We were not the only ones that Saturday afternoon who had come
(35)   to see the destruction. A steady line of cars crept up the twisting mountain road, like a gleaming artery through the charred flesh of the mountain. The landscape was blackened, covered with a smooth, uniform layer of ash.
(40)   Any trees left standing were bare, black, and livid against the cloudless sky. If not for the blue sky we could have been driving on the moon. The ranger station at the summit had been spared (whether by the efforts of the
(45)   rangers or by luck, I don't know), and we parked there to get out of the car and take pictures. A homeless raccoon ambled around among the parked cars and sightseers. My sister took pity and tossed him a piece of her
(50)   banana. And then we saw a tarantula a big, furry, golden-brown spider, just walking around as casually as the raccoon. It was as big as my father's hand. My dad took a picture of it, placing his sunglasses a few inches away
(55)   from the spider to provide perspective. I don't remember being scared, just amazed, fascinated at the huge spider that emerged from the dead landscape.
            But, of course, the distinction between
(60)   civilization and nature is a false one. Even in the heart of Chicago, where I now live, nature cannot be vanquished. People think the steel and glass canyons of the city offer protection from nature's destructive power, but, as I
(65)   once heard a Chicago TV meteorologist point out, the only thing that has kept a tornado from grappling with the Sears Tower is dumb luck. My relationship with nature has always been to keep this fact in mind, to allow myself
(70)   to be fascinated not only by Old Faithful and the Grand Canyon, but also by the sidewalk weed and trashcan raccoon.

GO ON TO THE NEXT PAGE

16. According to the passage, the cause of the fire was

(A) a camp fire that got out of control
(B) a spark from an airplane crash
(C) poor planning by forest rangers
(D) the combination of a drought and a storm
(E) never determined

17. The author mentions that he and his family watched the fire "from the comfort of our patio chairs" (lines 23-24) in order to

(A) remind the reader that his family was not in danger
(B) emphasize the nearness of a natural force to the author's home
(C) condemn his family for failing to call for help
(D) point out the humor in the situation
(E) illustrate his family's general indifference to nature

18. In line 60, the word "false" most closely means

(A) mistaken
(B) unfaithful
(C) dishonest
(D) counterfeit
(E) imitation

19. The author would most likely agree with which statement?

(A) Urban environments are rapidly depleting natural resources.
(B) People can escape from nature's destructive power, but not from its beauty.
(C) People in urban areas are not as removed from the forces of nature as they may think.
(D) The positive forces of nature will always overcome the negative forces of nature.
(E) Urban environments will exist only as long as good fortune prevents nature from intruding upon them.

20. The author describes the tarantula (lines 50-52) in order to

(A) illustrate the horror that his family felt at the destruction of the mountain
(B) show that his family felt compassion for the displaced animals
(C) provide a contrast to the description of the raccoon that his sister fed
(D) reveal the danger of a seemingly harmless situation
(E) demonstrate that nature exists even in hostile environments

21. The author mentions the "sidewalk weed and trashcan racoon" (lines 71-72) in order to

(A) show his distaste for city life
(B) contrast them to the natural surroundings he experienced in his childhood
(C) include them in his appreciation of nature
(D) dismiss the notion that nature can be enjoyed in the city
(E) compare their relative harmlessness to nature's more destructive forces

22. The author's attitude toward nature can best be described as

(A) reverent
(B) mocking
(C) uncertain
(D) respectful
(E) fearfulke

Questions 23–31 are based on the following passage.

Line The public imagination has always been captivated by dinosaurs, and many theories for their extinction some 65 million years ago have been advanced. Fewer people are
(5) aware, however, that another mass extinction has taken place in more recent times. Twelve thousand years ago, giant mammals roamed North and South America: the saber-toothed tiger, the mastodon, the giant
(10) sloth, as well as other less well-known species. By 8,000 B.C.E., virtually all the large mammals in North and South America had disappeared. As with the dinosaurs, several theories have been put forward to
(15) explain this mass extinction.

Climate change is an obvious culprit; most scientists believe that global cooling, whether caused by a volcano, the fall of a meteorite or comet, or some other force,
(20) was responsible for the death of the dinosaurs. The extinction of the American large mammals coincides with the end of the most recent ice age, so one theory holds that large animals were less able to adapt to
(25) global warming than the smaller ones and so died off. What is difficult to explain, however, is why animals of similar size in Europe and Asia experienced the same global warming without suffering the same
(30) massive extinctions.

Most scientists therefore believe that the advent of humans on the American scene around 11,000 years ago was responsible for the death of the large mammals.
(35) Large-animal extinctions in other areas—in Australia, long before the end of the last Ice Age; in New Zealand long after; in Madagascar as little as 2,000 years ago—also coincide with the coming of humans to those places.
(40) That this synchronicity is mere coincidence is unlikely, but the question remains: How could the coming of humans have caused so many deaths?

One possibility is that humans, with
(45) their superior intelligence and ability to use tools, simply hunted the large mammals out of existence. As they crossed over the Bering Strait and into the fertile New World, they encountered what must have struck
(50) them as a cornucopia of game—game, furthermore, that had never seen human beings and did not know how deadly these apparently defenseless two-legged animals could be. This theory holds that the new
(55) arrivals went on a hunting binge, killing everything in sight without worrying whether they killed more than they could eat.

Modern experience shows that humans
(60) are perfectly capable of hunting entire species to the brink of extinction and beyond. The near-extinction of the North American bison in the nineteenth century provides a perfect example. But the fact that
(65) there were humans already hunting the bison in that area also provides a counterexample that argues against the theory that humans overhunted the large mammals. Hunter-gatherer societies, whether nine-
(70) teenth-century Native Americans or Paleo-Indians of 11,000 years ago, are not prone to such excess. There is simply no reason for a group of humans primarily concerned with keeping themselves fed, warm, and sheltered
(75) to engage in mass slaughter of not one but hundreds of animal species.

Thus, other, less direct ways in which the humans might have caused the mass extinctions seem more likely. Changes in the
(80) ecosystem brought about by humans' attempts to make their new environment more livable seem a possibility, particularly in light of modern experience. Recently, a few researchers have even begun to argue
(85) that the humans brought a new disease with them as they came—an incredibly fast-

GO ON TO THE NEXT PAGE

moving and deadly virus that could leap across species lines. No such disease has so far been identified from fossil remains, but
(90) the recent emergence of such deadly cross-species viruses as *Ebola* lends new plausibility to this hypothesis. This would explain why Europe and Asia experienced no corresponding mass extinctions: The
(95) large animals there had developed immunities, as had the humans and their domestic animals. Smaller mammals, this theory holds, were less affected because they reproduce more rapidly than larger mammals. New,
(100) more resistant generations of small mammals could appear over the course of just a few years, before the previous generations were entirely wiped out.

23. The primary purpose of the passage as a whole is to

(A) analyze the processes that lead to mass extinction
(B) compare an early mass extinction with a later one
(C) examine hypotheses about the causes of a mass extinction
(D) caution human beings about meddling with the environment
(E) heighten popular awareness of a little-studied mass extinction

24. In line 4, the word "advanced" most nearly means

(A) hastened
(B) promoted
(C) increased
(D) put forward
(E) moved ahead

25. Which of the following pieces of evidence supports the idea that humans somehow caused the disappearance of many large-animal species in the Americas?

(A) Experience shows that humans are quite likely to hunt entire species to extinction.
(B) The extinction of the large animals happened at the same time that the last ice age ended.
(C) The predations of mammal species were also partially responsible for the death of the dinosaurs.
(D) The coming of humans in other areas at different times also caused massive large-animal extinctions.
(E) Small animals can both adapt to environmental changes and hide from human hunters more easily than can larger animals.

26. The question in lines 41–43 serves primarily to

(A) introduce several theories about the causes of the large-mammal extinction
(B) cast doubt on the idea that humans could have caused the large-mammal extinction
(C) express the author's astonishment over the cause of the large-mammal extinction
(D) lead into the author's theory that humans hunted the large mammals to extinction
(E) indicate that the scientific community remains confused over the cause of the large-mammal extinction

27. In line 60, the word "perfectly" most nearly means

(A) just
(B) quite
(C) exactly
(D) flawlessly
(E) skillfully

28. The passage discusses the North American bison in lines 62–68 primarily in order to

    (A) show that this near-extinction is different in both quality and quantity from the large-animal extinctions of twelve thousand years ago

    (B) argue that humans caused the large-animal extinctions not by hunting the animals but by changing their environment

    (C) refute the most important piece of evidence used to support the theory that human beings hunted many large animal species to extinction

    (D) illustrate the deadly effect of superior human weapons on animal species that have never encountered such weapons

    (E) give an example that supports the theory that humans hunted large animals to extinction while showing that this example also contradicts that theory

29. The passage's explanations of the theories about the large-mammal extinction suggest that one way of evaluating such theories is to

    (A) insist on verification by fossil remains

    (B) examine the forces that lead to global climate change

    (C) extrapolate from theories about the extinction of the dinosaurs

    (D) compare them with the causes of small-mammal extinctions

    (E) compare them with the more easily verified causes of modern phenomena

30. Viruses that can "leap across species lines" (lines 87–88) are apparently

    (A) generally fatal

    (B) relatively unusual

    (C) difficult to identify from fossil remains

    (D) more deadly to other animals than to humans

    (E) more deadly to wild animals than to domestic ones

31. The main difficulty mentioned in the passage with the disease hypothesis is that

    (A) there is no physical evidence for the existence of a likely disease

    (B) European and Asian mammals apparently were not affected

    (C) small mammals seem not to have suffered from such a disease

    (D) large mammals are known to have better resistance to disease than smaller mammals

    (E) other theories have the support of a larger portion of the scientific community

STOP If you finish before time is called, you may check your work on this section only. Do not turn to any other section in the test.

Section 3

Notes:

1. You may use a calculator. All of the numbers used are real numbers.

2. Figures accompany some problems. Assume that each has been drawn accurately and lies in a plane, unless the instructions indicate otherwise.

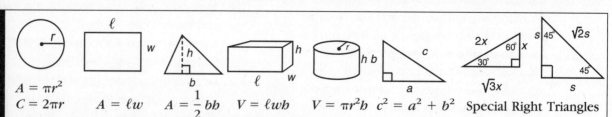

$A = \pi r^2$
$C = 2\pi r$ $\qquad A = \ell w \qquad A = \frac{1}{2}bb \qquad V = \ell w b \qquad V = \pi r^2 h \quad c^2 = a^2 + b^2$ Special Right Triangles

The number of degrees of arc in a circle is 360.
The measure in degrees of a straight angle is 180.
The sum of the measures in degrees of the angles of a triangle is 180.

Directions for Quantitative Comparison Questions

Questions 1–15 each consist of two boxed quantities, one in Column A and one in Column B. Compare them and select:

A if the quantity in Column A is greater;
B if the quantity in Column B is greater;
C if the two quantities are equal;
D if the relationship cannot be determined from the information given.

A response of E will be considered an omission.

Notes:

1. Some questions provide information about one or both of the quantities to be compared. This information is unboxed and centered above the two columns.
2. A symbol that appears in both columns represents the same value in each.
3. Letters such as x, n, and k stand for real numbers.

EXAMPLES

	Column A	Column B	Answers
E1	$\frac{1}{2}$ of 50	$\frac{1}{4}$ of 25	●ⒷⒸⒹⒺ
E2	The number of degrees in a circle	The number of degrees in a square	ⒶⒷ●ⒹⒺ
E3	$x > 0$		
	x	$\dfrac{1}{x}$	ⒶⒷⒸ●Ⓔ

Column A	Column B

1. $x - 3$ $x - (-4)$

2. The remainder when 876,543 is divided by 5 | The remainder when 876,543 is divided by 10

During a television show on Channel 2, 10 minutes of commercials were broadcast. During a television show on Channel 4, 8 minutes of commercials were broadcast.

3. The number of commercials broadcast during the show on Channel 2 | The number of commercials broadcast during the show on Channel 7

Column A	Column B

1.2345% of $33\frac{1}{3} = x$

123.45% of $33\frac{1}{3} = y$

4. x $\dfrac{y}{100}$

5. The number of degrees in a pentagon | 720

6. The number of distinct prime factors of 2,222 | The number of distinct prime factors of 3,333

GO ON TO THE NEXT PAGE

SUMMARY DIRECTIONS

Select: A if Column A is greater;
B if Column B is greater;
C if the two columns are equal;
D if the relationship cannot be determined from the information given.

Column A	Column B

Set $A = \{s, s, s\}$
Set $B = \{r, s, t\}$

7.

The average (arithmetic mean) of Set A	The median of Set B

$a - 3 < 4$

8.

$a - 2$	5

9.

a	b

Column A	Column B

An isosceles triangle has one side of length 5 and one side of length 7.

10.

The length of the triangle's third side	5

n is a positive integer.

11.

-1^{2n^3}	-1^{2n^5+1}

Peterson's SAT Success

Column A	Column B	Column A	Column B

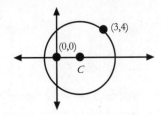

Note: Figure not drawn to scale.

C is the center of the circle above, and $(3, 4)$ lies on its circumference.

12.

The radius of circle C	5

$$xy > 0$$
$$yz < 0$$

13.

xz	0

$$ABC$$
$$+ \ CBA$$
$$\overline{DDD}$$

In the correctly worked addition problem above, A, B, C, and D represent distinct integers.

14.

B	5

A positive number, a, is decreased by $n\%$. The result is then increased by $n\%$, and the final amount is called z.

15.

a	z

GO ON TO THE NEXT PAGE

Directions for Student-Produced Response Questions

Enter your responses to questions 16–25 in the special grids provided on your answer sheet. Input your answers as indicated in the directions below.

Answer: $\frac{4}{9}$ or 4/9

Answer: 1.4
Either position is correct.

Write answer → in boxes.

← Fraction line

Decimal → point

Grid in → result.

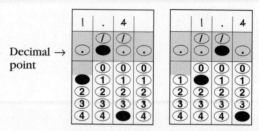

Note: You may begin your answer in any column, space permitting. Leave blank any columns not needed.

- Writing your answer in the boxes at the top of the columns will help you accurately grid your answer, but it is not required. **You will only receive credit for an answer if the ovals are filled in properly.**

- Only fill in one oval in each column.

- If a problem has several correct answers, just grid in one of them.

- There are no negative answers.

- **Never grid in mixed numbers.** The answer $3\frac{1}{5}$ must be gridded as 16/5 or 3.2.

If 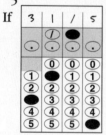 is gridded, it will be read as $\frac{31}{5}$, not $3\frac{1}{5}$.

Decimal Accuracy
Decimal answers must be gridded as accurately as possible. The answer 0.3333 . . . must be gridded as .333 or .334.
Less accurate values, such as .33 or .34, are not acceptable.

Acceptable ways to grid $\frac{1}{3}$ = .3333 . . .

Peterson's SAT Success

$$SSS$$
$$\times\ 4$$
$$\overline{TTT0}$$

16. In the correctly worked multiplication problem above, S and T represent distinct digits greater than 0. What is the value of $\dfrac{T}{S}$?

17. An 8-ounce, regular-sized bottle of shampoo costs $3.19. The 30-ounce, super-size bottle costs $8.99. If Carol uses 10 ounces of shampoo a month, how much will she save over the course of the year by buying the super-size bottles? (Disregard the $ sign when gridding your answer.)

$$x = \frac{y}{2}$$

$$x = 3z$$

18. What is the number of degrees in angle x?

19. If $9^3 = 3^x$, what is x?

20. A drawer contains 4 red socks, 3 black socks, 5 green socks, and 2 purple socks. What is the least number of socks that must be removed from the drawer to guarantee that a pair of the same color has been removed?

21. A number is called "special" if it is the sum of another number, n, and its reciprocal, $\dfrac{1}{n}$; n is then said to be the "generator" of the special number. For example, $\dfrac{10}{3}$ is special and 3 is its generator, because $3 + \dfrac{1}{3} = \dfrac{10}{3}$. Two is a special number; what is its generator?

GO ON TO THE NEXT PAGE

22. The average grade in a class of 9 people is 80. If a new student with a grade of 95 joins the class, what is new average grade of the class?

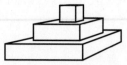

23. The figure above is created by placing a 5 by 5 by 1 slab on top of a table, placing a 3 by 3 by 1 slab on the center of the first slab, and placing a 1 by 1 by 1 block on the center of the second slab. What is the exposed surface area of this figure?

24. A certain school club has 50 members. Fifteen members worked on Project *A* and 32 members worked on Project *B*. If 13 members worked on both projects, what fractional part of the club worked on neither?

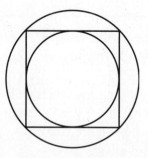

25. In the figure above, two concentric circles are shown. One is inscribed within a square; the other is circumscribed about the same square. If the ratio of the area of the circumscribed circle to the inscribed circle is x:1, what is x?

S T O P If you finish before time is called, you may check your work on this section only. Do not turn to any other section in the test.

[This page intentionally left blank]

Section 4

Time—30 Minutes
35 Questions

For each question below, choose the best answer from the choices given and fill in the corresponding oval on the answer sheet.

Each sentence below has either one or two blanks in it and is followed by five choices labeled (A) through (E). These choices represent words or phrases that have been omitted. Choose the word or phrase that, if inserted into the sentence, would best fit the meaning of the sentence as a whole.

Example:

Canine massage is a veterinary technique for calming dogs that are extremely _____.

(A) inept
(B) disciplined
(C) controlled
(D) agitated
(E) restrained   Ⓐ Ⓑ Ⓒ ● Ⓔ

1. The medical researchers had to abandon their project when they found that all of their blood samples had been _____ by foreign microbes.

   (A) disturbed
   (B) contaminated
   (C) overcome
   (D) arrested
   (E) mutated

2. In response to accusations that local educational standards were _____, district administrators announced their plan to implement more _____ procedures in hiring school teachers.

   (A) faltering..mediocre
   (B) moderate..scholarly
   (C) rigorous..compliant
   (D) lax..stringent
   (E) severe..useful

3. To consign materials that could be recycled to landfills is to _____ the earth's scarce resources.

   (A) utilize
   (B) appropriate
   (C) fabricate
   (D) undermine
   (E) squander

4. Despite the _____ of his mental processes, which were unbalanced by disease, Vincent Van Gogh produced paintings renowned for their _____ use of color and light.

   (A) clarity..remarkable
   (B) suppleness..intelligible
   (C) instability..capricious
   (D) obsessiveness..melancholy
   (E) chaos..judicious

5. Although television viewing has often been _____ by teachers and parents alike as a waste of time, the many good educational programs that are available can have _____ effect on minds of any age.

(A) extolled..a beneficial
(B) described..an enervating
(C) portrayed..an impractical
(D) disparaged..a salutary
(E) maligned..a desultory

6. Most primates are essentially _____; they spend most of their time in extended family groups engaging in social activities such as elaborate grooming rituals.

(A) gregarious
(B) innocuous
(C) passive
(D) fickle
(E) bellicose

7. Early computer programs were often so _____ that they _____ otherwise intelligent users with their complexity.

(A) advanced..reassured
(B) sophisticated..intimidated
(C) intricate..produced
(D) reliable..astounded
(E) innovative..mislead

8. Lupus is one of the more _____ human diseases; its symptoms can masquerade as many other less serious conditions, so that proper treatment is often delayed until after essential body systems have been damaged.

(A) momentous
(B) regressive
(C) insidious
(D) ephemeral
(E) quiescent

9. Though we are likely to censure people who engage in vicious behavior deliberately, we are more likely to _____ someone whose malicious deeds seem involuntary or unpremeditated.

(A) exculpate
(B) comprehend
(C) emulate
(D) extenuate
(E) redress

10. We felt sorry for the _____ speaker at the community center; while his speech would have been _____ to an audience of retired people, most of the people present were fully employed.

(A) animated..wearisome
(B) unrecognized..repellent
(C) unfortunate..irrelevant
(D) monotonous..attractive
(E) hapless..germane

GO ON TO THE NEXT PAGE

Each question below consists of two words that are related to one another in some way. Following these words are five sets of two words each, labeled (A) through (E). From these, you must choose the set that denotes a relationship <u>most similar</u> to the relationship expressed in the original set.

Example:
RUNNER : SPEED::
- (A) acrobat : height
- (B) dancer : grace
- (C) minister: holy book
- (D) waiter : order
- (E) landlord : rent

11. RALLY : LOSS ::

- (A) edit : essay
- (B) regain : market
- (C) salvage : wreck
- (D) purify : disinfectant
- (E) recover : disease

12. FRAMEWORK : CARPENTER ::

- (A) outline : writer
- (B) wall : muralist
- (C) message : recipient
- (D) hacksaw : plumber
- (E) ward : patient

13. FRET : ANXIETY ::

- (A) heed : warning
- (B) disdain : approval
- (C) demonstrate : competence
- (D) cherish : fondness
- (E) sleep : rest

14. ISLAND : ARCHIPELAGO ::

- (A) bay : inlet
- (B) animal : species
- (C) grass : meadow
- (D) mountain : chain
- (E) city : country

15. DROWSE : SLEEP ::

- (A) order : countermand
- (B) look : peruse
- (C) obstruct : proceed
- (D) attenuate :extend
- (E) practice : improve

16. COMPOUND : ELEMENTS::

- (A) drawing : composites
- (B) constitution : rulings
- (C) batter : ingredients
- (D) map : countries
- (E) book : series

17. INCARCERATE : FREEDOM ::

- (A) compensate : disability
- (B) restrain : mobility
- (C) remunerate : service
- (D) beware : hazard
- (E) vilify : opposition

18. AUDITORY : HEARING ::

- (A) tactile : response
- (B) responsive : stimulus
- (C) carnivorous : meat
- (D) material : soul
- (E) visual : sight

19. MEETING : CHAIRPERSON ::

- (A) trial : judge
- (B) rostrum : speaker
- (C) committee : nominee
- (D) seminar : student
- (E) tournament : winner

20. CAUTIOUS : HEADSTRONG ::

- (A) reticent : vocal
- (B) slow : lethargic
- (C) stormy : disquieting
- (D) prolific : productive
- (E) maturity : bond

21. FUEL : BLAZE ::

(A) burn : incense
(B) abuse : victim
(C) provoke : ire
(D) reward : achievement
(E) correct : oversight

22. SAFETY : HAVEN ::

(A) specialty : restaurant
(B) rehabilitation : hospital
(C) tree : branches
(D) confinement : prison
(E) adventure : guest

23. BEGUILE : TRICKERY ::

(A) enjoy : pleasure
(B) expunge : eraser
(C) discern : ambiguity
(D) accuse : offense
(E) study : memorization

GO ON TO THE NEXT PAGE

Read the passage carefully, then answer the questions that come after it. The answer to each question may be stated overtly or only implied. You will not have to use outside knowledge to answer the questions—all the material you will need will be in the passage itself.

Questions 24–35 are based on the following passage.

Line Between the melting pot and the salad bowl lies the reality of how ethnic cultures come together in the United States. The melting-pot metaphor, used during the massive
(5) waves of European immigration in the nineteenth and early twentieth centuries, shows immigrants melting in with the mainstream of American society—adding some bit of their own particular ethnic
(10) flavor, as carrots add to a stew, but in essence simply assimilating to dominant American culture. The salad bowl metaphor, born of ethnic pride following the civil-rights movement of the 1950s and 60s,
(15) shows various ethnic groups mixing to make a whole but without losing their essential identity: The carrots retain the flavor and texture of carrots.

The truth is that both metaphors are
(20) true simultaneously, particularly when it comes to grassroots cultural expression. Ethnic groups tend to keep aspects of their culture deemed relevant to their time and place for long periods. Simultaneously,
(25) cultural expressions of a given ethnic group borrow freely from those of other ethnic groups. New circumstances caused by migrations and historical developments, as well as individual innovation, also affect the
(30) development of ethnic cultures. Three new forms of music that emerged in a brief span of years after World War II provide examples of this mixture of cultural conservatism and eclecticism.
(35) In the Upper South and in urban areas to which Appalachian migrants moved, a new British-American style called bluegrass

took shape just after World War II. It is characterized by singing in the classic
(40) British-American style and use of acoustic stringed instruments—in conscious opposition to the more broadly popular singing style and electrified instruments already becoming standard in country music at the
(45) time. Thus bluegrass taps the most conservative stylistic preferences of British-American folk music. At the same time, it borrows songs and stylistic elements from African-American music. And from jazz and popular
(50) music it borrows such devices as breaks featuring different instruments in turn—devices unknown in earlier mountain string bands.

During the same period but quite
(55) independently, the contemporary African-American style known as rhythm and blues was taking shape in the Deep South and in urban centers where large numbers of African Americans had migrated. The chief
(60) characteristic of the new style was that it was plugged in. Amplified guitars and other stringed instruments expressed the new urban experience of African Americans from the Deep South. At the same time, amplifica-
(65) tion permitted creative extension of the traditional slide-guitar technique that had already become a hallmark of the older country blues style. Plugging in thus proved to be a deeply traditional innovation,
(70) simultaneously embracing new cultural experiences and asserting deeply held older values.

The parallels between bluegrass and rhythm and blues might suggest that both
(75) reflected a larger cultural fermentation in the South, which is the home region for both.

The American South is peopled by a variety of regional and ethnic groups, which have consistently engendered new grassroots (80) musical styles and exported them into the popular music of the whole nation. This long-standing pattern of cultural flow might account for bluegrass and rhythm and blues in the period after World War II. But there (85) are further parallels beyond the South.

The period following World War II also saw the development of the contemporary American Indian powwow throughout the American Plains. The musical style is (90) pan-tribal, in contrast with the separate tribal styles that preceded it. It probably evolved first in Oklahoma; then it spread quickly through the entire Plains region, and it continues to spread into other tribal (95) gatherings further west and east. The singing style of some Plains groups, characterized by a tense throat and pulsating voice, has been adopted as the Native American style in the contemporary powwow ceremonial con- (100) text—and is now seen as traditional by mainstream American culture. Tribal traditionalists fret about the intrusion of the powwow style into older traditional ceremonies, but it clearly represents a new pan- (105) Indian experience and world view and has strengthened Native American identity throughout much of America.

All three styles show an ethnic tradition reaching out to embrace neighboring (110) traditions, as well as elements of the mainstream culture. Yet each simultaneously reemphasizes fundamental stylistic elements of the group's traditional art. Furthermore, these new forms combine a group's cultural (115) expression with the possibility for versatility on the part of the individual performer. An energetic form like bluegrass, rhythm and blues, or the powwow style not only borrows from various cultures but also (120) attracts new adherents from outside the source group. This process can begin to redefine a group and its boundaries.

The phenomena of bluegrass, rhythm and blues, and the modern powwow style (125) should remind us that ethnicity is not doomed to extinction. Rather, it remains a potent creative factor in American culture, precisely because it allows for a fluid synthesis of the old and the new in the arts (130) and lives of Americans.

24. The passage supports its thesis primarily by

(A) providing examples from one time period
(B) examining the causes of a historical trend
(C) reasoning from the general to the specific
(D) contrasting different musical styles
(E) analyzing an extended metaphor

25. Which of the following best expresses the main idea of the passage as a whole?

(A) Ethnic culture is alive and well in the United States.
(B) Bluegrass and rhythm and blues came from the American South, while the powwow style came from the Plains.
(C) Individual creativity is more important than the traditions of a given ethnic group in forming new musical styles.
(D) The period immediately following World War II saw the formation of three new grassroots musical forms.
(E) Ethnic cultural expressions tend to keep elements of traditional styles while adapting elements from other cultures.

GO ON TO THE NEXT PAGE

26. The "carrots" in the metaphors of the first paragraph most likely stand for

   (A) mainstream American culture
   (B) ethnic pride
   (C) ethnic groups
   (D) musical styles
   (E) individual immigrants

27. The author of the passage most likely believes that the melting-pot metaphor described in the first paragraph is

   (A) a reliable description of how ethnic groups usually assimilate to mainstream culture
   (B) too often discounted by students of ethnic culture
   (C) partially accurate in describing the interactions among cultures
   (D) less useful than the salad-bowl metaphor to describe current cultural realities
   (E) an outmoded idea based on earlier immigration trends

28. The role of "historical developments" (line 28) in the development of ethnic cultures is best exemplified in the passage by the

   (A) development of electrified musical instruments after World War II
   (B) migration of large numbers of people from the South to the urban North after World War II
   (C) return of veterans who were members of minority groups from the battlefields of World War II
   (D) spread of the powwow style from the Plains to much of the rest of the United States
   (E) development of a pan-Indian world view among many Native American groups

29. In contrast to the bluegrass style, rhythm and blues

   (A) was more instrumental than vocal
   (B) appropriated stylistic elements from jazz
   (C) used primarily electric musical instruments
   (D) had its roots both in the South and in northern cities
   (E) borrowed elements from British-American folk music

30. The author discusses the powwow style in lines 86–107 primarily in order to

   (A) highlight the contributions of Native Americans to the music of the United States
   (B) refute the possible objection that the tendencies being examined were limited to the South
   (C) point out similarities between a musical style used in ceremonies and styles whose primary function is to entertain
   (D) provide an example that more closely corresponds to the melting-pot metaphor than to the salad-bowl metaphor
   (E) show that innovation in ethnic cultural expressions can come from within as well as outside the source group

31. The "tribal traditionalists" mentioned in lines 101–102 most likely object to the powwow style because

(A) they believe that new forms profane the old ceremonies
(B) they prefer older forms that are less accessible to non-Native American people
(C) its characteristic singing style is uncomfortable for singers unaccustomed to it
(D) it is replacing musical styles particular to their own tribes or nations
(E) it borrows stylistic elements from non-Native American music

32. Which of the following is an element of the new musical styles that was traditional in the music of the source group?

(A) The singing style used in bluegrass
(B) The singing style used in rhythm and blues
(C) The instruments used in rhythm and blues
(D) The singing style used in the powwow style
(E) The instruments used in the powwow style

33. Which of the following is an element of the new musical styles that was borrowed from some other ethnic culture?

(A) The stylistic devices used in bluegrass
(B) The stringed instruments used in bluegrass
(C) The electric instruments used in rhythm and blues
(D) The instrumental techniques used in rhythm and blues
(E) The singing style used in the powwow style

34. Which of the following is NOT mentioned in the passage as a force that contributes to the development of ethnic cultures?

(A) Historical circumstances
(B) The influence of other ethnic cultures
(C) Cultural conservatism on the part of ethnic groups
(D) Individuals with new ideas
(E) The geographic proximity of various ethnic groups

35. In line 128, the word "fluid" most nearly means

(A) liquid
(B) effortless
(C) easily distorted
(D) subject to change
(E) of smooth consistency

S T O P If you finish before time is called, you may check your work on this section only. Do not turn to any other section in the test.

Peterson's: www.petersons.com

373

Section 5

<table>
<tr><td>Time—30 Minutes
25 Questions</td><td>Solve the following problems, select the best answer choice for each and fill in the corresponding oval on the answer sheet. Use your test booklet for scratchwork.</td></tr>
</table>

Notes:

1. You may use a calculator. All of the numbers used are real numbers.

2. Figures accompany some problems. Assume that each has been drawn accurately and lies in a plane, unless the instructions indicate otherwise.

Reference Information

  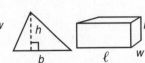 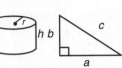

$A = \pi r^2$
$C = 2\pi r$ $A = \ell w$ $A = \frac{1}{2} bh$ $V = \ell wh$ $V = \pi r^2 h$ $c^2 = a^2 + b^2$ Special Right Triangles

The number of degrees of arc in a circle is 360.
The measure in degrees of a straight angle is 180.
The sum of the measures in degrees of the angles of a triangle is 180.

---

1. If n is an integer, which of the following expressions will ALWAYS produce an odd integer?

   (A) $n + 1$
   (B) $n + 2$
   (C) $2n + 1$
   (D) $2n - 2$
   (E) $2(n + 1)$

2. The number 12 has how many distinct prime factors?

   (A) 2
   (B) 3
   (C) 4
   (D) 5
   (E) 6

3. Lines a and b lie in the coordinate plane, such that line a is perpendicular to line b. If the slope of line a is $\frac{2}{3}$, what is the slope of line b?

   (A) $\frac{3}{2}$

   (B) $\frac{2}{3}$

   (C) $-\frac{1}{3}$

   (D) $-\frac{2}{3}$

   (E) $-\frac{3}{2}$

Peterson's SAT Success

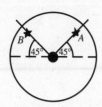

4. A radar sweeps out a screen in the clockwise direction every one minute. A plane is detected at point *A* during a down-sweep of the radar and at point *B* during the following up-sweep. How long did it take for the plane to move from *A* to *B*?

(A)   45 seconds

(B) $52\frac{1}{2}$ seconds

(C)   1 minute

(D)   1 minute $7\frac{1}{2}$ seconds

(E)   1 minute 15 seconds

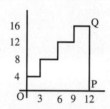

5. Keith follows the jagged path from O to Q, and Mia follows the path from O to P and straight up to Q. If all angles shown are 90°, how many units longer is Mia's trip?

(A)   0

(B)   1

(C)   2

(D)   4

(E)   8

6. Points *A*, *B*, *C*, and *D* lie on a line in that order, such that $AB = \dfrac{AD}{6} = \dfrac{AC}{2}$. *AD* is equal to all of the following EXCEPT

(A) $6AB$

(B) $3(AB + BC)$

(C) $\dfrac{3CD}{2}$

(D) $3AC$

(E) $AB + AC$

7. In a drawer, there are 3 white socks, 3 black socks, and 3 blue socks. If a blue sock is removed from the drawer, what is the probability that the next sock removed will also be blue?

(A) $\dfrac{1}{3}$

(B) $\dfrac{1}{4}$

(C) $\dfrac{2}{9}$

(D) $\dfrac{3}{8}$

(E) $\dfrac{1}{2}$

GO ON TO THE NEXT PAGE

8. Greg places a special order for a shelves at a kitchen supply store, leaving a deposit of b dollars. If the balance due on the shelves is c, how much does each shelf cost in terms of a, b, and c?

(A) $\dfrac{a + b}{c}$

(B) $\dfrac{b + c}{a}$

(C) $\dfrac{a}{b + c}$

(D) $\dfrac{b - c}{a}$

(E) $\dfrac{c}{a + b}$

$$x^2 = y^3$$

9. If x and y are both integers greater than 1, then the smallest value for xy is

(A) 8
(B) 16
(C) 32
(D) 40
(E) 64

10. Two clocks are set to the correct time at noon; however, one clock gains 5 minutes every hour and the other clock loses 5 minutes every hour. How long until the two clocks read the same time? (Note: The clocks do not distinguish between a.m. and p.m.)

(A) 6 hours
(B) 12 hours
(C) 24 hours
(D) 72 hours
(E) 144 hours

S T O P If you finish before time is called, you may check your work on this section only. Do not turn to any other section in the test.

[This page intentionally left blank]

Section 6

Questions 1–12 are based on the following passages.

These passages present two views of an exhibition sponsored by the American Folklife Center of the Library of Congress in the early 1990s. The exhibition focused on the role of Italian-Americans in the American West. Passage 1 was written by a staff member involved in organizing the exhibition and describes some of the purposes of the project. Passage 2 was written by a staff member who was not involved in this project. Herself an Italian-American from the West, she reflects on her feelings about the exhibition.

Passage 1

Line The truck from the Library of Congress pulled into the driveway of Kerry Nick Fister's home in Price, Utah, as the Nick family was gathering for its 1992 reunion. It
(5) was there to pick up items Mrs. Fister had agreed to lend for an exhibition sponsored by the American Folklife Center on Italian Americans in the West. The Nick family will be represented in a section of the exhibition
(10) on the transformation of Italians in the American West into Italian Americans. The very surname Nick (changed from Nicolavo)

encapsulates one part of that story. Many Italians felt obliged to change or anglicize
(15) their names, either to disguise the fact that they were Italians (and thus avoid discrimination) or simply to make the name easier to pronounce.

The Nicks and other contributors were
(20) puzzled at first that the Folklife Center wanted to display their garden tools, linens, photo albums, and such. What was so special about the hog-sticking knife Kerry Fister's father made using an old file from
(25) the Carbon County coal mine where he worked? But when field-workers explained how ordinary objects come to symbolize the experiences of a lifetime, most warmed to the idea. Field-workers discovered a deep
(30) sense of family pride in the western communities they investigated, and most Italian-American families agreed that their stories deserved to be told.

While most Americans associate
(35) Italian-American life, history, and culture with the urban East, this project was designed to uncover an important and much less understood aspect of Italian-American history—in the American West. In the
(40) mid-nineteenth century, large numbers of Italian immigrants settled in California and

other Western states. They brought with them a number of cultural skills and arts—agricultural techniques, wine culture, stone (45) masonry, and many others. More than most people realize, these Italian Americans helped shape the cultural landscape of the modern West.

David A. Taylor, project director, (50) explained his task: "Field-workers devoted attention to Italian-American involvement in the distinctive occupations of the several regions," Taylor explained. "For instance, research in coal and precious metal mining (55) communities shed light on the role Italian immigrant labor played in building extractive industries and revealed family and cultural connections between Italian-American settlements in the West, their counterparts (60) in the mining areas of the East, and the home communities in Italy.

"We also documented many other aspects of contemporary Italian-American culture, such as the centrality of extended (65) family, as well as food traditions that play an important role in Italian-American identity. We wanted to know if the informants contacted in the study communities were Italians or Westerners or both. Had they (70) shaped the contemporary culture of their Western subregion, or had it shaped them? These were the central questions the Center's researchers asked."

Passage 2

Line The history of the Italian side of my family is (75) typical of Italian immigrants to the West. My great-grandparents migrated from Italy to the San Francisco Bay Area in the late 1800s. My nonno's (grandfather's) parents ran a grocery store, and my nonna's father worked for a (80) winery. My mother and uncle grew up speaking Italian at home and English at school. For my sister and me, Italian-American cultural influences were one

generation removed and, thus, diluted. My (85) grandparents spoke English, so my sister and I didn't have to learn Italian to communicate with them. Yet there were plenty of cultural ties. We were a close-knit extended family. We saw my grandparents every weekend and (90) often visited my Aunt Eda Pedrizetti, whose husband owned vineyards and a winery. Pasta is the family staple dish, and as I grew up I learned how to make various sauces.

When I took a job with the American (95) Folklife Center, I didn't pay much attention to the Italian Americans in the West (IAW) project—even though I am both a folklorist and an Italian-American from the West. But one day, as I looked over the shoulder of a (100) colleague, I saw the name "Pedrizetti" on a photograph of a tombstone to be used in the IAW exhibition. The project field-workers had been working with my very family! Suddenly, I realized that my own family had been (105) identified as the folk, "the other"—the people I studied and sought to understand, but always stood apart from. I found myself symbolically on "the other" side of the microphone, transformed from folklorist to folk.

(110) I listened to the taped interviews the Center's researchers made with my cousins. As I heard their voices, I could see them in my mind's eye. I began to recall family memories, but my nostalgic mental journey (115) was interrupted by two unfamiliar voices asking questions. The answers revealed parts of my family history that I'd never heard. I wanted to ask more questions, but I also felt a strange sense of violation, as if the (120) presence of two field-workers with a microphone invaded my privacy and trespassed on my ownership of this family history. On the one hand, I was excited to have part of my life experience recognized (125) as important; on the other hand, I was

GO ON TO THE NEXT PAGE

ambivalent about my family being the topic of research. If my family's history was shared with the general public through inclusion in an exhibition, would it any longer have
(130) special meaning for me?

1. The first paragraph of Passage 1 serves primarily to

   (A) give concrete form to the focal ideas behind the exhibition on Italian Americans in the West
   (B) introduce the family that was the subject of the Italian Americans in the West exhibition
   (C) emphasize how cooperative families were in providing artifacts to be included in the Italian Americans in the West exhibition
   (D) sketch a contrast between one family and the majority of families studied by the American Folklife Center
   (E) outline the conflict felt by Italian people in the process of becoming Italian Americans

2. In lines 22–26, the author includes the detail of the hog-sticking knife primarily in order to emphasize the

   (A) ingenuity of Italian American crafts-persons in the West
   (B) lack of interest the Italian American families had in their heritage
   (C) care with which field-workers chose artifacts to be included in the exhibition
   (D) distinctive contributions of coal miners to Italian American culture in the West
   (E) initial incomprehension of the research subjects toward the field-workers' interests

3. In line 41, the word "settled" most nearly means

   (A) came to rest
   (B) made a decision
   (C) established residence
   (D) restored calmness
   (E) arranged definitely

4. Which of the following is most likely among the reasons why the American Folklife Center undertook the project on Italian Americans in the West?

   (A) The Center had already studied Italian Americans in the East.
   (B) The Center anticipated that the Italian Americans would be particularly cooperative with field-workers.
   (C) The Western immigration of Italians was recent enough that many physical artifacts were available for exhibition.
   (D) The project would reveal to the public an often-neglected facet of Italian-American culture.
   (E) The project focused on an ethnic group rarely studied by folklorists.

5. How does the first passage answer the question posed by David Taylor in lines 69–71?

(A) In some ways, Italian Americans adapted to the culture of the American West, but they also contributed to the formation of that culture.

(B) The culture of the American West had little impact on the close-knit Italian-American communities, but members of the majority culture adopted a few aspects of Italian culture from them.

(C) Italian Americans in the West mostly conformed to the majority culture around them, though they did add their own distinctive flavor to it.

(D) Because of the hostility of the environment, Italian Americans in the American West had little opportunity either to influence or to be influenced by the surrounding culture.

(E) The cultural traditions of Italian Americans in the West were so strong that they pervaded Western culture, making assimilation to the majority culture unnecessary for the Italian Americans.

6. The reaction of the author of Passage 2 to the discovery described in lines 98–103 is best characterized as one of

(A) delight
(B) astonishment
(C) indifference
(D) disbelief
(E) dismay

7. In line 103, the word "very" most nearly means

(A) truly
(B) extremely
(C) selfsame
(D) complete
(E) suitable

8. The "two unfamiliar voices" mentioned by the author of Passage 2 in line 115 are those of

(A) colleagues listening to the tape with the author
(B) field-workers interviewing her cousins on tape
(C) cousins that the author didn't know she had
(D) relatives that the author hears in her memory
(E) the author's own conflicting feelings

9. When the author of Passage 2 says that she felt "a strange sense of violation" (line 119), she means that she felt that

(A) the procedures for proper interviewing had not been followed
(B) the field-workers had intruded on her family
(C) her professionalism had been disregarded
(D) her train of thought had been interrupted
(E) her most sacred beliefs had been desecrated

GO ON TO THE NEXT PAGE

10. All of the following aspects of Italian-American culture in the West are mentioned in both passages EXCEPT

   (A) food
   (B) family ties
   (C) work in producing wine
   (D) work in agriculture
   (E) work in mining

11. Would the author of Passage 2 be likely to agree with the Italian American families mentioned in Passage 1 when they "agreed that their stories deserved to be told" (lines 32–33)?

   (A) Yes, because she finds a certain validation of her family history in its inclusion in the exhibition.
   (B) Yes, because she suggested that her family participate in the study.
   (C) Yes, because she is curious about parts of her own family story she has not heard before.
   (D) No, because she feels violated by the research done into her own family's history.
   (E) No, because she believes that her own family is not a valid subject for the exhibition.

12. The contrast in purpose between the two passages lies primarily in the difference between

   (A) the viewpoint of someone involved in the project and that of an outsider
   (B) a favorable and an unfavorable assessment of the project's goals
   (C) the opinions of a bureaucrat and those of a folklorist
   (D) an official description of the project and a personal reflection on it
   (E) the history of a nation and the history of a family

S T O P   If you finish before time is called, you may check your work on this section only. Do not turn to any other section in the test.

Quick-Score Answers

<table>
<tr><th colspan="7">Practice Test 2</th></tr>
<tr><th colspan="3">Math</th><th colspan="3">Verbal</th></tr>
<tr><th>Section 1</th><th>Section 3</th><th>Section 5</th><th>Section 2</th><th>Section 4</th><th>Section 6</th></tr>
<tr><td>1. C</td><td>1. B</td><td>1. C</td><td>1. C</td><td>1. B</td><td>1. A</td></tr>
<tr><td>2. D</td><td>2. C</td><td>2. A</td><td>2. C</td><td>2. D</td><td>2. E</td></tr>
<tr><td>3. A</td><td>3. D</td><td>3. E</td><td>3. C</td><td>3. E</td><td>3. C</td></tr>
<tr><td>4. B</td><td>4. C</td><td>4. A</td><td>4. B</td><td>4. E</td><td>4. D</td></tr>
<tr><td>5. C</td><td>5. B</td><td>5. A</td><td>5. C</td><td>5. D</td><td>5. A</td></tr>
<tr><td>6. D</td><td>6. C</td><td>6. E</td><td>6. B</td><td>6. A</td><td>6. B</td></tr>
<tr><td>7. E</td><td>7. D</td><td>7. B</td><td>7. E</td><td>7. B</td><td>7. C</td></tr>
<tr><td>8. B</td><td>8. B</td><td>8. B</td><td>8. E</td><td>8. C</td><td>8. B</td></tr>
<tr><td>9. C</td><td>9. B</td><td>9. C</td><td>9. A</td><td>9. A</td><td>9. B</td></tr>
<tr><td>10. C</td><td>10. D</td><td>10. D</td><td>10. D</td><td>10. E</td><td>10. E</td></tr>
<tr><td>11. B</td><td>11. A</td><td></td><td>11. A</td><td>11. E</td><td>11. A</td></tr>
<tr><td>12. E</td><td>12. B</td><td></td><td>12. E</td><td>12. A</td><td>12. D</td></tr>
<tr><td>13. D</td><td>13. B</td><td></td><td>13. A</td><td>13. D</td><td></td></tr>
<tr><td>14. A</td><td>14. B</td><td></td><td>14. B</td><td>14. D</td><td></td></tr>
<tr><td>15. A</td><td>15. A</td><td></td><td>15. D</td><td>15. B</td><td></td></tr>
<tr><td>16. D</td><td>16. 2/5 or .4</td><td></td><td>16. D</td><td>16. C</td><td></td></tr>
<tr><td>17. E</td><td>17. 11.89</td><td></td><td>17. B</td><td>17. B</td><td></td></tr>
<tr><td>18. E</td><td>18. 108</td><td></td><td>18. A</td><td>18. E</td><td></td></tr>
<tr><td>19. C</td><td>19. 6</td><td></td><td>19. C</td><td>19. A</td><td></td></tr>
<tr><td>20. A</td><td>20. 5</td><td></td><td>20. E</td><td>20. A</td><td></td></tr>
<tr><td>21. E</td><td>21. 1</td><td></td><td>21. C</td><td>21. C</td><td></td></tr>
<tr><td>22. E</td><td>22. 81.5</td><td></td><td>22. D</td><td>22. D</td><td></td></tr>
<tr><td>23. C</td><td>23. 61</td><td></td><td>23. C</td><td>23. B</td><td></td></tr>
<tr><td>24. B</td><td>24. 8/25 or .32</td><td></td><td>24. D</td><td>24. D</td><td></td></tr>
<tr><td>25. D</td><td>25. 2</td><td></td><td>25. D</td><td>25. E</td><td></td></tr>
<tr><td></td><td></td><td></td><td>26. A</td><td>26. C</td><td></td></tr>
<tr><td></td><td></td><td></td><td>27. B</td><td>27. C</td><td></td></tr>
<tr><td></td><td></td><td></td><td>28. E</td><td>28. B</td><td></td></tr>
<tr><td></td><td></td><td></td><td>29. E</td><td>29. C</td><td></td></tr>
<tr><td></td><td></td><td></td><td>30. B</td><td>30. B</td><td></td></tr>
<tr><td></td><td></td><td></td><td>31. A</td><td>31. D</td><td></td></tr>
<tr><td></td><td></td><td></td><td></td><td>32. A</td><td></td></tr>
<tr><td></td><td></td><td></td><td></td><td>33. A</td><td></td></tr>
<tr><td></td><td></td><td></td><td></td><td>34. E</td><td></td></tr>
<tr><td></td><td></td><td></td><td></td><td>35. D</td><td></td></tr>
</table>

Detailed explanations can be found on page 425.

Scoring the Test

Check your answers to the math sections against the answer key, and record the number of correct and incorrect answers for each section in the spaces provided. For sections 1 and 5, multiply the number of incorrect answers by .25, and subtract this from the number correct. This gives you your raw scores for sections 1 and 5. For questions 1–15 in section 3, multiply the number of incorrect answers by .33, and subtract this from the number correct. For questions 16–25 in section 3, simply record the number of correct answers; these questions are Grid-ins and have no wrong answer penalty. Adding these two numbers gives you your total for section 3. Now sum the raw scores of each math section, and round the total to the nearest whole number. This is your math raw score.

Check your answers to the verbal sections against the answer key, and record the number of correct and incorrect answers in the spaces provided. Multiply the number of incorrect answers by .25, and subtract this from the number correct. Round the result to the nearest whole number. This is your verbal raw score.

Use the score chart to translate your raw scores into scaled scores. However, remember that these scores are only approximations of how you might do on the real test. Lots of factors will affect your actual SAT scores: taking the test under controlled conditions, your preparation between now and test day, etc. Use these scores to get a rough idea of your score range on the exam and to decide how to focus your SAT preparation.

Scoring Worksheet

MATH				
	Number Correct	**Number Incorrect**	**=**	**Raw Score**
Section 1	_____	− (.25 × _____)	=	_____
Section 3				
1–15	_____	− (.33 × _____)	=	_____
16–25	_____	(no wrong answer penalty)	=	_____
Section 5	_____	− (.25 × _____)	=	_____
	Total Rounded Raw Score			_____
VERBAL				
Sections 2, 4, and 6	_____	− (.25 × _____)	=	_____
	Total Rounded Raw Score			_____

Score Charts

Math			
Raw Score	**Math Scaled Score**	**Raw Score**	**Math Scaled Score**
60	800	28	500
59	800	27	490
58	790	26	490
57	770	25	480
56	760	24	470
55	740	23	460
54	720	22	460
53	710	21	450
52	700	20	440
51	690	19	430
50	680	18	420
49	670	17	420
48	660	16	410
47	650	15	410
46	640	14	400
45	630	13	390
44	620	12	380
43	610	11	370
42	600	10	360
41	600	9	350
40	590	8	340
39	580	7	330
38	570	6	320
37	560	5	310
36	560	4	300
35	550	3	280
34	540	2	270
33	540	1	250
32	530	0	240
31	520	−1	220
30	510	−2	210
29	510	−3 and below	200

Verbal			
Raw Score	**Verbal Scaled Score**	**Raw Score**	**Verbal Scaled Score**
78	800	37	510
77	800	36	510
76	800	35	500
75	790	34	500
74	780	33	490
73	770	32	490
72	760	31	480
71	750	30	480
70	740	29	470
69	730	28	460
68	720	27	460
67	710	26	450
66	700	25	450
65	700	24	440
64	690	23	440
63	680	22	430
62	670	21	420
61	670	20	410
60	660	19	410
59	650	18	400
58	640	17	390
57	640	16	380
56	630	15	380
55	620	14	370
54	610	13	360
53	610	12	360
52	600	11	350
51	600	10	340
50	590	9	330
49	590	8	320
48	580	7	310
47	570	6	300
46	570	5	290
45	560	4	270
44	550	3	260
43	550	2	250
42	540	1	240
41	540	0	230
40	530	−1	220
39	520	−2	210
38	520	−3 and below	200

Answers and Explanations

Diagnostic Test

SECTION 1

1. **The correct answer is (D).** Substituting each set of values into the inequality, you find that only choice (D), $(-3, 4)$, makes the statement true: $4 \le (-3)^2$ or $4 \le 9$.

2. **The correct answer is (D).** The median is the middle value in a group of ascending or descending terms. Placing Olga's grades in ascending order gives you 75, 85, 90, 90, 95. The third and middle term, 90, is her median grade.

3. **The correct answer is (A).** To return to his starting point, the boy must reverse direction for each leg of his journey. Since he last traveled 2 miles east, he must reverse direction and travel 2 miles west. The first leg was 1 mile south, so the reverse of that is 1 mile north.

4. **The correct answer is (B).** An isosceles triangle has two angles that are the same. Let them be x. The three angles sum to $180°$, so $90 + x + x = 180$, $2x = 90$, and $x = 45$.

5. **The correct answer is (A).** The area of a rectangle is equal to the length times the width. In the diagram, the length of the rectangle is identified as 5 and its width as a. Since its area is 20, $20 = 5a$ and $a = 4$.

6. **The correct answer is (B).** When dividing powers with the same base, keep the base and subtract the exponents. So $\dfrac{x^{12}}{x^3} = x^{(12-3)} = x^9$. Statement I is not true; $x^{12} - x^3 \ne x^{(12-3)}$. Eliminate choices (A), (C), and, (E) for including it. Statement II is true; when multiplying powers with the same base, you add the exponents, so $(x^4)(x^5) = x^{4+5} = x^9$. Statement III is not true; when raising a power to a power, you multiply the powers, so $(x^3)^2 = x^{3 \times 2} = x^6$. Eliminate choice (D) for including it, which leaves choice (B) as correct.

7. **The correct answer is (C).** Since 5 people share the shifts, every fifth shift will be assigned to the fifth person, or Eli. Since 240 is evenly divisible by 5, Eli will be assigned the 240th shift. That means Ariel will be assigned the 241st, Brian the 242nd, and Cameron the 243rd.

8. **The correct answer is (E).** If there are x ways for one event to happen and y ways for a second event to happen, then there are $(x)(y)$ ways for the two events to happen together. Any of the three numbers can be first, and for each of these three possibilities the two remaining numbers can come second, leaving only one possibility for the last slot. There are a total of $(3)(2)(1) = 6$ possibilities. If you didn't remember the fundamental counting principal, you could simply list the different possibilities and count them.

9. **The correct answer is (C).** Solve for x by isolating it on one side of the equation

$$x + 3y = 4(3y)$$
$$x + 3y = 12y$$
$$x = 12y - 3y \text{ or } 9y.$$

10. **The correct answer is (D).** The area of the triangle $= \frac{1}{2}$ the area of the square. You know that the perimeter of the square is 36, and since a square has 4 equal sides, each side is 36 divided by 4 or 9. The area of a square is equal to a side length squared, in this case, 81. Half of 81 is 40.5, choice (D).

11. **The correct answer is (E).** This question is a snap if you remember that an exterior angle of a triangle is equal to the sum of its two remote interior angles. In this case, $140 = (x + 10) + (x - 10)$. This leaves you $140 = 2x$ or $x = 70$, but don't pick choice (D). The question asks for the measure of angle ABC, which is given as $x + 10$, so $70 + 10 = 80$ is the correct answer. You could also have solved for x by seeing that angle ACB is 40 degrees (since it is supplementary to the 140 degree angle) and setting all three angles of the triangle equal to 180 degrees.

12. **The correct answer is (D).** If the product of two numbers is zero, then one or both of the numbers must be zero. You are not given enough information to determine whether a or b equals zero, which is why choices (A) and (B) are incorrect, so choice (D) is the correct answer.

13. **The correct answer is (B).** $\frac{1}{2} : \frac{1}{3} : \frac{1}{4}$ is the same as 6:4:3. There are $6 + 4 + 3 = 13$ shares. Each share is worth $\$156 \div 13 = \$12$. The greatest piece is 6 shares and the smallest is 3, so the difference is $3 \times \$12 = \$36$.

14. **The correct answer is (C).** The full line of numbers on the star shows you that each group of four circles must sum to $2 + 6 + 8 + 4$, or 20. Therefore, $A + 8 + 5 + 6 = 20$ and $A = 1$. Therefore, $1 + 6 + 7 + B = 20$ and $B = 6$.

15. **The correct answer is (E).** The circumference of the circle is equal to $2\pi r = 2 \times 4 \times \pi = 8\pi$. The bug has walked around 25% or a quarter of the circle, which is 2π. Since he did this in 4 steps, each of his steps is equal to $\frac{2\pi}{4} = \frac{\pi}{2}$.

16. **The correct answer is (E).** There are 366 days in a leap year. $336 \div 52 = 7$, with a remainder of 2. Therefore, 2 of the 7 days in the week occur 53 times in a leap year, and the remaining 5 occur only 52 times, so choice (E) is correct.

17. **The correct answer is (B).** The volume of a cube is equal to an edge cubed, so the edge of this cube is $\sqrt[3]{64} = 4$. Since a cube has 6 equal faces, its surface area is equal to six times the area of one of its faces. The area of one face is simply 4^2, or 16, so its surface area is $6(16) = 96$.

18. **The correct answer is (C).** The amount of jam in each jar is simply the total amount of jam used divided by the total number of jars filled. Martha began with g gallons of jam, and 3 gallons remained after jarring, so she used a total of $g - 3$ gallons. She filled j jars, so each contains $\dfrac{g-3}{j}$ gallons of jam, choice (C). If this seems a bit abstract, you could also have solved the problem by picking values for the variables involved. Let $g = 33$ and $j = 10$. Martha used all but 3 gallons of the jam, or 30 gallons. Dividing 30 gallons among 10 jars gives you 3 gallons apiece. Substituting $g = 33$ and $j = 10$ into the answer choices, you see that only choice (C) gives you 3.

19. **The correct answer is (C).** A fraction is undefined when its denominator is zero, so find the answer where $ad = bc$. Since $(4)(6) = (8)(3) = 24$, choice (C) is correct.

20. **The correct answer is (B).** For the expression in the question to equal one of the answer choices, the difference $ad - bc$ must be the same in both cases. Working it through gives you $(4)(5) - (4)(3) = 20 - 12 = 8$. Only choice (B) matches this: $(2)(4) - (0)(6) = 8 - 0 = 8$.

21. **The correct answer is (B).** The maximum winnings would result from winning at the tables with the 40:1 odds and the 30:1 odds. Betting $10 at the 40:1 table and winning results in a prize of $(\$10)(40) = \$400$. Winning at the 30:1 table yields $(\$10)(30) = \$300$, making the maximum possible winnings $\$400 + \$300 = \$700$. The minimum winnings result from winning at the 10:1 table and the 30:1 table. Winning at the 10:1 table yields $(\$10)(10) = \$100$, making the minimum winnings $\$100 + \$300 = \$400$. The difference is $\$700 - \$400 = \$300$.

22. **The correct answer is (C).** Divide the octagon into pieces whose areas you can find. Drawing perpendiculars from the top to the bottom and from left to right breaks the figure into 5 squares and 4 right triangles, as shown below. Each of the squares has side length 1, for an area of $1^2 = 1$. Each of the right triangles is equal to half a square (they are isosceles right triangles with legs of length 1) and have an area of $\dfrac{1}{2}$. So the total area is $5(1) + 4\left(\dfrac{1}{2}\right) = 5 + 2 = 7$.

23. **The correct answer is (C).** Make a quick sketch of the figure. You can see that each side of the square is also the hypotenuse of a right triangle. Solve for the hypotenuse of one of these triangles, say the one in the first quadrant. Each leg of the triangle falls on one of the axes, so it's easy to see that each has length 2. Two equal legs makes it an isosceles right triangle, and its hypotenuse is equal to a leg times $\sqrt{2} = 2\sqrt{2}$. The area of a square is equal to a side length squared, or $(2\sqrt{2})^2 = 8$.

24. **The correct answer is (D).** If you picked $480 as the answer, you fell for the trap. You can't just add 20% of $400 to the sale price to find the original price. The percent decrease was taken off the original price, not the sale price. Let x = the original price. Taking a 20% decrease gives you a sale price of $x - .20x = .80x$ or $.8x$. You know that the result of the 20% decrease is a sale price of $400, so $.8x = \$400$. Solving for x, you find that the original price is $500, choice (D). You could also have found the answer by plugging in each choice as the original price and seeing which yielded $400 after a 20% decrease.

25. **The correct answer is (B).** To find the area of the shaded region, simply subtract the area of the hexagon from the area of the circle. The area of the circle $= \pi r^2$. Since the radius of the circle is 1, its area is $\pi(1)^2 = \pi$. Since you know that the area of the hexagon must be subtracted from the area of the circle or π, you can eliminate choices (D) and (E). The hexagon is composed of six equilateral triangles, so six times the area of one triangle will give you the area of the hexagon. The area of a triangle is one half base times height. The base of each triangle is 1, but you have to solve for the height. Dropping a perpendicular line from the top vertex of a triangle to its base divides it into two equal right triangles, whose common leg is the height of the triangle. Since the hypotenuse of each is 1 and the other leg of each is $\frac{1}{2}$, it is a 30:60:90 right triangle and the remaining side must be $\frac{\sqrt{3}}{2}$.

That means the area of one equilateral triangle is $\left(\frac{1}{2} \times 1 \times \frac{\sqrt{3}}{2}\right) = \frac{\sqrt{3}}{4}$.

So the area of the hexagon is $6 \times \frac{\sqrt{3}}{4} = \frac{3\sqrt{3}}{2}$. Therefore, the area of the shaded region is $\pi - \frac{3\sqrt{3}}{2}$, choice (B).

SECTION 2

1. **The correct answer is (B).** Think cause and effect. Key words are *startling use of vibrant colors* and *unusual subjects*. O'Keefe shocked people, so they didn't appreciate her art right away. That is the sense of this sentence, and it eliminates choices (A) and (C), because of the second word and choices (C) and (E) because of the first word. Choice (D) may be tempting, but it doesn't quite make sense. The best answer is choice (B).

2. **The correct answer is (D).** The key words here are *find it impossible*. That's your hint that the first half of the sentence is going to contrast the second. Choice (A) doesn't work because *Opponents* of an idea would not find it impossible to dispute the idea. Choice (B) is incorrect because *Disciples* are followers, so they would not find it impossible to teach Freud's idea. Choices (C) and (E) just don't make much sense, so eliminate them.

3. **The correct answer is (C).** Key phrases are *immersed in* and *daily contact*. Ruth is totally absorbed in her work, so look for an answer that refers specifically to work. *Colleagues* are people who work in the same profession, so choice (C) is the best answer.

4. **The correct answer is (A).** Go for the sense of the sentence and note key words *stubborn adherence to tradition*. Jerry's firm either likes his traditional stance or it dislikes it. Test the answers one by one in this type of sentence. Choice (A) makes good sense, so keep it. Choices (B) and (C) don't make sense because if his firm mistrusts anything *modern* or *innovative*, Jerry's adherence to tradition would be received positively. Choice (D) is similarly illogical. Choice (E) doesn't make sense because *conventional* means traditional. Only choice (A) makes complete logical sense.

5. **The correct answer is (A).** A sentence of contrast. Key words are *rather than enlarging, negative effects,* and *offering only*. This guy is showing us only happy outcomes with his new vaccine, and we require a contrast to the word *negative*. Choice (B), *ambiguous*, is not an opposite, and choice (C) is talking about practicality, which is off the mark, as is choice (D). Choice (E) is fair, but choice (A), *sanguine* (very optimistic and positive), makes the most sense.

6. **The correct answer is (E).** The real question here is whether a once radical theory has been proved or not, and logic is critical. Choices (A) and (D) are contradictory, so they are not correct. Choice (B) makes no sense. Choice (C) doesn't make sense because *implicated* means that the scientists were proved to be involved with something. Choice (E) says that the bold paleontologists have been *vindicated* (justified, proved correct) by new discoveries that *confirm* their once radical idea.

7. **The correct answer is (C).** Read carefully. Common sense should tell you that Stewart disapproved of *lax* (loose) *morality*. So choices (A), *endorsed*, and (B), *encouraged*, are highly suspect, and the second word choices contradict them. Choice (C) says Stewart *decried* (deplored, disapproved of) this behavior but didn't *malign* (bad-mouth) anybody. It's perfect—but always check all answers. Choice (D) shows contradictory words that don't make logical sense, and choice (E) offers weak choices.

8. **The correct answer is (C).** Because Juanita became a concert violinist, she must like or have a talent for classical music. The only choice that makes sense is (C), *predilection for*, because *predilection* means preference. Even if you didn't know that, you could eliminate most of the other choices.

9. **The correct answer is (E).** It might help to know that *bibliophiles* are book lovers, but you don't need to know it in order to solve this one. You're looking for something that means *out of place*. Eliminate choices (A) and (B) right away, because they just don't make sense. Choices (C) and (D) may be tempting, but the word you're looking for is out of place in the same way that a slate writing tablet is—that is, something from another time period. Choice (E), *anachronisms*, is the perfect answer.

10. **The correct answer is (B).** This sentence contrasts a human's life expectancy with that of an insect. Key words *lifetime* and *his own longevity* tell us that the subject is time, not whether an insect is choice (A), *interactive*; or choice (C), *compelling*; or choice (D), *unique*. Eliminate those choices because the first word is off the subject. Choice (E) is close, but the second word, *confronted*, doesn't make sense. *Contrasted*, in choice (B), makes the most sense, and so does *evanescent*, which means short-lived.

11. **The correct answer is (D).** Type: Portion related to the larger whole. A *shaving* is a small piece of *wood* . . . just as a *slice* is a small piece of *cheese*. None of the other pairs shows this relationship.

12. **The correct answer is (C).** Type: Object and its purpose. Try putting the words in reverse order to make a sentence. A *backpack* is for carrying *books* . . . just as a *portfolio* is for carrying *documents*. *Clothes* are kept in a *dresser*, choice (A), but they aren't being toted around. The other answer pairs show different relationships.

13. **The correct answer is (E).** Type: Object and its purpose. A *bonnet* is worn on the *head* to cover it or protect it from the elements . . . just as *boots* are worn on the *feet* to cover and protect them. Don't be fooled by choices that list an item of clothing but not the part of the body it clothes.

14. **The correct answer is (B).** Type: A living thing related to a portion of its anatomy. The *hawk* uses its *talons* to hold things . . . just as a *squid* uses its *tentacles* to hold things. All other choices show animals and their physical aspects, but not the same specific relationship.

15. **The correct answer is (A).** Type: Something related to its purpose, by definition. The purpose of an *editorial* (by definition) is to give an *opinion* . . . just as the purpose of a *license* is to give *permission*. In choice (B), *notation* and *postcript* are both written, yet for different purposes. An *essay* is part of a *publication* in choice (C), and the *newspaper* has many *headlines*, as suggested by choice (D). In choice (E), a *summary* is not expected to give an *index*.

16. **The correct answer is (D).** Type: A type of person and a matching quality, by definition. A *prodigy*, by definition, has *talent* . . . just as a *champion*, by definition, has *proficiency*. Remember that although a *physician* probably has *medicine*, medicine is not a quality.

17. **The correct answer is (A).** Type: Object and its purpose. An *unguent* is used to *soothe* . . . just as an *ornament* is used to *embellish* (dress up, adorn). None of the other answer choices shows this specific relationship of use or purpose.

18. **The correct answer is (C).** Type: Relationship by definition. To *salvage* something is to save it from *destruction* . . . just as to *recoup* something (generally money) is to save it from *loss*. The other choices fail to show the necessary relationship.

19. **The correct answer is (E).** Type: Relationship by definition. (This one is tough at first glance; consider all uses of the word *retiring*.) Someone of a *retiring* (shy, modest, or timid) nature, by definition, dislikes *publicity* . . . just as someone of a *misanthropic* nature by definition dislikes *people*.

20. **The correct answer is (B).** Type: Implied relationship, by definition. Something *prodigious* inspires *awe* . . . just as something *abhorrent* (revolting, hateful, disgusting) inspires *revulsion* (instinctive shrinking-away in hatred or disgust). In choice (A), someone *precocious* might exhibit lots of *curiosity*, but that trait isn't part of the dictionary definition. The other choices have a vague relationship to each other at best.

21. **The correct answer is (D).** Type: Degree. Something *bulky* has a lot of *girth* . . . just as something *pungent* (strong-smelling) has a lot of *odor*.

22. **The correct answer is (D).** Type: Relationship by definition. *Jurisprudence* is the study of *law* . . . just as *pedagogy* is the study of *education*. Most of the other choices can be eliminated simply because they show no clear relationship.

23. **The correct answer is (E).** Type: Opposite by definition. *Diffident* (shy, unassertive) people by definition don't *assert* . . . just as *ambivalent* (unsure, indecisive) people by definition don't *decide*. *Arrogant* (prideful) people may or may not *assume*, and *capricious* (whimsical) people may or may not *revolt*; there's no real relationship in choices (C) and (D). Choices (A) and (B) have no logical relationship at all, so eliminate them right away.

24. **The correct answer is (E).** Read the first four paragraphs to see what qualities the writer notes in spiders. Nowhere is generosity even suggested, and after the fourth paragraph, the essay moves on to discuss our human fascination with disaster/evil.

25. **The correct answer is (A).** The key here is paragraph 2, in which the author helps the spider escape, and muses that "a moralist a century ago would have crushed the little reptile to death." In this passage, the author makes the point that although people retain feelings of ill will, they learn over time not to act on them. That the author did not crush the spider despite his revulsion toward it was a demonstration of choice (A), human progress.

26. **The correct answer is (B).** See paragraph 3, especially lines 32-37, in which the author discusses how long it takes people to rid themselves of prejudice on any topic.

27. **The correct answer is (B).** Read lines 20-25. The author explains that we can control our actions even when we can't control our feelings. *Practical exertion* of malevolence refers to acting upon feelings of malevolence.

28. **The correct answer is (C).** Read lines 20-37, in which the essayist says how hard it is to modify our *feelings, imaginations,* and *prejudices.*

29. **The correct answer is (D).** The writer states in lines 58-59 that "hatred alone is immortal." Of the answer choices, *hostility* is closest in meaning to *hatred.*

30. **The correct answer is (E).** Remember that when you have a question about the author's tone, it's usually a safe bet to eliminate any extreme choices, which eliminates choices (B) and (E). Choice (A) doesn't work because the author isn't really endorsing (supporting) anything, which leaves choice (C), *resigned acceptance,* and choice (D), *general optimism,* as the most likely choices. The author clearly believes that humans have strong failings that are not likely to get better, so eliminate *general optimism.* The best answer is choice (C), *resigned acceptance.*

31. **The correct answer is (A).** Reread lines 62-64 where the author says that all of us read the accidents and offences in a newspaper as the "cream of the jest." Taken with material before and after this comment, only choice (A) is totally accurate. Remember that the cream of anything is always considered the best or tastiest part. Choices (B), (C), and (E) have no support in the passage, and choice (D) goes a little too far.

32. **The correct answer is (C).** Take a look at the lines leading up to line 62. The author claims that "hatred alone is immortal," and then proceeds to provide examples. Choices (A) and (B) are wrong because the author clearly believes that adults have plenty of malice. Eliminate choice (D) because there is no mention of punishment. Choice (E) doesn't make sense, so eliminate it. Choice (C) is the best answer.

33. **The correct answer is (D).** Choices (A), (C), and (E) have no support in the passage. Choice (B) is perhaps true, but not discussed by the author, whereas the entire essay supports choice (D).

Peterson's SAT Success

34. **The correct answer is (D).** Lines 70-74 discuss our fascination with tragedy or evil, even saying that people hate to see a terrible fire extinguished (lines 65-67). The author links our feelings and our passions (lines 68-70)—our emotions, choice (D)—and separates them from our understandings, which we infer to mean our factual, logical knowledge.

35. **The correct answer is (E).** Read the last paragraph. The author says we'll do anything to avoid indifference and ennui, which means boredom. This is a pure vocabulary question, although you could make a good guess using the context. Also, you can eliminate choices (A), (B), (C), and (D) because they are not supported by the passage.

36. **The correct answer is (B).** This question asks to you to look at the author's main conclusion, so a quick reread of the last paragraph is a good idea. The author says, "We cannot bear a state of indifference" (line 83). Choice (B), *conflict is the spice of life*, best sums up the author's conclusion.

SECTION 3

1. **The correct answer is (A).** Don't be careless and assume the columns are equal. If you don't intuitively see that $2^8 > 8^2$ (Column A can be rewritten as $2^3 \times 2^3 \times 2^2 = 8 \times 8 \times 4 = 8^2 \times 4$, which is obviously greater than 8^2), you can use your calculator to find their values.

2. **The correct answer is (C).** Don't assume Column B is larger because the integer values involved are greater, and don't waste time adding and dividing. Simplify each fraction by factoring a 2 out of each term in the numerator of Column A and a 3 out of each term in the numerator of Column B. Each fraction reduces to $1 + 2 + 3 + 4$, so they are obviously equal.

3. **The correct answer is (A).** If half of a number is 180, then the number itself is certainly greater than half of 180, or 90.

4. **The correct answer is (B).** The average of t and s is somewhere between t and s. Because $t < s$, s must be greater than the average.

5. **The correct answer is (B).** All prime numbers—except for 2—are odd, but not vice versa. Think of 9, 21, 35; all have factors other than 1 and themselves. Consequently, there are more odd numbers than prime numbers.

6. **The correct answer is (C).** Since calculating percents involves multiplication, the commutative law applies. That means $a\%$ of b is equal to $b\%$ of a. Think about it: 100% of 50 is equal to 50% of 100, etc. Therefore, the columns are equal.

7. **The correct answer is (D).** Since x could be a little under five and y could be 0 or vice versa—you can't determine their relationship.

8. **The correct answer is (A).** The unshaded area in Square R is greater than the unshaded area in Square S. Since the overlapping shaded region is common to both squares, the total area of Square R must be greater than the total area of Square S.

9. **The correct answer is (A).** The triangle inequality theorem states that the third side of a triangle must be greater than the positive difference of the other two sides but less than their sum. That means that XZ must be greater than $8 - 3 = 5$ and less than $8 + 3 = 11$. Although you can't find its exact value, you know that XZ is greater than 5 in Column B.

10. **The correct answer is (D).** If b is positive, then $a - b < a + b$. If b is negative, then $a - b > a + b$. Since either relationship is possible, the answer must be choice (D).

11. **The correct answer is (B).** This figure is a 5-12-13 right triangle. Since the side opposite angle b is greater than the side opposite angle a, angle b must be greater.

12. **The correct answer is (A).** This question isn't about figuring the exact value of each column—the displays on most calculators can't even show the values of such large numbers in a way that makes them easy to compare. This question is about factoring. When you multiply powers with the same base, you add the exponents. That means that in Column A, $1,800^{25}$ can be rewritten as $(1,800^{24})(1,800)^1$, which gives you $(1,800^{24})(1,800^1) - (1,800^{24})$. Factoring the expression gives you $1,800^{24}(1,800^1 - 1) = 1,800^{24}(1,799)$. This is obviously greater than $1,800^{24}$ in Column B, so Column A is greater.

13. **The correct answer is (B).** Don't assume that the columns are equal. Work out each to see its value. In Column A you get $\frac{(8+1)^2}{(4+1)^2} = \frac{81}{25}$, which is a little more than 3. In Column B you get $(2+1)^2 = 9$, which is greater.

14. **The correct answer is (A).** Notice that the numerator and denominator of both fractions are always positive. The fraction in Column A has a greater numerator and smaller denominator than the fraction in Column B, so Column A is greater.

15. **The correct answer is (B).** You're given $a - 1 = b$, so Column A can be rewritten as $(a - 1)^2$. Don't assume that the columns are equal though. In fact, $(a - 1)^2 \neq a^2 - 1$. $a^2 - 1$ factors to $(a + 1)(a - 1)$. Column A can be expressed as $(a - 1)(a - 1)$. Since you know that $a > 1$, you can factor an $(a - 1)$ from each column. This gives you $(a - 1)$ in Column A and $(a + 1)$ in Column B, so Column B is greater.

16. **The correct answer is 0.** Angles about a point sum to 360 degrees, so $w + x + y + z = 360$. The four angles of a quadrilateral sum to 360 degrees, so $(a + h) + (b + c) + (d + e) + (f + g) = 360$. The arithmetic problem can be regrouped as

$$a + b + c + d + e + f + g + h - w - x - y - z,$$

and then rewritten as

$$(a + b + c + d + e + f + g + h) - (w + x + y + z).$$

Substituting, you get $360 - 360 = 0$.

17. **The correct answer is 12.** Adding the two equations gives you $2x + y = 6$. The question asks for the value of $4x + 2y$, or $2(2x + y) = 2(6) = 12$.

18. **The correct answer is 1.5 or 3/2.** The angle adjacent to the 120 degree angle must be $180 - 120 = 60$, since adjacent angles are supplementary. When parallel lines are struck by a transversal, all of the acute angles formed are equal, as are all the obtuse angles. Therefore, acute angle ZXY must also measure 60 degrees. That means the third angle of triangle XYZ is $180 - 60 - 90 = 30$. That makes it a 30:60:90 triangle, with sides in a ratio of $1:\sqrt{3}:2$. Side XZ is opposite the 30 degree angle, so it is equal to half the hypotenuse, or $3 \div 2 = 1.5$.

19. **The correct answer is 156, 182, 210, or 240.** You're looking for a number between 150 and 250 that is the product of two consecutive integers. Your calculator will come in handy multiplying consecutive pairs of numbers, but you need to have some idea of where to start. You know that $(10)(11) = 110$, so you need to start slightly higher than that. You know that $(12)(12) = 144$, so the product of 11 and 12 would be too small, but the product of 12 and 13 should fall in the desired range: $(12)(13) = 156$. It does, so grid it in and move on. You won't get any extra points for knowing that $(13)(14) = 182$, $(14)(15) = 210$, and $(15)(16) = 240$ are the other possible answers.

20. **The correct answer is 53.** If you remembered that the average of a group of consecutive integers is equal to the middle term, you would quickly see that the third and middle integer is $\frac{245}{5} = 49$. It follows that the fourth is 51 and the fifth, 53. You could also have set up an equation to solve. Since the question asks for the greatest of the five integers, let it be x. That makes the other four $x - 2$, $x - 4$, $x - 6$, and $x - 8$. You know that they sum to 245, so

$$x + x - 2 + x - 4 + x - 6 + x - 8 = 245.$$

Combining like terms, $5x - 20 = 245$, $5x = 265$, $x = 53$.

Peterson's: www.petersons.com

21. **The correct answer is 10.** The cars' routes form two 3-4-5 triangles, so the distance between them is $5 + 5 = 10$.

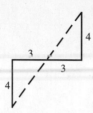

22. **The correct answer is 4.** The shaded triangle is a right isosceles triangle with a hypotenuse of 4, so its sides are $2\sqrt{2}$; therefore, its area is $\frac{1}{2} \cdot 2\sqrt{2} \cdot 2\sqrt{2} = 4$.

23. **The correct answer is 36/5 or 7.2.** The man's average speed is his total distance divided by his total time. The first half of the man's trip takes 1.5 hours and covers 6 miles. The second half of the trip takes 2.5 hours and covers x miles. The average is $6 = \dfrac{6 + x}{1.5 + 2.5}$. So, $x = 18$ miles. Hence, the man's speed during the second half of the trip was 18 miles in 2.5 hours, or $\dfrac{36}{5}$ miles per hour.

24. **The correct answer is 4.** The original price, x, of a ring increases by 20% each year. That means that in one year it will increase to 100% of x + 20% of $x = 120\%$ of x, or $1.2x$. To compute the increase of 20% each year, simply multiply the previous price by 1.2. Therefore, in two years the price will increase to $(1.2x)(1.2) = 1.44x$, in three years it will increase to $(1.44x)(1.2) = 1.728x$, and in four years it will increase to $(1.728x)(1.2) = 2.0736x$. Therefore, it will take four years for the price of the ring to exceed $2x$. If this seems too abstract, you could have picked a number for the price of the ring and figured the percent increases each year. Start with $100, since it's easy to figure percents of 100. The first year the price increases to $120, the next year to $144, the third year to $172.80, and the fourth year to $207.36. Since this is more than $(2)(\$100) = \$200$, it takes four years for the price to exceed twice the original price.

25. **The correct answer is 250.** Let $x =$ the number of mezzanine tickets sold. Since a total of 350 tickets were sold, $350 - x$ orchestra tickets were sold. You know the price of each ticket, and the total amount of money made from ticket sales, so you can set up an equation to solve for x

$$30x + 45(350 - x) = 12,000$$
$$30x + 15,750 - 45x = 12,000$$
$$-15x = -3,750$$
$$x = 250$$

SECTION 4

1. **The correct answer is (B).** Definition sentence. Everything following the colon is a specific example of a successful *mutation*, choice (B), so no other choice is possible.

2. **The correct answer is (C).** Read for sense and note the contrast. In order that everyone NOT appear at *widely divergent times*—those are the key words—we have to do WHAT to our schedules? The best choice is (C), *synchronize* them—arrange them so that they agree in time. Choice (D), *memorize*, is vaguely possible, but the real topic here is having participants appear at the same time.

3. **The correct answer is (C).** Sentence of contrast. Rather than *showering* the reader with (a ton of) description . . . the writer adopted a *minimalist* approach, offering *only a* certain kind of prose. Note those key words! One style of writing contrasted another. Only choice (C) contrasts a *torrent* of description with *sparest* prose (minimalist approach).

4. **The correct answer is (A).** This is a sentence of contrast, the key phrase being *a surprising departure*. You know that the first part of the sentence is going to have a meaning opposite to the second half. Choice (A) is the only one that fits the bill.

5. **The correct answer is (E).** Sentence of contrast and logic. *Witty, eloquent* campaign speeches from Lincoln are contrasted with today's speeches in a TV-dominated world. Do we need negative or positive words here? Logic requires negative words, so choices (A), (B), and (C) are not possible. Although *sound bites* are excellent in choice (D), we sense that *invigorating* is dead wrong.

6. **The correct answer is (D).** Definition sentence. The artist has *routinely defied convention*—key words—yet she is very popular. Her portraits are highly unusual, therefore, but not *devastating* (too negative). *Demure* (modest), *facile* (easily, simply accomplished), and *rebellious*, don't make much sense in context.

7. **The correct answer is (D).** This is a sentence of contrast, with the key phrase being *an unexpected leap*. The first blank is going to describe the past, in which Austen's books appeared mostly in classrooms, and the second blank is going to describe some kind of modern change. For the first blank, choice (B), *obscure* (uncommon), and choice (D), *parochial* (limited to a small area) are the best choices. Choice (A), *scholarly*, may seem tempting, but it doesn't really make sense for books to make a scholarly appearance. Eliminate choice (A) because a *leap into current cinema by way of the movies* is redundant and doesn't make sense. The best choice is (D).

8. **The correct answer is (A).** Logic and common sense tell you that Chris's grandfather is lecturing him (expounding) about money because the grandfather had to be so careful with his during the Great Depression. Many first-word choices are okay here, but *didactic* (meant to teach) is perfect, and a major depression most logically teaches people to be extremely thrifty with their money, which is the quality of *frugality*.

9. **The correct answer is (B).** Contrast and definition sentence. For a thing to become the opposite of what we expect is *ironic*. Thus, only choice (B) should tempt you. If rhetoric *once* (key word) denoted something excellent, it now means the opposite—something highly negative—which is a good definition of *pejorative* in choice (B).

10. **The correct answer is (D).** Type: Object related to its use. A *ramp* leads onto a *freeway* . . . just as a *gangplank* leads onto a *ship*. The other choices show different relationships.

11. **The correct answer is (D).** Type: Implied comparison—an object related to its place of creation. A *horseshoe* is typically made in a *forge* . . . just as a *tire* is made in a *factory*. Choice (B) might be tempting, but remember that a *spinning wheel* is an object, not a place.

12. **The correct answer is (B).** Type: Implied, customary relationship. An *agent* is hired to represent a *client* . . . just as a *lawyer* represents a *plaintiff*. The person in the first slot (agent or lawyer) works on behalf of the person in the second slot (client or plaintiff). None of the other choices exhibits this working relationship between people.

13. **The correct answer is (A).** Type: Implied comparison—creature related to its home. A *beaver* builds (and lives in) a *dam* that it has made . . . just as a *termite* builds (and lives in) a *mound* that it has built. No other pair satisfies this precise relationship.

14. **The correct answer is (E).** Type: Specific member of a general group. *Slang* is *language* at its most informal level . . . just as *doggerel* is *poetry* at its most informal level. Choice (A) says that one kind of *literature* is *Gothic*, but *Gothic* does not describe a lower level of literature. Choice (D) says one kind of speech is a *polemic* (forceful attack disputing another's ideas) but that is not speech at a degraded or slangy level.

15. **The correct answer is (C).** Type: Implied definition—behavior linked to its essential, defining quality. *Altruism* (thinking or acting for the good of others) is behavior that is *selfless* . . . just as *tenacity* (stubborn devotion to purpose) is behavior that is *stubborn*.

16. **The correct answer is (E).** This question tests your overall understanding of the passage. You need to find a choice that is neither too broad in scope nor too narrow. Choices (A), (B), and (C) are all too broad; the passage touches on each of those topics but does not focus primarily on any of them. The passage includes information about choice (A), *The Life of Grandma Moses*, but only a small part of her life. As for choice (B), the passage is really only about one style of American art: primitive. Choice (C) doesn't work because the passage does not cover a history of primitive art; it focuses on one artist. Choice (D) is too narrow; even though Grandma Moses' painting of small-town America is mentioned in the passage, it isn't the main focus. The best answer is choice (E), which lets you know that the passage is about Grandma Moses' role as an American painter.

17. **The correct answer is (B).** Take a look at lines 5-6. The author explains that the word *primitive* is *not the insult it may appear to be.* In other words, the author wants to make sure that the reader doesn't misinterpret the term *primitive*.

18. **The correct answer is (D).** This question requires you to have an overall understanding of the passage and to use this understanding to figure out which statement most closely matches the author's point of view. Choice (A) is a bit strong; the author speaks positively of Grandma Moses, but never claims that she is the greatest American artist. There is no evidence in the passage to support choice (B), and the passage outright contradicts choice (C). Eliminate choice (E) because the passage talks about people enjoying art that reminds them of a simpler time, not art that reminds them of their progress. The best answer is choice (D), which is supported throughout the passage, particularly in the last paragraph.

19. **The correct answer is (C).** Go back to the passage to answer this vocabulary-in-context question. If you read the sentences around the vocabulary word, you find out that Grandma Moses' style was *unpretentious and unpolished* and that her subject was simple scenes of rural life. You can anticipate that the correct answer will be something like *went well with,* or choice (C), *matched.*

20. **The correct answer is (A).** This detail question requires you to figure out why a particular detail is mentioned. Go back to the passage and read around the referenced line. Moses *created a new identity for herself* after a lifetime as a farm wife; in other words, she *reinvented herself.*

21. **The correct answer is (E).** The only one of those traits that is not mentioned in the passage is *love of art.* While the passage says that many people like American primitive art, it does not go so far as to say that love of art is an American trait.

22. **The correct answer is (E).** This question asks you to take a broad look at the general focus of the passage. The other choices name subtopics that come up in the passage, but choice (E) is the only one that is all inclusive.

23. **The correct answer is (C).** The key to solving this problem is the last paragraph, which says that the thousands of studies conducted by scientists suggest a neural cause of biological clocks, although hormones are thought to contribute. The paragraph makes clear the uncertainty scientists still have about the exact cause of circadian rhythms.

24. **The correct answer is (D).** Read lines 66–70, which support this answer. No other choice has support in the passage.

25. **The correct answer is (B).** The passage describes an experiment in which wood warblers adhered to their circadian rhythms long after their environment was changed.

26. **The correct answer is (A).** Read lines 55–60, which prove the dominance of the warblers' inner clocks.

27. **The correct answer is (B).** You can tell from context that *pronounced* means something like *strong* or *very noticeable.* The best choice is (B), *unmistakable.*

28. **The correct answer is (C).** Go back to the passage and read the vocabulary word in context. It clearly refers to animals' inborn, or *innate*, rhythms.

29. **The correct answer is (C).** Each paragraph in the essay supports this answer. While other choices may be scientifically correct, they are not proved in this passage.

30. **The correct answer is (D).** The passage says that humans appear to have pronounced biological rhythms—in other words, they *exhibit signs of endogenous rhythms*.

31. **The correct answer is (E).** Take a look at lines 82–83, which state that hormones are supposed to be an additional factor in the working of biological clocks.

SECTION 5

1. **The correct answer is (E).** If one fifth of a number is 20, then the number is $(5)(20) = 100$. Five times that number is $(5)(100) = 500$.

2. **The correct answer is (A).** Remember, $\dfrac{A}{B}$ is the same as $A \div B$.

3. **The correct answer is (B).** If $\dfrac{3}{4}$ the area of the square is 12, then the entire area of the square is $\dfrac{4}{3} \times 12 = 16$. The area of a square is equal to a side length squared, so the length of one side is $\dfrac{16}{4} = 4$.

4. **The correct answer is (E).** The angles adjacent to x are both $60°$. A straight angle is $180°$, so $x = 180 - 60 - 60 = 60$.

5. **The correct answer is (C).** The average of a group of terms is equal to the sum of the terms divided by the number of terms. Plugging in:
$$\frac{(a-2) + (a) + (a+2) + (a+4)}{4} = \frac{4a+4}{4} = \frac{4(a+1)}{4} = a + 1.$$

6. **The correct answer is (C).** From the first equation, $y = 2x$. $2x = w$, so $y = w$.

7. **The correct answer is (A).** Fifty percent of 80 is 40, 20% of 40 is 8.

8. **The correct answer is (B).** Starting from the right side, *Pride and Prejudice* is counted as the ninth book, so you know there are at least nine books; eliminate choice (A). If it's counted as the third book starting on the left side, there must be two books to the left of it. That means that a total of $9 + 2 = 11$ books are on the shelf.

9. **The correct answer is (E).** Notice that $\dfrac{a}{b-a}$ when multiplied by -1 can be rewritten $\dfrac{a}{a-b}$, so the expression can be rewritten as
$$\frac{b}{a-b} + \frac{a}{a-b} = \frac{a+b}{a-b}.$$

10. **The correct answer is (C).** If Sophie frosted $\frac{1}{2}$ of the cupcakes and Maureen frosted $\frac{1}{6}$ of the cupcakes, then $\frac{1}{2} + \frac{1}{6} = \frac{3}{6} + \frac{1}{6} = \frac{4}{6} = \frac{2}{3}$ of the cupcakes were frosted and $\frac{1}{3}$ were not. Therefore, the 12 unfrosted cupcakes represent $\frac{1}{3}$ of the total number of cupcakes, so a total of 36 cupcakes must have been baked.

SECTION 6

1. **The correct answer is (D).** This is the only answer that the passage supports. Note lines 7-8, where the author says, "Art can never match the luxury and superfluity of Nature," going on to say that all is clearly visible in Art, but not in Nature.

2. **The correct answer is (C).** Note lines 13-21, where the writer says that an evergreen is mightily attractive all by itself in a swamp, but fails to appeal to him in a normal yard. He prefers the tree in its natural state, so only choice (C) can be selected. Choice (D) is contradicted in the passage, as is choice (E).

3. **The correct answer is (B).** This answer is found in lines 36-40, where the author observes that we copy natural forms in our art. Choice (C) is out because as we're not discussing erosion, and the other answers are weak choices because the author has drawn a deliberate parallel by using the words "a similarity between Art's operations and human art" in lines 30-31.

4. **The correct answer is (E).** This answer is found in lines 39-44, where this answer is stated in other words.

5. **The correct answer is (A).** Vivian claims that it's fortunate Nature is such a mess or we wouldn't have Art at all. See lines 68-70. This answer alone is clearly supported by the passage.

6. **The correct answer is (B).** Vivian states that Nature's defects include choices (A), (C), (D), and (E) in lines 62-65, but nowhere does she suggest that Nature is unsatisfying for our emotions.

7. **The correct answer is (E).** This is a context question, so go back to the sentence to look at how the vocabulary word is used. Vivian says that "even the poorest workman could make you a more comfortable seat," so clearly she's talking about how well someone does a job.

8. **The correct answer is (C).** Read lines 75-77, where Vivian says that the infinite variety in Nature is probably found in the "imagination, or fancy, or cultivated blindness of the person who looks at her [Nature]." Only this choice has such clear support in the passage.

9. **The correct answer is (A).** In both passages, nature is personified as female and is always referred to with feminine pronouns. None of the other answers work in both passages. Remember that even if you didn't know that personification is giving a nonhuman thing human traits, you could find the answer by eliminating the other choices.

10. **The correct answer is (E).** Acerbic means biting or bitter. Vivian's tone definitely is more biting than the earnest, poetic tone of the author of the first essay.

11. **The correct answer is (D).** This is mainly a vocabulary question. However, even if you don't know all of the answer choices but have read Vivian's speeches carefully, you know that *lofty dismissal*, choice (D), suits her character best. Choice (A) is wrong because she wouldn't agree (*acquiescence*). She's not *indifferent* (unconcerned, aloof, or detached) from this subject either, so you can't pick choice (B). While she is somewhat *condescending*, she doesn't exhibit all of choice (C) *condescending pity*. Choice (E), *intense outrage*, is too extreme, so eliminate it.

Practice Test 1

SECTION 1

1. **The correct answer is (C).** Ten percent of 25 is 2.5, so 20 percent is two times that, or 5. That makes the price of the new candy bar $25 + 5 = 30$ cents.

2. **The correct answer is (E).** The Triangle Inequality theorem states that the third leg of a triangle must be greater than the positive difference of the other two legs and less than their sum. Therefore, $(4 - 3) < x < (4 + 3)$, and $1 < x < 7$. Since x must be less than 7, choice (E) is correct.

3. **The correct answer is (D).** Probability is equal to the number of desired outcomes divided by the total number of outcomes, or in this case, the number of green socks divided by the total number of socks. Therefore, the probability of removing a green sock is

$$\frac{3}{3 + 6 + 9} = \frac{3}{18} = \frac{1}{6}.$$

4. **The correct answer is (C).** Before you start multiplying, cancel where you can. Note that the denominator of each fraction is equal to the numerator of the fraction that follows it, so the 2s, 4s, and 8s cancel out, leaving $\frac{1}{16}$. Since $\frac{1}{16} = \frac{1}{y}$, $y = 16$.

5. **The correct answer is (D).** Adding one to the thousands' digit increases the original number by 1,000; adding 1 to the hundreds' digit increases it by 100; adding 1 to the tens' digit increases it by 10; and adding 1 to the units' digit increases it by 1. So the original number is increased by a total of 1,111.

6. **The correct answer is (E).** The school must purchase 12 dozen, or $(12)(12) = 144$ textbooks. Since the individual price is $\$9.89 - \$9.14 = \$0.75$ greater than the discount price, the school saves a total of $144(\$0.75) = \$108.00$ by buying in bulk.

7. **The correct answer is (D).** You're given that $XY = \frac{XZ}{3}$, or XY is $\frac{1}{3}$ of XZ. Since point Y lies between X and Z, $XY + YZ = XZ$. Therefore, YZ must equal $\frac{2}{3}$ of XZ. You know that $XY = \frac{1}{3}$ of XZ, so $YZ = 2XY$, choice (D). You could have picked a value for XZ and used it to determine the other lengths. If $XZ = 12$, then $XY = \frac{12}{3} = 4$, and $YZ = 12 - 4 = 8$. When you substitute $XY = 4$ in the choices, only choice (D) gives you 8.

8. **The correct answer is (B).** First, $10,000 must be paid from the estate, so $50,000 − $10,000 = $40,000 remains. Then half of this is donated to charity, so $\frac{40,000}{2}$ = $20,000 remains. This amount is divided among the 4 children, so each receives $\frac{\$20,000}{4}$ = $5,000. Working through each choice (following the rules of PEMDAS), you find that only choice (B) is equal to $5,000. Choice (A) is $22,500; choice (C) is −$15,000; choice (D) is $48,750; and choice (E) is $80,000.

9. **The correct answer is (E).** Since vertical angles are equal, you know that the angle opposite to the angle marked $3b$ must also equal $3b$. The three angles of a triangle sum to 180, so $3b + p + q = 180$ and $p + q = 180 - 3b$.

10. **The correct answer is (E).** When $x = 0$, then $x^3 = x^2 = 0$, so choices (A) and (D) are incorrect. When x is a positive fraction, then $x^3 < x^2$; for example if $x = \frac{1}{2}$, $\left(\frac{1}{2}\right)^3 = \frac{1}{8} < \left(\frac{1}{2}\right)^2 = \frac{1}{4}$, so choice (B) is incorrect. When x is negative, x^3 is negative and x^2 is positive (a negative raised to an odd power is always negative, and a negative raised to an even power is always positive), then $x^3 < x^2$, and choice (C) is therefore incorrect. Only when $x > 1$ will the inequality be true.

11. **The correct answer is (D).** Cross-multiplying gives you $y(x + 1) = 1$, which multiplies through to $xy + y = 1$. To solve for x, isolate it on one side of the equation:

$$xy + y = 1$$
$$xy = 1 - y$$
$$x = \frac{1 - y}{y}$$

12. **The correct answer is (A).** Since water must be mixed with concentrate in a ratio of 3 to 1, then the juice is composed of 4 parts: 3 parts water and 1 part concentrate. So water represents $\frac{3}{4}$ of the amount of juice, and concentrate represents the remaining $\frac{1}{4}$. Therefore, 12 liters of juice would require $\frac{1}{4} \times 12 = 3$ liters of concentrate.

13. **The correct answer is (E).** Since average $= \frac{\text{sum of terms}}{\text{number of terms}}$, then (average)(number of terms) = sum of terms. Vinny wants an average of 90 for the 6 tests, so the sum of all his test scores must be $(90)(6) = 540$. His average for the first 5 tests is 88, so he already has a total of $(88)(5) = 440$. Therefore, he must score $540 - 440 = 100$ on his sixth test.

14. **The correct answer is (D).** Don't be careless and select choice (A): $a^2 - b^2 = (a + b)(a - b)$, which is obviously not equal to $(a - b)(a - b)$. Using FOIL to multiply through, you find that $(a - b)^2 = a^2 - 2ab + b^2$. Neither choices (B) nor (C) is equal to this, so eliminate them. Multiplying through choice (D), you find that $(b - a)^2 = b^2 - 2ab + a^2$, so this answer is correct.

15. **The correct answer is (B).** Let $G =$ the number of CDs that Greg has. Mike has 5 fewer CDs than Greg, or $G - 5$. Greg has 2 more CDs than Thad, so Thad has $G - 2$. (Be careful here—many students incorrectly translate this as $G + 2$.) Together, the three have $(G - 5) + G + (G - 2) = 3G - 7$ CDs. The correct choice is the one that will yield an integer value for G when set equal to $3G - 7$ you can't very well own fractional parts of CDs. Only choice (B) does so: $3G - 7 = 17$, $3G = 24$, $G = 8$.

16. **The correct answer is (C).** Slope is equal to $\frac{y_2 - y_1}{x_2 - x_1}$, so the slope of line m is $\frac{4 - 0}{7 - (-1)} = \frac{4}{8} = \frac{1}{2}$. The point that lies on line m must also result in a slope of $\frac{1}{2}$ when paired with either of the original points. When plugging in, you find that only choice (C), (3, 2), yields a slope of $\frac{1}{2}$.

17. **The correct answer is (D).** Let $x =$ Jessie's income. She must pay 5 percent or $\frac{1}{20}$ of that amount in state taxes, or $\frac{1}{20} \times x = \frac{x}{20}$. She is able to claim 75 percent or $\frac{3}{4}$ of this as a deduction on her federal taxes, or $\frac{3}{4} \times \frac{x}{20} = \frac{3x}{80}$. You know that Jessie claimed a deduction of $1,800 so you can solve for x:

$$\frac{3x}{80} = \$1,800$$
$$3x = (80)(\$1,800) = \$144,000$$
$$x = \$48,000$$

18. **The correct answer is (C).** Start with the easier equation first. Since Margaret has n nickels, d dimes, and a total of 40 coins, then $n + d = 40$ would be one of the two equations necessary to solve for n and d. Only choices (C) and (D) include it, so eliminate the others. You know the total amount of money that Margaret has, so the sum of each coin multiplied by its value totals $3.00. Of the remaining choices, only choice (C) includes this equation, so it is correct.

19. **The correct answer is (C).** Start with 5 rocks, 2 stones, and 3 pebbles. Add 4 pebbles change to get to 5 rocks and 3 stones. Add another 4 stones change to get to 6 rocks.

20. **The correct answer is (E).** Cross-multiplying shows that $ad = cb$. To check the fractions in each choice, cross-multiply, remembering that $ad = cb$. All of the choices are true except choice (E).

21. **The correct answer is (C).** To find the area of the shaded region, simply subtract the area of the circle from the area of the square. Area of a circle is πr^2, so the area of this circle is $\pi(5)^2 = 25\pi$. The area of a square is s^2, where s is a side of the square. You aren't given s, but note that a diameter of the circle is equal to a side length. The diameter of a circle is twice its radius, so diameter = side length = 10. So the area of the square is $10^2 = 100$, making the area of the shaded region $100 - 25\pi$, choice (C).

22. **The correct answer is (E).** S is the sum of the consecutive odd integers from 1 through 99 inclusive, and T is the sum of the consecutive even integers from 2 through 98 inclusive. Start writing each set out, and you will notice a pattern:

    $$S = 1 + 3 + 5 + 7 + \ldots 95 + 97 + 99$$
    $$T = 2 + 4 + 6 + 8 + \ldots 96 + 98$$

    For each term in S, there appears to be a term in T that is 1 greater. The exception seems to be for the last term in S: there is no term in T greater than 99. This means that there is one more term in S than T. You can verify this by determining the number of terms in each set. The number of terms in an inclusive range is found by subtracting the first number from the last and then adding 1. In these cases, we're only dealing with half of the numbers in the range, (since each set is either exclusively odd or even) so you must divide the sum in two. Therefore, the number of terms in S is $\left(\dfrac{99 - 1}{2}\right) + 1 = 49 + 1 = 50$, and the number of terms in T is $\left(\dfrac{98 - 2}{2}\right) + 1 = 48 + 1 = 49$. The first 49 terms in S are each one less than their corresponding terms in T, $(S_1 - T_1 = -1. S_2 - T_2 = -1.$ etc.), so if it weren't for the fiftieth term in S, the difference $S - T$ would be $49(-1) = -49$. There is a fiftieth term in S however, with a value of 99, so the difference of $S - T$ is actually $-49 + 99 = 50$.

23. **The correct answer is (A).** If you sketch a diagram of the large triangle, you'll see that its perimeter is composed of 6 sides of the smaller triangles. The perimeter of an equilateral triangle is equal to 3 times side length, so each side is $\dfrac{1}{3}$ of its perimeter. Since you're given that the perimeter of the smaller triangles is x, then each side of the smaller triangle is $\dfrac{1}{3}x = \dfrac{x}{3}$. Since the larger triangle's perimeter consists of 6 of these sides, its perimeter must be $6\left(\dfrac{x}{3}\right) = \dfrac{6x}{3} = 2x$, choice (A).

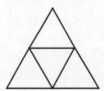

Peterson's SAT Success

24. **The correct answer is (E).** The amount of material that will remain after the circles are cut out is the area of the entire piece of material, minus the total area of the circles that were cut out. The total area of the circles that were cut out will be equal to the area of one of the circles times the total number of circles. To minimize the amount of wasted material, the diameter of the circle cut out should divide evenly into both the length and width of the cloth. Therefore, what you're really looking for is the greatest common factor of the length and width. To find the greatest common factor of 16 and 36, break down each number to its prime factorization and then multiply together all the prime factors that the two have in common. In this case, 16 and 36 share 2 prime factors of 2, so their greatest common factor is 4. Since 4 goes into 16 four times and into 36 nine times, a total of $(4)(9) = 36$ circles with diameters of 4 can be cut from the cloth. The area of each circle is equal to πr^2. Since the diameter of each square is 4, its radius is 2 and the area of each circle is $\pi(2)^2 = 4\pi$. So the material that will be left over is $(36)(16) - 36(4\pi) = 36(16 - 4\pi) = (36)(4)(4 - \pi) = 144(4 - \pi)$.

25. **The correct answer is (B).** The project would take a staff of 6 people 24 hours to complete, for a total of $(6)(24) = 144$ work hours. Getting the job done in 8 hours would require a total of $144 \div 8 = 18$ people. Since there is already a staff of 6, 12 additional workers need to be employed.

SECTION 2

1. **The correct answer is (E). Sentence of contrast.** The key words, "certain knowledge," need an opposite in order to make the sentence logical. The best opposite is choice (E), *speculation*. Other choices give journalistic terms that don't imply the uncertainty of *speculation*.

2. **The correct answer is (D). Sentence of contrast and definition.** We need an opposite to "just and well-considered decisions." The opposite of well-considered is choice (D), *arbitrary* (based on a whim).

3. **The correct answer is (B). Logic sentence.** Ask why the counselor is now reacting to what is only a harmless offense. Only choice (B), *flagrant* (highly noticeable in a negative way, glaring), explains why the counselor insisted on enforcing the rule this time. Choice (C), *unusual*, may have been tempting, but the sentence tells you that the violation was harmless, which doesn't sound too out of the ordinary.

4. **The correct answer is (B). Logic sentence.** Key words are *appalled*, *rundown tenement*, and *problem*. Determine what kind of conditions appall people. Will this be a calm, casual letter or one deeply felt? The first blank must have a very negative word, and the second blank must make logical sense. Choice (B) is best, although choice (E) is momentarily tempting—not tempting for long, because *unpleasant* is too weak for the first blank.

5. **The correct answer is (A). Sentence of contrast.** The sentence says that while Claude's early figures managed to disturb people, his later sculptures—note all of those helpful key words—revealed an "agreeable symmetry." What is the opposite of "agreeable symmetry?" Choice (A)—*skewed*, which means slanting, not coming together—is the best choice, although choice (B), *uneven*, may have been tempting.

6. **The correct answer is (C). Logic sentence.** Both choice (A), *mixture*, and choice (C) *blend*, seem like good choices for the first blank. None of the other choices makes sense, so eliminate them. Choice (A), *repudiate* (to refuse to accept something), doesn't work, so the correct answer is choice (C), *mirror*, which is used here as a verb that means "to reflect."

7. **The correct answer is (D). Sentence of contrast.** The phrase "or if they arise only after birth" gives you clues to the meaning of the word in the second blank. The word in the first blank is going to be an "opposite" word, which is indicated by the "or" in the middle of the sentence. Possible choices for the second blank are choice (C), *upbringing*, and choice (D), *environment*. Choice (A), *culture* and choice (E), *heritage*, are weak, and choice (B), *wishes*, makes no sense at all. Remember that the first half of the sentence has to contrast with the second, so the best answer is choice (D), *inherited*.

8. **The correct answer is (D). Definition, logic, and vocabulary sentence.** The last half of the sentence requires a second-word choice that refers to the writing of an "educated, witty man." Choice (D) gives us *enlightened humor*, which is perfect. The first word choice should be something that relates to an *autocrat*, a dictatorial, dogmatic person. Choice (D), *doctinaire* (dogmatic, dictatorial), is the correct answer.

9. **The correct answer is (E). Sentence of contrast and logic.** The first blank is going to be something similar to *dense*. (If you don't know that *dense* means "hard to move through," the word *plowing* is a clue.) While Janet enjoys this sort of reading, her students have a contrasting reaction, so look for a negative word. The best choice for the first blank is (E), *verbose*, which means "wordy." (Don't be fooled by *terse*, which means "brief or concise"). It makes sense that her students see the prose as *convoluted*, which means "complicated."

10. **The correct answer is (C). Analogy of degree.** *Exhausted* is the extreme of *tired*, just as *famished* is the extreme of *hungry*. The other choices indicate different relationships.

11. **The correct answer is (C). One of a kind analogy.** *Cinnamon* is one kind of *spice*, just as *cider* is one kind of *beverage*. No other set of words reflects this exact relationship.

12. **The correct answer is (D). Implied comparison—words linked by meaning or usage.** A *chuckle* is a sign of *amusement*, just as a *whimper* is a sign of *fear*. While you might experience a *tremor* (slight shaking) of *glee*, choice (C), *tremor*, isn't, by definition, a response to an emotion.

13. **The correct answer is (B). Relationship by definition.** *Edible* describes *food* that can be eaten, just as *potable* describes *water* that can be drunk.

14. **The correct answer is (E). Implied relationship by definition.** Something *fallacious* lacks *truth*, just as something *diminutive* (small) lacks *bulk*.

15. **The correct answer is (B). Implied comparison—words linked by definition.** To *jeopardize* something is to subject it to *danger*, just as to *lampoon* something is to subject it to *ridicule*.

16. **The correct answer is (C).** Read the first paragraph, and focus on the last sentence, which gives you the correct answer.

17. **The correct answer is (A).** Remember that when the question includes a reference line, you should read a little bit before and after that line to make sure you understand the context. The author describes both "social imperialism" and "economic imperialism" as what would happen if one discipline tried "to take over the subject matter of the other," (lines 10-11), which is exactly what choice (A) states.

18. **The correct answer is (D).** The correct answer can be found in lines 54-56. Eliminate choice (A) because there's no evidence that Comte and Smith had a "close" association. Choice (B) can be eliminated because there's no mention of biology in this passage. There are no facts to support choices (C) and (D).

19. **The correct answer is (E).** Read line 43, in which the author praises Mill's pragmatic (practical) attitude, then read the second paragraph, in which Mill, Smith, and Marx are commended for striking a happy balance, suggesting that they had open minds. All of the other choices are too narrow or unsupported.

20. **The correct answer is (B).** The passage gives you this answer in lines 33-39, but finding the correct answer is determined by your vocabulary knowledge. Choice (B), their *parochial* interests, means their "narrow," insular interests—the problem with recent professionals in both disciplines, according to the author.

21. **The correct answer is (B).** Always go back to refer to the context of a vocabulary question. In this case, *distinguished* means "set apart," choice (B).

22. **The correct answer is (A).** Reread the last sentence of the first paragraph, in which the author expresses the hope that economics and sociology will move toward open borders and free communication. The author goes on to describe a "happy balance" between the two disciplines (lines 23-24).

23. **The correct answer is (B).** The last sentence of paragraph 2 states that the real reason for concern is that the hot dogs contain 80 percent of the fat calories. Choice (C) is contradicted in lines 18-19, and the other choices are weak.

24. **The correct answer is (A).** Eliminate choice (C), *outraged*, because it is too extreme. Choice (B), *philosophical*, doesn't seem quite right for a passage that is so full of scientific facts. Choice (D), *amused*, may be true in the first few lines, but the author quickly switches to a more serious tone. Choice (E), *rebellious*, doesn't make much sense. The best answer is choice (A), *instructive*.

25. **The correct answer is (D).** Reread lines 78–81. This a straight research question.

26. **The correct answer is (C).** Reread the rest of the paragraph to answer this question. The paragraph is about the food components that usually accompany protein, and the author lists steak and cheese to inform the reader that while the foods contain a lot of protein, they also contain a lot of fat.

27. **The correct answer is (A).** There isn't any particular myth that the author is debunking, choice (B), and this isn't an opinion piece, choice (C). Choice (D) may be tempting, but remember that the passage isn't about Ralph Nader or any other expert. Eliminate choice (E) because the passage doesn't have much to do with conventional (traditional) wisdom.

28. **The correct answer is (B).** The clue to the answer is in the humorous sentence that begins with "The panic eventually subsided," telling you that the public was generally confused. A series of questions that occur early in any article is typically there to grab a reader's attention and forecast at least some of what is to follow. Here, the next-best answer is choice (D), but these questions fail to outline all that will be discussed.

29. **The correct answer is (D).** This question is answered in lines 57–75, which explain the role of proteins in the body.

30. **The correct answer is (E).** Reread the last paragraph to find the correct answer. All of the other choices cannot be supported by the material.

SECTION 3

1. **The correct answer is (B).** When powers with the same base are divided, the exponents are subtracted. So in Column A, the fraction reduces to $\frac{1}{2}(10^{6-4}), = \frac{1}{2}(10^2)$, which is obviously less than Column B.

2. **The correct answer is (C).** Since there are 60 seconds in a minute and 60 minutes in an hour, the value of both columns is $60x$.

3. **The correct answer is (B).** Since $8.2 > 8$ and $4.3 > 4$, you don't need to calculate to see that the product in Column B must be greater than $8 \times 4 = 32$ in Column A.

4. **The correct answer is (C).** It's apparent that $a = b$ because they are opposite equal sides marked k in the triangle, and therefore, the columns are equal.

5. **The correct answer is (D).** Multiplying through the expression in Column B shows that you are comparing $4z^2$ to $4z$ in Column A. Try some values for z to determine their relationship. If $z = 1$, then $4(1) = 4(1)^2 = 4$. If $z = 2$, then $4(2)$ or $8 < 4(2)^2$ or 16. Since more than one relationship between the columns is possible, the correct answer is choice (D).

6. **The correct answer is (B).** You should intuitively see that Column B is greater. Both columns have 5 factors, each with 2 factors of 2 and of 3. The only difference is that the fifth factor in Column A is 2, while the fifth factor in Column B is 3, making it greater. If you didn't see this, you could have used your calculator.

7. **The correct answer is (D).** Area of a square is equal to a side squared, so each side is $\sqrt{64} = 8$. A square has 4 equal sides, so its perimeter is $4(8) = 32$. The area of a rectangle is equal to length times width so there are many possible pairs of lengths and widths—with consequently different perimeters—for a rectangle of area 64. Consider for example, 1 and 64 (with perimeter $2(1 + 64) = 130$), 2 and 32 (with perimeter $2(2 + 32) = 68$), 4 and 16 (with perimeter $2(4 + 16) = 40$), etc. All these perimeters are greater than the perimeter of the square, so you might think Column B is greater. However if you do, you forgot that by definition all squares are rectangles; a square is just a special kind of rectangle. Therefore the value of Column B could also be 32, which would make the columns equal. Since Column B can either be greater than or equal to Column A, the correct answer is choice (D).

8. **The correct answer is (A).** Intuitively you should see that Column A is greater. If x is the coat's sale price, 25% less than its original cost, then x is obviously less than the original price. Therefore, $.75x$ or $\frac{3}{4}x$, which is less than x, must certainly be less than the coat's original price. If you didn't see this right away, you could have set the original price of the coat to \$100. The sale price x is 25% less than this, so $x = \$75$. Therefore, Column A is \$100, and Column B is $.75(\$75) = \$56.25$.

9. **The correct answer is (B).** The volume of the cylinder is equal to πr^2 (if you didn't remember this, it's printed with the reference material at the start of each math section). Since its diameter is 2, its radius is 1, and its volume is 4π. In Column B, the volume of the solid is $(2)(2)(4)$ or $(4)(4)$. Since $\pi < 4$, $4\pi < (4)(4)$.

10. **The correct answer is (C).** Rewrite $a!b$ or $\frac{1}{a} + \frac{1}{b}$ by finding a common denominator $\frac{a}{ab} + \frac{b}{ab} = \frac{a + b}{ab}$, and you see that the columns are equal.

11. **The correct answer is (A).** Isolating $x!y$ on one side of the equation, you see that it equals -9. Therefore, 9 in Column A must be greater.

12. **The correct answer is (C).** The distance formula for the coordinate plane is $D = \sqrt{(x_2 - x_1)^2 + (y_2 - y_1)^2}$. Because both x_1 and y_1 are a, it doesn't matter if you flip x_2 and y_2. You could also have made a sketch for each scenario, setting the origin as (a, a) and an arbitrary point for (p, q). In each picture, sketch in the right triangle that has the distance from (a, a) to the point as its hypotenuse. You'll see that in each case, one of the legs of the triangle has length p and the other q. Two right triangles with equal pairs of legs have equal hypotenuses.

13. **The correct answer is (A).** The sum of the lengths of two sides of a triangle is greater than the length of the third side. Draw in FB and you'll see that it is the third side of triangle FAB, and therefore less than $FA + AB$; draw in BD to see it is the third side of triangle BCD, and less than $BC + CD$. Therefore, Column A is greater. You could also have realized that the shortest distance between two points is a straight line, so the length FD (which is $FB + BD$) is obviously less than the circuitous route expressed in Column A.

14. **The correct answer is (D).**

$$
\begin{array}{r}
(x + y)^2 = x^2 + 2xy + y^2 \\
-(x - y)^2 = x^2 - 2xy + y^2 \\
\hline
= 4xy
\end{array}
$$

If x or $y = 0$, the columns are equal. If $x = y = 1$, then Column A is $4(1)(1) = 4$ and Column A is greater. Since more than one relationship is possible, choice (D) is correct.

15. **The correct answer is (D).** CD could be equal to, less than, or more than 4 without affecting any of the given relationships, so choice (D) is correct.

16. **The correct answer is 50.** From the given equations, $a = d + 25 + 15 + 10$ or $a = d + 50$. Therefore, $a - d = (d + 50) - d = 50$.

17. **The correct answer is 1/4 or .25.** Eating $\frac{1}{4}$ of the pie leaves $\frac{3}{4}$. Eating $\frac{1}{4}$ of the remaining $\frac{3}{4}$ leaves $\frac{2}{4}$. Eating $\frac{1}{2}$ of the remaining $\frac{2}{4}$ leaves $\frac{1}{4}$.

18. **The correct answer is 8.25.** A twelve-pound turkey costs $12(\$0.85) = \$10.20$. A three-pound chicken costs $1.5(\$1.30) = \$1.95$. The difference is $\$10.20 - \$1.95 = \$8.25$.

19. **The correct answer is 22.5 or 45/2.** Since they are opposite sides of equal length b, $\angle B = \angle C$. The angles of a triangle sum to 180, so $\angle A + 2\angle B = 180$, $45 + 2\angle B = 180$, $2\angle B = 135$ and $\angle B = 67.5$. So the difference is $67.5 - 45 = 22.5$.

20. **The correct answer is 71.** Since average $= \dfrac{\text{sum of terms}}{\text{number of terms}}$, then (average)(number of terms) = sum of terms. Since the average of all 3 number is 67, their sum is $(67)(3) = 201$. The average of two of the numbers is 65, so the sum of those two is $(65)(2) = 130$. That means that the third number must be $201 - 130 = 71$.

21. **The correct answer is 3.** To find the maximum value of $\frac{b}{a}$, use the greatest b and the smallest a. Subbing in you get $\frac{12}{4} = 3$.

22. **The correct answer is 1, 2, 3, or 4.** In both the units' place and the hundreds' place you're adding X to Z, and in each case you get the same one-digit result. For this to be true, there must not be any carrying over from the sum of the digits in the tens' column. In other words, $Y + Y$ or $2Y$ must be less than 10, and Y must be less than 5. You're not given any additional conditions about the values of X, Y, and Z (e.g. that they are distinct), so Y could be 1, 2, 3, or 4.

23. **The correct answer is 12.** Start writing down multiples of 6 and you'll notice a pattern: 6, 12, 18, 24, 30, 36, 42, 48, etc. The units' digits repeat in a pattern of 6, 2, 8, 4, 0. Since the fifth digit in the pattern is 0, every fifth multiple of 6 will end in a 0. Therefore the 85th house will have a street number that ends in 0, the 84th will end in the fourth digit in the pattern or 4 and the 83rd house will have a street number that ends in the third digit in the pattern, 8. So the sum of the units' digits of these three houses is $0 + 4 + 8 = 12$.

24. **The correct answer is 3/16 or .187 or .188.**

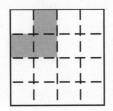

Add lines to the figure so it looks like a checkerboard. When you do so, you see that the area of square $ABCD$ is composed of 16 equal squares. Since the shaded region comprises 3 of these squares, it represents $\frac{3}{16}$ of the area of square $ABCD$.

25. **The correct answer is 8.** Figure out how many times each light will flash until they are in sync again. Start with the blue light since it flashes less frequently. After they have flashed together, the blue light will flash again in 90 seconds, then 180 seconds, then 270 seconds, etc. The red light will flash again in 20, 40, 60, 80, 100, 120, 140, 160, and 180 seconds. Therefore, they will flash again in 180 seconds. The blue light will flash alone once before that at 90 seconds; the red light will flash alone 8 times (at 20, 40, 60, 80, 100, 120, 140, and 160 seconds). Since the red light will flash alone 8 times and the blue light will flash alone 1 time, the number of times the red light will flash alone is 8 times as great.

SECTION 4

1. **The correct answer is (D). Sentence of contrast.** The key word is *despite.* You're looking for an answer that will contrast with Kevin's *blustery* (swaggering, acting tough) manner. At the same time, you want a word that means he can't stand the sight of his own blood. The best choice is (D), *squeamish*.

2. **The correct answer is (C). Sentence of contrast.** Key words are *odd duality,* which tell you to look for two things that typically do not go together. Only choice (C) gives you logical opposites for this context.

3. **The correct answer is (B). Definition sentence.** Determine what objects are created when function dictates form. Useful, practical objects is your answer, which point to choice (B), *pragmatists* (highly practical people).

4. **The correct answer is (B). Logic sentence.** Read for sense and plug in your own words before you hunt for the correct answer. Common sense says to pick either choice (B) or (C), and you can't *expedite* (speed up) a running injury, choice (C), so that leaves only choice (B). To *exacerbate* an injury means to make it worse.

5. **The correct answer is (E). Logic and vocabulary sentence.** Read for sense until you've got it, then eliminate choice (A) because *misunderstood* is a bad choice. Was he *maligned* (spoken badly of)? Not really. Choice (C) is close. Choice (D) is contradictory because *irascible* means "easily angered," the opposite of *placid*. Remember that *oracular* pronouncements (solemn, pompous, and dictatorial) would make someone *tedious* (tiresome). Choice (E) is a better choice than choice (C) because it provides more explanation for the fact that the family "tended to leave the scene" whenever the guy spoke.

6. **The correct answer is (B). Contrast sentence.** Key words are *a more private position.* Choice (B) *public* provides the perfect contrast.

7. **The correct answer is (C). Logic sentence.** Determine whether or not the director is protecting her young troupe from the toll of traveling. Reading the choices, only (C) contains the two words that make logical sense in this context. *Refrained* means held back and *reserved* means "held."

8. **The correct answer is (D). Logic sentence.** The key words, *eager to promote a piece of legislation*, indicate that the lawmakers are either annoyed if the bill takes forever or excited if it zips through the committee. Check all answer choices. The only choice that makes sense is (D). *Thwarted* means "defeated," or "kept from succeeding." To *languish* is to lose intensity or become weak.

9. **The correct answer is (A). Definition sentence.** An *autocrat* (dictatorial sole-ruler) runs things the way he or she sees fit. Choice (A) is the correct answer since *mandated* means "directed."

Peterson's SAT Success

10. **The correct answer is (E). Logic sentence.** All of the first-word choices are possible, so examine the second-word choices. The semicolon and the phrase "even after the wall fell" provide clues: the second part of the sentence will be similar to the first part, not in contrast with it. Choice (C) is possible, but it's a little awkward since cultural differences don't actually *separate* a nation, they *divide* it. Choice (E) is the best choice.

11. **The correct answer is (C). Type: Person connected to job.** A *pilot* is in charge of controlling a *jet*, just as a *captain* is in charge of controlling a *ship*. No other choices show this relationship.

12. **The correct answer is (E). Type: Object linked to its purpose/ use.** The "job" of a *furnace* is to provide *warmth*, just as the "job" of a *wall* is to provide *enclosure*.

13. **The correct answer is (A). Type: Part of a whole.** A *syllabus* is a brief overview of a full-length *course*, just as a *synopsis* is a brief overview of a full-length *novel*.

14. **The correct answer is (C). Type: Person related to job.** A *referee* settles disagreements in a *game*, just as an *arbiter* settles disagreements in a *dispute* (difference of opinion). Both persons in the first slot function in the same manner on the job. Other choices fail to show people functioning in this manner at work.

15. **The correct answer is (E). Type: Something related to its most desirable trait.** A *reason* that makes sense is *plausible*, just as an *argument* that makes sense is *cogent*.

16. **The correct answer is (D). Type: Implied comparison—person related to guiding document.** A *driver* follows a *map*, just as a *builder* follows a *blueprint*. Each document tells the person what to do. No other choice offers this exact relationship.

17. **The correct answer is (B). Type: Object related to use/purpose.** A *canister* is used for *storage*, just as a *vehicle* is used for *transportation*. No other pair exhibits this precise relationship.

18. **The correct answer is (A). Type: Degree.** A *voracious* person has a huge amount of *hunger*, just as an *exhausted* person has a huge amount of *sleepiness*.

19. **The correct answer is (D). Type: Relationship by definition.** To sweeten is to make less acerbic (sour or bitter). Try each answer in that sentence. To sugar is to make less caloric? No. To *anger* is to make less riled? *Riled* means "made angry," so that doesn't work. To *correct* is to make less accurate? No. To *relax* is to make less rigid? Yes. Just in case there's a better answer, try choice (E). Does provoking (irritating) something make it less languid (drooping, listless)? The best answer is choice (D), because sweetening something definitely makes it less acerbic.

20. **The correct answer is (D). Type: Relationship by definition.** Try reversing the words to make a sentence: *Glasses* correct *vision*, just as a *cane* corrects a *limp*.

21. **The correct answer is (A). Type: Implied comparison—by definition.** A *broad-minded attitude* is by definition wide-ranging, just as a *catholic education* is by definition wide-ranging. Remember that only Catholic (capital C) refers to a specific religion.

22. **The correct answer is (C). Type: Analogy of degree.** To *proliferate* is to *spread* like crazy, just as to *pour* is to seep (ooze, drip, or permeate very slowly) like crazy.

23. **The correct answer is (B). Type: Implied comparison—noun related to least likely quality.** One with *prejudice* is never *indifferent* (unbiased), just as someone with *effrontery* (boldness, temerity) is never *timid* (utterly lacking in boldness).

24. **The correct answer is (D).** Lady Windermere's joking, unserious attitude about fortune-telling can best be described as choice (D), *playful*. It is not choice (A), *wistful* (sad), choice (B), *reverent* (deeply respectful), or choice (E), *serious*. Choice (C), *dismissive* is the next-closest, but it implies contempt, and Lady Windermere clearly enjoys fortune-telling.

25. **The correct answer is (E).** Reread the opening paragraphs to infer this answer. No support is offered for any of the other choices, so this must be assumed or inferred by the reader.

26. **The correct answer is (A).** Mr. Podgers reads in the Duchess's hand that "economy is not the least of your Grace's virtues" (lines 68–69), which is an ironic remark meaning that it is a prominent character trait for her; in other words, she is stingy.

27. **The correct answer is (C).** Only this answer is possible, given the other poor choices, and realizing that Lady Windermere is shown here as a somewhat whimsical person. Reread lines 22–28, which tell us that Lady Windermere doesn't take any of this very seriously.

28. **The correct answer is (D).** Reread from line 31 through 36 again to see that Lady Windermere is merely enjoying herself with all of this palm-reading business.

29. **The correct answer is (B).** The correct answer must be inferred from lines 39–40 in which the Dutchess worries that telling bad fortune is "tempting Providence." In other words, saying that bad things will happen is tempting fate to make them happen.

30. **The correct answer is (D).** Again, deduce the correct answer by trying to understand the satiric, playful tone of the entire passage. If you have any doubt, check the last paragraph, in which Lady Windermere compares Mr. Podgers to a performing lion who will jump through hoops for her.

31. **The correct answer is (A).** This is partly a vocabulary question, partly inference by the reader. Surely Mr. Podgers is not *disdainful* (scornful) or *indifferent* (unbiased or uninterested). Nor is he *suspicious*. It is most *tactful* to say that the Duchess's intellect is not exaggerated, rather than saying she is of limited intelligence.

32.   **The correct answer is (E).** Since Mr. Podgers has just said that the Duchess's hand shows great permanence of affection, combined with a strong sense of duty, the Duchess naturally looks quite pleased at hearing herself described so positively. None of the other answers has such direct support in the passage.

33.   **The correct answer is (C).** Read the description Mr. Podgers gives of Lady Flora (lines 83–85) after she steps awkwardly out from behind the sofa. Self-confident people don't try to be inconspicuous by standing behind the sofa. Note that the other choices are all meanings of *reserved*, but not the meaning used in this specific context.

34.   **The correct answer is (A).** Only this answer is supported by the passage. Reread each description of a person to determine that all of the other choices are either wrong or unsupported.

35.   **The correct answer is (C).** This is vocabulary in context again. All of the choices are correct meanings for the word *declined*. Only choice (C), *refused*, makes sense in this particular context.

SECTION 5

1.   **The correct answer is (C).** By grouping the addends on the left side of the equation you see that $5 + 6 = 11$ and $3 + 4 = 7$, so $1 + 2$ must equal x, making it 3.

2.   **The correct answer is (B).** Two angles of the left triangle are identified as b and c. The third angle of this triangle is a vertical angle to the one marked a, so it must also be a. Since the three angles of a triangle sum to 180, $a + b + c = 180$.

3.   **The correct answer is (E).** You're filling three times as many jugs, so it takes three times as long. You're asked for the time in minutes, so convert 90 seconds to $\frac{3}{2}$ minutes: $3 \times \frac{3}{2} = \frac{9}{2} = 4\frac{1}{2}$ minutes.

4.   **The correct answer is (E).** Area of a triangle is $\frac{1}{2}bh$. You know the ratio of the two triangles' altitudes, or heights, but you know nothing about their respective bases. Therefore, choice (E) is correct.

5.   **The correct answer is (E).** Find the smallest number divisible by both 6 and 8, or their least common multiple. Check out the multiples of 8 until you find one that's also a multiple of 6: 8, 16, 24. Since 24 is also a multiple of 24, it is correct.

6.   **The correct answer is (B).** Average is equal to the sum of terms divided by the number of terms. In this case,

$$\frac{(8x + 5) + (-3x + 9) + 0 + (7x - 2)}{4} = \frac{12x + 12}{4}$$
$$= \frac{4(3x + 3)}{4}$$
$$= 3x + 3.$$

7. **The correct answer is (D).** Elizabeth runs m miles in h hours, so she runs $\dfrac{m}{h}$ miles each hour. Therefore, in x hours, she runs $\dfrac{m}{h} \times x = \dfrac{mx}{h}$ miles. You could also have solved this problem by picking values for the variables. If Elizabeth runs 10 miles in 2 hours ($m = 10$, $h = 2$), then she runs 5 miles an hour. Therefore, in 3 hours ($x = 3$) she runs $(3)(5) = 15$ miles. Plugging these values into the choices, only choice (D) gives you 15.

8. **The correct answer is (A).** To find out how many revolutions the truck's wheel makes each mile, divide one mile by the wheel's circumference. Circumference equals $2\pi r$, or $(2)(\pi)(2) = 4\pi$ feet. Since the wheel's radius is given in feet, convert 1 mile to 5,280 feet: $\dfrac{5,280}{4\pi} = \dfrac{1,320}{\pi}$, choice (A).

9. **The correct answer is (C).** The symbol x inside a circle equals $2x - 2$. The symbol x inside a square equals $2(x - 2) = 2x - 4$. Therefore, the symbol x inside a circle minus the symbol x inside a square equals $(2x - 2) - (2x - 4) = -2 - (-4) = -2 + 4 = 2$.

10. **The correct answer is (D).** Since the solution is made of equal parts of A and B, then it is 50% or $\dfrac{1}{2}$ each A and B. There are x ounces of the solution, so there are $\dfrac{1}{2} \times x = \dfrac{x}{2}$ ounces each of A and B. You're asked how many ounces of A, in terms of x, must be added to result in a new solution that is 40% or $\dfrac{2}{5}B$. A solution composed of only A and B that is $\dfrac{2}{5}B$ must necessarily be $\dfrac{3}{5}A$. Since percent is equal to part over whole, for the new solution to be $\dfrac{3}{5}A$, the total amount of A in the new solution divided by the total amount of the new solution must equal $\dfrac{3}{5}$. The total amount of A in the new solution will be equal to the original amount of A, $\dfrac{x}{2}$, plus the additional A, which we'll call a. The total amount of the new solution will be the original amount, x, plus the additional A, a. This gives you the equation $\dfrac{\dfrac{x}{2} + a}{x + a} = \dfrac{3}{5}$. Cross-multiplying gives you $5\left(\dfrac{x}{2} + a\right) = 3(x + a)$ and multiplying through gives you $\dfrac{5x}{2} + 5a = 3x + 3a$. To solve for a, isolate it on one side of the equation: $2a = \dfrac{6x}{2} - \dfrac{5x}{2}$ or $\dfrac{x}{2}$. Dividing both sides by 2 you find that $a = \dfrac{x}{4}$, choice (D).

SECTION 6

1. **The correct answer is (B).** Carefully read the first paragraph which makes the point that the Fourth Amendment applies when a police officer has stopped the suspicious person and has begun to search for something illegal, such as a weapon.

2. **The correct answer is (C).** In paragraph 2, the writer offers a typical scenario to explain why a police officer may become suspicious enough to feel compelled to stop a person and conduct a search, and that all of this is done to prevent crime (lines 37–46). This is a major theme of the majority opinion in Passage 1.

3. **The correct answer is (A).** Read the sentence, substituting the word *performing*, choice (A), if you have any doubt that this is the meaning intended here.

4. **The correct answer is (B).** Choice (A) repeats the question and choice (C) doesn't work because the officer had good reason to believe that he needed to search the suspect. Choice (D) is partly true, but doesn't address the topic of armed and dangerous. Choice (E) is broader than the context or question here. Choice (B) gives us the officer's observation that this suspicious person was actively planning to rob a store, and would logically be toting a weapon.

5. **The correct answer is (C).** Read the word *validly*, choice (C), in place of *properly* in this sentence and see how it preserves the meaning of the sentence. None of the other choices is as accurate or precise.

6. **The correct answer is (D).** Read the first and second paragraphs, where the writer of Passage 2 insists that loitering is the only crime that could actually have been observed by the officer. This writer apparently wants officers to stop and search at the precise moment a crime is about to be committed or while it's being committed, not in advance to protect the general citizenry.

7. **The correct answer is (B).** Reread lines 74–77. The writer says that a judge would not have been authorized to issue a search warrant since probable cause had not been established to make the officer believe the suspect was indeed carrying a concealed weapon. If a judge cannot authorize a search, says this writer, then the police can't perform the action without probable cause.

8. **The correct answer is (A).** Reread lines 81–82, which make this point.

9. **The correct answer is (E).** This remark acknowledges that modern forms of lawlessness may be harder to monitor or control, thus conceding that today's police officers may have to behave differently. But the remark does not persuade us that his reasoning is preferable, choice (A), nor does it support his argument, choice (B). Choices (C) and (D) also fail to be supported by the passage.

10. **The correct answer is (E).** All answers except choice (E) cannot be supported or are just plain incorrect. Choice (A) is not treated in the passage; neither is choice (B). Choice (C) is illogical, as citizens have never been asked to interpret the Constitution, and choice (D) has no basis in the passage. But, according to the author of Passage 2, this ruling by the court has interfered seriously with the intent of the Fourth Amendment, something it has no right to do. See lines 84-92.

11. **The correct answer is (C).** Reread lines 68-70. The writer insists that only loitering had true probable cause in this case, and not the crime of carrying a concealed weapon, yet the majority opinion upheld the right of the police officer to conduct the search even without clear probable cause.

12. **The correct answer is (D).** The entire length of Passage 2 focuses on whether or not this was a reasonable search. Passage 2 maintains that the officer had a strong hunch that a crime was about to be committed that involve the use of a hidden weapon, but that hunch was not enough to justify a search for that weapon.

13. **The correct answer is (D).** Reread the first paragraph of Passage 2. The "mystery" to which the author refers is how the search and seizure in question could be constitutional by the Fourth Amendment since there was no probable cause for it. Choice (D) best summarizes that idea.

Practice Test 2

SECTION 1

1. **The correct answer is (C).** Any number that divides evenly into 30 will produce an integer value for $\dfrac{30}{n}$, so pick the choice that's not a factor of 30. Four is not a factor of 30, so it's correct.

2. **The correct answer is (D).**

$$A + B - C - D = (A + B) - (C + D)$$
$$= 7 - 5 = 2$$

3. **The correct answer is (A).** The equation of a line can be written as $y = mx + b$, where m represents the slope and b represents the y-intercept. Therefore, the slope here is 3.

4. **The correct answer is (B).** Try a number for z. Since z leaves a remainder of 4 when divided by 6, use $z = 6 + 4 = 10$. Therefore, the remainder when $2z$ or 20 is divided by 6 is 2, choice (B).

5. **The correct answer is (C).** Rate times Time = Distance, so driving 50 mph for 2 hours results in a distance of 100 miles. Driving this distance at 60 mph would take $\dfrac{100}{60} = 1\dfrac{2}{3}$ hours. Therefore, it would take $2 - 1\dfrac{2}{3} = \dfrac{1}{3}$ hour or 20 minutes less driving at 60 mph.

6. **The correct answer is (D).** Seven, the number of days in a week, divides evenly into 364, so 364 days from now it will also be a Saturday. The next day, the 365th, is a Sunday.

7. **The correct answer is (E).** All of the choices are equal except for $\dfrac{16}{100}$, which is $\dfrac{1}{10}$ of the rest of the values.

8. **The correct answer is (B).** All of the variables must have a distinct or different value from 1 through 9. Starting with the second equation, C can't be 7 (D and E would both have to be 0), 6 (either D or E would have to be 0), 5 (D and E would both have to be 1), or 3 (both D and E would have to be 2, or one would have to be 3). Therefore, C must be 4. Checking the second equation, if $C = 4$, the other variables could be 8 and 9.

9. **The correct answer is (C).** Adding the two costs, you find that 5 cups of coffee and 5 bagels would cost $7.50. Therefore, one coffee and one bagel would cost one-fifth of this, or $1.50. If you didn't see this you could have written two equations based on the stated relationships, solved for one variable in terms of the other, and then plugged in to the other to solve.

10. **The correct answer is (C).** Ten percent of 75 is 7.5 so 20 percent is 15. You see that 15 is 50% or half of 30, choice (C).

11. **The correct answer is (B).** An even integer divisible by 5 is also divisible by 10. The positive integers less than 100 that are divisible by 10 are 10, 20, 30, 40, 50, 60, 70, 80, and 90, for a total of 9.

12. **The correct answer is (E).** Looking at the figure, you can see that the short side of the rectangle is equal to the diameter of the circle, while the long side of the rectangle is equal to two diameters. Let the diameter of a circle be d. That means the dimensions of the rectangle are d and $2d$. The area of the rectangle is 18, so $d(2d) = 18$ and $d^2 = 9$ or $d = 3$. The radius of a circle is half its diameter, so the radius of each circle is 1.5.

13. **The correct answer is (D).** Shipping rates are given in terms of ounces, so first convert the weight of the package to ounces: 4 pounds 5 ounces $= 4(16) + 5 = 64 + 5 = 69$ ounces. Shipping the first ounce costs a, and the remaining 68 ounces are charged at b cents each, making the total charge $a + 68b$.

14. **The correct answer is (A).** The perimeter of the star is composed of twelve sides of the triangle. The length of three sides of each triangle is $2\frac{1}{2}$ centimeters, so the perimeter of the star is $4 \times 2\frac{1}{2} = 10$ centimeters.

15. **The correct answer is (A).** The obvious and wrong answer is $33\frac{1}{3}\%$. Since the ratio of chocolate-covered pretzels to licorice sticks is 3:1, then the ratio of licorice sticks to the factory's total production is 1: (3 + 1) or 1 : 4. Therefore, the licorice sticks represent $\frac{1}{4}$ or 25% of total production.

16. **The correct answer is (D).** Since the product is positive that tells you something about the three numbers. They can't contain an odd number of negatives, since that would make their product negative. Choice (A) can't be correct since it would include three negatives. They also can't include 0, since this would result in a product of 0, which is neither positive nor negative. This eliminates choices (B) and (C) as being the middle number, since each would include 0 in the group. If 2 were the middle number, the other two would be 1 and 3. Since both their product and sum is 6, this is correct.

17. **The correct answer is (E).** The price of each pizza times the number of pizzas, pd, is the total spent on the pizzas. Dividing this by the total number of people, $b + g$, gives the cost per person. Multiplying this by the number of girls gives you the amount paid by the girls, or $\frac{gpd}{b + g}$. You could also have selected values for the variables and plugged them into the choices.

18. **The correct answer is (E).** The ratio of the areas of two squares is equal to the square of the ratio of their corresponding linear measures. Since you know that their perimeters are in a ratio of 1 to 4, their areas must be in a ratio of 1 to 16, choice (E). If you didn't remember the ratio principle above, you could have solved for the respective areas to come up with the correct answer.

19. **The correct answer is (C).** Since both 4 and 8 are powers of 2, the equation can be rewritten as $(2^{x+2})(2^{x+2}) = (2^{2x})(2^{2x})(2^{2x})$, which simplifies to $2^{2x+4} = 2^{6x}$. Since you're now working with the same base on each side of the equation, you can set the exponential expressions equal: $2x + 4 = 6x$, $4x = 4$, and $x = 1$. You could also have plugged in each choice for x to see which worked.

20. **The correct answer is (A).** The formula for slope is $\frac{y_2 - y_1}{x_2 - x_1}$, so plugging in gives you $\frac{S - R}{R - S} = -1$.

21. **The correct answer is (E).** Let B = the number of beanie babies Brenna has. Eileen has 8 fewer than Brenna, or $B - 8$. Brenna has one third as many as Ryan, which is the same as saying that Ryan has three times as many as Brenna, or $3B$. Together, they have a total of $5B - 8$ beanie babies. Therefore, the total number of beanie babies will be a multiple of 5, minus 8. Multiples of 5 end in either 5 or 0, and subtracting an 8 from numbers ending in these digits would result in final digits of 7 and 2, respectively. Based on this, either 22 or 67 seem like possibilities. Setting 22 equal to $5B - 8$, you find that $B = 6$. This is not possible; since Eileen has 8 fewer beanie babies than Brenna, Brenna must have at least 8. Setting 67 equal to $5B - 8$, you find that $B = 15$. Therefore, Brenna has 15, Eileen has 7, and Ryan has 45, and 67 works as the total number of beanie babies.

22. **The correct answer is (E).** Sketch a diagram of the situation, which should look like the one below. It's clear that you have a 30:60:90 triangle, with sides in the ratio $1 : \sqrt{3} : 2$. Since the side opposite the 30° angle is 12, the hypotenuse must be twice that, or 24.

23. **The correct answer is (C).** For positive integer n, $\frac{\sqrt{n}}{2} = \sqrt[3]{n}$. You're asked which of the choices could be the value of the cube root or c. In other words, which of the choices, when cubed, results in a number whose square root divided by 2 equals c? Simply try the choices. Choice (A) $1^3 = 1$, $\sqrt{1} = 1$, $\frac{1}{2} \neq 1$ so eliminate; choice (B) $2^3 = 8$, $\sqrt{8} = 2\sqrt{2}$, $\frac{2\sqrt{2}}{2} \neq 2$, so eliminate; choice (C) $4^3 = 64$, $\sqrt{64} = 8$, $\frac{8}{2} = 4$, so choice (C) is correct.

24. **The correct answer is (B).** The obvious and wrong answer is choice (A), decreasing n by 5%. You can't simply add or subtract percent changes when they're made on different amounts. To see this more clearly, let $n = 100$. Decreasing n by 25% results in 75. Increasing this result by 20% gives you $75 + 15 = 90$. Since you started with 100, this is an overall decrease of 10%, choice (B).

25. **The correct answer is (D).** In order for no material to be left over when the squares are cut, the side length of the square must divide evenly into both 54 and 117. The smallest possible number that does so is 1, which would result in squares of area 1. However, the question states that each square must have an area greater than 6, so 1 is not a possible side length. If you look at the factors of 54 and 117, you see that their smallest common factor is 3 and their largest common factor is 9. Since 3 goes into 54 eighteen times and into 117 thirty-nine times, the cloth could be cut into $(18)(39) = 702$ squares with a side length of 3. Since 9 goes into 54 six times and into 117 thirteen times, the cloth could be cut into $(6)(13) = 78$ squares with a side length of 9. Therefore, the difference between the number of the smallest squares and the number of the largest squares is $702 - 78 = 624$.

SECTION 2

1. **The correct answer is (C).** In contrast to her previous two-faced friends, Lisa now wants honest, or *candid*, friends.

2. **The correct answer is (C).** Either the house's wealthy-looking exterior is going to match the sumptuous (magnificent) furnishings on the inside, or the house's poor-looking exterior is not going to match the sumptuous furnishings on the inside. Choice (A) is out because *opulent* means wealthy, so the exterior would not have *contrasted* with the inside. Choice (B) doesn't make sense, because *Spartan* means very spare—the opposite of *sumptuous*—and such an exterior would not *suggest* a sumptuous interior. Choices (D) and (E) just don't make much sense, so eliminate them. The best choice is (C). An *austere* (very spare, not fancy) exterior would have *belied* (misrepresented) the sumptuous interior.

3. **The correct answer is (C).** If the scientists were studying something else when they made an important discovery, then the discovery was unexpected, a lucky break—*serendipitous*.

4. **The correct answer is (B).** The word in the first blank has to fit with the other adjective, "dry," which is joined to the blank with nothing more than a comma. That eliminates choices (A) and (D). The word in the second blank is defined in the rest of the sentence: where the characters seem completely, and ludicrously, out of place. *Incongruous* means out of place. *Pedantic* means instructive in a dull and narrow way, so the choice is a perfect fit.

5. **The correct answer is (C).** The contrast is between something durable, which lasts a long time, and something which lasts a fleeting instant—in other words, something *ephemeral*.

Peterson's SAT Success

6. **The correct answer is (B).** An idea that goes with another idea as a natural progression or deduction is a *corollary*.

7. **The correct answer is (E).** The last part of the sentence, which says that painterly abstractions are the norm, is your clue to the rest of the sentence. Ringgold's quilts are made of cloth, so they're not painterly. This implies that the word in the first blank will set up a contrast with "abstractions"—eliminate choices (B) and (D)—and that the phrase in the second blank has to describe something that stands out as different: an aberration.

8. **The correct answer is (E).** The phrases "At the beginning" and "but by the end" set up a contrast between the first half of the sentence and the second half, which says that we had mastered the rigors of trigonometry. So at the beginning of the course, we must not have been masters of this difficult subject. *Uncomprehending* emphasizes the novices' lack of mastery and *inscrutable* (hard to understand) shows just how difficult the subject was.

9. **The correct answer is (A).** Impersonating a sheriff's deputy is a bad thing to do, so you can eliminate as a candidate for the first blank any word with a positive or neutral meaning. That leaves you with choices (A), (B), and (C). For the second blank, you can rely on the context provided by the second half of the sentence: the duties of a sworn officer of the law are legal, lawful—or *licit*—duties.

10. **The correct answer is (D).** A *worshipper* is part of a *congregation* as a *pupil* is part of a *class*.

11. **The correct answer is (A).** A *surfeit* (an overabundance), by definition, lacks *scarcity*, just as a *haze*, by definition lacks *clarity*.

12. **The correct answer is (E).** The purpose of a *purgative* substance or device is to *purify* something else, just as the purpose of an *incendiary* substance or device is to *ignite* something else.

13. **The correct answer is (A).** The words define each other: a *swindle* is a *fraud* as a *ruse* is a *subterfuge*.

14. **The correct answer is (B).** A *votary* (a devotee or worshipper) is characterized by an attitude of *veneration* (worship) as a *skeptic* is characterized by an attitude of *incredulity*.

15. **The correct answer is (D).** To *pine* (to ache for) has the same meaning as to *long*, just as to *low* is the same as to *moo*.

16. **The correct answer is (D).** Take a look at the last two sentences of the first paragraph, which tell you that lightning struck the mountaintop, which was "dead-dry from the lack of rain."

17. **The correct answer is (B).** Go back to the line and read it in context. The author begins the sentence about the patio chairs by mentioning the saying about nature being "in your own backyard." He uses the example of the patio chairs to illustrate how close the fire was to being in his family's own backyard. In other words, he was emphasizing the nearness of a natural force to his home.

18. **The correct answer is (A).** This is a vocabulary-in-context question, which means that you need to go back to the passage and read the context in which the word is used. In this case, you need to read a couple of sentences past the one that uses "false." These sentences explain that the distinction between civilization and nature doesn't really exist—such a distinction would be mistaken.

19. **The correct answer is (C).** This question requires you to apply your overall understanding of the passage. Would the author agree that urban environments are rapidly depleting natural resources? Even if it's a true statement, it's not a topic the author discusses. Choice (B) might be tempting, but the author doesn't always describe nature as being beautiful—he seems more concerned with the idea that it's always present. There's no evidence to support choice (D), and choice (E) goes too far. The author says that nature can intrude upon an urban environment at any time, but he doesn't imply that as soon as it does the environment will be destroyed. The best answer is choice (C), because the author's point throughout the passage is that nature is never far removed from people's homes, even in urban areas. In the last paragraph, the author specifically points out that city people who believe themselves to be shielded from nature are incorrect.

20. **The correct answer is (E).** Go back to the referenced line and read around it. The answer comes at the end of the paragraph, in which the author expresses his fascination at seeing the spider emerge from the dead landscape, a "hostile environment."

21. **The correct answer is (C).** Look at the phrase as it's written in the last sentence. The author says that he is fascinated not only by Old Faithful and the Grand Canyon (natural wonders) but also by the sidewalk weed and trashcan raccoon. In other words, he includes the weed and raccoon in his appreciation of nature.

22. **The correct answer is (D).** This question tests your overall understanding of the author's purpose in writing the passage. Clearly, he admires nature in all its forms. *Reverent* (worshipping) might be tempting, but it's a bit strong. Keep looking to see if there's a better choice. *Mocking* is out, as is *uncertain*. *Respectful* is a strong choice; keep it. Fearful may be tempting because the author witnessed a large fire, but he doesn't express any fear in the passage. The best choice is (D), *respectful.*

23. **The correct answer is (C).** The entire passage is concerned with various theories about the large-mammal extinction. The other choices may be contained within the passage but only in small sections and not throughout.

24. **The correct answer is (D).** The context shows that the subject of "have been advanced" is theories. To advance a theory is to put it forward for consideration.

25. **The correct answer is (D).** See lines 77-79. Choice (A) is cited in the passage in support of the specific idea that humans hunted the animals until they were extinct, not for the broader concept that humans somehow caused the extinction. Choice (B) is mentioned in the passage but has nothing to do with the theory in question, and choices (C) and (E) are not mentioned in the passage.

26. **The correct answer is (A).** The rest of the passage after this question concerns itself with several theories on how humans might have caused the extinction. Nothing in the passage suggests that the author has any serious doubt, choice (B), or feels astonished, choice (C), about the human cause of the extinction, nor that the scientific community is confused, choice (E). The question leads into the theory that humans hunted the large mammals to extinction, choice (D), but this theory could not be described as the author's theory because the author clearly intends to cast doubt on this specific hypothesis.

27. **The correct answer is (B).** Only *quite* can be substituted for *perfectly* in the sentence without changing the meaning.

28. **The correct answer is (E).** The North American bison are both a perfect example (lines 62-64) of the lethal capabilities of humans and a counterexample (lines 65-66) that argues against the theory that early humans killed off all the large animals around them.

29. **The correct answer is (E).** The passage repeatedly compares the large-mammal extinction with more recent phenomena, in lines 37-38 (as recently as 2,000 years ago), line 59 (modern experience shows), line 83 (in light of modern experience), and lines 90-92 (the recent emergence . . . lends new plausibility).

30. **The correct answer is (B).** In introducing the disease hypothesis in line 84, the author says that researches "have even begun to argue for it," which implies that it is somehow unlikely. Add to that the facts that no cross-species virus has been identified from fossils, that such diseases have recently emerged, and that the author names only one such virus (line 91). You have what is apparently a rare phenomenon.

31. **The correct answer is (A).** See lines 88-89.

SECTION 3

1. **The correct answer is (B).** Since subtracting a negative is the same as adding a positive, Column B is equal to $x + 4$ and is greater than $x - 3$ in Column A.

2. **The correct answer is (C).** Multiples of 5 end in 0 or 5. When a nonmultiple is divided by 5, if its last digit is less than 5, the remainder is equal to that digit. Since $3 < 5$, when 876,543 is divided by 5, the remainder is 3. Multiples of 10 end in 0. When nonmultiples are divided by 10, the remainder is equal to the value of the number's last digit. Therefore, the remainder when 876,543 is divided by 10 is also 3, and the columns are equal.

3. **The correct answer is (D).** There could be 10 one-minute commercials on Channel 2 and 4 two-minute commercials on Channel 4, or 5 two-minute commercials on Channel 2, and 8 one-minute commercials on Channel 4. Since you have no idea how long any of the commercials are, you cannot determine the relationship between the columns.

4. **The correct answer is (C).** The only difference between x and y is that the decimal in the percentage in y is two places farther to the right. Each time you move a decimal one place to the right in a number, you increase that number's value by a factor of 10. Therefore, y is 100 times as great as x, so dividing y by 100 is equal to x.

5. **The correct answer is (B).** If you remember that the number of degrees in a polygon is $(n - 2)180$, where n is the number of sides, then you'd quickly see that 3(180) in Column A is less than 720. Otherwise, use the fact that a triangle has 180 degrees to solve. Sketch a pentagon and divide it into triangles. Since it can be divided into 3 triangles, it must contain 3(180) degrees.

6. **The correct answer is (C).** $2{,}222 = 2 \times 1{,}111$ and $3{,}333 = 3 \times 1{,}111$. Since 1,111 isn't divisible by either 2 or 3, both 2,222 and 3,333 have one more prime factor than 1,111, and the columns are equal.

7. **The correct answer is (D).** The arithmetic mean of a group of terms is equal to the sum of the terms divided by the number of terms. Since all 3 terms in Set A are s, the arithmetic mean must be s. The median is the middle term in a group of terms arranged in ascending or descending order. However, since you have no information about the relative values of r, s and t, there is no way to determine the median of Set T. Since you don't know the value of Column B, you cannot determine the relationship between the columns.

8. **The correct answer is (B).** Isolating a in the centered inequality, you find that $a < 7$. Since $7 - 2 = 5$, something less than 7 minus 2 must result in a number less than 5.

9. **The correct answer is (B).** Adjacent angles are supplementary, so the angle adjacent to the one marked 91° must be 89°. The three angles in a triangle sum to 180°, so the third angle in the triangle must be $180° - 89° - 45° = 46°$. Since b is opposite the 46° angle and a is opposite the 45° angle, b is greater.

10. **The correct answer is (D).** An isosceles triangle has two equal sides, so the third side of the triangle described must be either 5 or 7. If it is 5, the two columns are equal; if it is 7, Column A is greater. Since more than one relationship is possible, the correct answer is choice (D).

Peterson's SAT Success

11. **The correct answer is (A).** The product of an even number of negative numbers will be positive, while the product of an odd number of negative numbers will be negative. Therefore, this question boils down to whether the expressions in each exponent are even or odd. In Column A, $2n^2$ is always even; whatever the value of n^2, multiplying it by 2 will always result in an even product. In Column B, $2n^5 + 1$ is always odd; by the above reasoning, $2n^5$ is always even so adding 1 to it will always produce an odd result. Therefore, the value of Column A is positive and the value of Column B is negative, and choice (A) is correct.

12. **The correct answer is (B).** The radius of circle C is the same as the distance from C, its center, to $(3, 4)$, a point on its circumference. Since the origin is to the left of point C, the distance from the origin to $(3, 4)$ is greater than the distance from C to $(3, 4)$. If you sketch in the segment connecting the origin and $(3, 4)$, you see that dropping a perpendicular from $(3, 4)$ to the x-axis results in a 3-4-5 right triangle. This means that the distance from the origin to $(3, 4)$ is 5, so the distance from C to $(3, 4)$ must be less than 5.

13. **The correct answer is (B).** For xy to be positive, x and y are either both positive or both negative. For yz to be negative, either y or z, but not both, must be negative. If z is negative, then y must be positive, and, consequently x must be positive as well. This makes xz the product of a negative and a positive and therefore negative. Alternately, if z is positive then y must be negative, making x negative as well. Again, xz is negative, so 0 in Column B is greater.

14. **The correct answer is (B).** In both the units' place and the hundreds' place you're adding A to C, and in each case you get the same one-digit result, D. For this to be true, there must not be any carrying over from the sum of the digits in the tens' column. In other words, $B + B$ or $2B$ must be less than 10, and B must be less than 5.

15. **The correct answer is (A).** You can't combine percent increases and decreases that are made on different wholes. To make this clear, let $a = 100$ (because it's easy to find percents of 100) and $n = 50$. Decreasing 100 by 50 percent results in 50. Increasing this result by 50% means adding 25 to 50 for a final result, z, of 75. Therefore, Column A is greater.

16. **The correct answer is 2/5 or .4.** The only digit from 1 to 9 that will cause S times 4 to end in 0 is 5. Working through the problem knowing $S = 5$ reveals that $T = 2$. Therefore, $\frac{T}{S} = \frac{2}{5}$ or .4.

17. **The correct answer is 11.89.** Using 10 ounces of shampoo a month will result in 120 ounces used per year. Carol would have to buy 15 regular size bottles at $3.19 each, for a total of $47.85. She would have to buy 4 super size bottles at $8.99 each, for a total of $35.96, making her savings $47.85 − $35.96 = $11.89.

18. **The correct answer is 108.** From the given information, $y = 2x$ and $z = \dfrac{x}{3}$. Since angles about a point sum to 360, $x + 2x + \dfrac{x}{3} = 360$, $\dfrac{10x}{3} = 360$, $10x = 1,080$, $x = 108$.

19. **The correct answer is 6.** Since $9 = 3^2$, $9^3 = (3^2)^3 = 3^6$, and $x = 6$.

20. **The correct answer is 5.** To ensure that a pair of the same color socks is removed, one sock of each of the 4 colors must first be drawn. After that, whichever color sock is removed must match one of the 4 socks already drawn. Therefore, 5 socks must be removed to guarantee that a pair is removed.

21. **The correct answer is 1.** A special number is obtained by adding a number to its reciprocal or $n + \dfrac{1}{n}$, where n is the special number's generator. Since you know that 2 is special, $2 = n + \dfrac{1}{n}$, $2 = \dfrac{n^2 + 1}{n}$, $2n = n^2 + 1$, $n^2 - 2n + 1 = 0$, $(n - 1)(n - 1) = 0$, and $n = 1$.

22. **The correct answer is 81.5.** You can't simply average 80 and 95 to come up with the new class average. The grade of 80 represents the scores of 9 students, so it must be weighted as such when you figure the total average: $\dfrac{9(80) + 95}{10} = \dfrac{720 + 95}{10} = \dfrac{815}{10} = 81.5$.

23. **The correct answer is 61.** The exposed surface area from the top is a 5 by 5 square. The exposed surface from each of the sets of 4 sides is a 1 by 1 square, on a 3 by 1 rectangle, on a 5 by 1 rectangle. None of the bottoms are exposed, so the total surface area is $25 + 4(1 + 3 + 5) = 25 + 36 = 61$.

24. **The correct answer is 8/25 or .32.** Sketching a Venn diagram can help you visualize the solution to this problem. Draw two circles that overlap, labeling the one on the left A and the one on the right B. The overlap is the number of people who worked on both projects, or 13. Since the total number of people who worked on Project A was 15, then $15 - 13 = 2$ worked only on A; fill this in on the left circle. The total number of people who worked on Project B was 32 so $32 - 13 = 19$ worked only on B. So $2 + 13 + 19 = 34$ people worked on Project A, B, or both, and $50 - 34 = 16$ people worked on neither. This represents $\dfrac{16}{50} = \dfrac{8}{25}$, or .32, of the club.

25. **The correct answer is 2.** Let s be the length of a side of the square. Note that the diameter of the inscribed circle is equal to a side of the square, so it is s and its radius is $\frac{s}{2}$. Drawing in a diagonal of the square you see that it is equal to the diameter of the circumscribed circle. Diagonal of a square is equal to side length times $\sqrt{2}$, so the circumscribed circle's diameter is $s\sqrt{2}$ and its radius is $\frac{s\sqrt{2}}{2}$. Consequently, the area of the circumscribed circle is $\frac{1}{2}s^2\pi$ and that of the inscribed circle is $\frac{1}{4}s^2\pi$. Since the area of the circumscribed circle is twice as big as that of the inscribed circle they are in a ratio of 2:1, making x equal 2.

SECTION 4

1. **The correct answer is (B).** The key words in this sentence are *foreign microbes*. Blood samples containing microbes from the outside are contaminated.

2. **The correct answer is (D).** You can a pretty good feel for the answers before you even look at your choices. If the district administrators are implementing a change, something must be wrong with the educational standards, so look for a word that indicates a problem. The word in the second blank is going to describe the solution to the problem, so it's going to describe some kind of improved procedure. The only words that really make sense for the first blank are *faltering* (losing strength), choice (A), or *lax* (careless), choice (D). A *mediocre* (not very good) procedure would not be much of an improvement, but a *stringent* (tightly controlled) one would be, so your answer is choice (D).

3. **The correct answer is (E).** First of all, *consign* means turn over, commit—but you could probably figure that out from the context. Is it good to take things that could be recycled and instead put them in landfills? No, so you need a negative word—leaving you with choices (D) and (E). Since *squander* means waste, it's the choice that fits the context of the sentence. To *undermine* means to weaken.

4. **The correct answer is (E).** In the first blank, you need a word that indicates that Van Gogh's mental processes were unbalanced, which quickly eliminates choices (A), and (B). *Despite* lets you know that this is a sentence of contrast; the second half of the sentence says that the paintings' use of color and light is surprising in light of Van Gogh's illness. Choice (E) is the only remaining choice that sets up such a contrast.

5. **The correct answer is (D).** The first word, *Although*, lets you know that this is a sentence of contrast. In the first part of the sentence, waste of time signals that the first blank is a negative or, at best, neutral word. The contrast set up by *Although* and the word *good* to describe educational programs lets you know that the word in the second blank must be a good one. So, you're left with *disparaged*, which means put down, and *salutary*, which means contributing to health or well-being.

6. **The correct answer is (A).** This sentence defines the missing word in its second half. The word that describes beings that like to spend their time in social activities is *gregarious*.

7. **The correct answer is (B).** The key words here are *otherwise intelligent* and *complexity*: The old programs were so complex that they made smart people feel stupid.

8. **The correct answer is (C).** This is another sentence that defines its missing word. What would you call a disease that acts like other, less serious conditions until it's too late to do anything about the real disease? It's an imposter, something that does harm in a subtle or hidden way—something *insidious*.

9. **The correct answer is (A).** This sentence is full of hard words. Start with the easy one. *Though* sets up a contrast. Now, if the vocabulary gives you trouble, skip it for the moment and look at the sentence structure instead. See *we are likely to* in both halves of the sentence? The next word in the first half of the sentence is censure; the next word in the second half is the blank. If you know that censure means blame, you're home free—you want a word that's the opposite. If you don't, use the context to help you figure it out. If someone does a bad thing deliberately, is that better or worse than if they do it without meaning to (involuntary or unpremeditated)? Of course, it's worse; and now you know that *censure* means to blame, and you're prepared to choose *exculpate*, which means, find not guilty. And if you didn't know the meaning of *exculpate*, you could analyze its roots: *ex* means out; *culp-* (as in culpable, culprit) means guilty.

10. **The correct answer is (E).** If we felt sorry for the speaker, something must have gone wrong. Also, note the contrast between the real audience of fully employed people with the audience of retired people for whom the speech was meant. There's a discrepancy between the audience that would have been right and the audience that was really there. Too bad for the speaker. He's really unlucky, or *hapless*. The speech would have been appropriate and relevant, or *germane*, to a group of people who weren't there.

11. **The correct answer is (E).** To *rally* is to get over a loss; to *recover* is to get over a disease.

12. **The correct answer is (A).** A *framework* is a supporting structure from which a *carpenter* constructs a building (or structure), an *outline* is a supporting structure from which a *writer* constructs an essay or story.

13. **The correct answer is (D).** To *fret* is to have or show anxiety; to *cherish* is to have or show fondness.

14. **The correct answer is (D).** An *archipelago* is a group of islands; a *chain* is a group of mountains.

15. **The correct answer is (B).** To *drowse* is to sleep lightly or superficially; to *look* is to persue lightly or superficially.

16. **The correct answer is (C).** A *compound* is a new substnace made up of two or more elements; a *batter* is a new substance made up of two or more ingredients.

Peterson's SAT Success

17. **The correct answer is (B).** To *incarcerate* is to cut off or end freedom; to *restrain* is to end mobility (movement).

18. **The correct answer is (E).** *Auditory*, by definition, means having to do with the sense of hearing; *visual*, by definition, means having to do with the sense of sight.

19. **The correct answer is (A).** A *meeting* is presided over by a chairperson; a *trial* is presided over by a judge.

20. **The correct answer is (A).** A *cautious* person is the opposite of someone who is headstrong (strong-willed); a *reticent* (quiet) person is the opposite of someone vocal.

21. **The correct answer is (C).** You *fuel* a *blaze* to make it burn more hotly; you *provoke ire* (anger) to make it burn more hotly.

22. **The correct answer is (D).** A *haven* is, by definition, a place of *safety*, just as a *prison* is, by definition, a place of *confinement*.

23. **The correct answer is (B).** To use *trickery* is to *beguile*; to use an *eraser* is to *expunge* (wipe clean).

24. **The correct answer is (D).** The three musical styles that developed after World War II are the primary means that the passage uses to illustrate the way ethnic cultural expressions develop.

25. **The correct answer is (E).** The subject of the passage is the development of ethnic cultural expressions. The author's thesis, best expressed in the second paragraph, is that this development is both traditional in that ethnic groups keep aspects of their culture (lines 23–24) and innovative in that ethnic groups borrow freely from other ethnic groups (lines 25–26). Choices (A), (B), and (D) are contained in the passage but are not the main idea, while choice (C) does not accurately reflect the author's opinions.

26. **The correct answer is (C).** As stated in lines 1–3, the point of both metaphors is how ethnic cultures come together in the United States. The referent of the carrots in the melting pot metaphor is immigrants, line 10—not individual immigrants, but the groups that composed the massive waves of European immigration (line 5). The referent of the carrots in the salad-bowl metaphor is various ethnic groups (line 15).

27. **The correct answer is (C).** The author says in lines 19–20 that both the metaphors are true simultaneously. Since the two metaphors represent fundamentally opposing viewpoints, the author goes on to qualify this statement by showing in what sense each is true: Each is partially accurate.

28. **The correct answer is (B).** In lines 35-39 and 54-59, the author mentions the migration of members of the source groups of bluegrass and rhythm and blues to urban areas from the American South. The description of the development of each musical style that follows these lines implies that this migration was one reason for the borrowing from other ethnic cultures. The development of electrified instruments, choice (A), is a technological trend, not a historical one. Choice (C), which does represent a historical trend, is not mentioned in the passage. Choices (D) and (E) are culture trends, though they too may have been influenced by historical trends.

29. **The correct answer is (C).** Lines 40-45 say that bluegrass retained the use of acoustic stringed instruments despite the rise of electrified instruments at the time. Lines 59-61 point out that rhythm and blues appropriated these electrified instruments; it was a style that was plugged in.

30. **The correct answer is (B).** See the fifth paragraph, lines 73-76: The passage says that the two previous examples might suggest that a cultural fermentation in the South, rather than a broader trend, might be the reason for the rise of bluegrass and rhythm and blues. But in the final sentence of that paragraph, lines 84-85, the author cites further parallels beyond the South by way of introducing the powwow style.

31. **The correct answer is (D).** The tribal traditionalists fret about the intrustion of the powwow style into older traditional ceremonies (lines 101-103), which apparently represent the separate tribal styles mentioned in lines 90-91, in contrast to the powwow style, which is pan-Indian—representing all the Native American groups rather than the individual nations.

32. **The correct answer is (A).** See lines 39-40, which say that bluegrass is characterized by singing in, the classic British-American style. The other choices represent innovative rather than traditional elements, except for choice (E), which is not mentioned in the passage.

33. **The correct answer is (A).** Lines 47-49 mention several stylistic elements of bluegrass that are borrowed from other cultures.

34. **The correct answer is (E).** Choices (A) through (D) are all mentioned in the second paragraph.

35. **The correct answer is (D).** The fluid synthesis of lines 128-129 is a synthesis that is subject to change in its blending of the old and the new.

SECTION 5

1. **The correct answer is (C).** You see that $2n$ is always even, and adding 1 to an even number must result in an odd number. If you didn't see this, you could have tried values for n in the choices to see which always produces an odd integer.

2. **The correct answer is (A).** The prime factorization of 12 is $2 \times 2 \times 3$; there are 2 distinct or different prime factors.

3. **The correct answer is (E).** When two lines are perpendicular, their slopes are negative reciprocals. Since the slope of line a is $\frac{2}{3}$, the slope of line b must be $-\frac{3}{2}$.

4. **The correct answer is (A).** The radar moved $\frac{3}{4}$ of the way around the screen. This takes $\frac{3}{4}$ of a minute, or 45 seconds.

5. **The correct answer is (A).** As long as all the angles involved are 90°, no distance is saved by making turns.

6. **The correct answer is (E).** Since $AB = \frac{AD}{6}$, $6AB = AD$ and choice (A) is true. Since $\frac{AD}{6} = \frac{AC}{2}$, $6AC = 2AD$ and $3AC = AD$, so choice (D) is true. Since $AB + BC = AC$, $3AC = 3(AB + BC) = AD$ and choice (B) is true. Since $AC + CD = AD$ and $AC = \frac{1}{3}AD$, then $CD = \frac{2}{3}AD$. Therefore, $\frac{3}{2}CD$ or $\frac{3CD}{2} = AD$ and choice (C) is true. The only statement that is not true is choice (E).

7. **The correct answer is (B).** Originally, there are a total of 9 socks in the drawer, and 3 of them are blue. A blue sock is removed, which drops the total number of socks in the drawer to 8 and the number of blue socks to 2. Therefore, the probability of selecting a blue sock is now $\frac{2}{8} = \frac{1}{4}$.

8. **The correct answer is (B).** If Greg leaves a deposit of b dollars and still owes a balance of c dollars, the total cost of the shelves is $b + c$. There are a total of a shelves, so the cost per shelf is $\frac{b + c}{a}$. If this wasn't clear, you could have used values for the variables to find the cost of a shelf, and then plugged the values into the choices to see which yielded the desired result.

9. **The correct answer is (C).** The first integer greater than 1 that is both a square and a cube is 64, since $64 = 4^3 = 8^2$. If x is 8 and y is 4, then $xy = 32$.

10. **The correct answer is (D).** The two clocks are moving apart (and together) at 10 minutes per hour. After moving 12 hours together/ apart, they will read the same time. Twelve hours divided by 10 minutes or 720 minutes divided by 10 minutes is 72.

SECTION 6

1.   **The correct answer is (A).** In essence, the first paragraph is an introduction to the whole passage. It uses the concrete image of a truck pulling into a driveway to give form to the main idea of the passage.

2.   **The correct answer is (E).** The sentence immediately before the one about the hog-sticking knife, in lines 19–22, makes it clear that the question about the knife is one that the subjects of the study might have asked. The fact that the subjects might wonder what was so special about a knife indicates that they didn't understand why field workers would be interested in their everyday objects.

3.   **The correct answer is (C).** The context describes immigrants setting up residence in the American West.

4.   **The correct answer is (D).** Lines 36–39 contrast most people's association of Italian-Americans with the urban East with the project's goal to uncover an important and much less understood aspect of Italian-American history.

5.   **The correct answer is (A).** The passage nowhere specifically answers this question. However, it does mention the transformation of Italians into Italian Americans (lines 10–11) and describes how the Nicolavo family changed their name to Nick in order to assimilate (lines 11–18). These statements support the idea that Italian Americans conformed to the prevailing culture. The passage also says that Italian Americans helped shape the cultural landscape of the modern West (lines 46–48) and gives examples of that process.

6.   **The correct answer is (B).** The author's astonishment is apparant from her use of an exclamantion point in line 103 when she describes her discovery that the field-workers had been studying her family, as well as from her use in the next sentence of the word *suddenly*.

7.   **The correct answer is (C).** The author uses *very* here to mean selfsame—*my own family* would be another way to express this.

8.   **The correct answer is (B).** The author mentions the researches in line 111 and even specifies that there were two of them, with a microphone to record the conversation, in lines 119–121.

9.   **The correct answer is (B).** The author defines the sense of violation in the next part of the sentence: as if the presence of two field-workers . . . invaded my privacy and trespassed on my ownership of this family history (lines 121–123).

10.   **The correct answer is (E).** Passage 2 does not mention work in mines, though Passage 1 does.

11. **The correct answer is (A).** The author of Passage 2 says that she was excited to have part of her life experience recognized as important (lines 123–124). Eliminate choice (B) because the author, far from volunteering her family to participate in the study, was surprised to learn of their involvement. Choice (C) is weak; while the author says she would like to "ask more questions" of her family, it isn't reason that the stories deserve to be told. Eliminate the "no" answers; there is not sufficient evidence to justify them.

12. **The correct answer is (D).** Passage 1, though fairly informal in tone, is nevertheless an official descripion that defines the project's goals and even quotes the project director extensively. Psssage 2, as characterized by its use of first-person voice and its exploration of the author's feelings, is much more personal. Choice (A) may seem like a close second, but remembers that both speakers are involved in the project in some way. Choice (C) may seem tempting too, but remember that the first passage wasn't about the opinions of a bureacrat; it was an official description of the project.

Math Teaching Unit

Arithmetic

PRACTICE SET I

1. **The correct answer is (C).** The student body is $\frac{2}{3}$ male and $\frac{1}{3}$ female. So $\left(\frac{1}{4} \times \frac{2}{3}\right) + \left(\frac{1}{6} \times \frac{1}{3}\right) = \frac{1}{6} + \frac{1}{18} = \frac{2}{9}$ of the student body plays soccer.

2. **The correct answer is (C).** For N to be an integer, it must be a multiple of both 8 and 36. Four is a factor of 8 and 36, not a multiple, so eliminate choices (A) and (E) for including it. Sixty-four is a multiple of 8 but not 36, so eliminate choices (B) and (D). This leaves choice (C), 72, which is indeed a multiple of both.

3. **The correct answer is (A).** We know that 25% or one-fourth of 72 is 18. We also know that 18 is 150% or $\frac{3}{2}x$, so $x = \frac{2}{3}(18) = 12$.

4. **The correct answer is (B).** You can't simply average 90 and 80 since each average represents a different number of tests. You must weight the averages accordingly: $\frac{3(90) + 2(80)}{5} = \frac{430}{5} = 86$.

5. **The correct answer is (A).** Since 7 is prime, it is its only prime factor. The only prime factor of 81 is 3. Therefore 7 in Column A is greater than 3 in Column B.

6. **The correct answer is (A).** Rewrite the columns to make them easier to compare. Column A can be rewritten as $\frac{1,001}{13} - \frac{26}{13}$ or $\frac{1,001}{13} - 2$. Subtracting $\frac{1,001}{13}$ from each column leaves you comparing -2 and -26. Since $-2 > -26$, Column A is greater.

7. **The correct answer is (C).** Since Sum = (Average)(Number of quantities), $\frac{\text{Sum}}{\text{Average}}$ = Number of quantites and the columns are equal. If you didn't see this you could have picked some numbers.

8. **The correct answer is 5/3 or 1.66 or 1.67.** Set up a proportion: $\frac{\frac{1}{3}}{24} = \frac{x}{120}$. Cross multiply: $24x = 40$, $x = \frac{5}{3}$.

9. **The correct answer is 31.** The difference between the high and low temperatures is $19 - (-12) = 19 + 12 = 31$.

10. **The correct answer is 3.** Kate received 1 free woozle with every 5 she bought, so $\frac{1}{6}$ of the total number of woozles she left with were free. Since she bought 30, 5 were free and she paid for the other 25. Since she paid 75 dollars, each woozle sells for $\frac{75}{25} = 3$ dollars.

PRACTICE SET II

1. **The correct answer is (C).** Rate × Time = Distance, so $30T = 20$ and $T = \frac{2}{3}$ hour. On the return trip, $40T = 20$ and $T = \frac{1}{2}$ hour. Therefore, Carmela spent $\frac{2}{3} + \frac{1}{2} = 1\frac{1}{6}$ hours, or 1 hour and 10 minutes, driving.

2. **The correct answer is (C).** Since 60% of the class goes on the trip, 40% doesn't go. Therefore, $\frac{40x}{100}$ or $\frac{2x}{5} = 12$. Cross-multiplying, $2x = 5(12)$ and $x = 30$.

3. **The correct answer is (C).** Be sure to "weight" the average: $\frac{12(\$4.00) + 18(\$5.50)}{30} = \frac{\$48 + \$99}{30} = \frac{\$147}{30} = \$4.90$.

4. **The correct answer is (E).** Since 51 has factors 1, 3, 17 and 51, it is not prime. All of the other statements are true.

5. **The correct answer is (B).** A number divisible by 5 ends in either 0 or 5. If the last digit of a non-multiple of 5 is greater than 5, the remainder it leaves when divided by 5 is equal to its last digit minus 5. Therefore, the remainder, when 2,345,678 is divided by 5, is $8 - 5 = 3$. A number divisible by 10 ends in 0. The last digit of a non-multiple is equal to the remainder the number leaves when divided by 10. Therefore, the remainder when 2,345,678 is divided by 10 is 8 and Column B is greater.

6. **The correct answer is (A).** Both a and b result from taking 37.25% of a number. However, the number involved in the case of a is 10 times larger than the one from which b is derived. Therefore, $a = 10b$, making 10a in Column A 100b, and clearly larger than b in Column B.

7. **The correct answer is (A).** The numerators of the fractions are equal, so the one with the smaller denominator is greater. Since $3 < 6$, Column A is greater.

8. **The correct answer is 15.** Since the average of 5 numbers is 17, their sum is $5(17) = 85$. Since the average of 2 of the numbers is 20, their sum is $2(20) = 40$. That means the sum of the remaining 3 numbers must be $85 - 40 = 45$ and their average is $\frac{45}{3} = 15$.

9. **The correct answer is 24.** The number of possibilities for 3 people sitting in 4 seats is actually the same as the number of possibilities for 4 people sitting in 4 seats ($4 \times 3 \times 2 \times 1 = 24$), since leaving a seat empty seat can be thought of as an option. If the first seat is left empty, there are 3 possibilities for the second seat, 2 for the third, and 1 for the fourth, for a total of $3 \times 2 \times 1 = 6$ arrangements. There are 6 more arrangements when the second seat is empty, 6 when the third is empty, and 6 when the fourth is empty for a total of 24.

10. **The correct answer is 12/7 or 1.71.** Set up a proportion: $\frac{7}{1} = \frac{12}{x}$, $7x = 12$, $x = \frac{12}{7}$. Be sure to grid your answer as a decimal or an improper fraction, never as a mixed number.

PRACTICE SET III—*Real SAT Questions*

1. **The correct answer is (A).** There are three paths that start out from point A. The one on the left leads straight to point B, for one route. The middle path veers off midway, offering two routes to point B. The right path also veers off midway, offering two routes. Therefore there are 5 routes from A to B.

2. **The correct answer is (D).** Since m and n are both negative, their product mn must always be positive. This eliminates choices (A), (B) and (C). If both variables were greater than -1, that is, negative fractions, their product would be a positive number less than 1. But since m is less than -1, the product mn can be any positive number.

3. **The correct answer is (C).** Even if you're not sure how to solve you can eliminate some answers. The total driving time for the roundtrip was 2 hours, or 120 minutes. If each way were driven at the same speed, it would have taken 60 minutes for each leg of the trip. But since she drove at a higher speed to the museum, that leg must have taken less time and therefore be less than 60 minutes; eliminate choices (A) and (B). To solve, let t be the time it took to drive to the museum and write the equation $40t = d$. Since the roundtrip took 120 minutes, the time it took to drive back home can be expressed as $120 - t$. This enables you to write an equation about the drive back home, $35(120 - t) = d$. Since you have two different equations with the two variables, you can solve. Plugging in $40t$ for d in the second equation gives you $35(120 - t) = 40t$, and you can solve:

$$4,200 - 35t = 40t$$
$$4,200 = 75t$$
$$56 = t$$

4. **The correct answer is (B).** There are four "pairs" of opposite seats at the table: 1 and 5, 2 and 6, 3 and 7, and 4 and 8. For each of these pairs there are two possible seating arrangements: student A in seat 1 and student B in seat 5, or vice versa. That means there are a total of $4 \times 2 = 8$ possible arrangements.

5. **The correct answer is (B).** Let the store's cost of the sweater be x. Since the store charged 40 percent more than its cost, $\$28 = 1.4x$. Solving for x you find that the store cost is $\frac{\$28}{1.4} = x = \$20$. Employees receive a 30 percent discount off the store's price, so they actually pay 70 percent of the store's price: $\$20 \times .7 = \$14$, choice (B).

6. **The correct answer is (B).** The pattern consists of 3 repeating numbers so any term divisible by 3 will correspond to the 3rd number, or 0. That means the 18th term in the pattern must be the 0. Therefore the 17th term must be 1 and the 19th, -1, making Column B greater.

7. **The correct answer is (A).** Any number times 0 is 0, so there are 9 ways to represent 0 as the product of two different one-digit integers. There are only 2 ways to represent 12 as the product of two different one-digit integers: 2×6 and 3×4.

8. **The correct answer is (D).** There are 4 different prime numbers less than 10: 2, 3, 5, and 7. There are 4 different positive even integers less than 10: 2, 4, 6, and 8. If you compare the sum of the first 3 terms in each set ($2 + 3 + 5 = 10$ in Column A and $2 + 4 + 6 = 12$ in Column B), Column B is greater. But if you compare the sum of the last 3 terms in Column A ($3 + 5 + 7 = 15$) with the sum of the first 3 terms in Column B (12), Column A is greater. Since more than one relationship is possible, choice (D) is correct.

9. **The correct answer is 225.** You could set up an equation to solve for the values of the first 5 integers, but you won't have to if you remember that the average of a set of consecutive integers is equal to the middle term of that set. Since the sum of the first five integers is 200, its average and middle term must be $\frac{200}{5} = 40$. That means the fourth and fifth integers are 41 and 42. Therefore the last 5 integers are 43, 44, 45, 46 and 47, which sum to 225.

10. **The correct answer is 207.** Average times number of terms is equal to the sum of the terms, so the sum of these three different positive integers is $70 \times 3 = 210$. To find the greatest possible value of one of those terms, set the other two to the lowest possible values. The two smallest different positive integers are 1 and 2. That means the greatest possible value for the third integer is $210 - 1 - 2 = 207$.

Algebra

PRACTICE SET I

1. **The correct answer is (C).** $8(x + y) = 64$, so $x + y = 8$. Therefore, their average is $\frac{8}{2} = 4$.

2. **The correct answer is (E).** Evaluate each statement. Statement I must be true. Raising an even number to a power will always result in an even number. Eliminate choices (B) and (C) since they do not include statement I. For statement II, if $2n = 8$, $n = 4$. Since this statement isn't always true, eliminate choice (D) for including it. In statement III, since n is even, $2n$ will always be even. And since one less than an even number will always be an odd number, statement III must be true. Therefore, choice (E) is correct.

3. **The correct answer is (C).** If the greatest integer is x, the one that precedes it must be $x - 2$. Note that you must subtract in increments of 2 since the numbers involved are consecutive odd integers. The other 3 integers are $x - 4$, $x - 6$, and $x - 8$; $x - 8$ is the smallest. If this is too abstract you could have picked some numbers. Say that the 5 consecutive odd integers were 9, 7, 5, 3 and 1. If $x = 9$, then the smallest integer 1 would be represented as $9 - 8 = x - 8$.

4. **The correct answer is (D).** Pick values for the variables. If 5 baubles cost 10 dollars ($b = 5$ and $d = 10$), then each bauble costs 2 dollars. At this rate, $5 - 1$ or 4 baubles would cost 8 dollars. Plugging these values into the answer choices, only choice (D) gives you 8, so it is correct.

5. **The correct answer is (C).** Since $\frac{1}{x} + \frac{1}{y} = \frac{y}{xy} + \frac{x}{xy} = \frac{x + y}{xy}$ and $\frac{1}{x} + \frac{1}{y} = \frac{1}{z}$, $\frac{x + y}{xy} = \frac{1}{z}$. You're told that $xy = z$, so $x + y$ must be 1.

6. **The correct answer is (B).** Plugging in $a + 2$ for b in the second equation, $(a + 2) - 1 = c$, $a + 1 = c$, and $a = c - 1$. Therefore, Column B is greater.

7. **The correct answer is (B).** The columns are not equal. Since $\sqrt{14}$ is a little less than 4, then Column A is a little less than $\frac{4}{7}$. Since $\sqrt{2}$ is a little more than $\sqrt{1}$, it is a little more than 1 and therefore greater. You could have used your calculator if you weren't sure.

8. **The correct answer is 150.** Let $x = $ the number of each of the three types of coins the woman receives. Therefore $.25x + .10x + .05x = 20.00$, or $.40x = 20.00$, and $x = 50$. That means she has $3(50) = 150$ coins.

9. **The correct answer is 5/6 or .833** To find the maximum value of $\frac{x}{y}$, you want the largest value of x and the smallest value of y: $\frac{5}{6}$.

10. **The correct answer is 5:** $a^2 - b^2 = (a - b)(a + b)$. Plugging in the given values, $5 = 1(a + b)$ and $a + b = 5$.

PRACTICE SET II

1. **The correct answer is (C).** Cross-multiplying, $2p + 2q + 2r = 3p + 3q$. Isolating r, $2r = p + q$ and $r = \frac{p + q}{2}$.

2. **The correct answer is (A).** The formula $(x + y)^2 = x^2 + 2xy + y^2$ can be rearranged as $(x + y)^2 = x^2 + y^2 + 2(xy)$. Plugging in the given values, $(x + y)^2 = 15 + 2(5) = 25$. Since $(-5)^2 = 25$, choice (A) is correct.

3. **The correct answer is (D).** Let the amount of money Lori spends in each store be x. Ed spends $30 more than Lori does in the first store, or $x + 30$. In the second store, Lori spends $12 less than Ed does, so Ed spends $x + 12$. Therefore, Lori spends a total of $2x$ while Ed spends $2x + 42$, making choice (D) correct.

4. **The correct answer is (B).** Try values for the variables. Say Thad bikes 60 miles every 2 hours ($m = 60$ and $h = 2$). That means he bikes 30 miles in one hour and $\frac{1}{2}$ mile every minute. In 45 minutes, he would bike $45 \times \frac{1}{2} = 22\frac{1}{2}$ miles. Plugging these values into the answer choices, only (B) gives you $22\frac{1}{2}$, so it is correct.

5. **The correct answer is (A).** Since there are 100 cents in a dollar, Column A can be expressed as $\frac{100d}{33}$, which is greater than Column B.

6. **The correct answer is (D).** Try values for the variables. If $x = 2$ and $y = 1$, then 2 in Column A is greater than $\frac{1}{2}$ in Column B. But, if $x = -1$ and $y = -2$, then $\frac{1}{2}$ in Column A is less than 2 in Column B. Since more than one relationship is possible, choice (D) is correct.

7. **The correct answer is (B).** In Column A, $\frac{\sqrt{75}}{\sqrt{3}} = \sqrt{25} = 5$, so Column B is greater.

8. **The correct answer is 2.** Let x = the number. Translating, $x - 3 = 2x - 5$. Isolating x, $2 = x$.

9. **The correct answer is 5/8 or .625.** Since $\dfrac{a}{b} \times \dfrac{b}{c} = \dfrac{a}{c}$, $\dfrac{a}{c} = \dfrac{3}{4} \times \dfrac{5}{6} = \dfrac{15}{24}$. Since $\dfrac{15}{24}$ will not fit on the grid, reduce it to $\dfrac{5}{8}$, or grid it as a decimal.

10. **The correct answer is 2.** Subtracting the second equation from the first equation gives you $4a - 4b = 8$. When you factor out a 4, you find that $a - b = 2$.

PRACTICE SET III—*Real SAT Questions*

1. **The correct answer is (B).** Stack the two equations and you'll see that if you subtract the second from the first you'll have the answer:

$$\begin{array}{r} 10x + y = 8 \\ - (7x - y = 9) \\ \hline 3x + 2y = -1 \end{array}$$

2. **The correct answer is (D).** Simply plug into the formula prescribed for each symbol: $(5^2 + 5) - (4^2 - 4) = 30 - 12 = 18$

3. **The correct answer is (A).** Plugging into the formula prescribed for the rectangle symbol gives you:

$$(m + 1)^2 - (m + 1) = (m^2 + 2m + 1) - (m + 1)$$
$$= m^2 + 2m - m + 1 - 1$$
$$= m^2 + m$$

Since the triangle symbol directs you to sum the square of a number with that number, choice (A) is correct.

4. **The correct answer is (C).** To determine how many pints of jam Pam can make, simply divide the amount of berries set aside for jam by the number of grams required for each pint. If she uses 40 percent of the strawberries for pies, that means she has 60 percent or $\dfrac{3}{5}s$ to use for jam. Each pint of jam requires j grams: $\dfrac{3}{5}s \div j = \dfrac{3s}{5j}$.

5. **The correct answer is (B).** At the outset, the woman owns $\frac{1}{4}$ of the business and receives more shares in the course of the question. Therefore, she'll end up with more than $\frac{1}{4}$ of the business in the end; since $\frac{5}{24} < \frac{1}{4}$, choice (A) can't possibly be right. Since it's impossible for anyone to own more than 100 percent of the business, and $\frac{11}{6} > 1$, choice (E) is out as well. Originally, there are 4 equal shares in the business. The woman begins with 1 share, buys an additional $\frac{1}{2}$ share, then a $\frac{1}{3}$ share, for a total of $1 + \frac{1}{2} + \frac{1}{3} = 1\frac{5}{6} = \frac{11}{6}$ shares. This represents $\frac{\frac{11}{6}}{4} = \frac{11}{6} \times \frac{1}{4} = \frac{11}{24}$ of the entire business.

6. **The correct answer is (A).** Use values for the variables. Pick numbers that are easy to work with, and don't worry about whether you're coming up with a realistic price for a cup of coffee. Say that 8 ounces of ground beans cost 16 dollars, or $d = 16$. That means that each ounce costs $\frac{16}{8} = 2$ dollars. Say that each ounce of ground beans makes 4 cups of coffee, or $c = 4$. Therefore, the amount of ground beans necessary for one cup of coffee costs $\frac{2}{4} = \frac{1}{2}$ dollar. Plugging $d = 16$ and $c = 4$ into the answer choices, only choice (A) gives you $\frac{1}{2}$.

7. **The correct answer is (C).** Put the columns in the same form. Multiplying through in Column B you see that $3y + 6 = 15$. Since $3x + 6 = 15$, x and y must be equal.

8. **The correct answer is (C).** When multiplying powers with the same base, add the exponents. When raising powers to powers, multiply the exponents. Therefore, in Column A you have $(a^{30})(a^{36}) = a^{66}$ and in Column B you have a^{66}, making them equal.

9. **The correct answer is 25, 30, 35, or 40.** If x and y are different positive integers that sum to 5, there are 4 possible sets of values: $x = 1$ and $y = 4$, $x = 4$ and $y = 1$, $x = 2$ and $y = 3$, or $x = 3$ and $y = 2$. Plugging them into the equation $4x + 9y$, the respective values for each possibility are 40, 25, 35, and 30. Remember that for Grid-ins with more than one correct answer there's no reason to come up with all the solutions. Simply find one correct answer and move on.

10. **The correct answer is 2.** Recognizing the common factorable in this question makes solving a breeze. The equation $x^2 - y^2 = 10$ can be factored into $(x + y)(x - y) = 10$. Since you know that $x + y = 5$, $5(x - y) = 10$ and $x - y = 2$.

Geometry

PRACTICE SET I

1. **The correct answer is (D).** The ratio of the areas of similar figures is equal to the square of the ratio of their corresponding linear measurements. Since the ratio of the circles' diameters is 1:2, the ratio of their areas is 1:4. Therefore, the area of the circle with diameter $2d = 4A$.

2. **The correct answer is (D).** The angles opposite equal sides in a triangle are also equal; since $AB = AC$, $\angle ABC = \angle ACB = x°$. Since the three angles of a triangle sum to 180°, angle $BAC = 180° - 2x°$.

3. **The correct answer is (A).** Visualize the situation: rolling a cylindrical paint roller on the wall produces a rectangular region of blue paint, with one side of length 12. The length of its other side will be equal to the circumference of the roller. Since the area of the region is 48, the circumference must be $48 \div 12 = 4$. Circumference equals $2\pi r$, where r is the radius. Therefore $2\pi r = 4$, $r = \dfrac{4}{2\pi} = \dfrac{2}{\pi}$.

4. **The correct answer is (B).** Make a sketch for yourself:

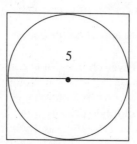

   Note that the diameter of the circle is equal to a side of the square. Area of a circle is πr^2 where r is the radius. The radius is $\dfrac{5}{2} = 2.5$, so the area is $\pi(2.5)^2 = 6.25\pi$.

5. **The correct answer is (B).** A line is defined by the equation $y = mx + b$ where m is the slope of the line. Subtract $2x$ from both sides to put the given equation into standard form: $y = -2x + b$. Therefore the slope is -2 and Column B is greater.

6. **The correct answer is (C).** The exterior angle of a triangle is equal to the sum of the two remote interior angles, so $z = x + y$. Subtracting x from both sides, $z - x = y$ and the columns are equal.

7. **The correct answer is (B).** Since OA and OB are both radii of circle O, they are equal. In a triangle, angles opposite equal sides are also equal, so $\angle OAB = \angle OBA = 59°$. The angles of a triangle sum to 180°, so $\angle AOB = 180 - 2(59°) = 62°$. Since the angle opposite AB is greater than the angle opposite OA, AB is greater.

8. **The correct answer is 36.** The angles of a triangle sum to 180, so $2x + 3x + 5x = 180$, $10x = 180$, and $x = 18$. The smallest angle is $2x = 2(18) = 36$.

9. **The correct answer is 7/2 or 3.5.** The line passes through point $(2,7)$ and the origin, which has coordinates $(0,0)$. Plugging into the slope formula: $\dfrac{(y_2 - y_1)}{(x_2 - x_1)} = \dfrac{7 - 0}{2 - 0} = \dfrac{7}{2}$ or grid it in as a decimal.

10. **The correct answer is 9.** Volume of a cube is equal to e^3 where e is an edge of the cube. Volume of a rectangular solid is equal to $l \times w \times h$, where l, w, and h represent, respectively, the length, width, and height of the solid. Therefore $6^3 = h(12 \times 2)$ and $9 = h$.

PRACTICE SET II

1. **The correct answer is (E).** Plug into the slope formula: $\dfrac{(y_2 - y_1)}{(x_2 - x_1)} = \dfrac{0 - (-3)}{5 - 3} = \dfrac{3}{2}$.

2. **The correct answer is (D).** When dealing with combined figures, look for pieces they have in common. If you sketch in a line connecting the centers of the two circles you'll see that it is also a diagonal of the square. This line is composed of a radius of each circle; since the circles are equal their radii are equal and the diagonal equals $2r$. The area of a circle is 18π, so $\pi r^2 = 18\pi$, $r^2 = 18$ and $r = \sqrt{18} = \sqrt{9} \times \sqrt{2} = 3\sqrt{2}$. Therefore, the diagonal is $6\sqrt{2}$. The diagonal of a square is equal to a side times $\sqrt{2}$ (since it is essentially made up of two isosceles right triangles with the leg/hypotenuse ratio of $1{:}\sqrt{2}$.) Since the diagonal is $6\sqrt{2}$, the side of the square must be 6. Perimeter of a square is equal to $4s = 4(6) = 24$.

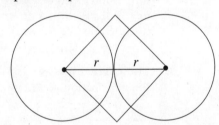

3. **The correct answer is (B).** Area of a rectangle is lw where l and w represent its length and width respectively. Therefore $64 = 16w$ and $w = 4$. Perimeter of a rectangle is $2(l + w)$ or $2(16 + 4) = 40$.

4. **The correct answer is (B).** Since DE is parallel to BC, $\angle ADE = \angle ABC$ and $\angle AED = \angle ACB$. Since both $\triangle ADE$ and $\triangle ABC$ contain $\angle A$, all three of their angles are equal and they are similar. The sides of similar triangles are proportional. Since $AD = \dfrac{DB}{2}$, $2AD = DB$. Since $AB = AD + DB$, $AB = 3AD$, and $AD = \dfrac{1}{3}AB$. Since the perimeter of $\triangle ABC = 24$, the perimeter of $\triangle ADE = \dfrac{1}{3}(24) = 8$.

5. **The correct answer is (A).** An isosceles triangle has 2 equal sides, so the third side of this triangle must be either 3 or 7. By the triangle inequality theorem, the third side of any triangle must be less than the sum of the other two sides and greater than their positive difference. In this case, the third side must be between $7 - 3$ and $7 + 3$, or $4 <$ third side < 10. Since the third side must be greater than 4, it must be 7 and Column A is greater.

6. **The correct answer is (B).** Area of a triangle is $\frac{1}{2}bh$ where b and h are its base and height, respectively. The base of $\triangle XYZ$ is 4, so its area is $\frac{1}{2}(4)(h) = 2h$. Its height is the perpendicular distance from Y to XZ. Sketching it in you see that is the leg of two right triangles with hypotenuses of 4. Without figuring its exact length you know that it must be less than 4, since the hypotenuse must be the longest side of a right triangle. Therefore the area of $\triangle XYZ$ must be less than $2(4) = 8$.

7. **The correct answer is (D).** A straight line has 180°, so $x + y + 90 = 180$ and $x + y = 90$. You don't know anything about their relative values, though. Both angles could be 45°, in which case the columns would be equal, or x could be 30° and y, 60°, in which case Column B would be greater. Since more than one relationship is possible, choice (D) is correct.

8. **The correct answer is 30.** Area of a square is s^2, where s is a side of the square. Since the area of each square is 25, $25 = s^2$ and $s = 5$. The rectangle's perimeter is composed of 6 square sides, so it is $6(5) = 30$.

9. **The correct answer is $10 <$ perimeter < 18.** Perimeter of a triangle is equal to the sum of its three sides, in this case, $4 + 5 + x$ or $9 + x$. The third side of a triangle must be greater than the positive difference of the other two sides and less than their sum. In this case, $5 - 4 < x < 5 + 4$ or $1 < x < 9$. Therefore the perimeter of the triangle must be between $9 + 1 = 10$ and $9 + 9 = 18$, or $10 <$ perimeter < 18. Any answer in this range would be acceptable.

10. **The correct answer is 1/3, .333, or .334.** Make a sketch to organize the information you're given.

Since Y is the midpoint of WZ, $WY = YZ$. Since X is the midpoint of WY, $WX = XY$. You can see that $XY = \frac{1}{4}WZ$. Since $XZ = XY + YZ$ and $YZ = \frac{1}{2}WZ$, $XZ = \frac{1}{4}WZ + \frac{1}{2}WZ = \frac{3}{4}WZ$. Therefore,

$$\frac{XY}{XZ} = \frac{\frac{1}{4}WZ}{\frac{3}{4}WZ} = \frac{1}{3}.$$

PRACTICE SET III—*Real SAT Questions*

1. **The correct answer is (D).** The area of the shaded region is the area of the rectangle minus the area of one circle (the sum of the areas of the two equal semi-circles). Since $AB = 12$ and $AD = 16$, the area of the rectangle is $12 \times 16 = 192$. Since AB is equal to the diameter of the circle, the diameter of the circle is 12, its radius is 6 and its area is $\pi(6)^2 = 36\pi$. Therefore, the area of the shaded region is $192 - 36\pi$, choice (D).

2. **The correct answer is (A).** Since line ℓ passes through point $(1, 3)$ and the origin $(0, 0)$, its slope is $\frac{3 - 0}{1 - 0} = 3$. Since (h, k) lies on line ℓ, it must also produce a slope of 3 when plugged into the slope formula with either of these points. Plugging point (h, k) into the slope formula with the origin you see that $\frac{k - 0}{h - 0} = \frac{k}{h} = 3$.

3. **The correct answer is (D).** Both figures are isosceles right triangles so they are similar. Corresponding lengths of similar figures are proportional. Since the ratio of the hypotenuses z and $\frac{1}{3}z$ is 3:1, the ratio of the legs must also be 3:1. Therefore, leg y of the larger triangle must be 3 times as great as leg x of the smaller triangle, and $y = 3x$.

4. **The correct answer is (C).** A line that rises from left to right has a positive slope. Two diagonals with positive slope can be drawn, AC and AD. None of the other diagonals that can be drawn rise from left to right.

5. **The correct answer is (B).** Area of a triangle is equal to $\frac{1}{2}bh$, where b is its base and h its height. Both the base and height of the triangle are radii of the circle, and therefore have length 10. The area of triangle AOB is $\frac{1}{2}(10)(10) = 50$.

6. **The correct answer is (E).** Sketch in length AB. Drop a perpendicular from A down to the bottom circumference of the cylinder and call this point C. Then connect C to B and you have a right triangle. The height of this triangle is AC, which is the height of the cylinder or 5. The base of this triangle is CB, which is the diameter of the cylinder. Since the radius of the cylinder is 2, its diameter is 4. To solve for AB, use the Pythagorean theorem:

$$5^2 + 4^2 = AB^2$$
$$41 = AB^2$$
$$\sqrt{41} = AB$$

7. **The correct answer is (D).** You might think that increasing the radius of each circle by the same amount would necessarily result in equal increases in area. If the circles originally have the same radius, that is indeed the case. If both circles originally had radii of 5, their original areas would be 25π; increasing the radii to 6 would result in areas of 36π. This would produce an increase of 9π in the area of each circle. But suppose that the original radius of circle A is 5 and the original radius of circle B is 10. The area of circle A would increase from 25π to 36π, a change of 9π, while the area of circle B would increase from 100π to 121π, a change of 21π. Since the relationship varies depending on the original values of the radii, choice (D) must be correct.

8. **The correct answer is (D).** Perimeter of a square is equal to $4s$ where s is a side of the square. A square with perimeter 12 has a side length of $\frac{12}{4} = 3$. Perimeter of a rectangle is equal to $2(l + w)$ where l and w represent its length and width, respectively. There are several possible values for l and w that will result in a perimeter of 12, for example 1 and 5. If the length is 1, then 3 in Column A is greater; if the length is 5, then it is greater than 3 in Column A. Since more than one relationship is possible, the answer is (D).

9. **The correct answer is (C).** Both ABC and ABD are right triangles, and both have hypotenuse AB. According to the Pythagorean theorem, the square of the hypotenuse is equal to the sum of the squares of the legs. Column A contains the sum of the squares of the legs of triangle ABC and Column B contains the sum of the squares of the legs of triangle ABD. Since the hypotenuses of these triangles are equal, the sums of the squares of their legs must also be equal.

10. **The correct answer is 3.5 or 7/2.** The distance from the center of a circle to its circumference is its radius. Since you're told that the figure is a semi-circle, you know that its center must lie on the x-axis. Since the y-coordinate of the x-axis is 0, the point on the semi-circle farthest from the x-axis will have a y-coordinate equal to the radius of the circle. From the figure you can see that the diameter of the semi-circle is 7, so its radius is 3.5.

Verbal Teaching Unit
Analogy

PRACTICE SET I

1. **The correct answer is (A).** A METER is a measure of LENGTH, as a pound is a measure of weight.

2. **The correct answer is (D).** Somebody RUTHLESS has no PITY, as somebody bewildered has no comprehension.

3. **The correct answer is (E).** The job of a PHILOSOPHER is to REASON, as the job of a speaker is to orate.

4. **The correct answer is (D).** A SCRIVENER's job is to create a SCROLL, as a seamstress' job is to create a garment.

5. **The correct answer is (A).** When a CHILD grows older it will MATURE, as when a bud grows older it will burgeon.

6. **The correct answer is (C).** TORTUOUS describes a winding PATH, as convoluted describes winding prose.

7. **The correct answer is (B).** A MENDICANT by definition is never WEALTHY, as an expert by definition is never inept.

8. **The correct answer is (A).** The purpose of an EMOLLIENT is to SOOTHE, as the purpose of a glaze is to finish.

9. **The correct answer is (A).** OBESE is an extreme degree of HEAVY, as distraught is an extreme degree of sad.

10. **The correct answer is (E).** Something TRITE has no NOVELTY, as something torpid has no energy.

PRACTICE SET II

1. **The correct answer is (C).** A BRANCH is a larger version of a TWIG, as a river is a larger version of a stream.

2. **The correct answer is (A).** A GRAM is a measure of WEIGHT, as an inch is a measure of length.

3. **The correct answer is (B).** A ROSE is a type of FLOWER, as an elm is a type of tree.

4. **The correct answer is (D).** A GLADE is an opening between TREEs, as a pass is an opening between mountains.

5. **The correct answer is (C).** WAN means lacking RUDDINESS, as vapid means lacking depth.

6. **The correct answer is (E).** A MANNER that is rudely short is called BRUSQUE, as speech that is rudely short is called curt.

7. **The correct answer is (A).** An ORACLE by definition has FORESIGHT, as a sage by definition has wisdom.

8. **The correct answer is (B).** A MUSEUM is the place for a DISPLAY, as a theatre is the place for a performance.

9. **The correct answer is (D).** This one's easier if you reverse the order of the words. When ENERGY fades it FLAGs; when light fades it wanes.

10. **The correct answer is (E).** Someone MENDACIOUS has no VERACITY, as someone conceited has no humility.

PRACTICE SET III—*Real SAT Questions*

1. **The correct answer is (B).** The purpose of EXPOSITION is to CLARIFY, as the purpose of refutation is to disprove.

2. **The correct answer is (B).** PARODY is an exaggerated form of IMITATION, as caricature is an exaggerated form of likeness.

3. **The correct answer is (D).** Something BULKY has a lot of VOLUME, as something hefty has a lot of weight.

4. **The correct answer is (D).** A FORD is the place where you cross a RIVER, as a crosswalk is the place where you cross a road.

5. **The correct answer is (E).** PRECIPITATE means having too much HASTE, as overwrought means having too much excitement.

6. **The correct answer is (C).** To ASK repeatedly is to IMPORTUNE, as to pursue repeatedly is to hound.

7. **The correct answer is (E).** CONVALESCENCE is a process of becoming HEALTHY, as reclamation is a process of becoming useful.

8. **The correct answer is (E).** A BRUISE is a mark on the SKIN, as a stain is a mark on fabric.

9. **The correct answer is (B).** POISON is always TOXIC, as sugar is always sweet.

10. **The correct answer is (C).** A POSTSCRIPT comes after the end of LETTER, as an epilogue comes after the end of a play.

Sentence Completion

PRACTICE SET I

1. **The correct answer is (E).** Either the large amount of fish made looking elsewhere unnecessary, or the small amount of fish made looking elsewhere necessary. It makes sense that the *abundance* (large amount) of fish *forestalled* (prevented) their need to look elsewhere for fish.

2. **The correct answer is (A).** If few people went to see the play, it must have had a *modest* (small) run.

3. **The correct answer is (C).** The first blank has to support the fact the clarinet is a popular instrument, and the second blank is going to be a word that means a good musician. *Appealing* and *virtuoso* (person with great skill) are the best answers.

4. **The correct answer is (A).** Start with the second blank—what effect would the cell's complexity have on the way scientists describe it? It would *defy* (challenge) description. The first blank, then, is going to be a word that shows the puzzling nature of the living cell. A *conundrum* is a riddle.

5. **The correct answer is (D).** This one's straight vocabulary. What would continue to puzzle physicians? An *enigma* (something baffling).

6. **The correct answer is (D).** This is a sentence of contrast. Once, the park was a great place, and now its purity has been ruined by pollution and neglect. *Idyllic* means peaceful and rural, and *compromised* in this context means weakened.

7. **The correct answer is (B).** This is a contrast sentence. If Shaker furniture is simple, it must lack *ornate* (showy) embellishments (decorations).

8. **The correct answer is (C).** It helps to know that dissention is fighting, but you can still figure this one out if you don't. Both words describe something plague-like. Virulent means poisonous, and tenacious means holding firmly, a good word to describe a strong grip.

9. **The correct answer is (B).** The word *unfortunately* in the middle of this sentence signals a contrast. What kind of worker thinks of new approaches to old problems? An *innovative* (introducing changes) one. The second blank has to be a word that means something like *didn't like*—or *discouraged*. Only choice (B) works for both blanks.

10. **The correct answer is (E).** This is a sentence of contrast. Once the exhibits sat behind glass, not moving—now, they are *accessible* (approachable). Sounds like the museum has undergone *noticeable* change, and the accessible exhibits encourage viewer *participation*.

PRACTICE SET II

1. **The correct answer is (D).** The word *although* is your clue that this is a sentence of contrast. What's the opposite of clear and direct? *Obscure* (unclear).

2. **The correct answer is (B).** The first blank goes together with *difficult concepts*, so it must mean something like *confusing*, and the second blank describes how this hard material was for students who previously had no trouble in school. Apparently they're having trouble now because the book is so difficult. *Dense* (difficult to get through) and *challenged* both work.

3. **The correct answer is (D).** Since Christopher *discarded* (threw away) the rest of his research, which information did he keep? The *relevant* (important) information.

4. **The correct answer is (C).** Start with the second blank—what word goes with *atonal* (without tone)? The best choice is *jarring* (having a harsh sound). Because jarring is a negative word, it makes sense that the critics *deplored* (disapproved of) the music.

5. **The correct answer is (A).** *Daunted* (intimidated) is the best choice. Choice (B), *threatened* is a close second, but it's a little too strong—a steep trail doesn't actually threaten, but it does intimidate.

6. **The correct answer is (B).** The word *despite* signals a contrast. Sarah must be a good public orator despite the fact that in private she rarely speaks. Choices (B), (C), (D), and (E) could all work for the first blank, but only choice (B) works for the second blank, as well. In private Sarah is *taciturn* (quiet).

7. **The correct answer is (D).** It makes sense that you would need to make sure the witness is telling the truth before you can ask him to testify. To *verify* is to check for correctness, or accuracy.

8. **The correct answer is (C).** The gist of this sentence is that the professor is trying to prove that a story other people say is a myth, is actually true. *Legend* is the best answer.

9. **The correct answer is (B).** This complicated sentence boils down to a simple contrast. Now, people can pick from many kinds of cars; in the past, there weren't so many kinds. If there weren't many choices, car-buyers did not have a *glut* (large amount, excess) of models from which to choose.

10. **The correct answer is (E).** This sentence contrasts a *benign* (harmless) personality with one *bent on evil*. A character that goes from harmless to evil undergoes a change, or *metamorphosis*. A *ruthless* (cruel) character would be bent on evil.

PRACTICE SET III—*Real SAT Questions*

1. **The correct answer is (B).** This is a straight definition sentence. The phrase *confining his remarks* tells you that he doesn't speak much, so he is *laconic* (using few words) and uses *concise* (brief) expression.

2. **The correct answer is (E).** If novelists have *forsaken* (left behind) complicated plots and descriptions, they now must use *unadorned* (simple) ones.

3. **The correct answer is (C).** The actress manages to show the wit of her characters even though her most *ingenious* (clever) lines have been cut.

4. **The correct answer is (D).** This sentence contains the phrase *on the contrary*, a giveaway that there's a contrast. The contrast is between what certain people said about Mr. Frank and the truth about him. These people said Mr. Frank was always *at odds with* (against) the officers, but the truth was the opposite: his ideas were pretty similar to theirs. What people would say these things about Mr. Frank? People who didn't like him. *Disparagers* are people who speak badly about someone. *Incompatible* means not going well together—if Mr. Frank's ideas are *not at all incompatible* with the officers', it means they pretty much agree on things.

5. **The correct answer is (E).** The first blank is defined by the phrase *its pointed movement toward a single moment of discovery*. The only choice that works is *compression* (being packed closely together). *Precariousness* (uncertainty) works for the second blank, as would any of the other choices.

6. **The correct answer is (D).** Simplify this sentence before you tackle it: People tend to fool themselves, so the need to *something* this tendency with respect for *something* is important. You can predict that the first blank means something like *temper* or *balance*, and the second blank is something like *truth*. Choice (D) fits perfectly.

7. **The correct answer is (D).** *Amorality* is a lack of morals, so Robert must be able to commit *odious* (hateful) acts without *evincing* (showing) even a hint of *compunction* (regret).

8. **The correct answer is (C).** If advances that were once undreamed of are now so common they seem dull, consumers must be *jaded* (bored, unimpressed).

9. **The correct answer is (C).** What kind of areas would make the herb *difficult to study*? *Inaccessible* (hard to get to) ones.

10. **The correct answer is (A).** The word *ironically* signals a contrast. It is ironic—the opposite of what you'd expect—that the people who brought bankruptcy are celebrated (praised). These people who did the praising, the contemporaries, somehow *cherished* (held dear) the idea that the executives were heroes.

Critical Reading

PRACTICE SET I

1. **The correct answer is (B).** The author of the passage is clearly a fan of Jane Austen. You can anticipate that the answer is going to be something like "admiring." Eliminate choices (A) and (D) because they both imply a hesitation that the author doesn't display. Choice (E) goes too far; the author likes Austen a lot but doesn't blindly worship her. You can eliminate choice (C) *clearly unbiased* because the author is biased in favor of Austen. The best answer is choice (B).

2. **The correct answer is (D).** The passage praises Austen for all of the choices except for choice (D) the realism of her plots. The last paragraph says that "Austen's novels are essentially fairy tales-fantasies" (lines 42–43). The paragraph goes on to describe Austen's novels as "grounded in realism . . . but fantasies nevertheless."

3. **The correct answer is (D).** Go back to the second paragraph, and reread the part in which the author compares Austen and Shakespeare. The passage says "Both the novels and the comedies demonstrate how much human nature may be revealed . . . within a limited plot" (lines 20–24). In other words, both authors created rich characters, even when their plots weren't very surprising.

4. **The correct answer is (A).** The very first line of the passage describes Austen's universal appeal: "Everyone loves Jane Austen's novels . . ." The passage goes on to discuss why the novels have such universal appeal, a fact that the author clearly admires. All of the other answer choices are contradicted in the passage.

5. **The correct answer is (A).** Go back to the passage, and reread the word *sound* in context. The passage says that Austen's novels are made credible (believable) by careful observation and sound precepts of moral behavior. Even if you don't know that precepts are rules, you can figure out that to make novels credible, they must be true, or choice (A) *based on truth*.

6. **The correct answer is (D).** This question requires you to understand and paraphrase lines 20–24. These lines say that Austen's novels and Shakespeare's comedies reveal a lot about human nature (in other words, create complex characters) within limited plots.

7. **The correct answer is (D).** The author says that although Austen seems rational at first, her work is "firmly rooted in the realm of the feelings." The sentence sets up a contrast between the appearance of being rational and the realm of the feelings. The next sentence says that Austen's novels are "essentially fairy tales." In other words, "the realm of the feelings" is the nonrational, fairy-tale aspect of Austen's work.

8. **The correct answer is (E).** The referenced sentence says that some of Austen's popularity may be due to a particular element in her books: the success of the weak over the powerful. You can translate "Austen's popularity" to "people like to read her books." You can infer that if people like to read about the success of the weak over the powerful, they like to read about people overcoming *adversity* (hardship). You can eliminate choice (A), because it goes too far; there's nothing in the text to support it. The passage contradicts choice (B) by saying that Austen's heroines do not have a great deal of power. There is no basis at all for choices (C) and (D), so eliminate them.

9. **The correct answer is (B).** The first paragraph of the passage says that Austen's "subject is courtship" (line 10) and that her stories all end in a happy marriage. Choice (B), *relationships*, is the best choice.

PRACTICE SET II

1. **The correct answer is (E).** You need to find an answer that is neither too broad nor too narrow. Choices (A), (C), and (D) are all too broad to be the correct answer. Choice (B) is too narrow; the passage does discuss psychological testing, but it also discusses physical tests. The best answer is choice (E).

2. **The correct answer is (C).** The passage says that astronauts, like argonauts, "were to sail into a new, uncharted ocean." This is a figure of speech, not a literal description, so eliminate choice (A). It may be true that both groups choice (B), *took great risks to benefit mankind*, but that's not the reason why the passage compares them. What's the best way to sum up "sail into a new, uncharted ocean?" It's choice (C) *ventured into unknown territory*.

3. **The correct answer is (A).** The second paragraph specifically explains that the astronauts did not appear to be an elite group; rather, they seemed like average people.

4. **The correct answer is (B).** Rereading around the referenced sentence, you can see that the astronauts did not appear to be members of an elite; they wore civilian clothing, spoke plainly, and were average-looking. As a result, the public "forgot that they were volunteer test subjects and military officers." In other words, the astronauts did not match the public's expectations of military officers.

5. **The correct answer is (E).** Remember that to infer is to use what is written on the page to figure out something that isn't. It's important not to go too far when you make an inference. You may have been tempted by choice (A), but there's no real reason to believe that NASA was "experimenting" when they performed these tests. Choice (B) may well have been true, but it doesn't follow logically from the fact that NASA performed many tests. The description of the tests—all physical in nature—indicates that the astronauts would have to endure difficult conditions like these when they went into space.

6. **The correct answer is (D).** If circumstances *whetted* an insatiable (too huge to be satisfied) appetite, they must have done something to cause or increase it. Choice (D), *stimulated*, is the best answer.

7. **The correct answer is (E).** The sentence after the referenced one provides some context. It says that as pilots advance in their careers, the standards for skills and health become even stricter. The fact that only the best pilots can meet these conditions is "the natural selection process."

8. **The correct answer is (A).** If you read further down in the paragraph, you find that the "parlor game" exercises required the subject to answer the questions "Who am I?" and that the results were used to elicit "information on identity and perception of social roles." The tests, then, were used to determine how the subjects viewed themselves and their social role.

9. **The correct answer is (B).** In order to understand the quote, you need to read what prompted it. If you go back a couple of sentences from the end, you can see that the quote was in response to the difficult questioning. You can infer that "Nothing is sacred anymore" because the astronauts are required to reveal a great deal of information to the testers; in other words, the tests felt psychologically invasive.

PRACTICE SET III—*Real SAT Questions*

1. **The correct answer is (D).** Passage 1 describes the traditional Black narrative, which starts with a state of imprisonment and "involves the character's attempt to break out" (line 7). Passage 2 is about "dramatizations of imprisonment and escape" (lines 1-2) in nineteenth-century literature by women.

2. **The correct answer is (D).** Passage 1 uses the specific example of Frederick Douglass' autobiography to discuss the Black narrative tradition. Choice (A) may have been a tempting choice, but the only quotes in the passage came from Douglass' Narrative, not from other texts. The best answer, then, is choice (D).

3. **The correct answer is (A).** Go back to the passage and reread the referenced lines (plus the context around them). The passage states that at the end of a Black narrative, "the character has seldom achieved a state of ideal freedom" (lines 9-10). In other words, there are no simple, happy endings in these passages. Each pair of nouns, "hope and despair," "madness and sanity," and "repleteness (fullness) and longing," illustrates the complexity of the endings. Choice (B) is a tempting answer because it mentions contradictions. While each noun pair can be described as a contradiction, the narratives do not explain the contradictions in the endings as the choice suggests.

4. **The correct answer is (B).** Find the part of the passage that discusses Douglass' arrival in New York (lines 44–45). He "is still unsure of himself" and "fearful of the omnipresent threat of capture." He behaves, then, like someone who choice (B), *is aware of the tenuous* (weak, easily threatened) nature of his freedom. Because the threat of capture is very real, eliminate choice (D). While Douglass took a great risk in getting to New York, the question asks specifically about his behavior upon his arrival, so eliminate choice (E). There is no evidence in the passage to support choices (A) or (C).

5. **The correct answer is (B).** Go back to the passage and read the sentence that uses "thoroughgoing." It's a tricky word, but you know that it's got to mean something negative, since Douglass goes to great lengths to avoid "the thoroughgoing 'justice' of the White world." (The fact that "justice" is in quotes, indicating that it's not really justice, is also a clue.) Immediately you can eliminate choices (A), (C), and (D). Choice (E) is the second-best choice, but it goes a bit too far and is a bit too specific. It's not specifically violence that Douglass fears; it is the entire legal system, which is biased against Blacks.

6. **The correct answer is (C).** The referenced quote says, "The Black narrative does not offer a comfortable majority report." In other words, reading it makes people uncomfortable. Choice (D) may have seemed tempting, but it reads too far into the text. The answer is right on the surface—it's choice (C).

7. **The correct answer is (D).** You'll definitely need to go back to the passage and read around the referenced lines to solve this one. The paragraph explains that in a certain type of literature, "paraphernalia of 'woman's place'" is used to "enact their central symbolic drama of enclosure and escape" (lines 9–10). This is a complicated way of saying that the things women used in their homes showed up as symbols of oppression in nineteenth-century literature. The objects listed in lines 11–15 are examples of these symbols. In other words, they suggest choice (D), the limitations placed on women.

8. **The correct answer is (A).** In solving this question, it may be helpful to paraphrase (restate) the Dickinson quote. Essentially, she says that she feels like her life has been confined to a small space, and the only way she can bear that feeling of confinement is to imagine explosive moments in which her soul escapes into freedom. Her language and her feelings are best described as choice (A), *hints at the intensity of the urge to be free*.

9. **The correct answer is (A).** This is a tricky question, because several of the answers seem possible. Notice that the referenced quote describes a woman's soul exploding like a bomb. This hint of possible violence is best expressed by choice (A). While choices (B), (D), and (E) may well have been true, there is no evidence in the passage to support them, as there is for choice (A).

10. **The correct answer is (E).** This vocabulary-in-context question is a difficult one. The female author wants to escape "male houses and male constructs." You can figure out that "male houses" are physical buildings, so "male constructs" must be something else. The passage isn't about architecture or inventions, so eliminate choices (C) and (D). The passage doesn't discuss literature written by men, so eliminate choice (A). Chocie (B) is out because the passage is concerned with definitions of femininity, not masculinity. The best answer is choice (E); in addition to escaping from houses, women wanted to escape from the ideas about their lives that men had established.

11. **The correct answer is (D).** This question asks you to look at the main idea that the two passages have in common. Both passage are about oppressed people's desire for choice (D) *freedom and power*.

12. **The correct answer is (C).** You'll need to go through each answer choice to solve this question. Eliminate choice (A), because each passage uses a specific case (Douglass and Dickinson) to demonstrate an idea. There is no evidence to support choice (B), so eliminate it. How about choice (C)? Passage 1 ends by talking about a process moving toward human dignity—an expression of optimism. Passage 2 ends with a description of anger so strong it can no longer be contained—not very optimistic. Choice (C), then, is a good choice. Just in case, look at the last two choices. Choice (D) is out—if anything, Passage 1 talks more about political and legal considerations. Choice (E) is a tricky one, but remember that line about "male constructs" in Passage 2? Both passages name an oppressor, so you can eliminate choice (E). The best answer is choice (C).

Answer Sheets

SECTION 1

1 Ⓐ Ⓑ Ⓒ Ⓓ Ⓔ 11 Ⓐ Ⓑ Ⓒ Ⓓ Ⓔ 21 Ⓐ Ⓑ Ⓒ Ⓓ Ⓔ 31 Ⓐ Ⓑ Ⓒ Ⓓ Ⓔ
2 Ⓐ Ⓑ Ⓒ Ⓓ Ⓔ 12 Ⓐ Ⓑ Ⓒ Ⓓ Ⓔ 22 Ⓐ Ⓑ Ⓒ Ⓓ Ⓔ 32 Ⓐ Ⓑ Ⓒ Ⓓ Ⓔ
3 Ⓐ Ⓑ Ⓒ Ⓓ Ⓔ 13 Ⓐ Ⓑ Ⓒ Ⓓ Ⓔ 23 Ⓐ Ⓑ Ⓒ Ⓓ Ⓔ 33 Ⓐ Ⓑ Ⓒ Ⓓ Ⓔ
4 Ⓐ Ⓑ Ⓒ Ⓓ Ⓔ 14 Ⓐ Ⓑ Ⓒ Ⓓ Ⓔ 24 Ⓐ Ⓑ Ⓒ Ⓓ Ⓔ 34 Ⓐ Ⓑ Ⓒ Ⓓ Ⓔ
5 Ⓐ Ⓑ Ⓒ Ⓓ Ⓔ 15 Ⓐ Ⓑ Ⓒ Ⓓ Ⓔ 25 Ⓐ Ⓑ Ⓒ Ⓓ Ⓔ 35 Ⓐ Ⓑ Ⓒ Ⓓ Ⓔ
6 Ⓐ Ⓑ Ⓒ Ⓓ Ⓔ 16 Ⓐ Ⓑ Ⓒ Ⓓ Ⓔ 26 Ⓐ Ⓑ Ⓒ Ⓓ Ⓔ 36 Ⓐ Ⓑ Ⓒ Ⓓ Ⓔ
7 Ⓐ Ⓑ Ⓒ Ⓓ Ⓔ 17 Ⓐ Ⓑ Ⓒ Ⓓ Ⓔ 27 Ⓐ Ⓑ Ⓒ Ⓓ Ⓔ 37 Ⓐ Ⓑ Ⓒ Ⓓ Ⓔ
8 Ⓐ Ⓑ Ⓒ Ⓓ Ⓔ 18 Ⓐ Ⓑ Ⓒ Ⓓ Ⓔ 28 Ⓐ Ⓑ Ⓒ Ⓓ Ⓔ 38 Ⓐ Ⓑ Ⓒ Ⓓ Ⓔ
9 Ⓐ Ⓑ Ⓒ Ⓓ Ⓔ 19 Ⓐ Ⓑ Ⓒ Ⓓ Ⓔ 29 Ⓐ Ⓑ Ⓒ Ⓓ Ⓔ 39 Ⓐ Ⓑ Ⓒ Ⓓ Ⓔ
10 Ⓐ Ⓑ Ⓒ Ⓓ Ⓔ 20 Ⓐ Ⓑ Ⓒ Ⓓ Ⓔ 30 Ⓐ Ⓑ Ⓒ Ⓓ Ⓔ 40 Ⓐ Ⓑ Ⓒ Ⓓ Ⓔ

SECTION 2

1 Ⓐ Ⓑ Ⓒ Ⓓ Ⓔ 11 Ⓐ Ⓑ Ⓒ Ⓓ Ⓔ 21 Ⓐ Ⓑ Ⓒ Ⓓ Ⓔ 31 Ⓐ Ⓑ Ⓒ Ⓓ Ⓔ
2 Ⓐ Ⓑ Ⓒ Ⓓ Ⓔ 12 Ⓐ Ⓑ Ⓒ Ⓓ Ⓔ 22 Ⓐ Ⓑ Ⓒ Ⓓ Ⓔ 32 Ⓐ Ⓑ Ⓒ Ⓓ Ⓔ
3 Ⓐ Ⓑ Ⓒ Ⓓ Ⓔ 13 Ⓐ Ⓑ Ⓒ Ⓓ Ⓔ 23 Ⓐ Ⓑ Ⓒ Ⓓ Ⓔ 33 Ⓐ Ⓑ Ⓒ Ⓓ Ⓔ
4 Ⓐ Ⓑ Ⓒ Ⓓ Ⓔ 14 Ⓐ Ⓑ Ⓒ Ⓓ Ⓔ 24 Ⓐ Ⓑ Ⓒ Ⓓ Ⓔ 34 Ⓐ Ⓑ Ⓒ Ⓓ Ⓔ
5 Ⓐ Ⓑ Ⓒ Ⓓ Ⓔ 15 Ⓐ Ⓑ Ⓒ Ⓓ Ⓔ 25 Ⓐ Ⓑ Ⓒ Ⓓ Ⓔ 35 Ⓐ Ⓑ Ⓒ Ⓓ Ⓔ
6 Ⓐ Ⓑ Ⓒ Ⓓ Ⓔ 16 Ⓐ Ⓑ Ⓒ Ⓓ Ⓔ 26 Ⓐ Ⓑ Ⓒ Ⓓ Ⓔ 36 Ⓐ Ⓑ Ⓒ Ⓓ Ⓔ
7 Ⓐ Ⓑ Ⓒ Ⓓ Ⓔ 17 Ⓐ Ⓑ Ⓒ Ⓓ Ⓔ 27 Ⓐ Ⓑ Ⓒ Ⓓ Ⓔ 37 Ⓐ Ⓑ Ⓒ Ⓓ Ⓔ
8 Ⓐ Ⓑ Ⓒ Ⓓ Ⓔ 18 Ⓐ Ⓑ Ⓒ Ⓓ Ⓔ 28 Ⓐ Ⓑ Ⓒ Ⓓ Ⓔ 38 Ⓐ Ⓑ Ⓒ Ⓓ Ⓔ
9 Ⓐ Ⓑ Ⓒ Ⓓ Ⓔ 19 Ⓐ Ⓑ Ⓒ Ⓓ Ⓔ 29 Ⓐ Ⓑ Ⓒ Ⓓ Ⓔ 39 Ⓐ Ⓑ Ⓒ Ⓓ Ⓔ
10 Ⓐ Ⓑ Ⓒ Ⓓ Ⓔ 20 Ⓐ Ⓑ Ⓒ Ⓓ Ⓔ 30 Ⓐ Ⓑ Ⓒ Ⓓ Ⓔ 40 Ⓐ Ⓑ Ⓒ Ⓓ Ⓔ

SECTION 3

1 Ⓐ Ⓑ Ⓒ Ⓓ Ⓔ
2 Ⓐ Ⓑ Ⓒ Ⓓ Ⓔ
3 Ⓐ Ⓑ Ⓒ Ⓓ Ⓔ
4 Ⓐ Ⓑ Ⓒ Ⓓ Ⓔ
5 Ⓐ Ⓑ Ⓒ Ⓓ Ⓔ
6 Ⓐ Ⓑ Ⓒ Ⓓ Ⓔ
7 Ⓐ Ⓑ Ⓒ Ⓓ Ⓔ
8 Ⓐ Ⓑ Ⓒ Ⓓ Ⓔ
9 Ⓐ Ⓑ Ⓒ Ⓓ Ⓔ
10 Ⓐ Ⓑ Ⓒ Ⓓ Ⓔ
11 Ⓐ Ⓑ Ⓒ Ⓓ Ⓔ
12 Ⓐ Ⓑ Ⓒ Ⓓ Ⓔ
13 Ⓐ Ⓑ Ⓒ Ⓓ Ⓔ
14 Ⓐ Ⓑ Ⓒ Ⓓ Ⓔ
15 Ⓐ Ⓑ Ⓒ Ⓓ Ⓔ

For Questions 16–25
Only answers entered in the ovals in each grid area will be scored. You will not receive credit for anything written in the boxes above the ovals.

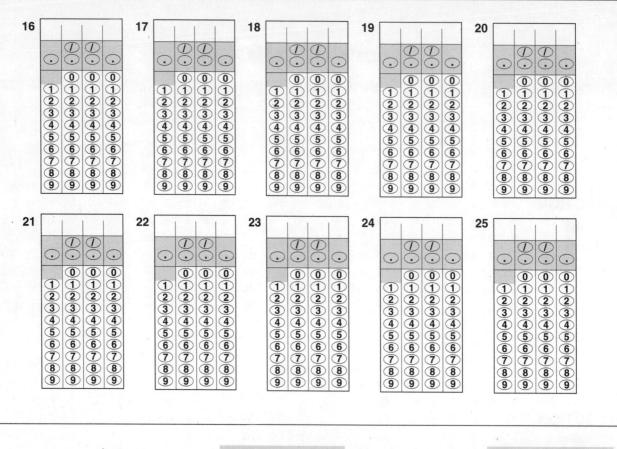

SECTION 4

1	Ⓐ Ⓑ Ⓒ Ⓓ Ⓔ	11	Ⓐ Ⓑ Ⓒ Ⓓ Ⓔ	21	Ⓐ Ⓑ Ⓒ Ⓓ Ⓔ	31	Ⓐ Ⓑ Ⓒ Ⓓ Ⓔ
2	Ⓐ Ⓑ Ⓒ Ⓓ Ⓔ	12	Ⓐ Ⓑ Ⓒ Ⓓ Ⓔ	22	Ⓐ Ⓑ Ⓒ Ⓓ Ⓔ	32	Ⓐ Ⓑ Ⓒ Ⓓ Ⓔ
3	Ⓐ Ⓑ Ⓒ Ⓓ Ⓔ	13	Ⓐ Ⓑ Ⓒ Ⓓ Ⓔ	23	Ⓐ Ⓑ Ⓒ Ⓓ Ⓔ	33	Ⓐ Ⓑ Ⓒ Ⓓ Ⓔ
4	Ⓐ Ⓑ Ⓒ Ⓓ Ⓔ	14	Ⓐ Ⓑ Ⓒ Ⓓ Ⓔ	24	Ⓐ Ⓑ Ⓒ Ⓓ Ⓔ	34	Ⓐ Ⓑ Ⓒ Ⓓ Ⓔ
5	Ⓐ Ⓑ Ⓒ Ⓓ Ⓔ	15	Ⓐ Ⓑ Ⓒ Ⓓ Ⓔ	25	Ⓐ Ⓑ Ⓒ Ⓓ Ⓔ	35	Ⓐ Ⓑ Ⓒ Ⓓ Ⓔ
6	Ⓐ Ⓑ Ⓒ Ⓓ Ⓔ	16	Ⓐ Ⓑ Ⓒ Ⓓ Ⓔ	26	Ⓐ Ⓑ Ⓒ Ⓓ Ⓔ	36	Ⓐ Ⓑ Ⓒ Ⓓ Ⓔ
7	Ⓐ Ⓑ Ⓒ Ⓓ Ⓔ	17	Ⓐ Ⓑ Ⓒ Ⓓ Ⓔ	27	Ⓐ Ⓑ Ⓒ Ⓓ Ⓔ	37	Ⓐ Ⓑ Ⓒ Ⓓ Ⓔ
8	Ⓐ Ⓑ Ⓒ Ⓓ Ⓔ	18	Ⓐ Ⓑ Ⓒ Ⓓ Ⓔ	28	Ⓐ Ⓑ Ⓒ Ⓓ Ⓔ	38	Ⓐ Ⓑ Ⓒ Ⓓ Ⓔ
9	Ⓐ Ⓑ Ⓒ Ⓓ Ⓔ	19	Ⓐ Ⓑ Ⓒ Ⓓ Ⓔ	29	Ⓐ Ⓑ Ⓒ Ⓓ Ⓔ	39	Ⓐ Ⓑ Ⓒ Ⓓ Ⓔ
10	Ⓐ Ⓑ Ⓒ Ⓓ Ⓔ	20	Ⓐ Ⓑ Ⓒ Ⓓ Ⓔ	30	Ⓐ Ⓑ Ⓒ Ⓓ Ⓔ	40	Ⓐ Ⓑ Ⓒ Ⓓ Ⓔ

SECTION 5

1	Ⓐ Ⓑ Ⓒ Ⓓ Ⓔ
2	Ⓐ Ⓑ Ⓒ Ⓓ Ⓔ
3	Ⓐ Ⓑ Ⓒ Ⓓ Ⓔ
4	Ⓐ Ⓑ Ⓒ Ⓓ Ⓔ
5	Ⓐ Ⓑ Ⓒ Ⓓ Ⓔ
6	Ⓐ Ⓑ Ⓒ Ⓓ Ⓔ
7	Ⓐ Ⓑ Ⓒ Ⓓ Ⓔ
8	Ⓐ Ⓑ Ⓒ Ⓓ Ⓔ
9	Ⓐ Ⓑ Ⓒ Ⓓ Ⓔ
10	Ⓐ Ⓑ Ⓒ Ⓓ Ⓔ
11	Ⓐ Ⓑ Ⓒ Ⓓ Ⓔ
12	Ⓐ Ⓑ Ⓒ Ⓓ Ⓔ
13	Ⓐ Ⓑ Ⓒ Ⓓ Ⓔ
14	Ⓐ Ⓑ Ⓒ Ⓓ Ⓔ
15	Ⓐ Ⓑ Ⓒ Ⓓ Ⓔ

SECTION 6

1	Ⓐ Ⓑ Ⓒ Ⓓ Ⓔ
2	Ⓐ Ⓑ Ⓒ Ⓓ Ⓔ
3	Ⓐ Ⓑ Ⓒ Ⓓ Ⓔ
4	Ⓐ Ⓑ Ⓒ Ⓓ Ⓔ
5	Ⓐ Ⓑ Ⓒ Ⓓ Ⓔ
6	Ⓐ Ⓑ Ⓒ Ⓓ Ⓔ
7	Ⓐ Ⓑ Ⓒ Ⓓ Ⓔ
8	Ⓐ Ⓑ Ⓒ Ⓓ Ⓔ
9	Ⓐ Ⓑ Ⓒ Ⓓ Ⓔ
10	Ⓐ Ⓑ Ⓒ Ⓓ Ⓔ
11	Ⓐ Ⓑ Ⓒ Ⓓ Ⓔ
12	Ⓐ Ⓑ Ⓒ Ⓓ Ⓔ
13	Ⓐ Ⓑ Ⓒ Ⓓ Ⓔ
14	Ⓐ Ⓑ Ⓒ Ⓓ Ⓔ
15	Ⓐ Ⓑ Ⓒ Ⓓ Ⓔ

Answer Sheets

SECTION 1

1 Ⓐ Ⓑ Ⓒ Ⓓ Ⓔ	11 Ⓐ Ⓑ Ⓒ Ⓓ Ⓔ	21 Ⓐ Ⓑ Ⓒ Ⓓ Ⓔ	31 Ⓐ Ⓑ Ⓒ Ⓓ Ⓔ
2 Ⓐ Ⓑ Ⓒ Ⓓ Ⓔ	12 Ⓐ Ⓑ Ⓒ Ⓓ Ⓔ	22 Ⓐ Ⓑ Ⓒ Ⓓ Ⓔ	32 Ⓐ Ⓑ Ⓒ Ⓓ Ⓔ
3 Ⓐ Ⓑ Ⓒ Ⓓ Ⓔ	13 Ⓐ Ⓑ Ⓒ Ⓓ Ⓔ	23 Ⓐ Ⓑ Ⓒ Ⓓ Ⓔ	33 Ⓐ Ⓑ Ⓒ Ⓓ Ⓔ
4 Ⓐ Ⓑ Ⓒ Ⓓ Ⓔ	14 Ⓐ Ⓑ Ⓒ Ⓓ Ⓔ	24 Ⓐ Ⓑ Ⓒ Ⓓ Ⓔ	34 Ⓐ Ⓑ Ⓒ Ⓓ Ⓔ
5 Ⓐ Ⓑ Ⓒ Ⓓ Ⓔ	15 Ⓐ Ⓑ Ⓒ Ⓓ Ⓔ	25 Ⓐ Ⓑ Ⓒ Ⓓ Ⓔ	35 Ⓐ Ⓑ Ⓒ Ⓓ Ⓔ
6 Ⓐ Ⓑ Ⓒ Ⓓ Ⓔ	16 Ⓐ Ⓑ Ⓒ Ⓓ Ⓔ	26 Ⓐ Ⓑ Ⓒ Ⓓ Ⓔ	36 Ⓐ Ⓑ Ⓒ Ⓓ Ⓔ
7 Ⓐ Ⓑ Ⓒ Ⓓ Ⓔ	17 Ⓐ Ⓑ Ⓒ Ⓓ Ⓔ	27 Ⓐ Ⓑ Ⓒ Ⓓ Ⓔ	37 Ⓐ Ⓑ Ⓒ Ⓓ Ⓔ
8 Ⓐ Ⓑ Ⓒ Ⓓ Ⓔ	18 Ⓐ Ⓑ Ⓒ Ⓓ Ⓔ	28 Ⓐ Ⓑ Ⓒ Ⓓ Ⓔ	38 Ⓐ Ⓑ Ⓒ Ⓓ Ⓔ
9 Ⓐ Ⓑ Ⓒ Ⓓ Ⓔ	19 Ⓐ Ⓑ Ⓒ Ⓓ Ⓔ	29 Ⓐ Ⓑ Ⓒ Ⓓ Ⓔ	39 Ⓐ Ⓑ Ⓒ Ⓓ Ⓔ
10 Ⓐ Ⓑ Ⓒ Ⓓ Ⓔ	20 Ⓐ Ⓑ Ⓒ Ⓓ Ⓔ	30 Ⓐ Ⓑ Ⓒ Ⓓ Ⓔ	40 Ⓐ Ⓑ Ⓒ Ⓓ Ⓔ

SECTION 2

1 Ⓐ Ⓑ Ⓒ Ⓓ Ⓔ	11 Ⓐ Ⓑ Ⓒ Ⓓ Ⓔ	21 Ⓐ Ⓑ Ⓒ Ⓓ Ⓔ	31 Ⓐ Ⓑ Ⓒ Ⓓ Ⓔ
2 Ⓐ Ⓑ Ⓒ Ⓓ Ⓔ	12 Ⓐ Ⓑ Ⓒ Ⓓ Ⓔ	22 Ⓐ Ⓑ Ⓒ Ⓓ Ⓔ	32 Ⓐ Ⓑ Ⓒ Ⓓ Ⓔ
3 Ⓐ Ⓑ Ⓒ Ⓓ Ⓔ	13 Ⓐ Ⓑ Ⓒ Ⓓ Ⓔ	23 Ⓐ Ⓑ Ⓒ Ⓓ Ⓔ	33 Ⓐ Ⓑ Ⓒ Ⓓ Ⓔ
4 Ⓐ Ⓑ Ⓒ Ⓓ Ⓔ	14 Ⓐ Ⓑ Ⓒ Ⓓ Ⓔ	24 Ⓐ Ⓑ Ⓒ Ⓓ Ⓔ	34 Ⓐ Ⓑ Ⓒ Ⓓ Ⓔ
5 Ⓐ Ⓑ Ⓒ Ⓓ Ⓔ	15 Ⓐ Ⓑ Ⓒ Ⓓ Ⓔ	25 Ⓐ Ⓑ Ⓒ Ⓓ Ⓔ	35 Ⓐ Ⓑ Ⓒ Ⓓ Ⓔ
6 Ⓐ Ⓑ Ⓒ Ⓓ Ⓔ	16 Ⓐ Ⓑ Ⓒ Ⓓ Ⓔ	26 Ⓐ Ⓑ Ⓒ Ⓓ Ⓔ	36 Ⓐ Ⓑ Ⓒ Ⓓ Ⓔ
7 Ⓐ Ⓑ Ⓒ Ⓓ Ⓔ	17 Ⓐ Ⓑ Ⓒ Ⓓ Ⓔ	27 Ⓐ Ⓑ Ⓒ Ⓓ Ⓔ	37 Ⓐ Ⓑ Ⓒ Ⓓ Ⓔ
8 Ⓐ Ⓑ Ⓒ Ⓓ Ⓔ	18 Ⓐ Ⓑ Ⓒ Ⓓ Ⓔ	28 Ⓐ Ⓑ Ⓒ Ⓓ Ⓔ	38 Ⓐ Ⓑ Ⓒ Ⓓ Ⓔ
9 Ⓐ Ⓑ Ⓒ Ⓓ Ⓔ	19 Ⓐ Ⓑ Ⓒ Ⓓ Ⓔ	29 Ⓐ Ⓑ Ⓒ Ⓓ Ⓔ	39 Ⓐ Ⓑ Ⓒ Ⓓ Ⓔ
10 Ⓐ Ⓑ Ⓒ Ⓓ Ⓔ	20 Ⓐ Ⓑ Ⓒ Ⓓ Ⓔ	30 Ⓐ Ⓑ Ⓒ Ⓓ Ⓔ	40 Ⓐ Ⓑ Ⓒ Ⓓ Ⓔ

SECTION 3

1 Ⓐ Ⓑ Ⓒ Ⓓ Ⓔ
2 Ⓐ Ⓑ Ⓒ Ⓓ Ⓔ
3 Ⓐ Ⓑ Ⓒ Ⓓ Ⓔ
4 Ⓐ Ⓑ Ⓒ Ⓓ Ⓔ
5 Ⓐ Ⓑ Ⓒ Ⓓ Ⓔ
6 Ⓐ Ⓑ Ⓒ Ⓓ Ⓔ
7 Ⓐ Ⓑ Ⓒ Ⓓ Ⓔ
8 Ⓐ Ⓑ Ⓒ Ⓓ Ⓔ
9 Ⓐ Ⓑ Ⓒ Ⓓ Ⓔ
10 Ⓐ Ⓑ Ⓒ Ⓓ Ⓔ
11 Ⓐ Ⓑ Ⓒ Ⓓ Ⓔ
12 Ⓐ Ⓑ Ⓒ Ⓓ Ⓔ
13 Ⓐ Ⓑ Ⓒ Ⓓ Ⓔ
14 Ⓐ Ⓑ Ⓒ Ⓓ Ⓔ
15 Ⓐ Ⓑ Ⓒ Ⓓ Ⓔ

For Questions 16–25
Only answers entered in the ovals in each grid area will be scored. You will not receive credit for anything written in the boxes above the ovals.

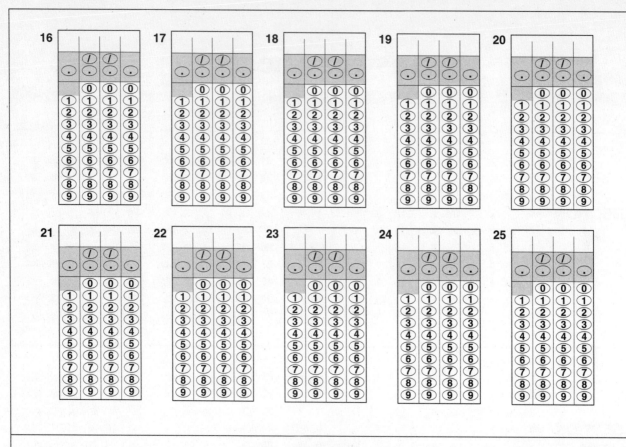

SECTION
5

SECTION
6

Answer Sheets

SECTION 1

1 Ⓐ Ⓑ Ⓒ Ⓓ Ⓔ
2 Ⓐ Ⓑ Ⓒ Ⓓ Ⓔ
3 Ⓐ Ⓑ Ⓒ Ⓓ Ⓔ
4 Ⓐ Ⓑ Ⓒ Ⓓ Ⓔ
5 Ⓐ Ⓑ Ⓒ Ⓓ Ⓔ
6 Ⓐ Ⓑ Ⓒ Ⓓ Ⓔ
7 Ⓐ Ⓑ Ⓒ Ⓓ Ⓔ
8 Ⓐ Ⓑ Ⓒ Ⓓ Ⓔ
9 Ⓐ Ⓑ Ⓒ Ⓓ Ⓔ
10 Ⓐ Ⓑ Ⓒ Ⓓ Ⓔ

11 Ⓐ Ⓑ Ⓒ Ⓓ Ⓔ
12 Ⓐ Ⓑ Ⓒ Ⓓ Ⓔ
13 Ⓐ Ⓑ Ⓒ Ⓓ Ⓔ
14 Ⓐ Ⓑ Ⓒ Ⓓ Ⓔ
15 Ⓐ Ⓑ Ⓒ Ⓓ Ⓔ
16 Ⓐ Ⓑ Ⓒ Ⓓ Ⓔ
17 Ⓐ Ⓑ Ⓒ Ⓓ Ⓔ
18 Ⓐ Ⓑ Ⓒ Ⓓ Ⓔ
19 Ⓐ Ⓑ Ⓒ Ⓓ Ⓔ
20 Ⓐ Ⓑ Ⓒ Ⓓ Ⓔ

21 Ⓐ Ⓑ Ⓒ Ⓓ Ⓔ
22 Ⓐ Ⓑ Ⓒ Ⓓ Ⓔ
23 Ⓐ Ⓑ Ⓒ Ⓓ Ⓔ
24 Ⓐ Ⓑ Ⓒ Ⓓ Ⓔ
25 Ⓐ Ⓑ Ⓒ Ⓓ Ⓔ
26 Ⓐ Ⓑ Ⓒ Ⓓ Ⓔ
27 Ⓐ Ⓑ Ⓒ Ⓓ Ⓔ
28 Ⓐ Ⓑ Ⓒ Ⓓ Ⓔ
29 Ⓐ Ⓑ Ⓒ Ⓓ Ⓔ
30 Ⓐ Ⓑ Ⓒ Ⓓ Ⓔ

31 Ⓐ Ⓑ Ⓒ Ⓓ Ⓔ
32 Ⓐ Ⓑ Ⓒ Ⓓ Ⓔ
33 Ⓐ Ⓑ Ⓒ Ⓓ Ⓔ
34 Ⓐ Ⓑ Ⓒ Ⓓ Ⓔ
35 Ⓐ Ⓑ Ⓒ Ⓓ Ⓔ
36 Ⓐ Ⓑ Ⓒ Ⓓ Ⓔ
37 Ⓐ Ⓑ Ⓒ Ⓓ Ⓔ
38 Ⓐ Ⓑ Ⓒ Ⓓ Ⓔ
39 Ⓐ Ⓑ Ⓒ Ⓓ Ⓔ
40 Ⓐ Ⓑ Ⓒ Ⓓ Ⓔ

SECTION 2

1 Ⓐ Ⓑ Ⓒ Ⓓ Ⓔ
2 Ⓐ Ⓑ Ⓒ Ⓓ Ⓔ
3 Ⓐ Ⓑ Ⓒ Ⓓ Ⓔ
4 Ⓐ Ⓑ Ⓒ Ⓓ Ⓔ
5 Ⓐ Ⓑ Ⓒ Ⓓ Ⓔ
6 Ⓐ Ⓑ Ⓒ Ⓓ Ⓔ
7 Ⓐ Ⓑ Ⓒ Ⓓ Ⓔ
8 Ⓐ Ⓑ Ⓒ Ⓓ Ⓔ
9 Ⓐ Ⓑ Ⓒ Ⓓ Ⓔ
10 Ⓐ Ⓑ Ⓒ Ⓓ Ⓔ

11 Ⓐ Ⓑ Ⓒ Ⓓ Ⓔ
12 Ⓐ Ⓑ Ⓒ Ⓓ Ⓔ
13 Ⓐ Ⓑ Ⓒ Ⓓ Ⓔ
14 Ⓐ Ⓑ Ⓒ Ⓓ Ⓔ
15 Ⓐ Ⓑ Ⓒ Ⓓ Ⓔ
16 Ⓐ Ⓑ Ⓒ Ⓓ Ⓔ
17 Ⓐ Ⓑ Ⓒ Ⓓ Ⓔ
18 Ⓐ Ⓑ Ⓒ Ⓓ Ⓔ
19 Ⓐ Ⓑ Ⓒ Ⓓ Ⓔ
20 Ⓐ Ⓑ Ⓒ Ⓓ Ⓔ

21 Ⓐ Ⓑ Ⓒ Ⓓ Ⓔ
22 Ⓐ Ⓑ Ⓒ Ⓓ Ⓔ
23 Ⓐ Ⓑ Ⓒ Ⓓ Ⓔ
24 Ⓐ Ⓑ Ⓒ Ⓓ Ⓔ
25 Ⓐ Ⓑ Ⓒ Ⓓ Ⓔ
26 Ⓐ Ⓑ Ⓒ Ⓓ Ⓔ
27 Ⓐ Ⓑ Ⓒ Ⓓ Ⓔ
28 Ⓐ Ⓑ Ⓒ Ⓓ Ⓔ
29 Ⓐ Ⓑ Ⓒ Ⓓ Ⓔ
30 Ⓐ Ⓑ Ⓒ Ⓓ Ⓔ

31 Ⓐ Ⓑ Ⓒ Ⓓ Ⓔ
32 Ⓐ Ⓑ Ⓒ Ⓓ Ⓔ
33 Ⓐ Ⓑ Ⓒ Ⓓ Ⓔ
34 Ⓐ Ⓑ Ⓒ Ⓓ Ⓔ
35 Ⓐ Ⓑ Ⓒ Ⓓ Ⓔ
36 Ⓐ Ⓑ Ⓒ Ⓓ Ⓔ
37 Ⓐ Ⓑ Ⓒ Ⓓ Ⓔ
38 Ⓐ Ⓑ Ⓒ Ⓓ Ⓔ
39 Ⓐ Ⓑ Ⓒ Ⓓ Ⓔ
40 Ⓐ Ⓑ Ⓒ Ⓓ Ⓔ

SECTION 3

1 Ⓐ Ⓑ Ⓒ Ⓓ Ⓔ
2 Ⓐ Ⓑ Ⓒ Ⓓ Ⓔ
3 Ⓐ Ⓑ Ⓒ Ⓓ Ⓔ
4 Ⓐ Ⓑ Ⓒ Ⓓ Ⓔ
5 Ⓐ Ⓑ Ⓒ Ⓓ Ⓔ
6 Ⓐ Ⓑ Ⓒ Ⓓ Ⓔ
7 Ⓐ Ⓑ Ⓒ Ⓓ Ⓔ
8 Ⓐ Ⓑ Ⓒ Ⓓ Ⓔ
9 Ⓐ Ⓑ Ⓒ Ⓓ Ⓔ
10 Ⓐ Ⓑ Ⓒ Ⓓ Ⓔ
11 Ⓐ Ⓑ Ⓒ Ⓓ Ⓔ
12 Ⓐ Ⓑ Ⓒ Ⓓ Ⓔ
13 Ⓐ Ⓑ Ⓒ Ⓓ Ⓔ
14 Ⓐ Ⓑ Ⓒ Ⓓ Ⓔ
15 Ⓐ Ⓑ Ⓒ Ⓓ Ⓔ

For Questions 16–25
Only answers entered in the ovals in each grid area will be scored. You will not receive credit for anything written in the boxes above the ovals.

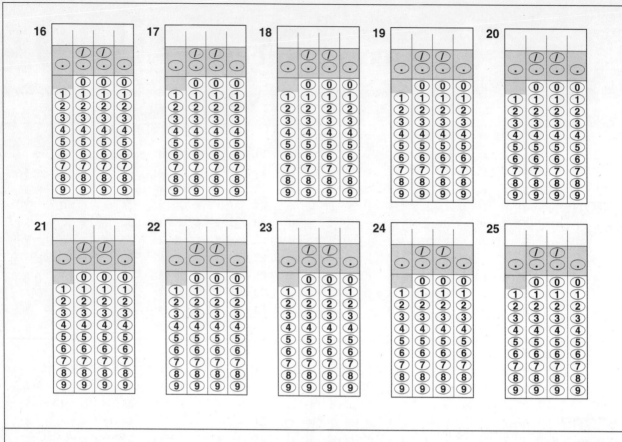

SECTION 4

1	Ⓐ Ⓑ Ⓒ Ⓓ Ⓔ	11	Ⓐ Ⓑ Ⓒ Ⓓ Ⓔ	21	Ⓐ Ⓑ Ⓒ Ⓓ Ⓔ	31	Ⓐ Ⓑ Ⓒ Ⓓ Ⓔ
2	Ⓐ Ⓑ Ⓒ Ⓓ Ⓔ	12	Ⓐ Ⓑ Ⓒ Ⓓ Ⓔ	22	Ⓐ Ⓑ Ⓒ Ⓓ Ⓔ	32	Ⓐ Ⓑ Ⓒ Ⓓ Ⓔ
3	Ⓐ Ⓑ Ⓒ Ⓓ Ⓔ	13	Ⓐ Ⓑ Ⓒ Ⓓ Ⓔ	23	Ⓐ Ⓑ Ⓒ Ⓓ Ⓔ	33	Ⓐ Ⓑ Ⓒ Ⓓ Ⓔ
4	Ⓐ Ⓑ Ⓒ Ⓓ Ⓔ	14	Ⓐ Ⓑ Ⓒ Ⓓ Ⓔ	24	Ⓐ Ⓑ Ⓒ Ⓓ Ⓔ	34	Ⓐ Ⓑ Ⓒ Ⓓ Ⓔ
5	Ⓐ Ⓑ Ⓒ Ⓓ Ⓔ	15	Ⓐ Ⓑ Ⓒ Ⓓ Ⓔ	25	Ⓐ Ⓑ Ⓒ Ⓓ Ⓔ	35	Ⓐ Ⓑ Ⓒ Ⓓ Ⓔ
6	Ⓐ Ⓑ Ⓒ Ⓓ Ⓔ	16	Ⓐ Ⓑ Ⓒ Ⓓ Ⓔ	26	Ⓐ Ⓑ Ⓒ Ⓓ Ⓔ	36	Ⓐ Ⓑ Ⓒ Ⓓ Ⓔ
7	Ⓐ Ⓑ Ⓒ Ⓓ Ⓔ	17	Ⓐ Ⓑ Ⓒ Ⓓ Ⓔ	27	Ⓐ Ⓑ Ⓒ Ⓓ Ⓔ	37	Ⓐ Ⓑ Ⓒ Ⓓ Ⓔ
8	Ⓐ Ⓑ Ⓒ Ⓓ Ⓔ	18	Ⓐ Ⓑ Ⓒ Ⓓ Ⓔ	28	Ⓐ Ⓑ Ⓒ Ⓓ Ⓔ	38	Ⓐ Ⓑ Ⓒ Ⓓ Ⓔ
9	Ⓐ Ⓑ Ⓒ Ⓓ Ⓔ	19	Ⓐ Ⓑ Ⓒ Ⓓ Ⓔ	29	Ⓐ Ⓑ Ⓒ Ⓓ Ⓔ	39	Ⓐ Ⓑ Ⓒ Ⓓ Ⓔ
10	Ⓐ Ⓑ Ⓒ Ⓓ Ⓔ	20	Ⓐ Ⓑ Ⓒ Ⓓ Ⓔ	30	Ⓐ Ⓑ Ⓒ Ⓓ Ⓔ	40	Ⓐ Ⓑ Ⓒ Ⓓ Ⓔ

SECTION 5

1	Ⓐ Ⓑ Ⓒ Ⓓ Ⓔ
2	Ⓐ Ⓑ Ⓒ Ⓓ Ⓔ
3	Ⓐ Ⓑ Ⓒ Ⓓ Ⓔ
4	Ⓐ Ⓑ Ⓒ Ⓓ Ⓔ
5	Ⓐ Ⓑ Ⓒ Ⓓ Ⓔ
6	Ⓐ Ⓑ Ⓒ Ⓓ Ⓔ
7	Ⓐ Ⓑ Ⓒ Ⓓ Ⓔ
8	Ⓐ Ⓑ Ⓒ Ⓓ Ⓔ
9	Ⓐ Ⓑ Ⓒ Ⓓ Ⓔ
10	Ⓐ Ⓑ Ⓒ Ⓓ Ⓔ
11	Ⓐ Ⓑ Ⓒ Ⓓ Ⓔ
12	Ⓐ Ⓑ Ⓒ Ⓓ Ⓔ
13	Ⓐ Ⓑ Ⓒ Ⓓ Ⓔ
14	Ⓐ Ⓑ Ⓒ Ⓓ Ⓔ
15	Ⓐ Ⓑ Ⓒ Ⓓ Ⓔ

SECTION 6

1	Ⓐ Ⓑ Ⓒ Ⓓ Ⓔ
2	Ⓐ Ⓑ Ⓒ Ⓓ Ⓔ
3	Ⓐ Ⓑ Ⓒ Ⓓ Ⓔ
4	Ⓐ Ⓑ Ⓒ Ⓓ Ⓔ
5	Ⓐ Ⓑ Ⓒ Ⓓ Ⓔ
6	Ⓐ Ⓑ Ⓒ Ⓓ Ⓔ
7	Ⓐ Ⓑ Ⓒ Ⓓ Ⓔ
8	Ⓐ Ⓑ Ⓒ Ⓓ Ⓔ
9	Ⓐ Ⓑ Ⓒ Ⓓ Ⓔ
10	Ⓐ Ⓑ Ⓒ Ⓓ Ⓔ
11	Ⓐ Ⓑ Ⓒ Ⓓ Ⓔ
12	Ⓐ Ⓑ Ⓒ Ⓓ Ⓔ
13	Ⓐ Ⓑ Ⓒ Ⓓ Ⓔ
14	Ⓐ Ⓑ Ⓒ Ⓓ Ⓔ
15	Ⓐ Ⓑ Ⓒ Ⓓ Ⓔ

Get Ready for College!

Peterson's offers students like you a wide variety of comprehensive resources to help you meet all your college planning needs.

4 Year Colleges 2002
This college-search classic features detailed profiles of every accredited college and university in the U.S. and Canada.

2 Year Colleges 2002
A comprehensive guide to more than 1,600 junior and community colleges.

Competitive Colleges:
Top Colleges for Top Students 2002
Describes nearly 500 institutions offering challenging educational opportunities for high-achieving students.

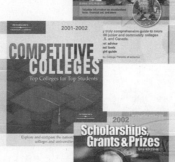

Scholarships, Grants & Prizes 2002
Identifies nearly 1.5 million financial aid awards worth nearly $5 billion! Includes CD with financial planning software and standardized test-prep.

College Money Handbook 2002
Explore financial aid opportunities offered by nearly 1,800 four-year colleges in the U.S. Plan expenses with Peterson's College Cost Chart.

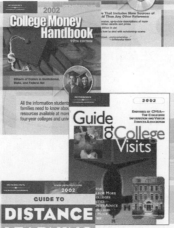

Guide to College Visits 2002
An exceptional resource for families planning campus visits. Packed with practical information on organizing your trip to more than 600 colleges and universities.

Distance Learning Programs 2002
Discover the convenience of learning via electronic media with this comprehensive sourcebook to more than 1,000 programs at 900 schools in the U.S. and Canada.

PETERSON'S ™
THOMSON LEARNING

Visit your local bookstore or call to order: **800-338-3282.**
To order online, go to **www.petersons.com** and head for the bookstore!

CollegeSelectionFinancialAidDistanceLearning